G.W. Carleton

The Suppressed book about slavery!

G.W. Carleton

The Suppressed book about slavery!

ISBN/EAN: 9783742817969

Manufactured in Europe, USA, Canada, Australia, Japa

Cover: Foto ©ninafisch / pixelio.de

Manufactured and distributed by brebook publishing software (www.brebook.com)

G.W. Carleton

The Suppressed book about slavery!

THE
SUPPRESSED BOOK
ABOUT
SLAVERY!

PREPARED FOR PUBLICATION IN 1857,—
NEVER PUBLISHED UNTIL THE PRESENT TIME.

NEW YORK:
CARLETON, PUBLISHER.
1864.

PREFACE.

THE people of the United States are a Slave-holding people. How much that term means we learn when we better understand what Slavery is, and what is the complicity of the people of the "*free* States" with it.

In the original draft of the Declaration of Independence one of the oppressive acts charged against the Mother country was the continuation of the Foreign Slave Trade, contrary to the interests and in spite of the remonstrances of the Colonists. It was afterwards omitted, at the dictate of those Southern Colonies who could not consistently complain of that as a wrong which they meant to claim as a privilege. When, at the close of the war, a Convention of Delegates from all the States met to form a Constitution, the two questions which threatened to be insurmountable obstacles in the way of a Federal Union were, whether the system of Slavery, which was cherished in some of the States, should be tolerated by those which had abolished or proposed to abolish it; and whether the traffic in African Slaves should be continued. The difficulty was evaded by a "Compromise." The Foreign Slave Trade was permitted, but only for twenty years. The rendition of fugitive Slaves was provided for by the Constitution, because they were "property;" but the Slaves were reckoned as three-fifths of the free population, as a basis of Congressional representation, because they were men. On the other hand, in case of direct taxation the same method of enumeration was observed. On the side of the Slaveholder was not only power, but "wisdom." The Foreign Slave Trade lasted as long as it was wanted, and till a more profitable Domestic Trade was about to arise to take its place. The Slaveholders have always had, by virtue of the three-fifths rule, a compact representation, as Slaveholders, in Congress, and have always held the balance of power. The Slave States, on the same basis of representation as the "free," would be entitled to only sixty-five representatives in Congress, yet they have ninety; that is, twenty-five extra. This discrepancy between population and representation arises from the fact that, in determining between the number of representatives to which each State is entitled, five Slaves are reckoned equal to three Freemen. The Slaves have a representation equal to that of the "free States" of New Hampshire, Vermont, Connecticut, Iowa, and Wisconsin?

The Slavehunter may pursue and take his prey wherever he can find him, between Canada and Mexico. The Northern man is punished with fine and imprisonment who gives the trembling fugitive a cup of water or a crust of bread.

These concessions to the Slaveholders, made for the sake of immediate harmony and union, were supposed to be merely temporary. Slavery, it was hoped, would speedily yield to the spirit of freedom, and, confined within narrow limits, necessarily and rapidly disappear. The leading men of that day have left upon record their strong condemnation of the system, and some of them were active members of associations formed for its extirpation. But with another generation came new circumstances and new ideas. The introduction of Cotton-culture opened a profitable field for the employment of Slave labour. The acquisition of new territory, permitting the extension of Slavery, and an economical calculation showing that a planter could profitably "work up" a gang of Slaves in seven years, and supply their place—not by natural increase, but by new importations from older Slave States —created an active Domestic trade, and secured to Virginia, Maryland, and the Carolinas an immense return for their "vigintial" crop of Negroes. The North was reconciled to share in the national iniquity by a commercial prosperity based upon the steadily increasing production of a great staple export. The admission of new Slave States to the Union added to the political strength of the Slaveholders—the power to acquire and use which the fatal concessions of the Constitution had put into their hands.

Thus the growth of this Slaveholding despotism has advanced with the growth and prosperity of the country. It has rarely excited the apprehension of the North. If, as at the time of the acceptance of the Missouri Compromise, she has seemed for a moment thoroughly aroused, it was easy to amuse and quiet her with some cunning scheme of a Southern politician, made only to be broken the moment the North demanded its promised advantage. The history of the Government from the beginning is a repetition of similar acts of Slaveholding domination, faithlessness, and pusillanimity.

In preparing this work the author has not depended on the facts or arguments of those who have been known as "Abolitionists," but has chosen rather to rely upon such authorities and sources of information as cannot be impeached for their relation to the Abolition party. For the character of Slavery the South is its own witness. The Southern clergyman and his Northern ally are permitted to show, in their own words, how they reconcile that system to the Divine Will. The Northern clergyman, whose standing in the Church and whose orthodox integrity are unquestioned, bears impartial testimony to the wickedness of an institution, the defender of which he, nevertheless, recognises as a Christian brother. The politician piles fact upon fact, and argument upon argument, in denunciation of Slavery and the Slave-power, through the organs of a party which denies that it has any wish or intention to interfere with Slavery where it already exists, or to withhold from the Slaveholder any of the privileges which the Constitution confers upon him. Against such witnesses there can be brought no charge of fanaticism. If there shall seem to be any glaring inconsistency between the avowal that Slavery is a gigantic wrong, or a heinous sin, and a position as a Christian or a citizen which gives to it that support without which it cannot exist, it is for those between whose faith and works such contradiction appears, to explain and justify it. The author of this work has done his part if by unimpeachable testimony he has shown the true character and the true relations of American Slavery.

A PAGE FOR 1864!

WHY SUPPRESSED?. Reader, would you like to know? Read the Book, and you will presently discover why. Would you have published it when it was written? Would you even have read it? Would you not have indignantly put it from you, muttering something about "those abominable abolitionists"?

This Book was written Anno Domini 1857. The stereotype plates from which it is now printed, were made then. Since that time, as the penalty for having been brought into the world seven years too soon, they have slumbered, unknown, unnoticed, and undisturbed, beneath the surface of the earth.

But, while they slept, the nation has been "marching on." Awake to its danger, it springs from its former lethargy, and wonders at its long-continued apathy to its true interests. We are not what we were seven years ago. We dare to read things at which we then would have looked with suspicion. We no longer tremble at the thought of what the slave power would do to us, were it to catch us doing any thing contrary to its bidding. We open our mouths to shout aloud what is right, instead of being almost afraid to whisper it. We can print, publish, read, speak, and listen to—exactly what we please.

And now, brought to the light of day, the Book discloses the hideous skeleton of the institution which we have fondled and petted till it has almost been the death of us. It reveals the dark deeds of slavery, and opens to view its hideous purposes, its revolutionary premeditations. It is no hackneyed hash of the worn-out things which for a generation have been said about slavery. It is fresh, vivid, sparkling, cutting to the very quick. Its pictures are true to the life. Its almost prophetic utterances are borne out by the light of the terrible deeds of the past three years.

You can read it now. You will not have to conceal it in your drawer, or furtively slip it into your waste-paper basket, or under the table-cover, if you are interrupted while absorbed in the thrilling interest of its pages. You can hold it open before your neighbor, for he wants to read it. The nation wants to see it. The world needs to *know* the truths contained in it.

AND NOW LET THE WORLD READ IT.

CONTENTS.

PART I.
THINGS PAST AND PRESENT.

	PAGE
CHAP. I.—How the Negro has been Treated......	9
II.—The unfortunate "Sons of Ham," as Slaves	37
III.—Commercial and "Union-Saving" Obedience to Slavery........................	63
IV.—The Imperious Demands of the Slave Power....................................	89

PART II.
SLAVES, HORSES, AND OTHER CATTLE.

CHAP. I.—The "Nigger Auction" Business.........	121
II.—Coffle Gangs, and the Separation of Families	159

PART III.
SLAVE LIFE ON THE PLANTATION.

CHAP. I.—The Barbarisms of the Institution....	187
II.—Stripes, Chains, and Tortures...........	209

PART IV.
SLAVE EDUCATION AND RELIGION.

CHAP. I.—Ignorance of the Slave Region.........	233
II.—Muzzling the Press and Mangling the Bible	251

PART V.

DOMESTIC AMUSEMENTS IN THE SLAVE STATES.

PAGE

CHAP. I.—FUGITIVES AND BLOODHOUNDS.............. 277
    II.—HUNTING "RUNAWAY NIGGERS"............ 313
    III.—RESTORING LOST "PROPERTY"................ 335

PART VI.

THE SLAVE POWER ADVANCING.

CHAP. I.—OSTEND, CUBA, AND KANSAS................... 353
    II.—SLAVERY TO REIGN SUPREME IN AMERICA. 367

APPENDIX A.—COLORPHOBIA IN FREE STATES......... 381
    B.—THE REV. JUDICIOUS TRIMMER, D.D.. 393
    C.—DOMESTIC AND FOREIGN SLAVE-TRADE 407
    D.—DOUGH-FACE RELIGION................... 417
POSTSCRIPT, 1864.. 427

PARTICULAR INDEX... 429

ILLUSTRATIONS.

HUMAN FLESH AT AUCTION (Frontispiece).
HALTING AT NOON.
THE COFFLE-GANG.
SOLD TO GO SOUTH.
THE LASH.
FLOGGING THE NEGRO.
THE BLOODHOUND BUSINESS.
RUNNING AWAY.

PART FIRST.

A GENERAL VIEW OF THE PAST AND PRESENT STATE OF THINGS.

CHAPTER I.

"When I reflect that God is just, and that his justice can not sleep for ever, I tremble for my country."—JEFFERSON.

"There is no power out of the churches that could sustain Slavery an hour, if it were not sustained in them."—BARNES.

UNDER the whole heavens there is not to be found a people pursued with a more relentless prejudice and persecution, than are the "colored" children of the United States of North America. Those who imbibe this prejudice against "color"— a practical denial of the Unity of the Human race as taught in the Bible—become infidels without suspecting it. Those who oppose it, and oppose Slavery, are driven into the infidelity that rejects the Bible by hearing the Bible appealed to in defence of them. In the New Testament, we are told that " God hath made of one blood all nations of men," (Acts xvii. 17;) and, that "he is no respecter of persons," (Acts x. 34; Eph. vi. 9.) "In Christ," says St. Paul, "all are one: there is neither Jew nor Greek, there is neither bond nor free." And Christ has laid down as the foundation of all true religion, and as the rule of our conduct toward him and his children, that we love the Lord our God with all our heart, and with all our soul, and with all our mind, and our Neighbor as ourselves. On these two commandments hang all the Law and the prophets. (Matt. xxii., 37–40.)

Senator Morrill, of New Hampshire, in a Speech, delivered in the United States Senate in 1820, said: "You excluded not only your Soldiers of Color from their Constitutional rights, but robbed them of the Patents of land you had given them. They fought your battles. They defended your country They preserved your privileges, but have lost their own. What did you say to them on their Enlistment? 'We will give you a monthly compensation, and, at the end of the war, one hundred and sixty acres of land, on which you may settle, and by cultivating the soil, spend your declining years in peace and in the enjoyment of those immunities for which you have fought and bled.' Now, sir, you restrict them, and will not allow them to enjoy the fruit of their labor. Where is the Public faith? Did they suppose, with a Patent in their hand, declaring their title to land in Missouri, with the Seal of the Nation and the President's signature affixed thereto, it would be said unto them, by any authority, 'you shall not possess the premises'? and yet this must follow if 'colored men are not citizens.'"

He that is not a Citizen is either an Alien or Slave. He that is not a Citizen can not inherit house or land. He can not receive them by devise while he lives, nor bequeath them by his Will when he dies. The property given to him reverts to the State. His wife has no dower. His children have no inheritance. He can not come into the Courts for redress. He can neither sue to recover rights nor to obtain debts. He can hold no trust and exercise no guardianship. He can be hanged or sent to jail, but he can not sit in the Jury-box. He can not be naturalized unless he is "white;" can not acquire rights by staying in the country, nor can he have a Passport to go to any other. Such is the condition of him who is not a citizen of the State under the Common Law, and such is defined to be the condition of every "free colored" man and woman, by the Supreme Court of the United States—that Supreme Court which strains every nerve to catch a single Slave, but does not scruple a moment to disfranchise seven hundred and fifty thousand freemen!

At the time of the Declaration of Independence there were but two States, South Carolina and Virginia, in which "free colored men" were excluded from citizenship. In all the other States no distinction was made as to the right of suffrage, on the ground of "color;" and so the matter also stood at the period of the adoption of the Federal Constitution, except in the case of little Delaware, she having adopted by that time the exclusive policy.

Thomas Jefferson, the immortal penman of the Declaration of Independence, ascribed Citizenship to the Slaves no less than to the "free colored men." The following passage, quoted from the "Proclamation" he issued in reference to the outrage of the British man-of-war Leopard upon the American frigate Chesapeake, relates to "free colored men." To understand the force of this quotation, it should be recollected that of the four seamen taken from the American service, the two born in the United States were "black men," natives of Maryland. The passage in the "Proclamation" is as follows:—

"This enormity was not only without provocation or justifiable cause, but was committed with the avowed purpose of taking by force from a ship-of-war of the United States a part of her crew, and that no circumstance might be wanting to mark its character, it had been previously ascertained that the seamen demanded were Native Citizens of the United States."

In his "Notes on Virginia," Jefferson shows what he thought as to the possibility of Slaves being Citizens of the United States. After enumerating some of the horrors of the atrocious concern called the "Peculiar Institution," he proceeds as follows:

"And with what execration should the statesman be loaded, who, permitting *one half of the Citizens thus to trample on the rights of the other*, transforms those into despots, and these into enemies, destroys the morals of the one and the *amor patriæ* of the other."

The Hon. Tristram Burgess, of Rhode Island, in a Speech in Congress, in January, 1828, said: "At the commencement of the war, Rhode Island had a large number of Slaves. A regiment of them were enlisted into the Continental service, and no braver men met the enemy in battle."

Governor Eustis, of Massachusetts, in his Speech against Slavery in Missouri, in 1820, bore this testimony to the bravery of the Colored Soldiers: "The blacks formed an entire Regiment, and they discharged their duty with zeal and fidelity. The gallant defence of Red Bank, New Jersey, in which the Black Regiment bore a part, is among the proofs of their valor."

The glory of the defence of Red Bank, which has been pronounced one of the most Heroic actions of the War, belongs in reality to black men; yet who now hears them spoken of in connection with it? Here are a few of the names of the Soldiers composing the Regiment:—

Cato Greene,	Philo Philipps,	Richard Cozzens,
Cæsar Power,	Primus Rhodes,	Richard Rhodes,
Cuff Greene,	Prince Greene,	Sampson Hazzard,
Gay Watson,	Prince Jenks,	Scipio Brown,
Henry Taylor,	Prince Vaughan,	Thomas Brown,
Ichabod Northrup,	Reuben Roberts,	York Champlain.

Gentlemen, who had at first held back from taking commissions, finding how matters were going, assumed commands, as readily of the Black Companies as if they had been pure Caucasian blood. The nephew of General Washington, Captain Humphreys — take notice, sham democrats of the nineteenth century — a nephew of General Washington, acting under the inspirations of his immortal uncle — commanded one of these battalions; notice, likewise, that their courage was equal to that of the white regulars.* The following is a list of some of the names of the "Black Heroes" commanded by Captain Humphreys. They belonged to the Second Company of the Ninth Regiment of the Connecticut Line of the Revolutionary Army:—

Alexander Judd,	Herman Rodgers,	Peter Lyon,
Andrew Jack,	Isaac Higgins,	Peter Mix,
Bill Sowers,	Jack Arabus,	Peter Morand,
Bristen Parker,	Jack Little,	Phineas Strong,
Cæsar Chapman,	James Dinah,	Philo Freeman,
Cato Wilbrow,	Jesse Rose,	Pomp Cyrus,
Cato Robinson,	Job Cæsar,	Pomp Liberty,

* It would seem from the record that some black men could lead off in a fight, on an emergency. A "descendant of Ham," named Crispus Attucks, was advertised in the Boston "Gazette" of Nov. 20, 1750, as a "runaway nigger." History does not inform us whether or not the "patriarch" who advertised him succeeded in catching him. Probably not. Crispus may have been smart enough to keep out of his way But on the 5th of March, 1770, the runaway proved that he was no coward. Captain Preston, with a body of British soldiers, undertook to repress symptoms of revolution then manifest in a crowd of Bostonians at Dock Square and near the Custom-House. The "white folks" hesitated a little, probably fearing to inaugurate hostilities with the mother-country. Attucks, seeing the need of a leader, placed himself at the head of the crowd, and urged them to drive the red-coats from the streets. He rushed forward, shouting, "Come on! Don't be afraid! We'll drive these red-coats out of Boston!" Two bullets pierced his breast, and the black man fell, the first martyr in the struggle for the freedom of the United States of America. No monument marks the spot where the body of this courageous man lies, simply because he was "*a nigger.*" An effort was recently made, in the Legislature of Massachusetts, to erect a monument to him, but it failed. Had his epidermis been of the sort commonly known as "flesh-color," a magnificent and costly monument would have commemorated his brave deed. "Who did sin, this man or his parents," that he was born with yellowish-brown skin?

Cæsar Bagton,   Joe Etis,   Pomp M'Cuff,
Cuff Freeman,   John Ball,   Prince Crosby,
Cuff Liberty,   John Cleveland,   Prince George,
Congo Zado,   John M'Lane,   Prince Johnson,
Daniel Bradley, John Rodgers,   Shapp Rodgers,
Dick Freeman,   Juba Dyer,   Sharp Camp,
Dick Violet,   Juba Freeman,   Solomon Lowtice,
Ezekiel Tupham, Lent Munson,   Shubael Johnson,
Gamelia Ferry,   Lewis Martin,   Tim Cæsar,
Harry Williams, Ned Freeman,   Tom Freeman.

Among the traits which distinguished the Black Regiments, was devotion to their Officers. In the attack made upon the American lines, near Croton river, Westchester County, New York, on the 13th May, 1781, Colonel Christopher Greene, the commander of the Regiment, was cut down and mortally wounded, but the sabres of the enemy only reached him through the bodies of his faithful guard of blacks, who hovered over him, fighting with the utmost daring to protect him until the last man of them was killed. No monumental piles distinguish their "dreamless beds;" not an inch on the page of History has been appropriated to their memory!

Not long ago, while the excavations for the vaults of a great retail dry goods store, north of the Park, New York, were going on, a large quantity of human bones were thrown up by the workmen. On inquiry it was ascertained that they were the bones of Colored American Soldiers, who fell in the battles of Long Island, in 1776, and of such as died of wounds then received. At that day, as at this, spite of the declaration that "all men are created equal," the prejudice against the "colored man" was intensely strong. The black and the white had fought against the same enemy, under the same banner, contending for the same object. But in the grave, they must be divided. On the battlefield, the blacks and the whites had mixed their bravery and their blood, but their ashes must not mingle in the bosom of their common mother.

The white man, exclusive and haughty even in his burial, must have his place of rest proudly apart from the grave of his black brother, whom he had once enslaved. Now, after seventy-nine years have passed by, the bones of these forgotten victims of the Revolution are shovelled up, and carted off, and thrown into the sea, as the rubbish of the City! Had they been white men's relics, they would have been honored with sumptuous burial anew. Now they are the rubbish of the Street. What boots it that the Colored man fought for American freedom; that he bled for liberty; that he died for his white brothers? Does the Colored man deserve a tomb? (See Appendix A.)

Three quarters of a century have passed by since the retreat from Long Island. What a change since then! From the Washington of that day to the world's Washington of this, what a change! Under the pavement of Broadway, beneath the walls of the Bazaar, there still lie the bones of the Colored Martyrs of American Independence! Dandies swarm gayly over the threshold, heedless of the dead Colored Soldier, contemptuous of the living. And while these faithful bones were being shoveled and carted to the sea, there was "a great Slave-hunt" in New England: a man was kidnapped and carried off to bondage.

The Hon. Charles Pinckney, of South Carolina, in a Speech delivered in the United States Senate, in 1820, bore the following testimony to the services rendered by the Colored Soldiers of 1776: "At the commencement of the Revolutionary struggle with Great Britain, all the States had this class of people. The New England States had numbers of them; the Middle States had still more, although less than the Southern States. They all entered into the great contest with similar views. Like brethren they contended for the benefit of the whole, leaving to each the right to pursue its happiness in its own way. They thus nobly toiled and bled together, really like brethren. *The colored portion of the population then were, as they still are, as valuable to the Union as any other equal number of inhabitants. They were in numerous instances the Pioneers, and in all, the Laborers of your Armies. To their hands were owing the erection of the greatest part of the Fortifications raised for the protection of our country. In the Northern States, numerous bodies of them were enlisted, and fought side by side with the whites the battles of the Revolution."*

The Hon. Robert C. Winthrop, of Massachusetts, in his Speech in Congress, on the Imprisonment of Colored Seamen, September, 1850, bore this testimony to the gallant conduct of the Colored Soldiers of the War of 1812 : " I have an impression that, not, indeed, in these piping times of Peace, but in the time of the War, when quite a boy, I have seen Black Soldiers enlisted, *who did faithful and excellent service.* But, however it may have been in the Northern States, I can tell the Senator what happened in the Southern States at this period. I believe that I shall be borne out in saying, that *no Regiments did better service at New Orleans, than did the Black Regiments, which were organized under the* direction of General Jackson himself."

While the British force was approaching Louisiana, General Jackson learned that among its ranks were Regiments of Colored Men, and he wished to excite the sentiments of loyalty in the bosoms of the " colored people" of that state. The condition of affairs was such, that not a man could be spared. The Government at Washington had left New Orleans utterly without defence, and the general had to avail himself of all the means within his reach to get together a force strong enough to make resistance with something like a chance in his favor of success. To this end, on the 21st of September, 1814, he issued from his Headquarters, at Mobile, Alabama, a " Proclamation," of which the following is a true copy :

Headquarters, 7th Military District,
Mobile, September 21, 1814.

To the Free Colored inhabitants of Louisiana :

Through a mistaken policy you have heretofore been deprived of a participation in the glorious struggle for National Rights, in which your country is engaged. This no longer shall exist. As sons of freedom, you are now called on to defend our most inestimable blessings. *As Americans, your country looks with confidence to her colored children for a valorous support. As fathers, husbands, and brothers, you are summoned to rally around the Standard of the Eagle, to defend all that is dear to existence.* Your country, although calling for your exertions, does not wish you to engage in her cause without remunerating you for the services rendered. In the sincerity of a Soldier, and in the language of Truth, I address you. To every noble-hearted man of Color, volunteering to serve during the present contest with Great Britain, and no longer, there will be paid the same bounty in money and land now received by the white Soldiers of the United States, viz.: $124 *in money, and* 160 *acres of land. The non-commissioned officers and privates will also be entitled to the same monthly pay and daily rations, and clothes, furnished to any white American soldier.* The major-general commanding will select officers for your government from your white fellow-Citizens. Your non-commissioned officers will be selected from yourselves. Due regard will be paid to the feelings of Freemen and Soldiers. You will not, by being associated with white men, in the same corps, be exposed to improper comparisons, or unjust sarcasm. As a distinct independent battalion or regiment, pursuing the path of glory, you will, undivided, receive the applause and gratitude of your countrymen. To insure you of the Sincerity of my Intentions, and my anxiety to engage your valuable services to our country, I have communicated my wishes to the Governor of Louisiana, who is fully informed as to the manner of enrolments, and will give you every necessary information on the subject of this address.

ANDREW JACKSON,
Major-General Commanding.

There is an elaborate Engraving of the Battle of New Orleans, eighteen by twenty inches, executed by M. Hyacinthe Laclotte, the correctness of which was certified to, by eleven of the Superior Officers in New Orleans, July 15, 1815, when the drawing was completed. In the battle, General Jackson and his staff were just at the right of the advancing left column of the British, and near him were stationed the Colored Soldiers. He is numbered " 6," and the position of the Colored Soldiers, " 8." The chart explanation of " Report, No. 8," from the American Army, reads thus: " 8. Captains Dominique and Bluche, two 24-pounders; Major Lacoste's battalion, formed of Men of Color, of New Orleans, and Major Daquin's battalion, formed of the Men of Color of St. Domingo, under Major Savery, second in command." When it is remembered that the whole number of Soldiers claimed by the Americans to have been in that battle reached only 3,600, it will be seen that the " Men of Color" were present in larger proportion than their numbers in the country warranted. General Jackson in his second " proclamation" said :

NEW ORLEANS, December 18, 1814.

TO THE FREE PEOPLE OF COLOR :

Soldiers! when on the banks of the Mobile, I called you to take up arms, inviting you to partake the perils and glory of your white fellow-Citizens, I expected much from you, for I was not ignorant that you possessed qualities most formidable to an invading enemy. I knew with what fortitude you could endure hunger and thirst, and all the fatigues of a campaign. *I knew well how you loved your Native country, and that you as well as ourselves, had to defend what Man holds most dear — his Parents, Wife, Children, and Property. You have done more than I expected. In addition to the previous qualities I before knew you to possess, I found among you a noble enthusiasm which leads to the performance of great things. Soldiers! the President of the United States shall hear how praiseworthy was your conduct in the hour of danger, and the Representatives of the American people will give you the praise your exploits entitle you to!* Your General anticipates them in applauding your noble ardor! The enemy approaches—his vessels cover our lakes—our brave Citizens are united, and all contention (about color) has ceased among them. Their only dispute is who shall win the prize of valor, or who the most glory, its noblest reward. By order.

THOMAS BUTLER, Aid-de-Camp.

How have these promises been kept? Alas! alas! What a spectacle do we witness in the year of our Lord, 1857. A country reaching from Sea to Sea, from the Gulf of tropic heat to Lake Superior's arctic cold, and not one inch of free soil all the way! A country 2,936,166 square miles, and not a foot where a poor heart-broken fugitive from Slavery can be free from the grasp of his " Master" or his agents! And this not the deed of a State reluctantly performing in her sovereign right a Constitutional obligation, but, in hurried obedience to despotic will!

Slavery, which was left to " die with decency," has become the vital and animating spirit of the National Government. The Slaveholders no longer conceal their purpose or deny their assumptions. They control the Foreign and Domestic policy, make War and Peace, enact and trample under foot Laws, and Treaties, and Constitutions, as suits their despotic wills. Their avowals are no less insulting than their acts are insufferable. In the " temple of liberty," Liberty herself is derided. In the Senate of the United States the dicta of its founders are denounced as a lie. The celebration of the " Fourth of July," in all the States, is looked upon as little else than a treasonable emeute. The laws of Congress and the " constitutional privileges" of the Citizens of the several States are alike denied validity when conflicting with the opinions or interests of the Slaveholders. Courts of justice, which are denied in one State for the liberation of Citizens, are perverted in another to the destruction of the liberties of all.

Jefferson's prediction is fulfilled. The danger he dreaded has come upon the people of the "*free* States." Here is his warning, written thirty-five years ago. Every line and word applies with startling distinctness, to the decision made by the Supreme Court of the United States in the case of Dred Scott, on the 7th of March, 1857 :—

" We already see the power installed for life, responsible to no authority, (for impeachment is not even a scare-crow) advancing with a noiseless and steady pace to the great object of consolidation. *The foundations are already deeply laid by their decisions for the annihilation of Constitutional State Rights.* This will not be borne. You will have to choose between reformation and revolution. If I know the spirit of this country, the one or the other is inevitable. Contrary to all correct example, *they go out of the question before them,* to throw an anchor ahead, and grapple further hold for future advances of power. They are, then, in fact, the corps of Sappers and Miners, steadily working to undermine the independent rights of the States. *Nothing in the Constitution has given them a right to decide for the Executive more than for the Executive to decide for them.* The opinion which gives to the Judges the right to decide what laws are Constitutional, and what not, not only for themselves in their own sphere of action, but for the Legislature and Executive also in their spheres, *would make the Judiciary a despotic branch.* If this opinion be sound, then, indeed, is our Constitution a complete *felo de se.* For intending to establish three departments coördinate and independent that they might check and counterbalance one another, it has given, according to this opinion, to one of them alone the Right to prescribe Rules for the Government of the others — and to *that one, too, which is unelected by and independent of the Nation."*

Such is the portrait of Chief-Justice Taney and his Slaveholding associates, drawn by the pen that wrote the Declaration of Independence. Acknowledging no control either by Congress, the Executive, or even "the People," this Court issues edicts to each, and directs or forbids the action of all.

Never did man speak more truly than did Daniel Webster, when he declared — "There is no North ;" for there is none. The South goes clear up to the Canada line. The *New York Tribune* of the 9th of March, 1857, says: "The people of the *free* States have been accustomed to regard Slavery as a 'local' matter for which we were in no wise responsible. As we have been used to say, it belonged to the Slave States alone, and they must answer for it before the world. We can say this no more. Now wherever the Stars and Stripes wave, they protect Slavery and represent Slavery. The cursed stain is on our hands also. From Maine to the Pacific, over all future conquests and annexations, wherever in the islands of western seas, or in the South American Continent, or in the Mexican Gulf, the Flag of the Union, by just means or unjust, shall be planted, there it plants the curse, and tears, and blood, and unpaid toil of this 'Institution.' The Star of Freedom and the Stripes of Bondage are henceforth one. American Republicanism and American Slavery are for the future synonymous. This, then, is the final fruit! In this all the labors of our statesmen, the blood of our heroes, the lifelong cares and toils of our forefathers, the aspirations of our scholars, the prayers of good men, have finally ended!"

There is not upon the face of the earth so despotic a Government as that of either of the Slaveholding States of the American Republic. Take, for example, the State of South Carolina. What are the "qualifications of a Representative"? *He must be legally seized and possessed, in his own right, of a settled freehold of five hundred acres of land, and ten Slaves; or, of real estate of the value of seven hundred and fifty dollars, clear of debt.* If a man does not own Slaves, he must own more land; because when a man owns a certain amount of land, he generally finds it necessary, in order to make it profitable, and increase its value, to purchase Slaves; and thus, as he increases the quantity of his land, he becomes interested in "Slave property." In this way, even those districts where there are but few Slaves will be represented by the owners of those Slaves in the legislature. They, therefore, will concur generally in measures for the support of the Slave interest — and thus *the whole House of Representatives must belong to the Slaveholders.* But to be a Senator requires twice the amount of freehold property qualification, that it does to be a Representative. It will, therefore, follow, that *both Houses must represent the Slave interest, not by a certain majority only, but with absolute unanimity.* And the Governor of the State, whose duty it is to recommend measures for the action of the legislature, must be worth not less than seven thousand dollars in settled estate. The governor, therefore, is the Executive of the Slave interest.

The two United States Senators are elected by the State Legislature. They must, therefore, represent the Slave interest of their State. Again, the Legislature divides the State Congressional Districts, *and it so does it that the Representatives in Congress shall represent the Slaveholding Districts, chiefly.* The State is entitled to seven Representatives in Congress. Now mark how these "Liberty-loving" Carolinians have arranged it. The lower country, with a White population of little over half that of the upper country, has *four* Representatives, while the latter has only *three* Representatives. In Congress, therefore, as well as in the State Legislature, it is the Slaveholding interest that is provided for.* Again, the Electors for President of the United States are chosen, not directly by "the People," but by the Legislature; and they, therefore, also represent the Slave interest. Again, the Judges and the ordinary Magistrates are chosen by the Legislature. Thus the Legislative, Executive, and Judicial departments of the Government are all the Representa-

---

* South Carolina has *seven* Representatives in Congress, while New Hampshire, with a free population greater by thirty-four thousand, has only *three;* and Virginia has *thirteen,* while Massachusetts, with a "*free* population" greater by forty-five thousand, has only *eleven;* and Mississippi has *five,* while Wisconsin, with about ten thousand greater "*free* population," has only *three.* The Slave States, on the same basis of representation as the "free," are entitled to only *sixty-five* Representatives in Congress; yet they have *ninety;* that is, twenty-five extra. This discrepancy between population and representation arises from the fact that, in determining between the number of representatives to which each State is entitled, *five* Slaves are reckoned equal to *three* Freemen! The Slaves have a representation equal to that of the "*free* States" of New Hampshire, Vermont, Connecticut, Iowa, and Wisconsin! Without the representation allowed to "Slave property" by the Compromisers of the "*free* States," the Slaveholders would have been kept in proper check.

tives of the Slaveholding interest. And to make it sure that this order of Government shall perpetually exist, the Constitution of the State provides that no part of this Constitution shall be altered unless a bill to alter the same shall have been read three times in the House of Representatives, and three times in the Senate, and agreed to by two thirds of both branches of the whole representation; neither shall any alteration take place until the bill so agreed to, be published three months previous to a new election for members of the House of Representatives, and if the alteration proposed by the Legislature shall be agreed to in their first Session, by two thirds of the whole representation in both branches of the legislature, after the same shall have been read three times, on three several days in each House, then and not otherwise the same shall become a part of the Constitution.

Now, we ask, when will this Slaveholding legislature, by a vote of two thirds of both Houses in two different Sessions, so alter the Constitution as to throw the majority of that body upon the side of the non-Slaveholding interests of the State, where it rightfully belongs? They will never do it so long as their Slaves can be of any profit to them. The non-Slaveholders or poor whites, therefore, who have no interest in Slavery, but whose interests are directly opposed to it, are tied down, "neck-and-heels," politically speaking, by the Slaveholding Power. They put their votes in the Ballot-box, it is true, *but can not vote for one of themselves.* They must make election from one of the Traffickers in Men, Women, and Children!

Of what account, then, is the vote of the non-Slaveholding portion of the white population of the State? It does not help them out in the least, but it serves to delude them with the idea that they are "freemen," that they may not raise a clamor about their "rights." And who are their "Masters"? Why, the Slaveholding gentlemen, who, living upon the labor, &c.,

&c., of Slaves, often their own Children, care not a straw what is the condition of the poor but industrious white man, nor what becomes of him or his family. If they can get some of them for their Overseers, these they will take interest in, according to their skill in "managing and driving" their "colored brethren." The poor whites have no social equality — no political force — no moral influence. Steeped in ignorance and poverty, the Slaveholders neither respect their opinions nor fear their power. The ostensible Representatives of "the People," in obedience to their "Masters," have not only reduced the "laboring masses" to servitude, but added insult to injury, by openly avowing that "Slavery is the rightful state of the laborer, everywhere, white or black."

The 32,000 Slaveholders in the State not only have Despotic Power over their 384,988 Slaves, but entire Political Power over 242,567 white native-born *freemen*, who can not by any Constitutional means redress themselves when oppressed by Legislative authority — who are so completely kept under the iron hoof, that they can not even have the question of their proper rights brought into discussion in the only body that can Constitutionally effect a change in the Government. Is there so great a despotism under the sun?

In the non-Slaveholding States, we do not often find a person who can not read; but in South Carolina *one fourth* of the adult whites can not read; and there are few of the other three fourths who can even do this with anything like correctness. Nor are the non-Slaveholding portion of the "genuine white population" of the other Slaveholding States highly celebrated for their learning. Yet the Democracy of the "*free* States" sympathize with this abhorrent power, which makes their Laws, builds their party Platforms, and makes their "Public Opinion." They are egregiously humbugged — are they not? or do they begin to understand it?

Concerning this class, the poor whites, Mr. William Gregg, of Charleston, in a pamphlet, called "Essays on Domestic Industry, or an Inquiry into the Expediency of establishing Cotton Manufactures in South Carolina," in 1845, says: "Shall we pass unnoticed *the thousands of poor, ignorant, degraded white people among us, who in this 'land of plenty,' live in comparative nakedness and starvation? Many a one is reared in South Carolina, from birth to manhood, who has never passed a month in which he has not, some part of the time, been stinted for meat. Many a mother is there who will tell you that her children are but scantily provided with bread, and more scantily with meat; and if they be clad with comfortable raiment, it is at the expense of these scanty allowances of food.* These may be startling statements, but they are nevertheless true; and, if not believed in Charleston, the members of our legislature, who have traversed the State in electioneering campaigns, can attest their truth. While we are aware that Northern and Eastern States find no difficulty in educating their poor, we are ready to despair of success in the matter, for even penal laws against the neglect of education would fail to bring many of our country people to send their children to school. *I have long been under the impression, and every day's experience has strengthened my convictions, that the evils exist in the wholly neglected condition of this class of persons.*

"Any man who is an observer of things could hardly pass through our country without being struck by the fact that *all the capital, enterprise, and intelligence, is employed in directing Slave labor;* and the consequence is, that our poor white people are wholly neglected, and are suffered to while away an existence in a state *but one step in advance of the Indian of the forest.* It is an evil of vast magnitude, and nothing but a change in 'public sentiment' will effect its cure. These people must be brought into daily contact with the rich and intelligent — they must be stimulated to mental action, and taught to appreciate education and the comforts of civilized life; and this, we believe, may be effected *only by the introduction of Manufactures.* My experience at Graniteville has satisfied me, that unless our poor people can be brought together in villages, and some means of employment afforded them, it will be an utterly hopeless effort to undertake to educate them. We have collected at Graniteville about 800 people, and as likely-looking a set of country girls as may be found — *industrious and orderly people, but deplorably ignorant, three fourths of the adults not being able to read.* It is very clear to me that the only means of educating and Christianizing our poor whites, will be to bring them into such villages, where they will not only become intelligent, but a thrifty and useful class in our community."

Governor Hammond, in an address before the South Carolina Institute, in 1850, describes these poor whites, or non-Slaveholders, as follows: "They obtain a precarious subsistence *by occasional jobs, by hunting, by fishing, by plundering fields or folds, and too often by what is in its effects far worse, trading with Slaves, and seducing them to plunder for their benefit."* Governor M'Duffie openly declared, in 1835, that the laboring population of any country, "bleached or unbleached," was a dangerous element unless reduced to Slavery. He predicted that the laboring people of the "free States" would be virtually reduced to Slavery within thirty years. Hear him:—

"If we look into the elements of which all political communities are composed, it will be found that servitude, in some form or other, is one of the essential constituents. In the very nature of things, there must be classes of persons to discharge all the different offices of society, from the highest to the lowest. Where these offices are performed by members of the political community, a dangerous element is obviously introduced by the body politic. *Domestic Slavery, therefore, instead of being an evil, is the Corner-Stone of our Republican edifice."* (Message to South

Carolina Legislature, 1835.) Of the Abolitionists he said: "The laws of every community should punish this species of interference with death, without benefit of clergy."

A mechanic, who was "doing well" in Massachusetts, but wanted to "do better," removed with his family to South Carolina, wrote back the following account of the country and its inhabitants: "You ask me how I like the country and the people thereof. As to the land, it is cheap as dirt, but the climate is rather *blowy* and sultry. The owners of 'the people' are distinguished for their *chivalrous* bearing. Cruelty, deceit, and cowardice, are unknown among them. They are extremely philanthropic and wonderfully religious. Human sacrifices are not very frequent, and cannibalism is scarcely ever heard of. The principal exports of the State are cotton, rice, and Negroes."

A man on Long Island, New York, a carpenter, who, as master-workman had become successful, by industry, honesty, and intelligence, in the pursuit of his business, and learning that there was great demand for his work in the " land of *gentle* gales," and thinking he might more rapidly acquire a competency there, closed up his business and went South for that purpose. He had hardly got into his shop, when a man sent for him to make a contract with him for repairing and in effect rebuilding some part of his establishment. He desired him to make a computation of the cost, and to let him know the lowest price at which he would undertake the business. The bill somewhat exceeded his expectations. He reflected a while, and at length told the man that on the whole he concluded not to engage him. The work would take two or three months, and he thought he could do better to *buy a carpenter, and sell him again in the spring.* The man left the house, went to his shop, packed up his tools, took passage for New York, declaring that a country where men could buy their carpenters and sell them again in the spring, was no place for him or for free-labor to live in.

The Slave-traders of Mississippi, Louisiana, Texas, &c., have made sad work with the Sons and Daughters of South Carolina. In 1790, the State had a "genuine white population" of 140,178 souls, and in 1850, only 274,567. What has become of the natural increase of the 140,178?

There ought to have been, in 1850, a population of 840,000. The "Peculiar Institution" is chargeable with the deficiency.

A book has recently been published in the South — a book that has been indorsed by *The Richmond* (Va.) *Enquirer*, the ablest organ of the Democratic party in the United States — an organ that sustained the Administration of Franklin Pierce, and sustains the Administration of James Buchanan. Here are a few extracts from the work:

1. Make the laboring man the Slave of one man, instead of the Slave of Society, and he would be far better off. Two hundred years of labor have made white laborers a pauper banditti. Free society has failed, and that which is not free must be substituted. Free society is a monstrous abortion, and Slavery is the healthy, and beautiful, and natural condition which they are trying unconsciously to adopt. Nature has made the weak in mind and body Slaves.

2. The Slaves are governed far better than the free laborers of the North are governed. Our negroes are far better off as to physical comfort than the free laborers, and their moral condition is better. Slavery, black or white, is right and necessary. Men are not born entitled to equal rights. It would be far nearer to truth to say that some were born with saddles on their backs, and others booted and spurred to ride them, and riding does them good. They need the reins, the bit, and the spur.

3. Life and liberty are not inalienable. The Declaration of Independence is exuberantly false and aborescently fallacious. Has not the experiment of universal liberty failed? Are not the evils of free society insufferable? We repeat, then, that policy and humanity alike forbid the extension of the evils of free society to a new people and coming generations. We would not have your rich, vulgar, licentious bosses, and your brutal insubordinate factory hands in our midst, for all "the wealth of Ormus and Ind." We would not exchange our situation for the count-

less millions of paupers and criminals who build up and sustain the cowardly, infidel, licentious, revolutionary edifice of free society.

4. Until recently, the defence of Slavery has labored under difficulties, but its apologists (for they are mere apologists), took halfway ground. They confined the defence of Slavery to the mere *Negro* Slavery; thereby giving up the Slavery *principle*, admitting other forms of Slavery to be wrong. The line of defence, however, is now changed. The South maintains that *Slavery is right, natural, and necessary, and does not depend upon difference of complexion.* The laws of the Slave States justify the holding of white men in bondage. Repeatedly have we asked the North, "Has not the experiment of liberty failed? Are not the evils of *free society insufferable?* And do not thinking men among you propose to subvert and reconstruct it?" Still no answer. This gloomy silence is another conclusive proof, added to many other conclusive evidences we have furnished, that free society in the long run is an impracticable form of society.

The people of Virginia certainly are "a people blessed above all other people." They might have Wealth; they might have Manufactures; they might have Commerce; but they do not want a Society that it would bring along with it! They are content now: give them territory enough so that they can extend their "Institution" and sell annually $25,000,000 worth of their Sons and Daughters, and that "Commonwealth" is content.

The party papers throughout the Southern States echo the sentiments of the Richmond Enquirer boldly, while at the North and West they do the same. No Democratic paper has dared to deny or controvert its position, nor will any do so. The Democracy of the South may be regarded as the Democracy of the Nation, for it has always given to the entire party shape and direction as well as Platforms. The party being, according to its own averment, exclusively "National," it must, of necessity, be the same North that it is South. *The Enquirer* says, in its issue of June 16, 1856:

> The South contends for the equal extension of Slavery with other social forms, and must contend that it is equally worthy of extension.

Her old grounds of apology and excuse will avail her nothing. She must prove that Slaves are as well provided, as happy and contented, as hired laborers. She can easily show that they are better off in all these respects than hirelings, and far less addicted to crime. She must also show, that Slaveholders are the equals in Morality, Piety, Courage, and Intelligence, to the Bosses and Employers of the Northern States. It will be easy to prove that they are their Superiors. *It will only remain for her to show that the Bible sanctions Slavery, and her victory will be complete.* The Democrats of the Slaveholding States can not rely on the mere Constitutional guarantees of Slavery, for such reliance is pregnant with admission that Slavery is wrong, and, but for the Constitution, should be abolished. Nor will it avail us aught to show that the *Negro* is most happy and best situated in the condition of Slavery. If we stop there we weaken our cause by the very argument intended to advance it; for we propose to introduce into new territory human beings whom we assert to be unfit for liberty, self-government, and equal association with other men. We must go a step further. We must show that *Slavery is a Moral, Religious, National, and a Necessary Institution of Society.* We know that we utter bold threats, but the time has arrived when their utterance can be no longer suppressed. The true issue stands out in bold relief, so that none may mistake it. This is the only line of argument that will enable the South to maintain the doctrines of State Equality and Slavery Extension.

The *South Side Democrat,* whose Editor was in the Winter of 1855, a Candidate for Clerk of the House of Representatives, and was supported by the Democratic members, says; "We have got to hating everything with the prefix *free,* from *free* Niggers down and up through the whole catalogue—*free* Farms, *free* Labor, *free* Society, *free* Will, *free* Thinking, *free* Children, and *free* Schools—all belonging to the same brood of detestable isms. But the worst of all these abominations is the system of *free* Schools." Another leading press of the Democratic party, and a worthy organ of Pierce, Buchanan, & Co., published in South Carolina, sustains the views taken by *The Enquirer.* It uses this plain language on the subject: "*Slavery is the natural normal condition of the laboring man, whether white or black.* The great evil of

Northern *free* Society is, that it is burthened with a *Servile class of Mechanics and laborers, unfit for self-government*, and clothed with the attributes of Citizens. Master and Slave is a relation in Society as necessary as that of Parent and Child; and the Northern States of this Republic will yet have to introduce it. Their *theory* of a 'free Government' is a delusion." Another prominent organ of the Democratic party, *The Muscogee* (Ala.) *Herald*, a journal which goes even further than its Virginia contemporaries, says: " Free society! We sicken of the name. What is it but a conglomeration of *greasy mechanics, filthy operatives, small-fisted farmers, and moonstruck theorists. All the Northern, and especially the New England States, are devoid of society fitted for a well-bred gentleman.* The prevailing class one meets with, is that of mechanics struggling to be genteel, and small farmers who do their own drudgery; and yet who are hardly fit for a Southern gentleman's body-servant. This is your *free* Society which the Northern hordes are endeavoring to extend into the Territories."

The New York *Day Book*, a journal which aspires to the leadership of the Democratic forces of the entire country, in its issue of June 21, 1856, says: "*Negro Slavery is the Basis of American Democracy. The insubordination of an Inferior race has secured and always will secure, the Equality of the Superior race.*" In its " Campaign Prospectus" (a copy of which was sent to every Postmaster in the United States and Territories, to be hung up in their respective Offices), occurs the following portentous announcement: " We have enlisted for the War against Abolitionism and its Impostures, and we do not intend to stop until *we* subdue them." The same Journal, in a leader on the " gallant conduct" of the " chivalrous Brooks," of South Carolina, for his assault on the defenceless Sumner of Massachusetts, says: " The time is close at hand when such statesmen as Sumner, Seward, Hale, and Wade, will have justice, full justice done them, when, in short, an Abolitionist will be lynched as readily in New York or Boston, as in Charleston or New Orleans."

The deadliest foe of the Northern Free Laborer is the Slaveholder; as one increases must the other decrease. They are natural antagonists. Yet so wily has the Slave power been that, while it has with one hand grasped the reins of government, it has with the other moulded the Free Laborer of the North into a willing subservience to its interests, and obedience to its commands.

At a "Mass Meeting" of the Democracy of Philadelphia, held September 17, 1856, in "Independence Square," in commemoration of the Federal Constitution, Governor Johnson, of Georgia, in a Speech on the "glories of Slavery," said: "The results of the Institution shows that it is a great instrument of *Providence*, intended to work out a magnificent destiny for the Democracy of the entire country—and the continent of Africa! And I would venture to throw out another idea: the great contest that is now being waged, call it by what name you will, is a contest between Capital on the one hand and Labor on the other; and the only question is whether it is better for the Southern States of our glorious Union to *own* their labor or to *hire* it. (Cheering and hissing.) The South did not interfere with the settlement of the Slavery question in the Northern States of our happy Union, and all I ask of the *free* States in return is, 'Hands off! in God's name stop this excitement, this outrageous agitation, and let us do as we please.' (Groans, hisses, and cries of 'Bravo!') The South has determined that Capital shall *own* Labor. Why? It is better upon this ground, if no other, that their Agricultural products are of such a *character* that they *can not* hire labor to cultivate them. They can not hire labor to cultivate rice swamps, ditch their low ground, or drain their morasses. (Laughter, hisses, groans.) And why? Because the climate is deadly to the white man — he could not go there and live a week, and therefore the vast territory would be a barren waste unless Capital *owned* its Labor."* (Applause.)

The calculation has been made, and not been disputed, that India could supply Cotton equal in staple to that of America, and twenty-five per cent. cheaper. A regular trade in that product, the raw material of England's most important branch of industry, has been established between the districts of Broach and Surat, and England. These territories lie along the sea-coast, the Cotton lands being in no case more than twenty miles from water-carriage to Bombay, where the shipments are made; but the produce is not of a high quality owing to the small demand, and the consequent limitation of price. A larger demand and higher prices would act naturally as encouragements to native agriculture. The lowest average price of American Cotton is seven cents (three pence halfpenny) per pound — sufficient to act as a powerful stimulus to its cultivation in India. Governor Adams, of South Carolina, in his "Annual Message" to the Legislature of that State, in November, 1856, said: "*Whenever England and the Continent can procure their supply of the raw material elsewhere than from us, and the Cotton States are limited to the Home market, then will our doom be sealed. Destroy the value of*

---

* At the same time, in this same city of Philadelphia, a cotton-ridden church was trying to get rid of its minister, a faithful servant of God, for having dared to speak from his pulpit plain words in reference to the giant power to which the nation and the Church had sold themselves. It was necessary, "in order to save the Union," that this minister should not rebuke certain Christians in his congregation, who were in receipt of large incomes from the unrequited toil of the colored brethren on their plantations in the South, whom they claimed to own. The slave power in the church succeeded in accomplishing its purposes. It almost killed the church, however, in the struggle. The valiant soldier of the Cross is now doing duty only a few blocks off, preaching to a congregation who are willing to listen to an undiluted gospel.

Slave labor, and *Emancipation follows inevitably*. This, England, our commercial rival, clearly sees, and hence her systematic efforts to stimulate the production of Cotton in the East. During the year 1855 the shipments of Cotton to Great Britain were, from the United States, in round numbers, six hundred and seventy-nine millions of pounds, and the East Indies, Egypt, and Brazil, two hundred and two millions of pounds! France, too, is encouraging and stimulating its growth in Algeria, with like advantages of soil and labor. *To maintain our position, we must re-open the African Slave-trade.*"

Governor Adams ought to be satisfied with the thirty-five Slavers now in the field. (See Appendix C.) So long as public opinion tolerates Slavery itself and the "Domestic" traffic connected therewith, laws against the stealing of Men, Women, and Children, from Africa, for the purpose of enslaving them in the "Model Republic," must necessarily be a farce.

The Hon. F. W. Pickens, of South Carolina, in a Speech in Congress, said: "All society settles down into a classification of Capitalists and Laborers. The former will *own* the latter, either collectively through the Government, or individually in a state of Domestic servitude, as exists in the Southern States of this glorious Confederacy. *If laborers ever obtain the political power of a country, it is in fact in a state of revolution. We have already not only a right to the proceeds of our laborers, but we own a class of laborers themselves.* But, let me say to gentlemen who represent the great class of Capitalists at the North, beware how you drive us into a separate system." Chancellor Harper, of the same State, in a communication to *The Southern Literary Messenger* (a religious periodical, published at Charleston), says: "Would you do a benefit to the horse, or the ox, by giving him a cultivated understanding, a fine feeling? So far as the mere laborer has the pride, the knowledge, or the aspiration of a freeman, he is unfitted for his situation. If there are sordid, servile, laborious offices to be performed, is it not better that there should be sordid, servile, laborious beings to perform them? Odium has been cast upon our legislature on account of its forbidding the elements of education being communicated to Slaves. But, in truth, what injury is done them by this? He who works during the day with his hands does not read in the intervals of leisure, for his amusement or the improvement of his mind."

Professor De Bow (the Compiler of the United States Census, of 1850), in the January number, 1850, of his Review, in an article on Manufactures in South Carolina, expresses his fears of bringing together masses of non-Slave-holding Southern white population even for Manufacturing purposes:—

So long as these poor but industrious people could see no mode of living except by a degrading operation of work with the Slave upon the plantation, they were content to endure life in its most discouraging forms, satisfied that they were *above* the Slave, though faring often worse than he. But the progress of the world is "onward," and though in some sections (New England, for instance) it is slow, still it is *onward*. The South hitherto has attempted to justify Negro Slavery as an exception to a general rule, or, if wrong, *as a matter of bargain between the North and the South*. The laws of God and Nature are immutable, and man can not bargain them away. While it is far more *obvious* that Negroes should be Slaves than Whites — for they are only fit to labor, not to direct — yet the principle of Slavery is itself right, and does not depend on difference of complexion.

When the mind once becomes familiarized with the process of Slavery — of Enslaving first, Black, then Indian, then Mulatto, then Quadroon, and when "blue eyes and golden hair" are advertised every day of the year as properties of *Negroes*, what protection is there for poor white people? "We boast," says General John H. Eaton, of Washington, D. C., "of Liberty and National justice! How frequently have I seen in the Southern States of our country weeping

Mothers leading guiltless Infants to the Sales, with as deep anguish as if they had led them to the Slaughter-house. When I see these enormities practised upon beings whose Complexion and Blood claim kindred with my own, I curse the perpetrators, and weep over the wretched victims of their rapacity."

A walk on the street in Washington is one of the best and most touching commentaries on the character of the "Peculiar Institution." A man's eyes are only needed to carry to his mind the conviction of the servitude it entails upon the descendants of the whites themselves. Along with the "blacks," side by side, stand the Mulatto, the Quadroon, the tenth part, the twentieth part, the thirtieth part black, absolutely undistinguishable from the white, all chained alike to the same inexorable and soul-breaking sorrows of Slavery. It results from this that there is a class of Slaves in all respects Equal, and in many cases Superior, to the "Master" or "Mistress" who owns or controls them.

CHAPTER II.

"SLAVERY," says the Hon. Charles J. Faulkner, of Virginia, "is an Institution which presses heavily against the best interests of the State. It banishes *free white labor; it exterminates the Mechanic, the Artisan, the Manufacturer. It deprives them of bread. It converts the energy of a community into indolence — its power into imbecility — its efficiency into weakness.* Sir, being thus injurious, have we not a right to demand its extermination? Shall society suffer that we Slaveholders may continue to gather our Crops of Human Flesh? What is the Slaveholder's mere pecuniary claim, compared with the great interests of the common weal. Must the country languish, droop, die, that the Slaveholder may flourish? Shall all interests be subservient to one? all rights subordinate to those of the Slaveholder? Has not the Mechanic, have not the middle classes their rights? — rights incompatible with the existence of Slavery? Sir, I am gratified to perceive that no gentleman has yet risen, in this hall, the avowed Advocate of Slavery. I even regret, sir, that we should find those among us who enter the list of discussion as its Apologists. Sir, if there be one who concurs with the gentleman (Mr. Golshon) from Brunswick County, in the 'harmless character' of this Institution, let me request him to compare the condition of the Slaveholding portion of this State — *barren, desolate, and seared as it were by the avenging hand of Heaven* — with the descriptions which we have of this same country from those who first broke its virgin soil. To what is this change ascribable? *Alone to the withering and blasting effects of Slavery.* Sir, if this does not satisfy him, let me request him to extend his travels to the Northern States of this Union, and beg him to contrast the happiness and contentment which prevail throughout that portion of our country—the busy and cheerful sound of Industry—the rapid and swelling growth of their Population—their means and Institutions of Education—their Skill and Proficiency in the Useful arts—their Enterprise and Public spirit—the Monuments of their Commercial and Manufacturing industry.

"To what, sir, is all this ascribable? To what vice in the organization of Society by which one half of its inhabitants are arrayed in interest and feeling against the other half—to that unfortunate state of Society in which *freemen* regard labor as disgraceful, and Slaves shrink from it as a burden tyrannically imposed upon them—*to that condition of things in which over half the population of the State can feel no sympathy with the Society in the prosperity of which they are forbidden to participate, and no attachment to a Government at whose hands they receive nothing but injustice.* If this should not be sufficient, and the curious and incredulous inquirer should suggest that the contrast which has been adverted to, and which is so manifest, might be traced to a difference of Climate or other causes distinct from Slavery itself, permit me to refer him to the two States of *Kentucky* and *Ohio*. No difference of soil, no diversity of Climate, no diversity in the original settlement of those two States, can account for the remarkable disproportion in the National advancement. Separated by a river alone, they seem to have been *purposely and providentially designed to exhibit in their future histories the difference which necessarily results from a country free from, and a country afflicted with, the curse of Slavery.* The same may be said of the two States of *Missouri* and *Illinois*. What, sir, have you lived for two hundred years without personal effort or productive industry, in extravagance and indolence, *sustained alone by the returns from the Sales of the Increase of Slaves, and retaining such a number as your now impoverished lands can sustain as Stock!*"*

The subsequent acquisition of new Slave States, and the consequent rise in the price of Slaves, appear to have decided Mr. Faulkner to "hold on a little longer," for he is now, in 1857, not only a Member of Congress, but one of the most determined advocates of the infamous traffic he so warmly condemned in 1832. (See Proverbs xxvi. 11, and St. Luke xi. 24–26.) Only the other day, six of his party-colored chattels — all of them the children, as a matter of course, of the "unfortunate Ham" — made their escape from his plantation, at Martinsburg, Virginia, to Canada.

The following "Circular" to the Postmasters, throughout the Union, will give the reader a more correct idea of Mr. Faulkner's position in July, 1856. It shows the effort that was made, and the means used to train the "foreign-born population," and bring them into rank and file for the purpose of electing Buchanan, and still further Extending the area of Slavery. It will be seen from the questions propounded that the National Executive were prepared for any kind of electioneering. If they but knew a man's religion they could meet his wants — exactly :—

DEMOCRATIC NATIONAL RESIDENTS' COMMITTEE ROOMS,
WASHINGTON, D. C., *July* 2, 1856.

To ——, Esq., *Chairman of Democratic Committee,*
    County of ——, State of —— :

SIR: Though the Executive National Committee have the most implicit reliance in the discretion and sound judgment of the people and the correctness of the principles maintained and asserted by the Democratic party, upon which they are to pass their verdict at the impending Presidential election, on the 4th November, 1856, they deem it, nevertheless,

* Speech in the Virginia House of Delegates, in 1832.

as a high duty, in view of the vast stake at issue — even the continuance of the Union — to do all in their power to secure the success of the Democratic cause, and the triumphant election of the nominees of the Democratic Convention. We are now sure that Victory will follow our banners [see chaps. i. and ii., of Part II.; and chap. ii., of Part V.], but to make Victory doubly sure, we invite you to send us an immediate answer to the following queries:—

First: What is the probable number of Voters in your County who speak the German language? Are they American-born or immigrants, and in what ratio?

Second: Are there any French, Dutch (Hollanders), Norwegians, or Swedes, in your County? and if so, what is approximately the number of votes cast by each respectively?

Third: Are there any German newspapers printed in your county? and if so, give the title of such paper or papers, and the place or places of such publication. You will confer a favor on the National Committee by sending, during the whole canvass, a number of the weekly issue of such paper or papers printed in the foreign language to the undersigned, Chairman of the National Resident Committee.

Fourth: To what religious denominations do the German, French, Dutch, Norwegian, or Swedish voters in your county belong?

Fifth: What are generally the political sentiments entertained by the adopted citizens in your county, especially in regard to principles now before the people, viz., the equality of the individual States in the settlement of our Territories; the equality of all Citizens in relation to Political rights, and the rights of Conscience?

Sixth: Have you appointed distributors in the different townships and School districts of your county, who will place the documents sent by the National Committee into the hands of your voters? or do you prefer to have them sent to you *franked* to be directed by you?

Seventh: Have you formed Democratic Clubs or Associations throughout your county? and if so, please to report the Officers to the National Committee, with their Postoffices.

Eighth: How are the Democratic nominations in your county received, and what is the probable vote the Democracy will cast?

Ninth: Will you furnish us with the names of two active and zealous Democrats contiguous to each Postoffice in your county, who can be relied upon to see the prompt distribution of documents forwarded to them?

Tenth: Will you inform us the grounds upon which the Democratic party is principally assailed in your county and suggest to us the *kind of documents* which would best promote the success of the Democratic party?

Please report the names and Postoffices of some reliable German citizens, living in the different townships of your county, in order to enable the National Resident Committee to enter into a correspondence with them. Please direct all communications to me.

CHARLES J. FAULKNER,
Chairman N. D. R. Committee.

Mr. Faulkner does not trouble his head about the Irish-American Vote, he merely addresses his German, French, Dutch, Norwegian, and Swedish "fellow-Citizens." As respects the Irish-Americans, they are "all right." There is no denying the fact. As a mass, they go for Slavery, and its Extension. The *Freeman's Journal*, the Archbishop's organ, is open for Slavery, for the degradation of that sort of labor, especially *unskilled* labor, which seven Irishmen out of every ten pursue in the United States; and thus these men are made to degrade their own *status* to the level of Slavery!

The Irish-Americans are great advocates of "European Liberty," and great friends of American Slavery. The "Irish patriots" of old were famous for making bulls; in modern times they would seem to be no less skilful in making asses — of themselves. This fact accounts for the extraordinary conduct of Mitchel, Meagher, & Co.

The shoe of Slavery will yet pinch the toes of the Irish-Americans. An able-bodied "Irish-American Nigger" can, even now, be purchased for about one third the price of an able-bodied "black Nigger." Only the other day, the Hon. P. T. Herbert, M. C., purchased from Judge Crawford, of Washington, the right of shooting an Irishman for three hundred dollars. "Irish-American Niggers" are preferred to either Dutch or German "Niggers," as being more "evangelical," and therefore, "more manageable" and "less likely to run away." Accordingly, *The Richmond* (VA.) *Enquirer*, after joining *The Charleston* (S. C.) *Mercury* and *The New Orleans Delta*, in declaring the revival of the African Slave-trade "necessary, inevitable, and desirable," now turns a short corner and opposes the introduction of "African Niggers."

$300 REWARD.—Ran away from the subscriber, on the 5th day of July last, a white *Negro* boy, 29 years of age; height 5 feet and 10½ inches; *has blue eyes, a very fair skin, and a Roman nose*. He will, no doubt, endeavor to pass himself off for a white man.

A. BEARD.

[New Orleans Picayune.]

$250 REWARD.—Ran away from the subscriber, on or about the 29th of November last, a *Negro* girl, named Biddy, about sixteen years of age, *quite white, and reddish hair*. She has three front teeth bucked out and a cut on her upper lip; about five feet and seven inches high; has a scar on her left buttock; *she passes for free;* talks English, French, and Mountain-Irish or "Bog-Latin." She will try to pass herself off for an Irish girl.

57 Common street, New Orleans.   THOMAS FOSTER.

$500 REWARD.—Ran away from the subscriber, on the 15th of May last, a *Negro* girl, named Fanny. Said girl is twenty years old; is rather tall; can read and write, and, consequently, can forge passes for herself. She carried away with her a pair of ear-rings and a Bible with a red cover. She is very pious; she prays a great deal, and was, as supposed, contented and happy. *She is as white as most white women, with straight light hair and blue eyes, and can pass herself for a white woman.* I will give $500 for her apprehension and delivery to me. She is very intelligent.

JOHN BALCH.

$100 REWARD.—Ran away from the subscriber, in Randolph county, on the 18th of October last, a boy, named Jim. This boy is 19 years of age, *of a light color, with sun-burned hair, inclined to be tolerably straight;* he is about five feet and seven inches high, and slightly made. He had on when he left, a black-cloth cap, black-cloth pantaloons, a plaid sack-coat, a fine shirt, and brogan shoes. One hundred dollars will be paid for the recovery of the above-described Nigger, if taken out of the State, or fifty dollars if taken in the State.

Huntsville, Missouri.   MRS. S. P. HALL.

We might go on giving advertisements and multiplying proofs, of this sort, until our task swelled into a dozen volumes, instead of one; but enough has been said (see chapters i., ii., and iii., of Part V.), to prove that White Slavery not only actually but Legally exists in the United States of North America. Will not those, then, whose ears are closed to the cry of anguish of the millions of the despised and hated black, brown, orange, drab, yellow, straw, and peach-blossom colored " Niggers," extend a helping-hand to relieve the anguish of the tens of thousands of " White Niggers," who are now in chains in eleven of the Slave States of the Union?

The Hon. S. W. Downs, late Senator from Louisiana, has just published an elaborate Speech, on the " peculiar advantages of Slave labor over free labor." In his discourse, this " enlightened statesman" assumes that the white laborers of the North are not so happy, contented, or comfortable, as the colored and party-colored " Niggers" of the South. Reduce, therefore, the white laborer of the North to the condition of the Southern Slave, and the sum of human happiness will be promoted.

If this be the treatment reserved for the Democracy of the North, it may well be supposed that the poor immigrants, who are classed with " Niggers," can scarcely look for more favorable treatment. Here is the remedy proposed for persons of this class who may be found unable to support their families — mark, it is not said for acknowledged mendicants, or for persons who have applied for relief from the public funds, but simply for those who may fall into poverty, and be unable to support their families. Says Mr. Downs:

" Sell the parents of these children into Slavery. Let our Legislature pass a Law, that, whoever will take these parents and take care of them and their offspring, in sickness and in health, clothe them, feed them, and house them, shall be Legally entitled to their services; and let the same Legislature decree, that, whoever receives these parents and their children and obtains their services shall take care of them as long as they live."

"Sir," said James M'Dowell, jr., " Virginia is withering under the leprosy which is piercing her to the heart. Proud as are the names, for intellect and patriotism, which enrich the volumes of our history, and reverentially as we turn to them at this period of waning reputation — *that name — that man — above all parallel would have been chief who could have blotted out this curse from his country.** In this investigation there is no difficulty — nothing has been left to speculation or inquiry; for, however widely men have differed upon the power and justice of touching this 'property,' they have yet united in a common testimony to its character. It has been frankly and unequivocally declared from the very commencement of this debate, by the most decided enemies of Abolition themselves, as well as by others, that this 'property' is an 'evil.' Yes, Sir, the danger is inevitable and is increasing.†

---

* What has been the conduct of the people of Virginia, and the other Slave States, toward the man who has been battling, to this end, for the last twenty-seven years? It has been most atrocious. Nor has he fared better at the hands of the people of the "*free* States." He has sought nothing for himself — neither office, nor money, nor praise. He has aimed to do his duty to his Neighbor and his God; who ever did both more manfully? See what his reward has been! Outwardly, abuse, scorn, hatred, loathing, from the State, and the hot curses of the "evangelical Churches." But he has that inward recompense which fails no man — the satisfaction of duties done, yes, of cruel sorrows, innocently and nobly borne. In the history of mankind, there is no man who has more courageously gone on a forlorn hope, none who has borne a cross so heavy with more sweetness and generous forbearance. Coming generations will do justice to his memory.

† Every three and a half minutes that passes witnesses a "colored" native American born to be a Slave. That child whom God made free, and for whose happiness Christ suffered, bled, and died, is seized by the Slaveholder, perhaps its own father, and blotted out from the Human race.

"Who that looks upon his family with the Slave in its bosom, ministering to its wants, but knows and feels that this is true — who but sees and knows how much the safety of that family depends upon forbearance, how little can be provided by defence? *Sir, you may exhaust yourself upon schemes of domestic defence; and when you have examined every project which the mind can suggest, you will, at last, have only a deeper consciousness that nothing can be done.* The curse which, in combination with others, has been denounced against man as a just punishment for his sins — the curse of having an enemy in his household — has come upon us. We have an enemy there to whom our dwelling is at all times accessible — our persons at all times — our lives at all times, and that by manifold weapons, both visible and concealed. But, Sir, I will not expatiate further on this view of the subject. Suffice it to say, that the defenceless situation of the 'Master,' and the sense of injured rights in the Slave, are the best possible preparatives for conflict — a conflict, too, which may be considered as more certainly at hand whenever and wherever the numerical ascendency of the Slave shall inspire him with confidence in his force."*

If Virginia had not a settler within her territory, and should be opened at once to free Settlement, *in ten years she would have nearly as many white inhabitants as she now has*, two hundred and fifty years after her Settlement, and *in twenty years she would have nearly as many whites as the whole number of Slaveholding States now have*, provided 60,000 settlers should go in the first year, and that the rate of increase should be as great as that of Wisconsin, Iowa, or Minnesota. Even with this population of twenty years, she would not be so densely peopled as Massachusetts was in 1850. The figures prove it: thus, Wisconsin had, in 1840, 30,749 whites; in

---

* Speech in the Virginia House of Delegates, in 1832.

1850, 304,756. Ratio of increase 89.11 *per cent.* Assume 60,000 whites in Virginia at the close of the first year, and the rate of increase as above, in ten years she would have 594,660 white inhabitants, and in twenty years 5,793,475. Number of whites in Virginia in 1850, 894,800; in the Slaveholding States, 6,184,477. Thus, as to population, *Slavery in two hundred and fifty years has done the work of twenty.* As to the value of lands, it has done still worse. Thus, in little more than ten years, Wisconsin had brought up the value of her farms per acre to $9.54; Virginia, in two hundred and fifty years, had barely raised the price of her lands to $8.27 per acre.

Only a little while ago an auction of Virginia lands took place at the Philadelphia Exchange. Some 40,000 acres situated in the Counties of Doddridge, Gilmer, and Monongalia, near Ohio and Pennsylvania, brought two cents (a penny) an acre, and some 70,000 acres in the Counties of Montgomery and Washington, near North Carolina and Tennessee, sold for one cent (a halfpenny) an acre. The whole quantity sold on the occasion, 150,000 acres, brought $1,800. Both prices show the blighting influence of Slavery. Think of it! Lands lying near Navigable rivers and Railroads, in the oldest State of the Union, endowed with Unsurpassed Fertility and Unbounded Mineral Wealth, selling in an open market, where there are millions of capital for any tolerable speculation, for one or two cents by the thousand acres!

The Hon. Willoughby Newton, of Virginia, in his Agricultural Address, in 1850, said: "I look upon the introduction of Guano, and the success attending its application to our barren lands, in the light of a *special interposition of Divine Providence, to save Virginia from reverting into its former state of wilderness and utter desolation.* Until the discovery of Guano—more valuable to us than the mines of California— I looked upon the possibility of renovating our soil, of ever bringing it to a point capable of producing remunerating crops, as utterly hopeless."

Is Virginia, then, "saved" by Guano? Mr. Newton recommends the application of two hundred pounds per acre. The number of acres of land under cultivation in Virginia in 1850, was 26,152,311. The amount of Guano requisite to cover this land, at the rate of two hundred pounds per acre, would be 2,615,231 tons. This, at $50 per ton, would cost $130,761,550. Guano must be applied every other year. This would give the annual amount, 1,307,615 tons, and the annual cost, $65,380,775. *Where is the money to pay this annual tax to come from?* How long would it take the permanent registered tonnage of Virginia (9,246 tons in 1855) to import enough for one year's use?

"Mr. Speaker," said Henry Berry, "coming from a county [Jefferson] in which there are over 4,000 Slaves, being myself a Slaveholder — and I may say further, that the largest 'property' I have in Virginia lies about a hundred miles east of the Blue Ridge, and consists of land and Slaves — under these circumstances I hope I shall be excused by my brethren of the North for saying a few words on this important and deeply-interesting subject. That Slavery is a grinding curse upon this State, I had supposed would have been admitted by all, and that the only question for debate would have been the possibility of removing the evil. But, Sir, in this I have been disappointed. I have been astonished that there are advocates here for Slavery, with all its effects. Sir, this only proves how far, how very far, we may be carried by pecuniary interest; it proves what has been said by an immortal bard:

> "'That man is unco weak, and little to be trusted
>   If self the wavering balance shake, 't is rarely right adjusted.'

"Sir, I believe no cancer on the physical body was ever more certain, steady, and fatal, in its progress, than is this cancer on the political body of the State of Virginia. It is eating into her very vitals. Like a mighty avalanche the evil is rolling toward us, accumulating weight and impetus at every turn. And, Sir, if we do nothing to avert its progress, it will ultimately overwhelm and destroy us for ever. And although I have no fears for any general results from the efforts of this class of our population now; still, Sir, the time will come when there will be imminent, general danger.* Pass as severe laws as you will to keep these unfortunate creatures in ignorance, it is in vain, unless you extinguish that spark of intellect which God has given them. Let any man who advocates Slavery, examine the *System of Laws* that we have adopted (from stern necessity, it may be said) toward these creatures, and he may *shed a tear upon that*, and would to God, Sir, the memory of it might thus be blotted out for ever.

"Sir, we have, as far as possible, closed every avenue by which light might enter their minds; we have only to go one step further — to extinguish the capacity to see the light — and our work would be accomplished; they would then be reduced below the level of the beasts of the field, and we would be safe; and I am not certain that we would not do it if we could

---

* The late Rev. John O. Choules, D. D., of Newport, Rhode Island, who, while attending a Baptist Convention at Richmond, Virginia, had a conversation with an Officer of the Baptist Church in that City, at whose house he was a guest, says: I asked him if he did not apprehend that the Slaves would eventually rise and exterminate their Masters? "Why," said the gentleman, "I did use to apprehend such a catastrophe, but *God* has made a providential opening, *a merciful safety-valve*, and now I do not feel alarmed, in the prospect of what is coming." What do you mean, said Mr. Choules, by Providence opening a merciful safety-valve? "Why," said the gentleman, "I will tell you. The Slave-traders come from the Cotton and Sugar plantations of the South, and are willing to buy up more Slaves than we can part with. *We must keep a Stock for the purpose of Breeding*, but we part with the most dangerous, and the demand is very constant, and is likely to be so, for when they go to those Southern States, the average existence is only five years."

HALTING AT NOON. (*See page* 159.)

find out the necessary process, and that under the plea of necessity. But, Sir, this is impossible; and can man be in the midst of *freemen* and not know what freedom is? Can he feel that he has the power to assert his liberty, and will he not do it? Yes, Sir, with the certainty of the current of time, will he do it whenever he has the power. Sir, to prove that the time will come, I need offer no other argument than that of Arithmetic; the conclusions from which are clear demonstrations of this subject. The data are before us all, and every man can work out the process for himself. Sir, a death-struggle must come between the two classes, in which one or the other will be extinguished for ever. Who can contemplate such a catastrophe as even possible and be indifferent or inactive?"*

The neighborhood of Slavery lessens the value of lands in the Free States; the neighborhood of Freedom increases it in the Slave States. *To such an extent is this true, that in Virginia, for example, the lands in counties naturally poor, are, by the proximity of freedom, rendered more valuable than the lands in the better portions of the State.* The value, per acre, of land in the Slave States, on the dividing line between Freedom and Slavery, is suggestive: thus, in the Free States, the value of Farms, per acre, is as follows, viz.: New Jersey, $43.67; Pennsylvania, $27.27; Ohio, $19.99; Indiana, $10.66; and Illinois, $7.99: average, $22.17. In the border Slave States, the value is as follows, viz.: Delaware, $19.75; Maryland, $18.81; Virginia, $8.27; Kentucky, $9.03; and Missouri, $6.49: average, $9.25. If we take the Slave States which by position, population, or intercourse, feel least the influence of the Free States, we find the value of farms, per acre, is, in North Carolina, $3.24; South Carolina, $5.08; Tennessee, $5.16; Florida, $3.97; Georgia, $4.19; Alabama, $5.30; Arkansas, $5.87; Texas, $1.44; and Mississippi, $5.22: average, $3.74.

* Speech in the Virginia House of Delegates, in 1832.

If Tennessee had been a Free State, her lands would have been worth as much as those of Ohio—$19.99 per acre, instead of $5.16 as now; and who can not see that, in that event, the lands of North Carolina, South Carolina, and Georgia, would have been worth more, per acre, than the sums of $3.24, $5.08, $4.19, respectively?

"New England" (says "A Perfect Description of Virginia," published in London, in 1649) "is in a good condition of livelihood; but for matter of any great hope but fishing there is not much." Compared to Virginia, "it is as Scotland is to England, so much difference, and lies upon the same land northward as Scotland does to England; there is much cold, frost, and snow; their land is barren, except a herring be put into the hole when you set the corn in it, it will not come up; *and it was a great pity all those planters, now about* 20,000, *did not seat themselves at first in Virginia, in a warm and rich country,* where their industry could have produced Sugar, Indigo, Ginger, Cotton, and the like commodities." Said Sir Thomas Dale, in 1612, speaking of Virginia: "Take four of the best kingdoms in Christendom, and put them all together, they may in no way compare with this country either for commodities or goodness of soil." Says Beverley, at a later period: "In extreme fruitfulness Virginia is exceeded by no other portion of the earth. No seed is sown there but it thrives, and most of the northern plants are improved by being transplanted thither.". Says Lane, the Governor of Raleigh Colony, in 1585, speaking of Virginia and Carolina: "It is the goodliest soil under the heaven, the most pleasing territory of the world. The climate is so wholesome that we have not one sick since we touched the land. If Virginia had but horses and kine, and were inhabited with English, no realm in Christendom were comparable to it."

Who would have dreamed that in Virginia, the Eden of the Republic, the average price of farms per acre would be, on the 1st day of January, 1850, $8.27, while in Massachusetts it was $32.50

The Hon. Thomas Marshall, another Slaveholder, bore this testimony: "Slavery is ruinous to the whites; it retards improvement—roots out an industrious population—banishes the yeomanry of the country—*deprives the Spinner, the Weaver, the Smith, the Shoemaker, the Carpenter, of employment and support.* It is increasing, and will continue to increase, until the whole country will be inundated by one *black* wave, covering its entire extent, with a few genuine white faces here and there floating on the surface. The Master has no capital but what is vested in Human flesh; the Father, instead of being richer for his Sons, is at a loss to provide for them. There is no diversity of occupations, no incentive to enterprise. Labor of every description is disreputable, because performed mostly by Slaves. Our towns are stationary, our villages everywhere declining; and the general aspect of the country marks the curse of a wasteful, idle, reckless population, who have no interest in the soil, and care not how much it is impoverished. Public improvements are neglected; and the entire continent does not present a region for which nature has done so much, and art so little. If cultivated by free labor, the soil of Virginia is capable of sustaining a dense population, among whom labor would be honorable, and where the busy hum of men would tell that all were happy, and that all were free."*

Virginia, free, and as thickly settled as Massachusetts, would have had, in 1850, 7,751,324 whites, instead of 894,800. Massachusetts, a Slave State, and as thinly populated as Virginia, would have had, in 1850, 102,351 white inhabitants, instead of 985,450. Virginia, free, would have had an annual product of Manufactures amounting to $1,190,072,592, instead of $29,705,387. Massachusetts, a Slave State, would

* Speech in the Virginia House of Delegates, in 1832.

have had manufactures amounting to $3,776,601, instead of $151,137,145. Virginia, free, would have been worth, in real and personal property (on the basis of the Census estimate), $4,333,525,367, instead of (value of Slaves deducted) $203,635,238. Massachusetts, a Slave State, would have been worth $48,604,335, instead of $551,106,824. Boston, with Slavery, according to the increase of population in Virginia, would have contained 3,489 people, instead of 136,881. In the whole South there are less than fifty cities with a population of 3,500. Richmond, Virginia, free, according to the increase of population in Massachusetts, would have contained 1,076,669 free people, instead of 17,643. (See Appendix D.)

The Hon. Henry A. Wise, of Virginia, now Governor of the State, in 1855, during the canvass for Governor, speaking to the Virginians, said: "You all own plenty of land, but it is poverty added to poverty. Poor land added to poor, and nothing added to nothing, makes nothing; while the Owner is talking Politics at Richmond, or in Congress, or spending the summer at the White Springs, the lands grow poorer and poorer, and this soon brings land, Slaves, and all, under the hammer. *You have the owners skinning the Slaves, and the Slaves skinning the land, until all grow poor together.* You have relied alone on the single power of Agriculture, and such Agriculture! Your sedge-patches outshine the sun; your inattention to your only source of Wealth has seared the bosom of Mother Earth. Instead of having to feed cattle on a thousand hills, you have to chase the stump-tailed steer through the sedge-patches to procure a tough beef-steak."

While such admissions come from Slaveholders — while the evils, social and moral, of Slavery are so deprecated by those who have been reared amid its influences — while its blighting effects are so abundantly and constantly manifest — is it not enough to disgust one with Human nature to find men styling themselves "Ministers of the Gospel of Jesus Christ" writing

Eulogies on the blessedness of bondage. They will not allow that "Niggers" are Men, because, if they did, it would show that they themselves were not Christians. They have the effrontery to say, " Slavery is right, natural, and necessary, and does not depend upon difference of complexion;" that "the Slaves are far better off, physically and morally, than the laborers, black or white, of the free States;" that "policy and humanity alike forbid the extension of the evils of free society to a new people and coming generations." After persecuting the "*free* Negroes," and driving the wretched fugitives from their doors (see chaps. i., ii., and iii., of Part V., and Appendix A), they turn round and tell us that the Slaves are the happiest class of laborers in the world, and the most perfectly contented! Hear them:

"The free Negro is in a worse condition than the Slave, physically and morally — less happy, less healthy, less contented, less secure, less religious. Many of those that have escaped have returned to their *Masters* of their own accord, glad to escape from the wretchedness of their freedom." (See chaps. i., ii., and iii., of Part V., and Appendix A.) "It is notorious that in the Southern States the Slaves look down upon the free Negroes with pity, and often with disdain, as being altogether in a position inferior to their own. For they feel themselves to be connected for life with the family of their *Master*, sure of protection, sure of a comfortable home, sure of a plentiful subsistence, sure of kind attendance in sickness and old age, and sure of affection and confidence, unless they forfeit them by unfaithfulness or rebellion. These advantages are lost to the free Negro, and the Slaves have no difficulty in understanding that he has nothing to replace them. True, they must work. But so must the free Negro: so must the laboring class in every civilized community. And when we compare their condition with that of our hirelings" (that is, the free white laborers of the North), "there are many points which seem to be greatly in their favor. For their work is light and regular, as a general rule. They have abundant time allowed for recreation and for holidays. They are not, like the free laborer, liable to be dismissed at a moment's warning, and forced to beg or suffer for want of work to do. They are not tempted to strike for higher wages, when the ordinary rates are too low for the necessaries of life.

"The Slaves are not exposed to the melancholy refuge of the poorhouse, and turned out to die in poverty and neglect, after their strength has been exhausted in a long struggle with hardship and toil. They are not sent adrift among the dens of infamy and pollution which contaminate all our cities" (that is, of the North), "bidding defiance to the hands of the police and the hearts of the benevolent. And if it be indeed a disadvantage that they can not change their *Masters,* it is in most cases more than a counterbalance for this that they could gain nothing by the change; since every laborer must have a Master in order to live, and the Slave possesses the only security of always having a Master who is bound to keep him from destitution, for years after the decays of nature have taken the power of earning his livelihood away. When philanthropy, therefore, gets rid of prejudice, and surveys the comparative advantages of the two systems" (that is, Slavery and Freedom), "with impartial candor, and casts aside the odium which attaches to the name of Slave, it will not appear so easy to determine that Slavery is a calamity to the race of Africa.* On the contrary, it

---

* "That our Slaves," says the Presbyterian Synod of Kentucky, "will be worse off if emancipated, is, we feel, but a specious pretext for lulling our pangs of conscience, and answering the arguments of the philanthropist. None of us believe that God has so created a whole race that it is better for them to remain in Slavery. But it is not the Slaves alone that suffer." No, Slavery crushes not only 5,000,000 souls of "the race of *Africa*" to the level of the swine in the gutter, but dooms the 6,500,000 poor whites in the Slaveholding States to "hopeless ignorance."

exhibits the nearest approach to the Patriarchal times, when Abraham had 318 Servants"* (meaning Slaves) "born in his own house, over whom he ruled with absolute power, but with far more substantial comfort and advantage to them than if they had been a band of ordinary hirelings.

"These statements may appear too highly colored or otherwise, just as my readers may have been accustomed to regard the subject. But however this may be, the fact remains undeniable that the Slaves of the South are, on the whole, the happiest class of laborers in the world, and the most perfectly contented with their own condition, and this *fact* is of more value than all the reasonings of abolitionism."†

Where did " the race of *Africa*," now in the North American Republic, come from? Yellow, straw, Jersey-white, and apple-blossom colored "Niggers" do not grow in "Africa." No, these poor children of the "cursed seed of *Ham*" are natives of the United States—Sons and Daughters of the Slaveholding nobility and their drivers or "hirelings," and are as justly entitled to the "Rights" of American citizenship as are the native-born white sons and daughters of New England; and infinitely more so than are nine tenths of the Irish and Dutch immigrants who crowd the Docks and flood the Naturalization offices for their "Papers"— to enable them not only to vote away the rights of the true "Sons of the Sires of 1776," but to "rivet more firmly the chains" of the poor Slaves!

When we shall see a Slaveholder arm his "318 *Servants*," and lead them hundreds of miles, over mountain, river, and desert, unto a foreign country where no law or power can

---

* The Pro-Slavery definition of the word "Servant" is given in chap. ii., of Part IV.

† "The American Citizen: his Rights and Duties according to the *Spirit* of the Constitution of the United States. By John Henry Hopkins, D. D., LL. D., Bishop of the Protestant Episcopal Church in the Diocese of Vermont," (pp. 131.) "New York: Pudney & Russell, 79 John street, 1857."

bind them to his service — when we shall see him thus leading his own trained and equipped household, for the rescue of an unfortunate kinsman, and dividing with them the spoils of war, we may begin to trace in that " Slaveholder" some resemblance to the patriarch Abraham. (See Gen. xiv. 13–24.) Or when we shall see Henry A. Wise of Virginia, William Aiken of South Carolina, the " Right Reverend Father *in* God, Leonidas Polk, D. D., LL. D., of the Protestant Episcopal Church in the Diocese of Louisiana," or any other " evangelical" Slaveholding Democrat, commissioning a Slave to go to Canada — beyond the reach of " plantation discipline," equipped with southern mules and a lot of other "likely niggers" to take care of them—laden with Jewels and Gold— having every facility for escape—yet trusted to choose a Wife for his Master's son, and to negotiate the Marriage contract, then again we may discern the features of patriarchal *Slavery* in the Slavery of " Christian America." How palpable it is, that Abraham did not hold his " Servants" as chattel-Slaves.*

No sane man or non-"hireling" will question the competence of the Rev. Robert J. Breckenridge, of Kentucky, to describe what the Northern " evangelical"† Pro-Slavery D.

* We have no record of any auction sale of Eliezer, or of the other "likely fellows," after the death of Abraham, in order to settle that patriarch's estate. See Gen. xv. 2, 3.

Had Abraham died childless, Eliezer's prospects would have been very different from those of the Southern " chattel."

† It is not the thing to use the term "evangelical" in connection with a Slave-trafficking religion. True evangelical religion is that which claims the most entire accordance with the Gospel in faith and practice. It is a religion which takes the Gospel view of sin; a religion which insists upon laying the axe at the root of every form of iniquity; a religion which regards selfishness as supreme wickedness, and insists upon the need of regeneration; a religion which would bring the precepts and "spirit" of Christ to bear against every evil in the heart and the life, in the individual and society.

D. s and LL. D. s call the "heaven-born Institution" — as it is. And how does he — a Slaveholder himself — describe it? He says: "The man who can not see that involuntary domestic Slavery, as it exists among us, is founded upon the principle of taking that which is another's, has simply no moral sense. Hereditary Slavery is without pretence except in avowed rapacity." After enumerating the defences of Slavery by his Southern brethren and their Northern "hirelings," he adds: "These are reasons for a Christian land to look upon and then ask, 'Can any system which they are advanced to defend be compatible with virtue and truth?'" He gives the following analysis of Slavery:

What is Slavery as it exists among us? We reply, it is that condition enforced by one half of the States of this confederacy, in which one portion of the community called "Masters," is allowed such power over another called "Slaves;" as, 1. To deprive them of the entire earnings of their own Labor, except only so much as is necessary to continue labor itself by continual *healthful* existence, thus committing robbery. 2. To reduce them to the necessity of universal Concubinage, by denying to them the civil rights of Marriage, thus breaking up the dearest relations of life and encouraging universal Prostitution.* 3. To deprive them of the means and opportunities of moral and intellectual culture, making it a high penal offence to teach them to read; thus perpetuating whatever of evil there is that proceeds from ignorance. 4. To set up between Parents and their Children an authority higher than the impulse of Nature and the Laws of God; which breaks up the Authority of the Father over

---

* The form of Marriage in use among the Slaves of Kentucky is that in general use in all the Slaveholding States, and is as follows: "Sambo! do you take Dinah to be *your* wedded Wife, to live together in God's holy ordinance of Matrimony until death shall you part, *or as long as circumstances will permit?*" "Yes, mass'r." The Rev. Doctor then puts the same question to Dinah, and receives the same response, when he stretches out his hands with due solemnity, and says, "I pronounce you man and *wife* according to the laws of God — *and the State of Kentucky.*" The Georgia method of "Marrying by the Blanket" (described in chap. ii., Part III.) is an improvement on the Kentucky plan.

his Offspring, and at pleasure Separates the Mother at a returnless distance from her child; thus abrogating the clearest laws of nature, thus outraging all decency and justice, and degrading and oppressing hundreds of thousands of beings created like themselves in the image of God. *This is Slavery as it is daily exhibited in the Slave States of this Republic.* A system which is utterly indefensible on every correct human principle, and utterly abhorrent from every law of God.*

Does any one point out the crying evils of this frightful system of iniquity — political, economical, and moral, and insist that "something ought to be done," if not for its immediate abolition, at least for restraining in some degree the "absolute dominion" of the "Master," and, by bestowing upon the Slaves the privilege of Marriage and of permanent family ties, providing the first basis of social advancement for what constitutes in many of the States of the Union the larger half of the entire population — the man who makes these moderate demands on behalf of humanity, Christianity, and civilization, finds himself met by some "evangelical" Cat's-paw or "hireling" of the Slave Power, and his mouth attempted to be stopped by the cry:

"Sir, these Slaves for whose benefit you would thus undertake to legislate, are *property*, and property is a sacred thing — a gift from *above* — a Patriarchal Institution, and in strict accordance with Natural and Revealed religion, and can not be touched!"

---

* The Presbyterian Synod of Kentucky, describing the extent of the "Domestic Slave-trade," its barbarities, &c., informs us, that "professors of the religion of mercy, who hold to our communion, have torn the Mother from the Children, and sent them into returnless exile. Yet acts of discipline have never followed such conduct." In the General Assembly of that Church, it was stated by Mr. Stewart, and without contradiction, that "even Ministers of the Gospel and Doctors of Divinity may engage in this unholy calling." "Elders," said he, "Ministers and Doctors of Divinity, are, with both hands, extensively engaged in the practice." Yet nothing was done or said by the Assembly in condemnation of it!

This cry of "property!" is the least objectionable thing about Slavery. It labors under the more serious objections of being false, hypocritical, and intended to deceive. It is the cry of stop thief! raised by those who have just committed a robbery, and who, in hopes of committing many others, raise this cry by way of saving themselves from immediate arrest. Wise fellows they, those Slaveholders and their Cat's-paw "hirelings," to set themselves up as the champions and advocates of "property" in Men as good, if not better, than themselves. What saith the Rev. Nathan Lord, D. D., LL. D., President of Dartmouth College, New Hampshire? Listen:

I. "Slavery is an Institution of God according to *Natural* religion." II. "Slavery is a positive Institution of *Revealed* religion." III. "The holding of Slaves, or the Carrying on of a System of Slavery" (that is, breeding and selling Slaves), "by Civil regulations, *in accordance with the Divine plan*, as understood by Natural and Revealed religion, is not inconsistent with any ideas or principles suggested or enjoined by Providence or the Word of God." IV. "The Nebraska bill, passed by the Congress of 1854, was a politic measure and suited, by extending the area of Slavery, to promote the best interests of the country." V. "It is unwise and hazardous for Christian men to denounce or oppose the Institution of Slavery, or to give encouragement, directly or indirectly, to romantic and excited persons, who would subvert it." VI. "Ministers of the Gospel of Jesus Christ, and all other *Christian* men, should take the doctrines of the Abolitionists into serious consideration, and use the most effectual means in their power to withstand them, and save the Nation from their *pernicious* influences." (See the Doughface and the Rev. Judicious Trimmer, D. D., Appendix B.) VII. "Whether a Minister of the Gospel of Jesus Christ, who has become convinced that Slavery is a Divine Institution, and who could without *conscientious misgivings*, and who with gratitude to God for such an opportunity of *benefiting* his degraded and suffering creatures, become himself a Slaveholder, may not still hope for the forgiveness and charity of his brethren, though he differs from them in the *honest* profession of his views."

It is difficult to treat the ludicrous idea and wicked refuge of oppression that "God devoted Ham to perpetual Slavery," either with patience or gravity; for, in the first place, it was not God, but Noah, who—immediately after waking from a drunken debauch—pronounced the curse; in the second place, the curse fell, not upon Ham, but upon Canaan, *whose descendants were as white as the Hebrews themselves, or the people of New England;* in the third place, the descendants of Ham, as the Pro-Slavery Doctors of Divinity, North and South, claim the Africans to be, *have nothing to do with this curse.* Their pretensions to a right from Heaven to lay this curse upon them, and hold them as their " property," is the wildest, most sweeping and diabolical forgery ever conceived or committed. They pretend to be, by charter from Heaven, the ministers of God's vengeance against a whole continent of men — a whole race of mankind — whom, in the execution of that vengeance, they are to hold and sell as their " property."* Where is the sentence in which God ever appointed them, the Anglo-Saxon race — they, who can not tell whether the blood of Shem, Ham, Japhet, St. Patrick, Dick Turpin, or Job Von Pronk, mingles in their veins — they, the asserters of a right to traffic in Human flesh? The whole thing is a forgery. " Ah, very true," says the trafficker in his fellow-men, " I admit that Ham's race are not *foreordained* strangers, but *Slaves*, and I am only executing God's predestination in turning Pirate for the benefit of the Kingdom of Christ Jesus. The *foreign* heathen must be brought in."†

The Southern view of "Foreign Missions" is an exceed-

---

* " Some people" appear to imagine that because an event has been foretold, therefore all the parties concerned in bringing about that event must be set down as free from *sin*, but this is not true. " It must needs be," said Christ, " that offences come, but cursed be he by whom they come! Better for him were it that a millstone were tied about his neck and that he were cast into the depths of the sea."

† There is no word for *sin* in the Chinese language. When a Chinaman commits Burglary, Arson, Rape, or Murder, he does not feel that he has committed sin, because his " Book of Discipline" is silent on "the sin question "

ingly comfortable doctrine. The Slaveholders point to the savage condition of unenlightened Africa, and to the meagre results of missionary labor there. Then, looking at the converted Slaves in their midst, they say, "See what Slavery has done for these poor benighted niggers! It has accomplished more than Foreign Missions." So, purely for the purpose of converting these heathen, and converting them here, rather than in their native land, they say that God subjected Ham to bondage, and that they — the "evangelical" Pro-Slavery Churches — are God's appointed instruments to fasten the chains upon him, the curse, the vengeance, of perpetual Slavery. But then, in another breath, in order to excuse themselves for this instrumentality, and under a galling sense of its odiousness and shame, they say that "God is a God of wondrous mercy and love," and has appointed the poor Africans to be Christians, and has made them no longer the executioners of his wrath, but the almoners of his bounty, to convert them, by means of Slavery, to Christ Jesus! They are appointed to put chains upon them, and buy and sell them as their "property" for ever, in order to make freemen of them, in Christ! They are God's appointed missionaries, to Christianize them by the Gospel of Slavery!

Now is it to be supposed that God does not see to the very bottom of such hollow — such diabolical professions, or that His indignation against such hypocrisy is any less at this day than it was when He told the Jews that all their obligations, and their approaches to Him, were an offence to him, instead of gaining his approbation; and that even when they burned incense to Him, it was no better than if they blessed an idol? "Yea they have chosen their own ways, and their soul delighteth in their abominations." They fasted, but refused to break a single yoke. They prayed, they made long prayers, and then turned and gave their influence against all preaching and all efforts to establish Freedom instead of Slavery, which was quite equivalent to making long prayers and then "devouring widows' houses." Just so now the "evangelical" Slaveholding and Slave-breeding Churches of the South, and their allies in the "*free* North," pray for "Revivals of Religion," but if any "brother from the country," too simple-hearted to understand the atmosphere and the currents of the prayer-meeting, happens to pray for the deliverance of the oppressed and the enslaved, a feeling runs through the room as if a "foreign heathen" had appeared in the assembly.

The vital principle of the Bible is to love God with all your heart and your Neighbor as yourself, and every "Law" that interferes with this, pierces the vitals of the Christian religion as the spear of the Roman soldier pierced the heart of the Saviour on the Cross. Dr. Lord's idea of holding Christian men in Slavery, to preserve them from a worse fate, is founded neither on Scripture, nor on common sense. No worse fate is possible. He that is a Slave, has lost all that he had to lose, except life, and that is his only in a very qualified sense. As an animal he might suffer more in the hands of one "Master" than in the hands of another; but his rights as a Man are sacrificed to the same extent, whatever may be the character of his "Master." The Slaveholder who recedes from the "property" principle, does not execute the "Law," and in so far, is not a Slaveholder. If the "Christian" respects his Slave, and counts him a "brother"—as he must do—the Slave law is no longer in force, and he can not be said to hold a Slave. But if he does apply the "Law," and reduce the Man or the Woman to a "chattel," what better is he than another —than the common run of Slaveholders? It is no matter what hand does the deed. Robbery, committed by "a pious man" is just as much robbery as if committed by a professional highwayman. The assassin's knife, plunged to the heart by the hand of a "friend," is not less fatal than if driven there by the hand of an enemy.

CHAPTER III.

ALL the commercial cities of the "*free* States" are threatened with the loss of " Southern trade" unless they consent to remain true to the interests of Slavery. By this means Boston is made to vie with New York, and New York to vie with Philadelphia, and Philadelphia to vie with Cincinnati, in doing whatever work the Slave power may require at their hands. The tariff is also a most effective instrument in the hands of the Slave power in controlling Northern capitalists. The North desires protection for her Manufactures; the Slave power will grant it only on condition of the most faithful allegiance on her part to its one great interest—its own preservation and aggrandizement. Here, then, we have the two dominant classes of society—the wealth and talent—placed entirely at the disposal of the Slave power, and ever listening to catch its word of command. Whatever crime is perpetrated against freedom, it is done to "save the Union." Is a Slave to be recaptured, it must be done to "save the Union." Is a Christian fined, imprisoned, or murdered for hiding the outcast, it is done to "save the Union." Is the freedom of speech cloven down by the lawless violence of a ruthless mob, or by a shameful perversion of the law by a faithless Court, it is done to "save the Union." Does a Doctor of Divinity offer up his Mother or Son on the altar of Slavery (see Appendix B), to serve in the harem, or toil in the rice swamps, it is to "save the Union." Indeed, no language can describe the depth of degradation to which this guilty connection with Slavery has reduced "the People." It has led them into the perpetration of crimes at the bare mention of which all Christendom turn pale with horror.

"Great men," says Elihu, "are not always wise; neither do the aged understand judgment. Therefore I said, Hearken to me; I also will show you mine opinion." (Job xxxii. 9, 10):

"Many Southern Slaveholders," says the Rev. Moses Stuart, D. D., LL. D., of Andover, Massachusetts, "are *true* Christians, and sending back a fugitive from Slavery to them is not like restoring one to an idolatrous people. We may *pity* the fugitive, yet the Gospel does not authorize the rejection of the claims of the Slaveholders to *their* stolen property."*

Is this in accordance with "Laws" of Him who said: "Thou shalt not deliver unto his Master the Servant which is escaped from his Master unto thee; he shall dwell with thee, among you, in that place which he shall choose in one of thy gates, where it liketh him best; thou shalt not oppress him." (Deut. xxiii. 15, 16.) And in Isaiah xvi. 3, 4: "Hide the outcast; betray not him that wandereth. Let mine outcasts dwell with thee; be thou a covert to them from the face of the spoilers." Such were the commands of God to his own "chosen people." The Golden Rule does not enjoin us to "do unto white men [only] as we would have them do to us;" the Good Samaritan was not commended for humanity to one of his own relations, but for cherishing a wronged fellow-man of a despised and detested race. The rights of Humanity know no distinction founded on a difference of "color."

Professor Stuart served the Slaveholders, not by rebuking

---

* A runaway Slave assigned as his reason for not communing with the Church to which he belonged, that the Church had Silver furniture for the administration of the Lord's Supper, to procure which they sold his Mother, and he could not bear the feelings it produced to go forward and receive the Sacrament from vessels which were the purchase of his poor Mother's blood.

them and calling them to repentance for their sins, but by showing them how, with Christ's name upon their lips, they could most effectually serve their employer, and "rivet more firmly the chains" of the poor Slaves. To be sure he does not assert that Christianity was positively friendly to Slavery. The Slaveholders did not ask him thus to stultify himself for their sake. They only wanted to be assured that Slaveholding, under the " peculiar" circumstances in which *they* were placed, were not offences that should exclude them from the "evangelical Churches;" and this assurance Professor Moses Stuart, D. D., LL. D., of Andover, Massachusetts, with the "full weight" of his authority, as "a learned interpreter of the Word of God," ventured to give them!

Another " evangelical " Pro-Slavery Doctor of Divinity, the Rev. Samuel B. How, D. D., of New Brunswick, New Jersey, speaking of the " divine origin of Slavery," thinks the tenth Commandment places Wives, Maid-Servants, Men-Servants, Oxen, and Asses, on the same Platform :—

"The objection that the New Dispensation had abolished all this was of no avail since Christ himself had, in many instances, held fellowship with Slaveholders. The Apostle Paul, in his remarks to believing Slaveholders, did not command them to liberate their Slaves. Suppose that Onesimus, the *Slave* of Philemon, the *Slaveholder*, should come to us and ask to sit at the Communion-table with us, would we reject him? I trust we have not come to that point in the Church in which we make the holding of a Slave a term of communion. Abraham was a Slaveholder, and, indeed, at one time owned three hundred and eighteen Slaves. Still God made the Covenant with him, that Covenant which, alienated by the Jews in the crucifixion of Christ, has descended to the visible Church, of which we" (Samuel B. How & Co.) "*are* a portion. Christ has pictured the happiness of Heaven as consisting in lying in Abraham's bosom, and I hope to lie in the bosom of that good old Slaveholder. The tenth Commandment proves that 'Servants' and

'Maid-Servants' stood on precisely the same footing as other chattels enumerated in that Commandment" (viz.: Wives, Oxen, and Asses). "This not only forbade depriving a man of property, which the Law of the land secured to him, but even the secret thought of so doing. It taught us" (Samuel B. How & Co.) "that there were rights of *property*" (that is, in Human flesh). "That there were Masters and that there were Slaves. This distinction of property lay at the foundation of Civilization. Slavery is one of the penal effects with which God, in his wrath, visits the sins of *his* people. If we were pure there would be no such thing as Slavery."*

The Mormons vindicate Polygamy by precisely the same arguments. They with great gusto appeal to the civilized world, saying: "Have we not Abraham to our Father?" If Abraham be good authority in the one case he ought to be in the other. These "evangelical" Pro-Slavery D. D.'s and LL. D.'s know well enough that the Dispensation under which men now live, abrogates everything in the Old which is not moral in its nature. But that feature of the Old Dispensation which allowed the existence of "bond-service" was no part of the moral law. Hence even the Jews under the New Dispensation, can have no warrant for the institution of "bond-service" arising out of Mosaic allowance; much less can a "Christian nation" have such a warrant. Who would think of pleading for the lawfulness of Polygamy for any cause now, simply because it was tolerated under the Old Dispensation?

With regard to Slavery, Moses himself was an Abolition-

* It would have been nearer the truth to have said: If it had not been for Cotton there would have been no such an animal as a Doughface or Time-server in New-Jersey. Show us the balance on the wrong side of the ledger, and we will find you thousands of Doctors of Divinity who would not only "pray" for the "cursed seed of *Ham*," but maintain that Onesimus was not a Slave. Pro-Slavery piety, therefore, begins and ends in Cotton. It is an exceedingly convenient religion. It can be worn as a dress, or thrown over the shoulders as a wraprascal.

ist of the most ultra type, for he killed a Slave-driver on the premises (see Exodus ii. 11–14), and "ran" about two millions of Slaves out of Egypt. Egyptian theologians and politicians may have said hard things of him for not respecting the "rights of property" which had been recognized for some time in Egypt. But he, having the right on his side, could afford to listen in patience to their arguments and their abuse. The controversy was settled beyond dispute by the settlement of a certain army under the waters of the Red Sea.

Nor does the New Testament, so often alluded to by the Pro-Slavery D. D.s and LL. D.s, and their employers, give any comfort, for we find that Christ denounced Slavery in such words as these: "Thou shalt love thy neighbor as thyself." "Do unto others as you would they should do unto you." The Parable of the good Samaritan, and nearly everything else he uttered, condemned both Slavery and Polygamy, by enunciating principles and rules of conduct which inevitably forbid them. He did not frame a Code; he inculcated a "Spirit" that showed forth a life with which all moral evil — all that degrades or imbrutes our weaker or more benighted fellow-beings — is incompatible. The Bible disciplines the Moral sense to the intent that we may judge of right and wrong without the aid of Specific precepts. The Roman Empire was Slaveholding, and the Apostles to the Gentiles were brought into daily contact with it. Watched as they were by the jealous and bitterly hostile Jews — hunted by accusations of conspiracy, implacable hostility to the existing sway, and "setting up another King, whose name is Jesus" — they were constrained to great circumspection, especially in their published writings. Why did the Herodians take counsel against Christ to destroy him? why did the Nazarenes rise up and thrust him out of their city? why were the Galileans filled with madness against him? why did the Jews take up stones and stone him? why did the chief Priests and Pharisees send

Officers to take him? Why? Because he preached no abstract Gospel emasculated of all reference to the crimes of his hearers.

Another prominent Pro-Slavery Doctor of Divinity, the Rev. Nehemiah Adams, D. D., of Boston, in the "*free* State" of Massachusetts, speaking of the atrocious Fugitive Slave Law, of 1850, says:—

"It seems hard, if some good understanding can not be had, to the effect that travellers" (that is, Slaveholders) "from the South, visitors, are to be protected in the enjoyment of services rendered by *Members* of their families. Now they must stay at home, or leave their favorite *Servants* behind them." (By no means, thanks to Dr. Adams and his co-workers in the "free States"—see Appendix A.) "Are we afraid that the sight of the happy relation subsisting between *Masters* and *Slaves* will make our people in love with the Institution? We must put a stop to the unlawful seizure of colored *Servants* passing with their *Masters* through a *free* State."* "Whatever our repugnance to Slavery may be, there is a law of the land, a Constitution to which we must submit, or employ suitable means to change it. While it remains, all *our* appeals to a 'Higher Law' are fanaticism." "We have been the assailants, she (the South) the mark; we the persecutors, she the defendant; we the accusers, she the self-justifying respondent." "The best thing which we at the North can do to pacify the country, to *help* the *colored* race, to prevent further Nebraska Measures, and promote *our* common interests, is to reconsider *our* feelings and conduct in times past toward the South. A penitent state of mind becomes *us*."

"The Apostolic spirit with regard to Slavery, surely is not of the same tone with the spirit which encourages Slaves to run away from their owners, and teaches them *his* boat, *his* purse, are theirs, if they wish to escape. Philemon travelling with Onesimus, was not annoyed by a

---

* Is it not as "hard" that a Citizen of Massachusetts — Dr. Adams's own State — can not travel into either North or South Carolina, or into either *Indiana* or *Illinois*, attended by his "free colored Servant," without running the risk of losing him altogether? A "free Nigger," on entering either of these States, is imprisoned, and in case, at the end of that imprisonment, he is not able to pay a heavy "fine," and bill for "board" and "jail-fees," he is liable to be sold into perpetual Slavery. (See chaps. i. and ii., of Part V., and Appendix A.)

Vigilance Committee of Paul's Christian friends, with a '*habeas corpus*' to rescue the *Servant* from his *Master;* nor did these friends watch the arrival of ships to receive a fugitive consigned by 'the saints and faithful brethren which were at Colosse' to 'the friends of the *Slave*' at Corinth. True, these disciples had not enjoyed the light which the Declaration of American Independence sheds on the subject of Human rights. Moses, Paul, and Christ, were their authorities on moral subjects; but our *infidels*" (that is, the friends of the oppressed) "tell us that we should have a far different New Testament, could it be written for us now."— *A South-Side View of Slavery, by Nehemiah Adams, D. D.*, pp. 128, 156, and 199.

Only a little while ago, while the Members of one "evangelical" Church, in Boston, were Kidnapping the Members of another Church, there was hardly a "respectable" Clergyman in the City to lift up his voice against the hideous iniquity. Husbands and Fathers were torn from their Families; and Mothers, with poor, helpless Children, fled at midnight, with bleeding feet, through snow and ice, toward Canada; and, in the midst of these scenes, which have made America a byword and a hissing and an astonishment among all nations, there were found men, "Christian men," "Ministers of the Gospel"—alas! that this should ever be written—who, standing in the Pulpit in the name of Jesus Christ, justified and sanctioned these enormities, and used that most loving and simple-hearted letter of the captive Paul to Philemon, to justify these atrocities! St. Paul speaks of this very Onesimus as his own Son; and beseeches Philemon to receive him as such, to receive him not as a "Servant;" not as a "runaway nigger" is received when his master recovers him, but as a Brother, beloved both in the flesh and in the Lord. If Onesimus *owed Philemon anything*, the Apostle tells him to set that to his (St. Paul's) account; but intimates a strong belief that no claim of that sort would be preferred. And he expresses the fullest confidence that Philemon would readily do all he had requested, and more. And there is every reason to believe that his wishes and expectations were fully realized; that the former "Master" and "Servant" met together in the faith and fellowship of the Gospel, as Brethren in the Lord, mutually delighting to promote each other's happiness.

If Judas was worthy of his reward for betraying one whom he knew had the power to extricate himself from the hands of his crucifiers, then much more is he worthy of his reward who casts — or helps to do it — into the hands of men more brutal than Jewish crucifiers thousands of unoffending, weak, and helpless Fathers and Mothers, Sons and Daughters, accused of no infraction of Religious or Civil Law, and whose blood is called for by no maddening populace, but by cold-blooded avarice and the foulest of passions.*

At the "Commencement of Rutgers College," New Brunswick, New Jersey, on the 1st of July, 1856, the "Orator of the Day," the Rev. Dr. Junkin, President of Washington College, Lexington, Virginia, on being introduced by Rodman M. Price, Governor of the State, said:—

"Our first duty is to spread the Bible among the heathen Nations of the *old* world. The *Bible* has made us what we are! We are bound to contend against the atheistic systems of European nations. Our great and glorious expansion, our Prospective population, our Tremendous power and high Moral position among the nations of the earth, enforce the question, 'What will the *foreign* heathen expect of us?'" [Sensation.]

---

* In the "Memoir of Mrs. Ann R. Page," sister of Bishop Meade, of Virginia (see chap. ii., of Part IV.), we are told that by her Marriage she came into the relation of Mistress to some two hundred Slaves, the "property" of her husband; and her efforts for their improvement and emancipation occupy the first two chapters of the book. She portrays the "*heaven*-born Institution" in these words: "Have you considered, my friends, the full amount of the evils of Slavery? No; they can not be seen by Human eyes. They form a part of those hidden things of darkness, which are linked by a chain which reaches into the dominion of Satan, not only here on earth, but into his more complete dominion in the realms of deepest hell.

"Slavery is represented as the great bar to the continuance of our glorious Union. Look at it! God has painted some five millions of people *black*,* and *brought* them here! They are more thoroughly Christianized and Civilized than the people of the Old World this day!" [Applause.] "More converts have been made to Christianity among this people, *during their dwelling among us,* than in the rest of the World."

Here the speaker sketched the progress of what he was pleased to call "our American territory," and spoke of the time when "our people would be obliged to throw the protection of the Stars and Stripes over the benighted countries on our Southern border, to preserve them from civil suicide." Nay, more, "we must turn Northward and carry forward the work of *benevolence* — of regeneration, until British America is brought under the influence of our glorious Institutions, and '*E Pluribus Unum*' covers our misguided runaway *Servants* (see chaps. i. and ii., of Part II.), and this Continent from the frozen pole to the burning zone!"

In February, 1856, the Rev. William S. Plumer, D. D., of Richmond, was invited by the Cleveland (Ohio) Young Men's Christian Association to deliver a lecture in the course then before them. Dr. Plumer was absent from Richmond when the letter of invitation reached his residence. On his return, he lost no time in communicating to the Chairman of Correspondence the following precious sample of Slave-holding theology: —

"I have carefully watched the Anti-Slavery movement from its earliest existence, and everything I have seen or heard of its character, both from its patrons and its enemies, has confirmed me, beyond repentance,

---

* Since they have been brought here, however, they have been painted so many other shades of color, that the original "*black*" has well nigh faded out. Perhaps it is their "conversion to Christianity" that has taken away the Hamite curse of the darker shades of complexion. When they shall have "dwelt among us" till they are *all* converted, the whole race may be bleached white.

in the belief that, let the character of the Abolitionists be what it may, in the Sight of the Judge of all the Earth, this is the most meddlesome, impudent, reckless, fierce, and wicked excitement I ever saw. If the Abolitionists will set the country in a blaze, it is but fair that they should receive the first warming at the fire."*

Can the Missouri ruffians and cut-throats do more! Have they attempted, or ever threatened to do, anything more than carry out the principles here so piously advocated? It is an old maxim, that "like Priest, like People." Is it any wonder that the Country is filled with Atchisons and Stringfellows thirsting for the blood of freemen, when she is taught her religion by such kind of Christians as the Rev. William S. Plumer, D. D.? Charity compels us to believe that the Young men who invited this ferocious Slave-breeding "minister" of the "*heaven*-born Institution" to insult the Anti-Slavery sentiment of Cleveland, by his lecturing, were entirely unacquainted with his character, and deceived by his position. Let us compare the sentiments of this advocate of fire and fagot — this pretended "minister" of the blessed Saviour — with that of the "infidel Jefferson," who says, "All men have inalienable rights, among which are liberty and the pursuit of happiness" (heavenly sounds compared with the cruel breathings of the Rev. William S. Plumer, D. D.) Speaking of Slavery, he says :—

" When I reflect that God is just, I tremble for my country ;"

and in view of the possibility of a Slave insurrection, he says : " There is no attribute in the character of the Deity that can take part with us Slaveholders in such a contest." The Al-

---

* At a public meeting of the American Bible Society, held in the Rev. George B. Cheever's Church, Union Square, New York, on the 6th of April, 1856, this man (William S. Plumer, D. D., of Richmond, Virginia,) " acted a prominent and acceptable part." The object of the meeting was to consider the expediency of giving a copy of the Bible to every poor white family in the United States. (See I Cor. xv. 33.)

mighty has left us an unmistakable indication of his hatred of Slavery in the destruction of an immense army of Slaveholders in the Red Sea, who were obeying their Fugitive Slave Law. "Proclaim," saith the Lord, "liberty throughout all the land to all the inhabitants thereof." That is Abolitionism of the strongest kind; plain and positive. Yet the Rev. William S. Plumer, D. D., raises his defiant arm, shakes his fist in the face of the God of eternal justice, and, Slaveholder like, says: "That is impudent!"

Liberty for the white man; slavery for the "nigger," so long as the white man is able to hold him. Let the Reverend Doctor be in the power of a very big black man, and the question might be opened, who should be Master and who should be "Servant."

The Rev. Thornton Stringfellow, D. D., of Richmond, Va., has published in that city what he calls " *Scriptural and Statistical Views in favor of Slavery,*" which has met with so much favor in that latitude as to have reached its fourth edition. In this edition, he undertakes to answer a letter written by a man called Elder Galusha to the Rev. Richard Fuller, of S. C. Here is a specimen of his logic : —

"His second Scripture reference to disprove the lawfulness of Slavery in the sight of God, is this : 'God has said a Man is better than a sheep. This is a Scripture truth which I fully believe — and I have no doubt, if we could ascertain what the Israelites had to pay for those Slaves they bought with their money according to God's law, that we should find they had to pay more for them than they paid for Sheep, for the reason assigned by the Saviour; that is, that a Slave-man is better than a Sheep; for when he is done ploughing, or feeding cattle, and comes in from the field, he will, at his owner's bidding prepare him his meal, and wait upon him till he eats it, while the owner feels under no obligation even to thank him for it, because he has done no more than his duty. (Luke xvii. 7, 8, 9.) This, and other important duties, which the people of God bought their Slaves to perform for them, by the *permission* of their Maker, were duties which Sheep could not perform."

This "evangelical" apologist and trafficker in his "colored

Brethren and Sisters," must know that the Bible recognizes no such traffick as that of property in Man, except as a wicked oppression; and the Mosaic legislation guarded the people at every point against such oppression, and was admirably contrived to render it impossible. In consequence of these careful and humane Statutes, both the spirit of the Hebrew constitution and the letter of the Law so effectually secured Freedom as a personal Birthright, that the idea of Slavery, *in the American sense of the term*, was never embodied in the language. There is no word to signify what we call a Slave — a Human being degraded into an article of " property." And the laws were minute and specific in regard to the treatment of Servants, and their rights, to such a degree, with such explicitness and exactness, in order that there might never be any temptation to introduce or establish Slavery in the land, it being from the outset made so impossible, that without direct defiance of Almighty God, no man could intend such a thing, and no tribe could accomplish it. And accordingly, notwithstanding all the oppression of which the Jews were guilty, and the instances and forms in which they evaded the law, and at length attempted to establish Slavery itself instead of the system of voluntary paid service prescribed by law, yet never at any time in Palestine was there a Slave-mart or public Slave-traffick. Babylon and Tyre, Greece and Rome, and other heathen nations, maintained the Slave-trade; and never a philosopher, unenlightened by God's Word, rose high enough to see its wickedness; but in Judea, its violation of the first principles of justice and humanity was so manifest by the Law of God, and so many Statutes combined to render it impossible, that though the idol altars of the heathen world were at length naturalized in Israel, and in the seductions of idol worship the people were carried headlong, yet the Slave-traffic and the Slave-marts never once obtained a footing.

At Platte City, the county-seat of Platte county, Missouri,

Senator Atchison's home, on the 5th of March, 1855, a Pro-Slavery "Mass-Meeting" was held. Several speakers addressed it, among them the *Rev. Leander Kerr, D. D.*, United States Chaplain to the Army at Fort~Leavenworth, who said:—

"And now to ascertain your position and what are your *duties* in the contest before you; let us ascertain the cause for which you are contending! What is that cause? It is the most just, *righteous*, and *holy* in which men were ever engaged! Go, then, to Kansas as men, as patriots, as Christians, and do your duty to yourselves, your country, and your God! Do you talk of 'lawful and honorable means' to prevent these New England infidel Abolition vagabonds from entering among you! If a midnight robber were to attempt to break into my quarters I would avail myself of the most efficient means at my command to expel him. I would not sit down to ponder upon 'honorable and lawful means;' the only law I would recognize, in the case, would be the law of self-preservation. Talk not of 'honorable and lawful means,' save the law of self-preservation, against men who trample alike the laws of heaven and your country under their feet; men who know as little of honor in their souls as a monkey knows of the mechanism of a steam-engine! Away with such paltry sentimentalism! It is as much out of place as lullaby songs and nursery tales are out of place in the heat of battle, or in the midst of storm and shipwreck! Honorable warfare is for honorable heroes, not for robbers and banditti, and such these Abolition infidels are!"

How this "minister of the Gospel of Jesus Christ" must have rejoiced at the success of his teachings and the faithful practice of them, by his fellow-Ruffians, shooting unarmed men in cold blood, bayoneting single disarmed, wounded men, shooting men by placing musket muzzles in their mouths, scalping living citizens, cutting out, tearing, and mangling the hearts of freemen, whom they hunted from their homes, by going to their houses to commit rape upon their defenceless Christian wives and daughters! Well have they practised on the preaching of a "minister of the Gospel of Jesus Christ" who stigmatizes honor and justice as "paltry sentimentalism!" Nor is the "*Rev. Leander Kerr, D. D.*," the only cut-throat "minister of the Gospel of Jesus Christ" in Missouri, for we find the *Rev. John Bull, D. D.*, a "distinguished Clergyman" of Weston, Missouri, "engaged, soul and body, in the good cause." Hear him:—

"I could stand by and not have one nerve quiver, and see any man cut up into inch pieces, who would say one word in defence of Abolitionism, or a Northern Emigration Aid Society."

The Church Session of the First Presbyterian Church (New School) in St. Joseph, Missouri, advertise in *The Christian Observer* for a Pastor, to take the place of the Rev. T. S. Reeve, who had resigned. Hear them:—

"We will give from five to eight hundred dollars a year; but we want a man who is strictly religious and *Southern* in his feelings, and care not where he was born or educated."

It is very evident that neither St. Paul nor any of the other Apostles would suit the " First Presbyterian Church in St. Joseph, Missouri." Not one of them would have been " Southern" in his " feelings"—only cosmopolitan and Christian. Neither was the admiration of Paul for " bonds" of the N. S. Order. He held them as the last thing one man should invoke for another. In his magnificent appeal for Religion and Liberty before the Roman Governor he has left nothing for the scourges of party-colored Men, Women, and Children, to build a theory upon. The Saint Joseph Christians should have an edition of the Bible prepared to be read to them by this " strictly religious" man, if they should get one of sufficient education to read without skipping the hard words. This edition should omit the history of Moses, the Ten Commandments, the Psalms, the Book of Proverbs, the prophecies of Isaiah, Jeremiah, and Ezekiel, the Life of our Saviour, and the epistles of Paul, Peter, James, John and Jude; and should cut out such passages from other parts of the Sacred Word as speak of God's justice, and His hatred of sin. They should inscribe over the pulpit, "*Prophesy unto us smooth things, prophesy deceits.*"

The Rev. James Smylie, a minister of the State of Mississippi, in a Pamphlet written in defence of Slaveholding, alluding to the charges of the Abolitionists, admits the facts adduced by them, but denies their criminality. "If Slavery be a Sin," says he, "and *advertising* and *apprehending* Slaves with a view to restore them to their *owners*, is a direct violation of the Divine law, and if the *buying, selling, and holding Slaves, for the sake of gain*, is a heinous sin and scandal, then, verily, three fourths of all the Methodists, Episcopalians, Baptists, and Presbyterians, in the Slave States of this Union, are of the Devil. They hold, if they do not buy and sell Slaves, and they do not hesitate to apprehend and restore runaway Slaves, when in their power. The *right* to buy, sell, and hold Men, Women, and Children, for purposes of gain, was given by express permission of God. The laws which forbid the education of the Slave are right, and meet the approbation of the reflecting part of the Christian community."

To call such a man a Christian, still more a Christian minister, is to libel Him who came to deliver men from bondage, not to enslave them.

What is it with which these Reverend Doctors are so desperately in Love? It is that System of iniquity which denies the right of a man to himself—to his Wife, to his Children! It is that System of Satan which reduces a man, born in the image of his God, with a soul immortal, to a condition below the beasts of the field! He possesses nothing in the world that he can call his own, and serves a "Master" who may beat him, blister him, bruise him, and burn him, and do whatsoever he will with him and *his* "Wife and Children." This is the System the "evangelical" Pro-Slavery Churches call a "*heaven*-born Institution"—"a gift from *above*," and to refuse to bow down to which is "blasphemy in the sight of God."

The Rev. Mr. Nelson, a conscience-stricken Slaveholder, of North Carolina, says:—

"I have resided in North Carolina forty years, and been intimately acquainted with the System" (that is, Slavery), "and I can scarcely think of its operations without shedding tears." (See chap. ii. of Part IV.) "It causes me excessive grief to think of my own poor Slaves, for whom I have for years been trying to find a free home. *It strikes me with equal astonishment and horror to hear Northern people make light of Slavery.* Had they seen and known as much of it as I, they could not thus treat it, unless callous to the deepest woes and degradation of humanity, and dead both to the religion and philanthropy of the Gospel of Christ Jesus. But thousands of them are doing what the hard-hearted tyrants of the South most desire. *If it were not for the support of the North, the fabric of blood would fall at once.* Of all the upholders of this frightful system of iniquity, none is so potent as that of the Pro-Slavery 'religious Periodicals and Newspapers' of the free States. They afford just the kind of succor demanded by the Slaveholders. *The abuse of the Abolitionists is music in Southern ears which operates as a charm.* But nothing is equal to their harping upon the 'religious privileges and instructions' of the Slaves of the South. And nothing could be so false and injurious (*to the cause of freedom and religion*) as the impressions they give on that subject. I say what I know when I speak in relation to this matter.

"I have been intimately acquainted with the religious opportunities of Slaves — in the constant habit of hearing Sermons which are preached to them. And I solemnly affirm, that, during the forty years of my residence and observations in this State, I never heard a single one of these Sermons but what was taken up with the obligations and duties of Slaves to their masters. Indeed, I never heard a Sermon to Slaves but what made *obedience to Masters by the Slaves the fundamental and supreme law of Religion.* Any candid and intelligent man can decide whether such preaching is not, as to religious purposes worse than none at all." (See chap ii. of Part IV.) "It is wonderful how the credulity of the North is subjected to imposition in regard to the 'kind treatment' of Slaves. For myself, I can clear up the apparent contradictions found in writers who have resided at or visited the South. 'The majority of the Slaveholders' say some, 'treat their Slaves with kindness.' Now this may be true in certain districts, setting aside all questions of treatment, except such as refer to the body. And yet, while 'the majority of Slaveholders' in a certain section may be 'kind,' the majority of Slaves in that Section will be treated with cruelty. This is the truth in many such cases, that while there may be thirty men who may have but one Slave a piece, and that a house Servant, a single man in their neighborhood may have three hundred Slaves — all field-hands, *half-fed, worked excessively, and whipped most cruelly.*"

We have frequently heard it denied that there are any Slaveholding and Slave-breeding "ministers" in the Northern Methodist Episcopal Church. No one denies but there are thousands of Slaveholding members, but it is stoutly denied that there are "Slaveholding preachers" in the Northern Church. Listen to the testimony of the Rev. B. F. Sedgewick, a Presiding Elder in Western Virginia, as published in the Richmond journals, in 1855:

"'There are many Members of the Methodist Episcopal Church North, residing in Slave States, *who are Slaveholders for gain, and who buy and sell Slaves.* Such things, I know, have occurred and are still occurring. I speak of that which I do know, and declare that the buying of Men, Women, and Children, for the purpose of Enslaving them is of more frequent occurrence in the M. E. Church, North, of late years, than it was in former times, and that their crime is passed by in every case with an apology, 'That to buy and sell Slaves is not buying Men to enslave them;' and so the work goes on pleasantly. Deny it who dare! And it can be proven that Slavery has for years, and does at this moment, exist in the ministry of the Church, North."

The Rev. J. Cable, of Indiana, in a letter to *The Mercer* (Pa.) *Luminary*, says: "I have lived eight years in Virginia, and received my Theological education at the Union Theological Seminary, Hampden Sidney College. Those who know anything about Slavery, know that the worst kind is 'jobbing Slavery' — that is, *the hiring out of Slaves from year to year,* while the *Master* is not present to protect them. It is the interest of the one who hires them, to get the worth of his money out of them, and the loss is the *Master's* if they die. What shocked me more than anything else was the Church engaged in this jobbing of Slaves. The College Church which I attended, and which was attended by all the students of

Hampden Sidney College and Union Theological Seminary, held Slaves enough to pay their Pastor, Mr. Stanton, one thousand dollars a year, of which the Church members did not pay a dollar. The Slaves, who had been left to the Church by some "*pious* Mother in Israel," had increased so as to be a large and still increasing fund. These were hired out on Christmas day of each year, the day in which they celebrate the birth of the Saviour, to the highest bidder! This was the Church in which the professors of the Seminary and the College often officiated. There were four Churches near the College Church, that were in the same situation as this, when I was in that country, that supported the pastor, in whole or in part, in the same way, viz.: Cumberland Church, John Kirkpatrick, Pastor; Briny Church, *William S. Plumer*, Pastor; Buffalo Church, Mr. Cochran, Pastor; Pisgah Church, near the peaks of Otter, J. Mitchell, Pastor."

Strange as it may seem, it is nevertheless true, there are some Members of the Methodist Church, who believe that, since the "Division" they are now entirely free from all connection with Slavery and Slaveholders. For the benefit of all such "simple souls," we give the following statement of one who has recently returned from a visit to Missouri. The author is a highly-esteemed member of the North Indiana Conference:—

"A person, who is in good standing in our Church, a few months since" (in April, 1855), "sold a Member of the Church to a Southern Slave-trader. When the poor fellow was delivered to his new owner, they had to tie him, hand-and-foot, and throw him upon a dray, and send him in this way to the Steamboat that was to convey him to the New Orleans Slave-Market. And in the same city where this occurred, there was, for many days, in that Slave-pen or prison, a colored man left for sale to the highest bidder, whoever he might be, either a St. Clair or a Legree, all the same; after a few days, he was purchased by one of his old neighbors, who was not willing to see him sold to the Southern Slave-driver; and this man that was thus sold was not only the *property* of a Methodist, but also a Methodist preacher, of the Church, North. I stood by on one occasion, and saw a Member of our Church, a *Class-*

leader, purchase a Slave girl, the last and only Child that a Slave mother had left. I stood and looked upon that poor mother, as she kneeled before him; I heard her say, as she sobbed bitterly, 'Oh, massa, spare my Child! Oh, please spare my last earthly comfort!' And in this way she continued to pray. It seemed to me almost enough to move a heart of stone; but he soon turned scornfully away, saying he had not bought her to sell again, and thus tore her Child away where they would never meet again in this world.

"I might continue and enumerate many similar cases that I could vouch for their truth, but the above is sufficient.

"J. G. D. PETTIJOHN."

President Blanchard, of this Church, in a letter to the *Cleveland* (Ohio) *True Democrat*, September 26, 1851, said: "The Methodist Episcopal Church North, *has about one fifth part as many Slaveholding Churches as the entire South.* It reports in the Slave States three Annual Conferences, 857 Preachers, 86,627 Members, all in actual and full fellowship with Slaveholders." At the present moment (5th July, 1857), the Church North is "about" one third part owner of the "race of *Africa*," or "cursed seed of *Ham*," in the Slaveholding States.

The Rev. D. R. M'Annaly, in a letter to *The St. Louis* (Mo.) *Advocate*, speaking of the Methodist Episcopal Church, North, says:

"You could not make them more indignant than to intimate that they had any sympathy with the Anti-Slavery cause. 'They operate against Slavery!' I would like to know when, where, or how? We have had some knowledge of the operations of these Missionaries for some two or three years past to the present time" (July, 1855), "and if ever one of them preached, lectured, or exhorted, for the overthrow of Slavery, we have never heard of it. *Slavery is no bar to Communion in the M. E. Church, North,* any more than in the Church, South.

The Charleston (S. C.) Baptist Association, in a Memorial to the Legislature of the State, insisted that "the Divine Author of our holy religion adapted the Institution of Slavery as one of the allowed relations of Society. And neither Society nor individuals have any authority to demand a relinquishment of *this species of property* without an equivalent, We would resist, to the utmost, every innovation of this right, come from what quarter and under what pretence it may." Of course, " Why should God's people part with Endowments with which their Creator has blessed them, or the money and Niggers inherited from their Ancestors ?"

In the settlement of the estate of the Rev. Dr. Furman, of the same sect, in the same State, his legal representatives exercised this " right" in an advertisement of a public sale of his *property* at Auction. Hear them:

" A plantation or tract of land on and in Wateree Swamp, a tract of the first quality of fine land in the town of Camden ; a Library of Miscellaneous character, chiefly Theological; twenty-seven Negroes, some of them very Prime articles ; two Mules, one Horse, and an old Wagon."

This is Baptist religion at the South. What is it at the North ? The late Rev. Lucius Bolles, D. D., of Massachusetts, Corresponding Secretary of the American Baptist Board for Foreign Missions, said : " There is a pleasing degree of Union among the multiplying thousands of Baptists throughout the land. Our Southern brethren are generally, both Ministers and People, Slaveholders."

The Baptist Churches and Associations have repeatedly, and publicly, decided that Slaves separated by Sale or Removal from their " Wives" or " Husbands" might " Marry again," without any violation of the " Book of Discipline," such separation being equivalent to death ; and that every Slave Husband or Wife may thus " Marry again *as often as the separation is repeated.*" A similar morality prevails in all the Slaveholding Churches of the South. Why are these Churches so inconsistent as to deny Mormonism a " privilege" which they claim for Slavery ? They all allow the " privilege" of Bigamy or Polygamy " to all persons similarly situated." Yes, and to all persons not similarly situated.

A Slaveholder, of Charleston, brought to Pennsylvania a Slave-mother and two of her Children and emancipated them, being unable to secure their freedom in South Carolina. This woman, before her emancipation and since, has borne a high character for integrity and intelligence. She was Married by the Church according to the usual method of marrying "all persons similarly situated" (see chap. ii. of Part III.), to a man whom she loved with the devotion of a true wife, and together they were members of the M. E. Church, of Charleston, and it was the only grief that darkened the brightness of her joy that she was separated from him. By the assistance of friends, arrangements were made for his purchase, and some three hundred dollars were collected toward the object. Her hope brightened, the satisfaction of her heart's yearning seemed almost at hand, when the news fell upon her, crushing and consuming to ashes all her anticipations, that her husband had "*married another woman.*" She got a friend to write to his Class-leader in the Church, to secure his and the Church's aid in bringing her husband to see the cruelty of his course, and inducing him to abandon it. The Class-leader laid the case before the Church, and afterward wrote to the heartbroken wife the following letter, communicating their views of the case:

CHARLESTON, *May* 26, 1853.

I duly received your letter desiring me to inform you of the reasons by which your husband justified his recent conduct. I regret, indeed, that such should ever have been the case, but considering the circumstances by which he is surrounded, I can not think him wholly unjustifiable. It is a fact known to you, that he is not Master of his own time, and can not, therefore, employ it at his will. He has been separated from you two years, and has not the possibility of ever again seeing you. It is out of his power to go to you, if so disposed. Conscious of this, and having been assured of your comfort and happiness, he availed himself of the privilege the Church allows all persons similarly situated, and took to himself another wife. It is natural to mankind to seek and desire companionship, and when deprived of this high privilege by circumstances beyond his control, and for so long a time, he becomes literally a widower. Such being the case, it seems to me that one would be pardonable if he sought those pleasures of sympathy and companionship in the bosom of another. The precedent he has given leaves it optional with you to follow his example if desirous. Sympathy and charity cover a multitude of sins, and to these ennobling qualities of the mind this case loudly appeals. Think not, Madam, from what I have said, that it is my wish to defend or justify him. It is my desire only to present the matter in a plain and reasonable light, and to reconcile you to the change, if possible. Concerning his feelings, and the rest of his conduct, I can not assure you of anything with the certainty of truth, but must leave you to decide, as, in your judgment, his conduct justifies you. Yours, &c.

JACOB WESTON.

A truly Christian spirit of resignation to surrounding circumstances. Cool comfort to the worse than agonized wife. Mr. Weston's letter is a signal illustration of the moral pollution and death which Slavery has wrought in the Churches. The Church does not yield to a necessity it deplores, and is striving to avert. So far from it, the Slave system, with its traffic in Human beings, its merciless sundering of Families, and its degradation of soul and prostitution of purity, *finds its strongest bulwark in the Churches.* The State makes it "Legal," Custom makes it "Expedient," Avarice pronounces it "Necessary and Profitable," but the Churches consecrate it as "Divine;" the especial object of Heaven's favor, to oppose which is "Infidelity" and "Blasphemy." They seek to perpetuate and extend the "Institution" to multiply its victims, both in and out of the Churches, "rivet their chains for ever;" and that, too, while hourly witnessing its character and results, ay, while actively helping to form that character and produce those results! Thus, then, these self-styled "Christian Churches" commit themselves before the world to the righteousness of Bigamy and Polygamy! It is an odious Monopoly; since it is mathematically certain that every "genuine white brother" can have as many "colored sisters" as he may desire; and all this the Churches proclaim as a "beautiful arrangement," and "in perfect conformity to the Laws of *God*."

If Polygamy, and the continual practice of it among "all persons similarly situated," affords no ground for refusing to those who give other "credible evidence of piety" admission into the Churches, how can it be made an objection to admitting Utah and the Mormons into political and social religious fellowship and brotherhood? If a "converted" Slaveholder may still "take" with safety to his soul, and without scandal to his brethren, five, ten, twenty, forty, eighty, one hundred and sixty, or three hundred and twenty "wives," on what principle is the same privilege to be denied to Brigham Young, or any other who may expound God's law after this fashion?

Professor W. T. Brantly, a "leading Southern Baptist," has published an article to show that his denomination is gaining more rapidly in the Slave States than in the Free. He infers from this that "Slavery is consistent with the purest form of Christianity, and can not therefore be sinful." This is the way that the moral sentiment of the world is occasionally outraged by those who disgrace the office of the Christian Ministry. What wonder then infidelity should increase, and the most fearful immorality should stalk abroad in open day, when the pretended embassadors of our holy religion are propagating such views! Who that has a soul worth saving would not turn away in disgust from a religion that could by any course of reasoning be brought to acknowledge Slavery as "consistent with its purest forms!" In the "great day of accounts," when the hidden purposes of all hearts shall be made known, and the outraged Slave with his chains stricken from his redeemed limbs, shall stand before the "great white throne," side by side with his oppressor and this "leading

Southern Baptist," the wickedness and blasphemy of such men will meet their reward. In that "final day of reckoning," will such men take their blasphemy with them, as they stand before the Judge of all the earth?

The following query was propounded to the Savannah River (Georgia) Baptist Association of Preachers: "Whether in case of involuntary separation of such a character as to preclude all further intercourse, the parties may be allowed to Marry again?" To this query the answer was as follows: " That such separation, among persons situated as our Slaves are, is civilly a separation by death, and we believe that, in the sight of God, it would be so viewed. To forbid Marriages, in such cases, would be to expose the parties not only to greater hardships and temptations, but to Church censure for acting in obedience to their owners, who can not be expected to acquiesce in a regulation at variance with justice to the Slaves, and to the spirit of that command which regulates Marriage between Christians." *The Slaves are not free agents*, and a dissolution by death is not more entirely without their consent and beyond their control than by such separation. *Resolved*, therefore, " That without a new Revelation from *Heaven*, no Man is entitled to pronounce *Slavery* wrong."

"Brethren," such a religion came not down from "heaven" — "wafted hither on fragrant gales" — but steamed up from the bottomless pit, laden with foulest exhalations, and pregnant only with curses. May the Friend of the poor, the wretched, the oppressed, send it to its "own place," that Mankind may no longer be deceived by its wiles or bewitched with its sorceries.

> " Down let the shrine of Moloch sink,
>   And leave no traces where it stood:
> No longer let its idol drink
>   His daily cup of Human blood;

> But rear another altar there,
>   To Truth, and Love, and Mercy given,
> And Freedom's gift, and Freedom's prayer,
>   Shall call an answer down from Heaven!"

James M'Dowell, Jr., of Virginia, a Slaveholder, in a Speech in the House of Delegates of that State, in 1832, said :—

"You may place the Slave where you please — you may dry up, to your utmost, the fountain of his feelings, the springs of thought — you may close up his mind to every avenue of knowledge, and cloud it over with artificial night; — you may yoke him to your labor, as the ox which liveth only to work; — you may put him under any process which, without destroying his value as a Slave, will debase and crush him as a rational being — you may do this, and the idea that he was born to be Free will survive it all. It is allied to his hopes of immortality; it is the eternal part of his nature, which oppression can not reach. It is a torch lit up in his soul by the hand of the God of eternal Justice that can never be extinguished by the hand of the oppressor."

If in the countenances of their "Masters" only the Slaves discovered the visage of a foe, not another sun would go down upon an unbroken fetter. "We of the South," says the *Marysville* (Tenn.) *Intelligencer*, "are emphatically surrounded by a dangerous class of beings — degraded, stupid savages — who, if they could but once entertain the idea that immediate and unconditional death would not be their portion, would react the St. Domingo tragedy. But the consciousness, with all their stupidity, that a tenfold force, superior in discipline, if not in barbarity, would gather from the four corners of the United States and slaughter them, keeps them in subjection. But to the non-Slaveholding States particularly are we indebted for a permanent safeguard against insurrection. Without their assistance, the white population of the South would be too weak to quiet that innate desire of Liberty which is ever ready to act itself out with every Rational creature."

The *Charleston* (S. C.) *Religious Telegraph* says : "Hatred to the whites, with the exception in some cases of attachment to the person and family of the Master, is universal among the Slave population. We have then a foe cherished in our own bosoms — a foe willing to draw our life-blood whenever the opportunity is offered."

If there be any mandate of Christianity binding on man, it is that which commands us to "do unto others whatsoever we would have them do unto us;" and he who holds his fellow-man as "property," while he himself is unwilling to be converted into a brute, is an infidel.

CHAPTER IV.

SLAVERY is advancing. In 1776, it only reached on the Atlantic coast from Massachusetts to the Gulf of Mexico; but in no case did it extend two hundred and fifty miles into the interior. Now it has spread over every foot of Territory in the Union; it has crossed the Alleghanies, and finds a home in the great basins of the Mississippi. It is to be found even in California; and notwithstanding their Constitution prohibits bondage, yet Slaves, black, red, and white, are to be found there, and their owners are protected by the authorities of the United States.

It is no longer a question of Slavery and Anti-Slavery, but of Liberty on one side and Despotism on the other. The viper, warmed into life by mistaken sympathies, has recovered its ancient venom, and threatens to drive from the home of the United States Constitution the rightful owners of the hearthstone!

The question is not, "Shall there be Slavery in one part of the Nation?" but if it is, then the question is, "Shall there be Freedom in the other part?" It is not possible. Slavery is not and can not be a "local" influence, simply because it is an "Institution." A morass may have a local position, but the malaria which it exhales will poison the whole atmosphere, and be wafted by winds in every direction :—

FREE STATES.	Sq. Ms.	SLAVE STATES.	Sq. Ms.
○ Maine	31,766	Delaware	2,120
○ New Hampshire	9,280	Maryland	11,124
○ Vermont	10,212	Virginia	61,352
○ Massachusetts	7,800	North Carolina	50,704
○ Rhode Island	1,306	South Carolina	29,385
○ Connecticut	4,674	Kentucky	37,680
○ New York	47,000	Tennessee	45,600
● New Jersey	8,320	Alabama	50,722
● Pennsylvania	46,000	Georgia	58,000
○ Ohio	39,964	Florida	59,268
● Indiana	33,809	Mississippi	47,156
● Illinois	55,405	Louisiana	41,255
○ Michigan	56,243	Arkansas	52,198
○ Wisconsin	53,924	Missouri	67,380
○ Iowa	50,914	Texas	257,504
● California	155,980		
Total Square Miles	612,597	Total Square Miles	871,448

TERRITORIES.		TERRITORIES.	
● District of Columbia	60	● New Mexico	207,007
● Kansas	114,798	● Oregon	185,030
● Minnesota	166,025	● Utah	299,170
● Nebraska	335,882	● Washington	123,022

Who has not seen a thorn in the finger produce fever, increase the pulse, and destroy the appetite? And whoever has seen this, has seen the brain, the heart, and the stomach, three most vital organs, disturbed by a little irritation in the end of the finger. A scratch has been known to produce lock-jaw and death. Every surgeon knows the wide range of sympathies which ever attend wounds and injuries. The brain suffers in a very marked degree, the stomach loses its tone, the action of the heart becomes fitful and irregular. When the secondary fever sets in, the skin is hot, the face flushed, the pulse increased in frequency, the appetite poor, and the tongue furred. And if all these sympathies may come from a trifling "local" injury in an unimportant part of the Human body, surely we ought to feel no surprise that the cancer Slavery, festering and ulcerating so vital an organ as "the South" or "lower extremities" of the Republic, should set up a chain of morbid sympathies involving the entire Union.

Slavery is felt in every fibre of the Nation. It has deadened the public feeling to *that* Liberty which was purchased with the blood of the Sires of '76 — purchased, too, with the blood of "Our Colored Fellow-Citizens." It has suppressed every generous expression of Liberty except when cautiously guarded and limited to a certain description of white men. "It sits" — to use the words of the Rev. George B. Cheever — "like a nightmare on the genius of the Gospel. It is a mountain of despotism and the fear of man upon the truth." It has taught the young men of the Rising generation to use all specious reasoning that the despots of bygone ages employed in defence of oppression. There has not been since the days of the first Man-stealer, to this hour, a plea for injustice, a sophistry in favor of the absolute power of one man over another, that the young "Democrats," North and South, have not been taught to employ. That sense of the sacredness of Man's natural rights, which every one of the old Revolutionary documents breathe, and of which the Declaration of Independence is a type, has become unpopular (practically so), and is very widely regarded as a "patriotic flourish." What says *The Washington* (D. C.) *Union*, the recognized Organ of the Government — of Franklin Pierce, James Buchanan, and the National Democratic Party?

"There is no equality among Men, except in the universality to obey the laws" (that is, of the traffickers in Men, Women, and Children) "of the land. Freedom and equality are necessarily determined in any given society or community by the varying influences of the origin of caste, numbers, geographical position, and contact with other societies and communities. The terms 'Liberty' and 'Freedom' are not in themselves expressive of a standard of freedom which excludes the *Idea* of dependence or Slavery."

Was this the "Idea" of the Declaration of Independence?

Was this the "Idea" of the founders of the Republic? Was this the "Idea" which combined the "Sires of '76" on Bunker Hill; which carried Washington through a seven years' war; which inspired Lafayette; which touched with coals of fire the lips of Otis, Adams, and Patrick Henry? In the days of the Revolution, men held with Franklin, that " Slavery is an atrocious debasement of human nature"—with Adams, that "consenting to Slavery is a sacrilegious breach of trust"—with Jefferson that "one hour of American Slavery is fraught with more misery than ages of that which we rose in rebellion to oppose"—with Madison, that "Slavery is a dreadful calamity," that "imbecility is ever attendant upon a country filled with Slaves"—with Monroe, that "Slavery has preyed upon the vitals of the community in all the States where it has existed"—with Patrick Henry, that "we should transmit to posterity our abhorrence of Slavery," and with Montesquieu, that "even the very earth, which teems with profusion under the cultivating hand of the free-born laborer, shrinks into barrenness from the contaminating sweat of the Slave." But the sentiment is changed now. The whole power of the Government is wielded for its benefit. The Administration never sends an "appointment" to the Senate for confirmation, that the question is not asked, "Is he sound on the Slavery question?"

This abhorrent power puts its hand upon the Pulpit, and it is dumb; upon the Press, and it is silent; upon Capital, and straightway, for the sake of its *per cent.*, it parts with its birthright; upon Literature, and it is self-emasculated.

In the whole length and breadth of the country (2,936,166 square Miles) there is not a man, holding a Government office, who says anything against Slavery. They do not dare. Was there a breath of "freedom" in the Federal officers—Secretaries, Judges, &c. of the Administration of Franklin Pierce? Ask the Cabinet; ask the Supreme Court; ask the Federal officers; they were almost without exception, "Servants" of

Slavery. Out of 43,000 Government officers 40,000 were strongly Pro-Slavery; and from the other 3,000 who were at heart Anti-Slavery, we have never heard the first Anti-Slavery lisp. We listened from the 4th of March, 1853, until the 4th of March, 1857, and heard not a word. On that "most glorious day of his life"— the 4th of March, 1853, President Franklin Pierce said:—

"I believe that involuntary servitude, as it exists in different States of this confederacy, is recognized by the Constitution. I believe that it stands like any other admitted right, and that the States where it exists are entitled to efficient remedies to enforce the Constitutional provisions. I hold that the laws of 1850, commonly called the 'Compromise Measures,' are strictly Constitutional, and to be unhesitatingly carried into effect."

Consider, for a moment, some of the atrocities which one of these "Measures"— the infamous Fugitive Slave Law of 1850— solemnly requires the Authorities and People "unhesitatingly" to commit: 1. It subjects the wretched fugitive or runaway from bondage, to the power of the Man-stealer or a perjured person, who may seize him by stratagem or violence. 2. It grants to the Man-stealer in this pursuit the aid of the Nation; the aid of Statutes, the Courts, and Treasury, together with the Executive, Naval, and Military power of the Nation. And the National Legislature demands that "All good Citizens" shall say Amen! 3. It offers to Slaveholders facilities, helps, inducements, and therefore strong temptations, to pursue those whom otherwise they might have suffered to go free.

This atrocious "Law" knows no "color" or condition. It puts it in the power of any stranger to swear that any person whom he chooses *was* or *is* his Slave, and a Commissioner must be satisfied and deliver him or her up in a "summary manner." Say not this will never be done. It has been done (see chapters i., ii., and iii., of Part V.), and while you sleep your Son or Daughter may be doomed to hopeless bondage—

"according to Law." Let the young woman of "bilious temperament," and the young man with "sun-burnt hair," be cautious about travelling where they are personally unknown. The time has come when "Ladies and Gentlemen" must carry Certificates of Freedom in their pockets, and let them take good heed lest they be lost or stolen from them.

The process of intermixture of the races is now so far advanced, and is so rapidly going forward, that a "perfectly white complexion, light blue eyes, and flaxen hair," are scarcely presumptive evidence of freedom. Persons thus described are advertised as runaway Slaves, and are liable to be pursued with Muskets and Bloodhounds, shot, maimed, captured, brought before the United States Marshals, sworn to be Slaves, given up, and sent to the Rice-swamp, and Cotton and Sugar plantations of the South, without trial by Jury, and by a "summary process" that precludes anything deserving the name of an investigation. Sometimes, under a peremptory refusal to wait a few minutes for witnesses (see chapters i. and ii. of Part V.) Yet "the People" of the Northern States imagine themselves "free," and their "liberties" secure under the enactment of what Presidents Fillmore, Pierce, and Buchanan, call the "Compromise Measures"—enacted under cover of the infamous Fugitive Slave Law of 1850; which, while it makes no distinction of "color" forbids them under pains and penalties to harbor or entertain each other when thus pursued!

"Is it not to deal thy bread to the hungry, and that thou bring the poor that are cast out to thy house? when thou soest the naked, that thou cover him; and that thou hide not thyself from thine own flesh?" Isaiah 58, 7.

Whoso does this, says the Fugitive Slave Law of 1850, whoso shall harbor a fellow-man, accused of no crime, fleeing from the vilest system of Slavery that has ever cursed the earth, and seeking only freedom without molestation or oppression, he shall be fined one thousand dollars, and shall be imprisoned six months for each and every instance in which he thus transgresses; and shall furthermore pay to the owner or owners of such Slave or Slaves the assessed Money-value of every fellow-man whom in obedience to the Gospel of Christ, he has fed, or clothed, or sheltered, or visited.

It would seem that such a law must have been passed by mistake; or that, if passed in a time of heated excitement culminating in the escape of a few Slaves of a Southern Senator, it would be suffered to remain as a dead letter on the Statute-Book of a "free" Nation. But the Slave power, ruling the Nation, set the Nation at work doing its will. It was supposed by many, at the time of the passing of the Law, that no case would ever occur of its being put into operation, and under this supposition some gave their consent, for the sake of peace, to the enactment of that which they would otherwise have opposed. The law was enforced, as everybody knows, amid scenes of violence disgraceful to a Christian Nation. There is no denying the fact that every Fugitive-Slave case made thousands of Abolitionists, of those who witnessed and read the proceedings. What low creatures could have been found, so debased as to take delight in carrying into execution the fiendish details of such a law? Not merely obscure country magistrates, but no less persons than Franklin Pierce, President of the United States, and Caleb Cushing, his Attorney-General. Read Caleb's letter, for evidence of the fixed purpose of "The President of the United States and all others in authority."

"WASHINGTON, *Saturday, October* 29, 1853.

"Dear Sir, **************. If there be any purpose more fixed than another in the mind of the President and those with whom he is accustomed to consult, it is that the dangerous element of Abolitionism under whatever guise or form it may present itself, *Shall be Crushed Out*, so far as his Administration is concerned. This the President declared in his Inaugural Address — this he has declared ever since, at all times, and in all places where he had occasion to speak on the subject. While he does not presume to judge of the hearts of men who publicly avow sound principles" (that is, Sound on the Slavery question), "he only needs overt acts to show where they are, in order that his settled policy in the conducting the affairs of the Government shall be unequivocally manifest! Those who have apprehended halting or hesitation on the part of the President, in treading any path which *Truth* and *Patriotism* open to him, Depend upon it, no matter what consequences may impend over him, he will never allow it to be shaken by Abolitionism! but will set his face like flint as well against right-handed backsliding as against left-handed defections" (that is, against the friends of liberty and justice), "which may embarrass the onward" (and downward) "progress of the Republic!

"I remain very truly yours,
"C. CUSHING, Attorney General.
"Hon. R. Frothingham, *Boston, Mass.*"

The Rev. George B. Cheever, of New York, in a Sermon on the atrocious "Law" which gave rise to the above letter to Mr. Frothingham, said: "To what conceivable degradation or abuse can immortal beings be subjected more detestable than to be put to a service which degrades even the animals employed in it, the Bloodhounds trained with ' peculiar' scent and ferocity for the pursuit of Human victims? The most odious tyranny that ever existed never had such an atrocious feature as that of compelling its subjects to execute the wickedness of enslaving one another. Such a law is an execrable tyranny, debasing every man beneath the swine in the gutter that obeys it; it is a hundred-fold worse than physical compulsion,

THE COFFLE GANG. (See page 164.)

for it makes the man the acquiescent instrument in his own infamy. A being in the form of Humanity to be changed into a Hound on the track of poor wo-begone fugitive Men, Women, and Children!—pointed and ordered by the Slaveholder, and his Northern allies, to precisely the same hunt on which he unleashes the keen and hungry tigers of his kennel! The veil of the forms of 'Law,' the refinement of its process, the change of scene from swamp, forest, or river, to the City or Court-House can not conceal the reality. The mind looks through the deception and sees at the bottom the victim and the hound! And to think of the 'Sons of Sires of '76' engaging in such a work ' unhesitatingly!' "

"The Slave feels," says the Rev. Henry Ward Beecher, "that God never gave to anybody the 'right' to own anybody. Every one of these poor hunted children of poverty and shame have just as much right to freedom as you or I. There are Men and Women among them who, through day and night, have performed unrecorded heroism. When such Men and Women come from the Slave States, seeking the yet further North, I think that a man who would not, in such circumstances, stretch out his hand to help them, is, before God, 'worse than an infidel.' And if that is Christianity it is a Christianity only of Satan; for a Christianity that teacheth me to deny every instinct of my nature and of humanity, to deny every sympathy which a struggling Man craves from the bosom of love, needs another Christ to die for it."

The Hon. Charles Sumner, of Massachusetts, in a Speech delivered in the United States Senate, said: "As the throne of God is above every earthly throne, so are his Laws and Statutes above all the laws and statutes of man. To question these, is to question God himself. But to assume that human laws are beyond question, is to claim for their fallible authors infallibility. To assume that they are always in conformity with the laws of God, is presumptuously and impiously to exalt man to an equality with God. Clearly human laws are not always in such conformity; nor can they ever be beyond question from each individual. When the conflict is open, as if Congress should command the perpetration of murder, the office of conscience as final arbiter is undisputed. But in every conflict the same Queenly office is hers. By no earthly power can she be dethroned. Each person, after anxious examination, without haste, without passion, solemnly for himself must decide this great controversy. Any other rule attributes infallibility to human laws, places them beyond question, and degrades all Men to an unthinking passive obedience. * * * The mandates of an earthly power are to be discussed; those of Heaven must at once be performed; nor can any agreement constrain us against God. Such is the rule of Morals. Such, also, by the lips of Judges and Sages, has been the proud declaration of the English law.

"And now, Sir, the rule is commended to us. The good citizen, as he thinks of the shivering fugitive — guilty of no crime — pursued — hunted down like a wild beast, while praying for Christian help and deliverance, and as he reads the requirements of this Act, is filled with horror. Here is a despotic mandate, to aid and assist in the prompt and efficient execution of this ' Law !' Again, let me speak frankly. Not rashly would I set myself against any provisions of law. This grave responsibility I would not lightly assume. But here the path of duty is clear. By the Supreme law, which commands me to do no injustice; by the comprehensive Christian law of Brotherhood; *by the Constitution, which I have sworn to support, I am bound to disobey this Act.* Never, in any capacity, can I render voluntary aid in its execution. Pains and Penalties I will endure, but this great wrong I will not do. 'I can not obey, but I can suffer,' was the exclamation of the author of Pilgrim's Progress, when imprisoned for disobedience to an earthly statute. Better suffer injustice than do it.

Better be the victim than the instrument of wrong. Better be even the poor Slave, returned to bondage, than the unhappy Commissioner.

"There is, Sir, an incident of history which suggests a parallel, and affords a lesson of fidelity. Under the triumphant exertions of that Apostolic Jesuit, St. Francis Xavier, large numbers of the Japanese, amounting to as many as 200,000 — among them Princes, Generals, and the flower of the Nobility — were converted to Christianity. Afterward, amid the frenzy of civil war, Religious persecution arose, and the penalty of Death was denounced against all who refused to trample upon the effigy of the Redeemer. This was the Pagan law of a Pagan land. But the delighted historian records that scarcely one from a multitude of converts was guilty of this apostacy. The law of man was set at naught. Imprisonments, torture, death, were preferred. Thus did this people refuse to trample on the painted image. Sir, multitudes among us will not be less steadfast in refusing to trample upon the living image of their Redeemer.

"Sir, less by genius or eminent services, than by sufferings, are the fugitive Slaves of our country now commended. For them every sentiment of humanity is aroused. Rude and ignorant they may be, but in their very efforts for Freedom, *they claim kindred with all that is noble in the past.* They are among the heroes of our age. Romance has no stories of more thrilling interest than theirs. Classical antiquity has preserved no examples of adventurous trial more worthy of renown. Among them are men whose names will be treasured in the annals of their race. By their eloquent voice they have already done much to make their wrongs known, and to secure the respect of the world. History will soon lend them her avenging pen. Proscribed by you during life, *they will proscribe you through all time.* Sir, already judgment is beginning. A righteous public sentiment palsies your enactment!"

It relieves the humiliating picture of human weakness and cupidity, to contemplate the image of a Man whom gold could not bribe, nor honors seduce. Such a Man is Charles Sumner.

"Of all evil things," says the Rev. George B. Cheever, "a law that embodies in itself the example of wrong, the instruction, the authority, sanction, justification, and command of injustice and oppression, in principle and in act, it is the highest and the worst. It is worse than arsenic in the fountain; it is poison for the souls of men, poison for the great heart of society—running through all the veins and corrupting the whole system. Well did Edmund Burke say, that of all bad things bad laws are the very worst, and that they derive a particular malignity from the good laws in their company, under which they take shelter. If a system of wicked laws be deliberately contrived, and fastened on a people for the purpose of consolidating and rendering immovable the Governmental despotism, and if, under those laws, a system of Immorality and Cruelty is inaugurated as the Central fountain of the Country's policy, to enter into both the Domestic and Civic life of the People, to regulate all their Institutions, to impose conditions on the Gospel itself; to compel Men in every sphere of Society, every branch of Commerce, every agency of active Business, to swear faithfulness to that immoral interest; and if the Word of God itself, *for the sake of shielding all this iniquity,* is either suppressed or perverted, what really is the attitude of such a people toward God, and what their character in his sight? can anything cover up this wickedness? Can any professions of Religion induce him to wink at it, or to connive at the Prostitution of religion itself for its support? God's own voice shall answer; here is his judgment from the Prophets:—

"'Wo unto them that decree unrighteous decrees, and that write grievousness which they have prescribed, to turn aside from judgment, and to take away the right from the poor of my people. Shall the throne of equity have fellowship with thee, which frameth mischief by a law?'

"If a man could take the bolt of God's thunder in his hand and could flash the lightning in the face of the tyrannical, usurping legislator, there could not be anything more direct than this. *And is not this to be preached?* And if the Government of any Nation be guilty of this sin, *is it not to be charged upon them?* And on whom rests the responsibility of doing this, and who have the right and authority from God to do it, but the Preachers of the Word? And will any man dare to call this 'political preaching'? It is indeed the bringing of Religion into politics, according to God's command, and the application of the instructions and principles of God's Word to the conduct of the nation and the people. And such application the prophets Isaiah and Jeremiah were commanded to make, and the Son of God enjoined upon the Preachers of the Gospel the same faithfulness. 'Cry aloud, spare not, lift up thy voice like a trumpet, show *my* people their transgressions, and the house of Jacob their sins?'

"The conservatism that would prevent the utterance of God's Word on this fearful system of iniquity is a conservatism that stands in the ways of righteousness, and yet it makes great pretensions to sobriety and uprightness. It reminds one of the prophet Jeremiah's satirical description: '*They are upright as a palm-tree, but speak not.*' It preserves a sober and dignified silence, when God commands a fearless, outspoken rebuke of cherished sins. Preaching religion in politics, is God's own command, both in the Old and New Testaments; but the *Preaching of politics in religion* is quite another thing—the work of intriguing politicians and of Satan, seeking to blind the minds of men, and keep God's light and God's authority away from their hearts and consciences. If religion be *not* preached and practised in the politics of a Nation, that Nation is on the high road to perdition. It is not possible for the individuals of a nation to support the nation's sins or apologize for them, or ward off the light of God's Word from rebuking them, and not put in peril their own piety and salvation. Already over more than seven eighths of the Pulpits in the North American Republic, there hangs the ban of Excommunication if a single page of God's Word be applied against Slavery; the thing must not be mentioned, and a Political silence prevails. The drums of God's Word are muffled, and they beat a Funeral march instead of a Gospel onset. The conservative Christians have turned Sextons; they are for Burying the truth instead of Publishing it. Their whole terror is against the living truth, dead Men's bones and all uncleanness have less that is repulsive for them than rousing, cutting, and exciting truth—the truth of God, that brings religion into their Cotton and Dry Goods speculations and their Politics.

" 'My people ask counsel at their *stocks*, and their staff declareth unto them. Ephraim is a Merchant; the balances of deceit are in his hands; *he loveth to oppress.* Yet he saith, I am become Rich; I have found out substance; in all my labors they shall find none iniquity in me that were sin.'

"There may be iniquity in the 'abstract,' but nothing is sin '*per se*' if there be great profit in it; and where the pecuniary interest of any system becomes vast there are enough of such prophets as Nehemiah Adams, Nathan Lord, Moses Stuart, John Henry Hopkins, to justify Ephraim in its preservation. Now, then, let such dead as these bury their dead, but the Gospel is not to walk as a mourner at the Grave-digger's bidding. Preach thou the kingdom of God. Undertakers for the dead; Preachers for the living. Let not the first presume to give instructions to the last. It is a different process, that of nailing up Truth in a coffin, and putting it five feet under ground, lest it be a stench in the nostrils of Cotton-Brokers and Dry Goods Jobbers, and that of revealing its grand and noble forms, as glorious Messengers from the Creator of Heaven and Earth. Now, who have any interest to keep Religion out of Politics except those who wish to serve Satan by Politics?"

In the judgment-hall of Pilate, Christ Jesus himself transcendently glorified and illustrated the duty of bearing testimony to oppressed and persecuted Truth, by declaring that his own object, even in becoming incarnate, was to give it utterance, and to stand up in behalf of it: "To this end was I born, and for this cause came I into the world, that I should bear witness unto the truth."

John Randolph predicted that the Slaveholding Democracy of the Union would be obliged to run away from their party-colored brethren long before this time. He did not foresee the events which have given a new impulse to Slavery, and made Slave-breeding the most profitable occupation in the country. Some of them, indeed, nobody could foresee. The opening of new and rich Cotton-fields on the Lower Mississippi, and the extension of Slavery into Texas, were far beyond the reach of human foresight. But could Mr. Randolph, with all his contempt for Northern dough-faces, have imagined it to be possible that fifty Members of the United States House of Representatives — from the "free States" — would be found voting to admit Slavery into Territories, from which it was excluded by a Solemn and time-honored compact, entered into in 1820? Could Mr. Randolph, with all his patrician disdain for Northern pettifoggers, have imagined it to be possible that a Northern President would, if he had the power, plunge the country into a War with Spain, or pay five times the price of Louisiana and Florida for the acquisition of Cuba, *and this for the simple and avowed purpose of propping up the Institution of Domestic Slavery?* In short, could Mr. Randolph, with all his knowledge of the means and appliances by which the

Slaveholders maintain their power, have imagined it to be possible that, in 1857, with two thirds of the White population in the "free States," the Government of the country should be administered as if it had but one object—of extending and perpetuating the traffic in Men, Women, and Children?

The annexation of Texas, the passage of the Fugitive Slave bill, in 1850, and repeal of the Missouri Compromise, of 1820, *have had the effect to advance at least one third the price of "Slave property."* So by these "beneficent and righteous acts," obedience to which is proclaimed by the Pro-Slavery Churches and Press, "the Slaves States will be greatly enriched." The demand for Slaves will be increased ten-fold. The injunction to "multiply and increase"—"Niggers" will be obeyed by the "race of *Africa*" and the race of the Slave States, with a zealous alacrity, since lust and profit lie in the same direction. Few "Southern farmers" will vex the unwilling earth as long as "Nigger-raising is less laborious and more profitable."

This furnishes the "Key" to the extraordinary exertions of the older Slave States in behalf of Slavery extension. It has been a subject of marvel why such States as Virginia and Maryland are so much fiercer advocates of the "Peculiar Institution" now than Louisiana, Tennessee, or Texas. The vulgar or North side View explanation is that "the Abolitionists have wrought this mischief." Preposterous notion! Virginia was infinitely more interested in introducing Slavery into Kansas and Nebraska than Louisiana, for it opened a New source of Life to her in her decrepitude; so that while her Representatives voted unanimously *for* the repeal of the Missouri Compromise, of 1820, the foremost and ablest member of the latter voted *against* it, and with the approbation of his constituents. The rankest defenders of the Slave Power in Congress are not from Louisiana and Texas, but from Virginia, Georgia, and the Carolinas. While Senator John Bell, of Tennessee, and Senator Sam Houston, of Texas, have substantially stood by the North, Senator George E. Badger, of North Carolina, and Senator Robert Toombs, of Georgia, have been leading champions of Slave aggression. In fact, the ground taken by Virginia now is — Slavery for ever, and its extension over the whole country. *The Richmond Examiner*, a leading Journal of the State, says:—

"It is all hallucination that we are ever going to get rid of Slavery or that it will be desirable to do so. It is a thing that this glorious Republic can not do without. It is *righteous*, profitable, and permanent, and belongs to Southern society as inherently, intrinsically, and durably, as the white race itself. Southern men should act as if the canopy of heaven were inscribed with a covenant, in letters of fire, that the *Negro* is here, and here for ever — is never to be emancipated — is to be kept hard at work and in rigid subjection all his days. * * * * * * * * * * * * In the early days of our glorious Republic, the superior sagacity of Virginia statesmen enabled them to Rivet so firmly the Shackles of the Slave, that all the Abolitionists, and other Infidels in the world, will never be able to unloose them! A wide and impassable Gulf separates the Proud and glorious South from her Northern traducers." (See St. Luke xvi. 25–26.) "The Mastiff dare not willingly assail the Skunk! When Virginia takes the field, she Crushes the whole Abolition or Infidel party; her slaughter is Wholesale, and 100,000 Anti-Slavery fanatics are cut down — Crushed Out — and trampled in the dust when she issues her commands! She makes and unmakes Presidents; she dictates her terms to the Northern Democracy, and they bow down and obey her!"*

---

* Of thirteen Presidents, *eight* were born in the Slave States, and *five* in the Northern States; and of these the one most Northern in his birth is Southernmost in his *principles*. For he who was born nearest the North Star of Liberty, went down like the Serpent in the Book of Genesis, crawling on his belly, that he might do his "Master's" will. Who could have believed that "a Son of New England" would be found to head movements that trailed her honors in the dust, brought reproach upon her good name, and caused the Christian world to blush over the coerced degradation of her Children? Of the Southern Presidents, *five* have been re-elected; of the *five* Northern, not one has been chosen twice. The South has had her sons for President fifty-two years; the North twenty.

There was a time when Virginia produced great Men, but the breed of noble blood is lost. In the Federal Convention which drew up the Constitution, Virginia counted members like Washington, Madison, and Mason. So sincere was his love of freedom, that Washington, besides being a gentleman, was an avowed Abolitionist;[*] Madison, another gentleman, considered it disgraceful for the Constitution to mention the word Slave ; and what that great man, Mason, also a polished gentleman, thought of Slavery we cite as novel and commendable to Slave-breeding Virginia at this moment:—

" The present question concerns not the Slave importing States alone, but the whole Union. The evil of having Slaves was experienced during the late war. Had Slaves been treated as they might have been by the enemy, they would have proved dangerous instruments in their hands. But their folly dealt by the Slaves as it did by the Tories. Slavery discourages Arts and Manufactures. The poor whites despise labor when performed by Slaves. *They prevent the immigration of whites, who really enrich and strengthen a country.* They produce the most pernicious effects on manners. Every owner of Slaves is born a petty tyrant. They bring the judgment of Heaven on a country. By an inevitable chain of causes and effects Providence punishes National sins by National calamities. I lament that some of our eastern brethren, from a lust of gain, have embarked in this nefarious traffic. As to the State being in the possession of the right to import Slaves, that was the case with many other rights now to be given up. I hold it essential in every point of view that the General Government should have power to prevent the increase of Slavery."

Such was the language of a truly great man, whose National reputation is not such as his genius deserves, for he was in nowise second to Jefferson in constructive power. Compare such nobility of sentiment and clearness of mental vision on

[*] In a letter to Robert Morris, dated Mount Vernon, April 12, 1786, Washington said: "I can only say that there is not a man living who wishes more sincerely than I do to see a plan adopted for the Abolition of Slavery; but there is only one proper and effectual mode in which it can be accomplished, and that is by Legislative authority; and this, so far as my suffrage will go, shall never be wanting."

the effect of Slavery — on it as a thing which the Nation has to deal with, because the Nation will be punished by the irresistible Moral law of the universe. Compare this with the coarse-mouthed rant of Henry A. Wise, who bullies Abolitionists, and foams about his "property" in Men as good, if not better, than himself — and think that such a person has been chosen Democratic Governor of Virginia — and then measure, if you can, the depth of her fall.

"If the people of the '*free* States,'" says the New York *Evening Post*, "must be governed by the Slaveholders, it would be far better that they should govern them directly in their own name, than through a set of canting dependants on their favor, recruited from the Northern politicians, and pretending to impartiality in the differences which have arisen between the Slave States and the 'Free.' It is better to live under a rule which is simply unjust, than under one which is both unjust and hypocritical."

To-day, July 5, 1857, twenty-seven millions of people, "free" and enslaved, "colored," party-"colored," and "pure white," are under the feet of the Slaveholders. The South now claims, and is constitutionally right in claiming, that the election of James Buchanan instead of John C. Fremont, has settled the question that the majority of "the People" of the United States are willing that Kansas, and the other Territories, should be "cut up into strips" and brought into the Union as Slave States. It will be useless for the people of the "*free* North" to deny that they intended any such thing by their votes. The reply will be, and it will be unanswerable: "This was the issue between the two Parties — between James Buchanan and Millard Fillmore, on the one side, and John C. Fremont on the other; and if you did not so understand it, you have only yourselves to blame. This was the issue plainly made, and we never denied it. It is on this plain issue that we gained the battle (on the 4th day of November, 1856), and now you have nothing to do but submit. If you are opposed to the measures, which we intend to pursue, you should have voted against us when your vote would have effected something. It is now too late. You ought to have understood better."

By reference to the following Table it will be seen that there is a Majority of fifty-six Electoral votes in favor of the "*free* States." With this remedy at hand, "the People" of the "*free* States" who voted against Fremont—to wit, of New Jersey, Pennsylvania, Indiana, Illinois, and California—have proven to the world how utterly unworthy they are of the name of "freemen":—

FREE STATES.	Vote.	SLAVE STATES.	Vote.
Maine	8	Delaware	3
New Hampshire	5	Maryland	8
Vermont	5	Virginia	15
Massachusetts	13	North Carolina	10
Connecticut	6	South Carolina	6
Rhode Island	4	Georgia	10
New York	35	Kentucky	12
New Jersey	7	Tennessee	12
Pennsylvania	27	Louisiana	6
Ohio	23	Mississippi	7
Indiana	13	Alabama	8
Illinois	11	Missouri	9
Michigan	6	Arkansas	4
Iowa	4	Florida	3
Wisconsin	5	Texas	4
California	4		
		Total	120
Total	176	*Free* State majority	56
Grand total	296	Necessary to a choice	149

The election returns prove that Fillmore, and " our Southern customers," threw the election into the hands of Buchanan. New Jersey and Pennsylvania alone could have prevented Buchanan's election. Here are the figures :—

FOR FREMONT.	Vote.	FOR BUCHANAN.	Vote.
Maine	8	New Jersey	7
New Hampshire	5	Pennsylvania	27
Massachusetts	13	Indiana	13
Rhode Island	4	Illinois	11
Connecticut	6	Delaware	3
Vermont	5	Virginia	15
New York	35	North Carolina	10
Ohio	23	South Carolina	8
Michigan	6	Georgia	10
Wisconsin	5	Alabama	9
Iowa	4	Mississippi	7
		Florida	3
Total	114	Texas	4
		Arkansas	4
		Kentucky	12
		Tennessee	12
		Missouri	9
		Louisiana	6
		California	4
FOR FILLMORE.			
Maryland	8	Total	174

The Popular vote of the States going for Fremont is 47 per cent. of all. His Electoral vote is only 39 per cent. Buchanan's States cast only 51 per cent. of all the votes, yet give him 59 per cent. of the Electors. Counting all the scattering Votes not returned until too late to be put in the "Official," we may call the aggregate vote of the Union 4,200,000, divided thus:— Fremont 1,400,000; Buchanan, 1,900,000; Fillmore 900,000.

There were tens of thousands of men in the South who sympathize with the Republicans, but had no opportunity to express their sentiments at the Ballot-box.

The Chronicle and Sentinel, Augusta, Georgia, is unwilling to let the Nullifiers of Virginia and South Carolina take to themselves the entire credit of defeating Fremont by threatening to "dissolve the Union." It insists, very fairly, that a share of the honor is to be accorded to its Fillmore brethren, saying:—

"These valiant gentlemen deceive themselves. They have had no hand in the defeat of Fremont. The same men among them, if any such there are, know very well that if Mr. Fillmore had not divided the North — if the Fillmore men had not stood firmly against the Free-Soil host — Mr. Buchanan would have been utterly overwhelmed, in spite of all the Government patronage, all the bribery and corruption unscrupulously used in his favor. To Mr. Fillmore and his men, and to them alone, is due the credit of defeating Fremont. The Free-Soil candidate would have been at this moment President elect of the United States, but for Fillmore. Not a Northern State would have voted for Buchanan."

In the same spirit *The Richmond* (Va.) *Enquirer* exults that " All danger of a dissolution of the Union is now over. Slavery will hereafter be, as it always has been, the Strongest bond and Cement of our Union ;" and proceeds to show that Slavery is growing popular at the North : for

"In the year 1800 more than six per cent. of the population of New Jersey were Slaves, but the public opinion was opposed to Slaveholding, and she found no difficulty in abolishing it. Now" (November, 1856), " Delaware does not own half as many Slaves in proportion to population as New Jersey did then, yet Delaware clings to Slavery, and which is another striking evidence of the growing popularity of Slavery.* In talking of disunion, in the event of Fremont's election, we were advocating the cause of union, while those who talked of submission were disunionists of the worst character. Union man as Governer Wise has always been, his patriotism was put to the hardest test when he found it necessary to threaten a dissolution of the Union, in order to save it. Here again he took the lead, and was more exposed to misconstruction, abuse, and obloquy, than any other man in Virginia. But he did not stand alone ; *the whole Democracy of the North and the South stood by him and fought shoulder to shoulder with him.* We notice him especially because he has been most vilified and abused."

---

* *The Newark* (N. J.) *Daily Advertiser*, of November 7, 1856, says: " The Students of Princeton College on Wednesday" (November 5, 1856), " had a torchlight procession for the purpose of *burying John C. Fremont*. After parading the streets carrying a coffin, and groaning and shouting to their hearts' content, they had a general oration, burnt the coffin and then dispersed. The procession consisted of 75 students, one of whom was dressed in woman's apparel" — to represent New Jersey.

Thus the Slave Power everywhere understands that it has succeeded in electing Buchanan to the Presidency of the United States by cracking its whip over the head of the Commercial and Officeholding classes at the North. And it will infer that in case of future resistance to the revival of the African Slave-Trade, the annexation of Nicaragua, the seizure of Cuba, or any kindred project, it has only to crack " a little louder" and the North will succumb.

It will be seen from the following document that as the " President and Council" of the Fillmore-men issued their " express and positive orders" to all the faithful to vote for Fillmore *with a view of electing Buchanan*, so the " President and Rulers" of Great Salt Lake, Utah Territory, issued their orders " to all the Saints throughout the Union" to vote for Buchanan; he, old Bachelor though he is, being the "destined instrument in the hands of Providence" for the fulfilment of the prophecy of the coming of the day "when seven Women shall lay hold of one man and shall say, ' Let us eat of our own bread and wear our own apparel; only let us be called by thy name to take away our reproach.'" Perhaps Mr. Buchanan will now renounce his Bachelorship, and make up for lost time by taking seven " Wives." But the Elders and Rulers of " The Church of Latter-Day Saints" do not rely on Scripture or Prophecy alone. They cite likewise a clause of the " Cincinnati Platform." Hear them: —

This was a "keen move" of the faculty of the College, for " Southern patronage." They had an eye to that passage of Scripture which says, " Make unto yourselves friends of the mammon of unrighteousness." The Empire Club of New York turned out in procession in honor of the victory, with a transparency representing the scourging of three black men, and headed " Bleeding Kansas." We thought that was the depth of degradation; but it has been exceeded, in the Metropolis of the Nation, and under the eye of the Executive. A procession passed through the streets of Washington, headed by a Government official, bearing a transparency inscribed " Sumner and Kansas, let them bleed."

"TO THE LATTER-DAY SAINTS.

"*The Elders and Rulers of the Church of Jesus Christ of Latter-Day Saints to the Saints in the United States of America:*

"Dear Brethren, Faithful Followers of the L—— and the Recipients of his Grace : We call upon you to stand firm to the principles of our Religion in the coming contest for President of the United States. Our duty is plain. There are Two principal Parties in the field — one for us, the other against us. The Democratic Convention in Cincinnati, which nominated James Buchanan for President, passed the following resolution :

"'*Resolved*, That Congress has no power under the Constitution of the United States to interfere with or control the Domestic Institutions of the several States, and that all such States are the sole and proper judges of everything appertaining to their own affairs, not prohibited by the Constitution of the United States.'

" This is a principle of the *Democratic Party*, which they have extended to Territories as well as States, and the doctrine of Squatter Sovereignty" (invented by Og, the king of Detroit, Michigan) " applies to us in Deseret as well as to the settlers in Kansas and Nebraska. The Democratic party is the instrument, in *God's* hand, by which is effected the recognition as a sovereign State, with the Domestic Institutions of Slavery and Polygamy, as established by the Patriarchs and Prophets of old, under *Divine* authority, and renewed to the Saints of Latter days, through *God's* chosen Rulers and Prophets. In the Republican Convention assembled at Philadelphia, which nominated John C. Fremont for President, it was

"'*Resolved*, That the Constitution of the United States confers upon Congress sovereign power over the Territories of the United States for their Government, and that in the exercise of that power it is both the right and the imperative duty of Congress to prohibit in the Territories those twin relics of barbarism, Polygamy and Slavery.'

AND PRESENT STATE OF THINGS. 113

"This is a blow aimed directly at our rights as Citizens of one of the Territories, at our *sacred* Institutions" (Slavery and Polygamy) "and our *holy* religion. Saints of the latter days! to whom God reveals his will through his chosen prophets" (that is, through Young, Kimball, Grant, & Co.), "stand steadfast in the ancient Scriptures!— And in that day shall seven Women lay hold of one Man, and they will say, 'Let us eat our own bread and wear our own apparel; only let us be called by thy name to take away our reproach.'*

* The members of the Morman Council (13 persons) have 171 "Wives." Of these Heber C. Kimball, President of the Council, has 57; Daniel H. Wells, 19; Albert Carrington, 21; Orson Pratt, 7; Wilford Woodruff, 12; John Stoker, 8; Lorin Farr, 3; Lorenzo Snow, 25; Leonard E. Harrington, 3; Isaac Morley (72 years old), 5; John A. May, 2; George A. Smith, 5: total 171. The Members of the House of Representatives (26 persons) have 167 "Wives." Of these the late J. M. Grant, Speaker, had 7; W. W. Phelps, printer, 9; A. P. Rockwood (an old man), 8; Edwin D. Woolley (a small man), 5; J. W. Cummings, 10; Hosea Stout, a Lawyer, 4; S. W. Richards, a young Lawyer, 15; Jesse C. Little, a Lawyer from Boston, Mass., 3; William Snow, from Vermont, 8; P. H. Young, elder brother of Brigham, tailor, 5; C. V. Spencer, a small man from Boston, Mass., 2; Ezra S. Benson, an old and homely fellow, 15; James C. Snow, 3; Aaron Johnson, 6; three of them are sisters. Lorenzo H. Hatch, wagon-maker, 2; Jacob G. Bigler, farmer, 10; George Peacock, farmer, 10; John Eldredge, phrenologist, 3; Isaac C. Haight, coal-digger, 12; Jesse N. Smith, Lawyer, 2; John D. Parker, an old deaf fellow, 3; Jesse Hobson, ox-teamster, 10; J. C. Wright, hotel-keeper, 5; James Brown, dairyman, 7; Enoch Reese, farmer, 2; W. A. Hickman, 3: total 167. To which add the officers of the House, to wit: Thomas Bullock, Clerk, 4; J. Grimshaw, Assistant Clerk, 5; Chandler Holbrook, Foreman, 4; Jacob F. Hutchinson, Messenger, 2; Joel H. Johnson, Chaplain, 7: total 22. To which add 76, the number now living of Governor Young's "Wives," and you have the whole number of females thus represented by the members of the Legislature, Officers of the same, and his Excellency, amounting to 438; or, in other words, 40 Men have 438 "Wives." The Mormons boast or exult in calling things, as they say, "by their right names;" all parts of the human body are spoken of familiarly, in terms that would make any but a Mormon blush, and they say it is a part of

"Given by Order of the President and Rulers, at Great Salt Lake, Utah Territory, on the 14th day of August, 1856.
"BRIGHAM YOUNG, PRESIDENT.
"HEBER C. KIMBALL,
"JEDIAH M. GRANT, } RULERS."

While the election of Buchanan " is sure to make the fortune of the King of Dahomey," it will bear hard on Maryland, Virginia, the Carolinas, Kentucky, &c. What will become of "Old Virginia" and her "Home Markets" for her "surplus Stock?" What will become of Governor Wise and the "evangelical Churches?" Re-open the Trade with Africa direct, and the King of Dahomey would so far undersell Governor Wise that the party-colored "Stock" of the latter would soon become a drug in the Market. His kidnapping Majesty could deliver a cargo of "black Niggers" in Norfolk, Charleston, Savannah, or New Orleans, at a Hundred Dollars a head, and make money by the operation. The consequence, in a short time, would be such a glut of "*black* Niggers" in all the Slave States—including California, Illinois, Indiana, Pennsylvania, and New Jersey—as to reduce Governor Wise and his co-breeders to utter poverty and bankrupt the State.*

The (New Orleans) *Delta*, speaking of the "glorious fields" opened up, through Buchanan's election to the Presidency of the United States, says: "Numbers of Slaveholders have already written to us to know if they could safely take their Slaves into Nicaragua to cultivate sugar, coffee, rice, indigo, or chocolate plantations, as the case might be. We have always assured our correspondents that though Slaves were not their duty, if not of their religion, to teach their Children a knowledge of the "issues of life," as they term it.

* It is reported that the King of Dahomey has sent two of his sons to the College at Marseilles, France. A prominent Pro-Slavery Journal, of New York, commenting upon this "piece of intelligence," says: "What effect it will have upon the price of our *Southern* Slaves—no mortal man can foresee." (See Appendixes A and B.)

recognised by law in Nicaragua, we had no doubt they would be secured to their owners during Gen. Walker's administration, and that *ultimately Slavery would have an established existence there of law as well as fact.*"

This " Walker" is the same who went to Nicaragua to " regenerate a fallen race," and commenced his " holy mission" by plunder, and confiscation, and the introduction of Slavery.

The Carolina Times fears that the New York, Boston, and Philadelphia capitalists and shipowners who have given such ardent support to Buchanan, would rush into the traffic with such eagerness to make money out of it as not only to run away with all the profits, but by their recklessness "to give some cause for the reprehension of cruelty."

The South now proposes to " parcel off" twenty-eight additional Slave States, in the following order: Kansas to give three; Nebraska, two; Texas, three; Washington Territory, two; Oregon Territory, two; New Mexico Territory, four; Utah Territory, four; Minnesota Territory, two; South California, one; Nicaragua, two; Cuba, three.

It would seem to be impossible that people in their senses should vote for their worst enemies, the Slaveholders, annihilating themselves. But still it is so, and the blame of it belongs to corrupt demagogues and an equally corrupt press. Formerly the masses had political morality enough to keep corrupt men out of office, and to elect only men of probity and character. But this ceased under the operation of the principle, " the spoils to the victors." The popular conscience expired. Men of character had fair play, and now, characterlessness and consciencelessness, so to speak, have become the two indispensable recommendations of an " Office-seeker." The country is in such a state that a good Citizen is compelled either not to vote at all or from a number of " tall men" choose the shortest. Really good and true men seeking the welfare of the people, are as rare as white crows or " black Niggers" in the Slave States; and if corruption progresses in the ratio in which it has for the last twenty-five years, there will be no more such to be found, as no good man will longer care to have any "Office."

"Human nature," says the Rev. George B. Cheever, "never sunk to a greater debasement than it has in those men who, under the light of Christianity, will, for the sake of an imagined greater security of property, establish, or vote to establish, the frightful curse of Slavery where it has not gone. To set this cancer in the vitals of a new land, to inoculate with this awful plague the heart of a new society, with the full knowledge of all the evils it will entail, generation after generation, is a climax of wickedness, a sublimity of crime, such as no other nation under heaven before ever had a possibility of attaining. Divine Providence has never once committed such a possibility to mortals, and would not have done it now except to 'a nation educated, trained, disciplined under the light of the Gospel,' and therefore prepared to repel the evil and elect the good. And now, for such a nation, having the power to determine the policy, the social and civil institutions of another State or States, and, in the words of God in Isaiah, to raise up the foundations of many generations, deliberately, after long dispute and discussion, to set the atrocious system of Slavery at the heart of it or them, is a crime so gigantic, a cruelty so infinite, that eternity alone can reveal its enormity. It is a transaction without a parallel on the face of the earth.

"Nations have made Slaves, have practised Slavery; but to compel another Nation abhorring it into the endurance and establishment of this iniquity, puts a complication and intensity of malignity into the transaction beyond the power of the imagination to measure and of language to describe. If the 'good Democrat' could take one immortal being, and set within the circle of his faculties, for his profit, regardless of his fate, a spring and machinery of incessant sin and misery, *that* would be the supernatural wickedness of a fiend; but who can adequately illustrate or characterize the enormity of setting such a spring at the heart of a whole Nation—of placing there this productive cause of all miseries—this fountain and creative agency of fraud, robbery, and murder?"

But deep as is the guilt of the South, the North is still more responsible for the existence, growth, and extension of Slavery. In her hands—in the hands of the Northern Churches—has been the destiny of the Republic from the beginning. They could have Emancipated every Slave long ere this had they been upright in heart and "free" in spirit. They have given respectability, security, and the means of subsistence and attack, to their deadliest foe. And if ever the Union is dissolved or the Republic destroyed, the Christian world, and the Historian, will hold the American Churches, and not the Abolitionists, responsible for it.

"Let the time come," says the Rev. Albert Barnes, of Philadelphia, "when in all the denominations of Christians, it can be announced that trafficking in the bodies and souls of Men, Women, and Children, is ceased with them for ever, and let the voice of each denomination be lifted up in kind, but firm and solemn testimony against the system—with no mealy words, with no attempt at apology, with no wish to blink it, with no effort to throw the shield of religion over the hideous system—and the work is done. There is no public sentiment in the country—there could be none created—that would resist the power of such testimony. There is no power out of the Churches that could sustain Slavery an hour, if it were not sustained in them."

Can the Churches do less than this, without incurring the charge of "holding the truth in unrighteousness"? 'Can the language of the one Master whom alone they acknowledge, "All things whatsoever ye would that men should do to you, do ye even so to them," be so interpreted as to require less?

If the relative positions of the Slaves and the Church members were the reverse of what they are — if those who are now the Slaves were invested with the rights and franchises of the Church members, and if those who are now the Church members were enslaved — what would the latter desire that the former should do for them? That desire, whatever it might with propriety be, is the measure of their present duty — a duty which they may not neglect without the guilt of "holding the truth in unrighteousness." It is because this duty is so shamefully neglected that Slavery is perpetuated. It continues to exist, and its domain is extended, and its power is augmented, from year to year, *because the Churches are, on the whole, and with some rare exceptions, willing that it should be so!* A few despised Samaritans — "infidels," who have been driven out from the Churches, or who are likely to be, bear testimony against this gigantic system of iniquity, and are doing what they can to relieve its lacerated and bleeding victims. But the Priest and the Levite, as of old, together with the great ecclesiastical and other religious organizations that acknowledge their leadership, pass by on the other side.

The position taken by Dr. Barnes is one which no man of intelligence will have the hardihood to question or deny, as the facts which go to substantiate it are patent to all the world. If Dr. Barnes and his "evangelical" *Anti*-Slavery brethren would only act consistently in their opposition to Slavery, the infamous "Peculiar Institution" could not live over a dozen years. But alas! their garments are red with the Slaves' blood! Over four millions five hundred thousand of their fellow-men — of the "cursed seed of *Ham*" — natives of the United States of North America, "walk in darkness and grope for the wall at noonday like them that have no eyes," while those whose business it is to enlighten their "benighted souls" devote their time and money to the cultivation of the arid soil of "foreign paganism."

So long as trafficking in Men, Women, and Children, is regarded at the North as compatible with a Christian profession; so long as Abolitionism is branded as an "Infidel" movement, so long as the Bible continues to be interpreted on the side of Slavery, and yet accepted as the inspired Word of God; so long as Church-fellowship and denominational unity exists between the Episcopalians, Presbyterians, Congregationalists, Baptists, and Methodists of the North and South, just so long will the Slave Power succeed in lengthening its cords and strengthening its stakes, and accomplishing all its purposes, however desperate and diabolical.

Dr. Adam Clarke, the learned commentator, said: "How can any Nation pretend to fast, or worship God, or dare profess to believe in the existence of such a being, while they traffic in the souls, blood, and bodies of men? Oh, ye most flagitious of knaves and worst of hypocrites! Cast off at once the mask of religion, and deepen not your endless perdition by professing the faith of Jesus Christ, while you continue in this traffic." (Comment on Isaiah xlviii. 6.)

"The advocates of oppression," says the Rev. George B. Cheever, "are always saying to those who open the batteries of truth, when noise and fury follow the cannonading, 'Had you kept silence there would have been nothing of this agitation; you are stirring up nothing but contention and wrath.' This was the very accusation brought against Jeremiah himself, when he proclaimed the Word of God in Jerusalem and Judea against sins which the Government commanded, and which the people declared they would defend and practise, and which not a few among prophets and priests themselves affirmed were no sins at all, but just a profitable policy:—

"'Wo is me, for I am become a man of contention and strife. I love peace, and I love my people, and I love my country, and out of love I speak to them this Word of the Lord! I have neither lent on usury, nor men have lent to me on usury, yet every one of them doth curse me.'

"Ah, Jeremiah, there are other ways to touch men's pockets, and invite their avarice, beside charging two-and-a-half per cent. a month for your money. Lay the tax of the Word of God upon their profitable, legalized, and cherished sins, and instantly they cry out violence and spoil, and the Word of God itself will be made a reproach unto you and a derision, daily:—

"'Then, said they, Come and let us devise devices against Jeremiah; for the law shall not perish from the priest, nor council from the wise, nor the word from the prophet. Come, and let us smite him *with the tongue*, and let us not give heed to any of his words.'"

The only hope for the deliverance of the land from bondage is from the Northern Churches; and if the Churches in the North will not act and hold up the mirror, that their reflections may tell upon the Churches in the South, the Satanic system will be perpetuated for ever.

PART SECOND.

AUCTION SALES OF SLAVES, HORSES, AND OTHER CATTLE.

CHAPTER I.

"Cursed be he that oppresseth the Poor and they that Sell the Poor for Silver, and the Needy to increase their Wealth." "The pride of thine heart hath deceived thee, thou whose habitation is high; that saith in thine heart, Who shall bring me down to the ground? Though thou shalt exalt thyself as the *Eagle*, and though thou set thy nest among the *Stars*, thence will I bring thee down, saith the Lord."

THE friends of the oppressed are accused of using harsh language. They admit the charge. They confess the "sin." They have not been able to find soft words to describe villany, or to identify the perpetrator of it. The man who makes a "chattel" of his brother—what is he? The man who keeps back the hire of his laborers by fraud—what is he? They who prohibit the circulation of the Bible—what are they? They who compel nearly five millions of Men and Women to herd together, like brute beasts—what are they? They who sell Mothers by the pound, and Children "in lots to suit purchasers"—what are they? We care not what terms are applied to them, provided they do apply. If they are not thieves, if they are not tyrants, if they are not Men-stealers, what is their true character, and by what names may they be called? It is as mild an epithet to say a thief is a thief, as it is to say that a spade is a spade. Strong denunciatory language is consistent with gentleness of spirit, long-suffering, and perfect charity. It was the God whose name is Love, who could speak, even to his chosen people, in the following terms :—

"An end, the end has come upon the four corners of the land. I will send mine anger upon thee, and will judge thee according to thy ways, and will recompense upon thee all thy abominations. And mine eye shall not spare, neither will I have pity." "A third part of thee shall die with the pestilence, and with famine shall they be consumed in the midst of thee : and a third part shall fall by the sword, round about thee, and I will scatter a third part into all the winds, and I will draw out a sword after them?" It was the Lamb of God who could exclaim, "Wo unto you, Scribes and Pharisees, hypocrites! for ye devour widows' houses, and for a pretence make long prayers : therefore ye shall receive the greater damnation. Ye blind guides! which strain at a gnat and swallow a camel. Ye serpents, ye generation of vipers, how can ye escape the damnation of hell?—"Why do ye not understand my speech? even because ye can not hear my words. Ye are of your father the devil, and the lusts of your father ye will do : he was a murderer from the beginning, and abode not in the truth ; because there is no truth in him. When he speaketh a lie, he speaketh of his own : for he is a liar, and the father of it." It was the martyr Stephen, who, though in his dying agonies, supplicated forgiveness for enemies, and, a few moments before his cruel death, could address his countrymen in the following strain :—"Ye stiff-necked and uncircumcised in heart and ears, ye do always resist the Holy Ghost : as your fathers did, so do ye. Which of the prophets have not your fathers persecuted? and ye have slain them which showed before of the coming of the Just One : of whom ye have been now the betrayers and murderers."

If Jefferson trembled for his country when he thought that God is just, in view of the enormous injustice of the Slave system, how much more may we tremble for Christianity, when it becomes its apologist and defender. Let those "South-side View" preachers and professors, who have not considered the matter, open their eyes to the undeniable fact, that infidelity gloats upon their admission that Slavery is sanctioned by Revelation. Let them consider how millions of deluded men, judging of the

Bible more by its interpreters than by its own teachings, have been, and are now, bewildered by the zeal of "evangelical ministers of the Gospel of Jesus Christ" put forth in behalf of the most atrocious system of iniquity that ever cursed the earth, and the venom with which they pursue the defenders of the oppressed. When "Christian ministers" abjure the plainest teachings of common sense, in sustaining such an infamous "Institution;" when, with the language of piety on their lips, they are recreant to every obligation of the religion of the meek and lowly Jesus, so far as to vindicate on Scriptural grounds the right to hold those for whom He suffered, bled, and died in bondage, and the consistency of oppression with religious character, what wonder that men should be disgusted, and exclaim, "Away with such a religion!"

Wo to the Churches when the moral standard of the "infidel" is higher than the standard of the professed Christian!

Men will not receive, and love, and cherish, as from Heaven, a religion that allows men to impose the yoke upon the necks of their fellows; that sanctions outrage upon human rights, in the persons even of the least of God's children; that will not freely and heartily lend its sympathy and advocacy openly and boldly to the cause of the oppressed. All the laws of God against oppression, all the manifestations of his abhorrence of it, go to show his intense feeling and judgment against Slavery. Listen:—

"Cursed be he that Oppresseth the poor, and they that Sell the poor for Silver, and the needy to increase their Wealth."—"Cursed be he that useth his neighbor's Service without Wages, and giveth him not for his hire."—"He that getteth riches, but not by right, shall leave them in the midst of his days, and at his end shall be a fool."—"Blessed is he that considereth the poor: the Lord will deliver him in time of trouble. The Lord will preserve him, and keep him alive; and he shall be blessed upon the earth: and thou wilt not deliver him unto the will of his enemies. The Lord will strengthen him upon the bed of languishing: thou wilt make all his bed in his sickness."

Ten dollars a pound is about the Selling price for a common article. " Choice specimens" sell for fifteen dollars, and " extra fine," for twenty-five dollars a pound. We quote the Market Report of *The Washington* (D. C.) *Union*, the recognized Organ of the President of the United States:—

"At Charlotte Courthouse, on Monday of last week, fifty Slaves, belonging to the estate of John M. Thomas, were sold at Public Auction for the aggregate sum of $35,400. Some other Slaves were sold at the same time. A likely Girl, 18 years of age, weighing 113 pounds, brought $1,776. Two boys, weighing 95 pounds, brought $950."

The Lynchburg Virginian, speaking of the state of the Market in Maryland, says: " C. C. Magruder, Esquire, administrator of Margaret A. Ghiselin, sold at Public Sale on Wednesday last, in Prince George's County, a lot of Slaves, some of whom brought very high prices. One Boy sold for $1,365; another for $1,425; one for $1,150, and a fourth for $1,120. In the present state of the Money-market these may be considered as high prices, being Sold for Cash. These are about the rates at which Men, Women, and Children, have been Selling for some time in our own State. It was predicted, by some of our Northern friends, that the passage of the Compromise Measures of 1850, would have the effect of cheapening, if not rendering valueless, this species of property Behold the result!"

This is a strong argument in favor of the " Compromise Measures." The people of the "*free* States" must be very obstinate, indeed, if they can any longer oppose a " Law" which Enhances the value and Quickens the Sale of Men, Women, and Children! There must be something potent in the elements of a " Law" which enables the Slaveholder to sell a Slave-husband for $1,425. And why should not all men be denounced as traitors who refuse to shout hosannas to a series of " Measures" which run up the value of a Boy to $1,365.

HORSES, AND OTHER CATTLE.

The Wilmington (N. C.) *Journal*, speaking of the condition of the Markets, says :—

"We know not to what cause to attribute it, but better prices have been offered by Traders for this description of property, than we have ever before known. Niggers, of ordinary appearance, are bringing $1,000 very readily. Women, from 16 to 20 years of age, are selling for very large prices, varying from $1,000 to $2,000. Boys, weighing about fifty pounds, can be sold for $500. This is the time for selling, if any one is so disposed. We know one Broker (Mr. M. Conly), who sold a number of Men, Women, and Children, last week, at prices ranging from $825 to $1,350; and we learn that he has also sold Men without any trade, as high as $1,500. One fancy Girl, 18 years of age, weighing one hundred and thirty-one pounds, brought $1,750. It really seems that there is to be no stop to this upward tendency of things. Good breeders are at least 30 *per cent.* higher now (in the dull season of the year) than they were in January last. What our Servants will bring next year, no mortal man can tell. An intimate acquaintance of ours had occasion, on Saturday last, to buy an ordinary house Girl, and the price was $1,000."

That boys weighing only "50 pounds" should fetch $500 a piece, shows that Human flesh, when young and tender, is worth about $10 a pound, though it is not usual to sell it so — out of the Feejee Islands. That those ordinary looking "Niggers" should fetch $1,000, who probably weigh, on the average, 150 pounds, proves that their flesh is hardly worth $7 a pound, the odds being the difference as to toughness. Young Women, weighing, say, 130 pounds, are fetching $1,750. This is a fair price a pound: their flesh is tender again. Altogether, the prices are extraordinarily favorable.

Another prominent Carolina Journal cautions its readers to be wide-awake as the Traders are about: "Speculators in Slaves are to be found in every Court-yard, and at every Corner, where Men, Women, or Children, are to be disposed of. We would, therefore, recommend to such of our friends as have Men, Women, or Children, to Sell to keep a steady eye upon the Market, as this species of property seems to be 'looking up,' constantly improving in value."

The Hon. J. R. Giddings, of Ohio, in a Speech delivered in Congress, in 1853, said: "You, Sir, lately saw an Advertisement in the leading Whig Journal of this City, in these words: '*For Sale a Handsome and Accomplished Lady's Maid — aged just Sixteen years.*' Now, Sir, except in this City of Washington, D. C., and Terra del Fuego, I do not think any Government within the bounds of Civilization would have permitted such an outrage upon decency. I speak of Terra del Fuego without intending any disrespect to the people of that Island by comparing their habits with ours. They buy Men and Women for Food only.* The object is far more honorable and 'Christian-like' than that for which the young Women of this City are Advertised and Sold."

The advertisement above referred to by Mr. Giddings, appeared in *The National Intelligencer*, and was as follows:—

"*For Sale:* An accomplished and handsome Lady's Maid. She is just Sixteen years of age, was raised in Maryland; and is now offered for Sale, not for any fault, but simply because the Owner has no further

---

* An Officer of the United States Navy, in a letter to *The National Intelligencer*, in August, 1855, says: "In Terra del Fuego every man has at least two Wives, some of them more, probably each as many as he requires to take care of him, to paddle his canoe and collect his food, for the whole labor devolves upon the Female portion of the community. We were informed that *these* Savages were never Cannibals unless when driven to it by absolute starvation, and they only eat their old Women. Upon being asked why they did not kill and eat their Dogs, of which animals they have great numbers, in preference to their old Women, a gallows-looking fellow replied that Dogs were useful in helping them to catch Otters, but old Women were good for nothing. On being interrogated as to which they preferred for dinner, an Englishman or a Yankee, they spoke strongly in favor of the former, for the reason that he was 'more juicy.'"

use for her. A note directed to O. K., Gadsby's Hotel, Washington, D. C., will receive prompt attention."

The Editor of the *Worcester* (Mass.) *Spy*, commenting upon this advertisement, says: "This man offers for Sale an accomplished and handsome Girl of sixteen, simply because he has no further use for her! Now what does this plainly and unmistakeably mean? It means that an American democrat — the father of this girl — under the Sanction of and with the Authority of the United States Government, will consign a young and accomplished girl to Prostitution, for a Pecuniary consideration, to be agreed upon by him and her purchaser. She has been hitherto instructed in all the graces and accomplishments of a refined and cultivated woman, and doubtless the inborn modesty and purity of her maiden sensibilities have been quickened and increased by her education, but now she is Publicly doomed to a fate from which she must recoil with horror, and which no Man, who ever had a Daughter or Sister, can contemplate, but with loathing and indignation. The consignment of this accomplished and handsome girl to Prostitution, it must be borne in mind, is not accidental. *It is an act Deliberately perpetrated by Professing Christians, under the full Authority and Sanction of the Government.* It is not the mere act of Southern Slave-breeders, either, but it is an act deliberately consented to by every Northern man who recognises the legality of Slavery, in any shape or form whatever."

The case of this young girl is only a living illustration of the "Compromise," or bargain between the "free" and Slave States, which has been made the standing test of the Politicians and Rhetoricians for several years past. It reveals what that perdition-begotten word conceals, and what it is meant to conceal. What does the "Compromise," and "perpetuity of the Compromise," signify, in connection with this particular illustration of Slavery in the District of Columbia?

Does it signify the "perpetuity" of the assumed right to sell innocent girls for purposes denounced in the law of God, completely subversive of the Sanctities of Social Life, and met with utter reprobation and disgust by even the most savage tribes of men? Every "minister of the Gospel" in the United States, or elsewhere, who has preached or spoken in favor of this Bargain or Compromise, and every Citizen who has consented to it, as a Legal and Constitutional basis of Law, has consented to ignore the seventh Commandment, and to consign this innocent young Woman, and tens of thousands like her, to the clutches of the wretches who sell and buy them.

It was no doubt easy, in many cases, to consent to the passage of the "Compromise" in the abstract. "Compromise" is only a word, and to millions of minds never seemed anything else but a sound. But when we draw it aside, like a veil, and see below it the pretended "Abolition of the Slave-trade in the District of Columbia" resolved into the Sale of "handsome and accomplished" young Women — and when we see the Fugitive Slave Law become authority for Kidnappers to murder the Citizens of what are called by courtesy, the "*free* States," we find the word "Compromise" become a Sword, and the abstraction turned into an act of Rebellion against Heaven and Humanity, and a Practical Disgrace to the American name as Men and Freemen. Did you endorse the "Compromise," Northern father and brother? If you did, then you endorsed this sale, and the primary and ulterior purposes of it. You legitimatized, as far as in you lay, the cupidity of the wretch who offered this Girl for Prostitution, and the lust of the equally execrable Monster who Bought her. Think of this as you look upon your beautiful Daughters and innocent Sisters; think of this as you contemplate what they are, and what they may be; think of this in connection with their future Joys and Loves, and feel, if you can, when you do think so, that your allegiance to a Political party demands the Ruin of such beings, and all Domestic joy that God and Love promised them.

> "What means that sad and dismal look,
> And why those falling tears?
> No voice is heard, no word is spoke,
> Yet naught but grief appears.
> Ah! Mother, hast thou ever known
> The pain of parting ties?
> Was ever Infant from thee torn
> And sold before thine eyes?"

Is there a Woman with Woman's heart and Woman's love, whose soul does not bleed for the wrongs of the Slave? How could the Woman be lovely or attract virtuous love who should fail to do this? How could she respect herself, how could a wise and manly husband confide in her, or how could she claim for herself the respect due a Woman should she be justly charged or suspected of indifference when Woman shrieks under the Lash, when Woman's affections are outraged, when Woman is torn from Husband and Child, when Woman is crushed and Polluted by lawless and domineering lust, when Woman is transformed into a beast?

And this is all done for what? For place, for Official honors; for a temporary lease of high station; for a day of authority. Here they go! and there they go! From every "*free* State," and from every County in every "*free* State," the examples of this humiliation crowd forward with a disgraceful alacrity. They come from hill and valley. High and low throng in supple subserviency around the throne of Slavery. They are called upon to disavow and repent of every sentiment in favor of Freedom they ever expressed, and they do it! They apostatize from the faith of their fathers. They repudiate their principles. They renounce their opinions. They learn, embrace, and repeat the "Catechism" of the Power at whose feet they cower. They begin, "*I believe in one polit-*

ical god, and that god is *Slavery*. '*I'will not resist nor obstruct his sway. 1 will perform his services according as I shall be ordered. I will set up the symbols of his worship in every Office. I shall hold under him,*" &c.

The moral degradation which has been reached in these efforts is unspeakable. The apologies which are made by Northern men for having entertained sentiments favorable to Freedom make a man blush to own himself a Citizen of a "free State."

"*Auction Sale*.—On Saturday morning, Dec. 11, 1853, in front of the Auction-rooms, Washington City, D. C., I shall Sell, without reserve, at 12 O'clock; One Boy, 18 years of age; one Girl, 10 years of age; three Horses, Saddles, Bridles, and Harness; one Carryall; two Carts; one Wheelbarrow; one Hay-rake; two Ploughs; one Cultivator; one Hay-cart; and a lot of Farm-harness. Terms Cash.
"JAMES C. MAGUIRE, *Auctioneer*."

The above advertisement appeared in *The National Intelligencer*, Washington, D. C., for several days prior to the Sale. Pursuant thereto a crowd collected at the corner of Pennsylvania Avenue and 10th Street. After the Sale of several Horses, Cows, and Farming utensils, the Human cattle were called for. On putting up the Boy, the Auctioneer said that he would give any man $25 if he would relieve him of the disagreeable duty of Selling those Children. No one offering to relieve him, he proceeded to sell them. He stated that the boy was deaf, had a running of the ears, and was an invalid; that he was the pet of his Mother, who was present, in great distress, and desired not to be separated from him. These children were part of the estate of Jesse Brown, deceased, late proprietor of Brown's Hotel, and it was known that Marshall Brown (one of the heirs) was present for the purpose of buying the Boy, if sold at a reasonable price, that he might not be separated from his Mother. The bidding commenced, and he was struck off to Mr. Brown at $325, when a man by the name of Naylor, a Slave-trader, claimed the bid as his, and insisted upon the Boy being struck off to him. Mr. Brown averred that the bid was his, and claimed the Boy. Naylor threatened to prosecute the Auctioneer, if he did not get him. After much cavilling amongst the bidders, the poor Boy was again put up. The Slave-trader advanced the bid to $330, when the Auctioneer, prompted by feelings of humanity, offered him $25 if he would not bid any more. This offer was accepted by Naylor, with the Satanic-like remark, that he " would as lief make $25 in that way as to make it out of a Nigger." So the $25 was paid over, and the poor trembling Boy was delivered to Mr. Brown.

The little Girl was next set up, and in the presence of her agonized Mother, was struck down to Judge Sturgis, of Georgia, where she is now leading the most wretched life that can be imagined, with

> "No arm to guard her from oppression's rod,
> Her will subservient to a tyrant's nod!
> No gentle hand, when life is in decay,
> To soothe her pains, and charm her cares away;
> But helpless left to quit the horrid stage,
> Harassed in youth, and desolate in age!"

Reader, this all took place in a " Christian country"—under the shadow of the Capitol of the American Republic, where sat, at the very hour this disgraceful scene was going on, the Representatives of a people whose " laws are based on the principle of equal rights and privileges," and who declare to the world that " all men are created free and equal!"

The Hon. J. R. Giddings, speaking, during the recent Session of Congress, of the flourishing condition of this abominable traffic in the District of Columbia, said: " Yesterday afternoon a servant man came to my room (at Brown's Hotel, Washington, D. C.), saying a colored woman wished to see me. I told him to show her up. He soon returned with her.

She was sobbing and in great distress of mind. I asked the cause of her grief. It was some time before she could so far compose her mind as to relate to me her misfortune; which consisted in living under the barbarous 'Fugitive Slave Law,' or 'Compromise Measures' enacted by Congress in 1850, for the government of this District. She said her Husband had just been Sold to a Slave-dealer and taken to the Barracoons of Alexandria—that his purchaser would take him to Alabama in two or three days—that she had four Children at home. At this point she burst into tears, exclaiming, 'O my Saviour! O Jesus, pity me! O my dear Children! O my husband!' Then appealing to me, 'O Sir, for the blessed Saviour's sake, do try to get back the Father of my Babes!'

"I learned that her Husband's name was George Tooman. His former 'owner' being a female named Martha Johnwood, living east of the Capitol some half mile. George went to work in the barn, at husking or shelling Indian-corn, without any suspicion of the fate which awaited him. The Slave-dealer and an assistant went to the barn, seized him, handcuffed and hurried him off to one of the Slave-pens of Alexandria. The poor Wife hearing of it followed him on foot, and returned, and then sought me in the vain hope that I should be able to assist her. The day was said to be the coldest known in Washington for years, yet she was exposed to the keen piercing winds, although wretchedly clad. She had not seen her children since morning, when she left them without firewood. I endeavored to soothe her sorrows by expressing some faint hope that her husband might yet be redeemed—that I would make inquiry, and ascertain if I could find some one who would repurchase him, and permit him to remain in the District. It was dark when she left my room to return to her desolate home. The cold winds rocked the Hotel, and howled mournfully about the corners. I reflected upon the barbarous 'Compromise Measures' by which Congress had authorized and encouraged such fearful crimes and inflicted such misery upon the down-trodden of God's poor. I trembled for my country when 'I reflected that God was just, and that his justice will not sleep for ever.' I asked myself the question, will Heaven permit such dreadful wickedness, such barbarous cruelty, to go unpunished?"

> " Oh, when shall Columbia's 'colored' sons find grace,
> And know their dreadful bondage o'er?
> When shall the unoffending race,
> Be bought and sold no more!"

At the conclusion of the Sermon in " Plymouth Church," Brooklyn, New York, on Sunday morning, June 1, 1856, the Pastor — the Rev. Henry Ward Beecher — announced to his congregation that he was about to perform an action of a most extraordinary nature, which he would preface by reading a portion of the 12th Chapter of St. Matthew. He accordingly read the 10th, 11th, and 12th verses of that Chapter, after which he proceeded to give a sketch of the later history of a Slave girl, Sarah by name, an appeal in whose behalf he had lately received. "She was," he said, "the daughter of a Southern planter, acknowledged by himself as his own offspring, and reared in his own family until his other daughters growing up had treated her so cruelly that she attempted to escape. She was captured and taken back to her paternal 'Master,' who made immediate preparations to sell her to the Extreme South, refusing to dispose of her to any one who would permit her to remain in her native State. Many persons in the vicinity knowing her to be a most faithful, efficient, and therefore 'valuable piece of property,' were anxious to purchase her; but her owner utterly refused to sell her to them, his object being to have her removed to so great a distance that her near relationship to his other children could occasion them no further mortification. She was accordingly sold to a Southern man, who held her at $1,500, but who finally consented to part with her for $1,200. A Slaveholder in Washington, pitying the girl, bought her for the latter sum, immediately, however, setting on foot a subscription to enable her to purchase her freedom, he himself contributing $100, another man, also a Slaveholder, gave $100, and $700 were finally obtained. At this juncture," said Mr. Beecher, "I received a letter asking if we could do anything toward making up the rest of the money, to which I replied, 'that I would promise nothing unless we could see her here.'"

The reverend gentleman here stepped from his desk, and with an encouraging, "Come up, Sarah," he led upon the altar a young, intelligent-looking mulatto-girl, whom he presented to the crowded audience as the Slave-girl in question. She was apparently about twenty-three years of age, probably five eighths white, and of very pleasing and modest appearance. Mr. Beecher seated her in a chair by his side, while he continued his remarks. "She was here," he said, "on her parole of honor. She had promised to go back, and she must return, either with or without the five hundred dollars which were yet necessary to make her a free woman. A collection would be taken up, and the result would show their verdict." By this time there was hardly a dry eye in the congregation of nearly three thousand people. Men wept, and women sobbed — not shamefacedly, but openly and without any attempt at concealment. All seemed to be touched to the very heart. The like scene has never been witnessed in any of the nations of the old world. In the "Model Republic," on the Christian Sabbath, in the "*free* State" of New York, in the Pulpit of a Christian Church, by the lips of a Christian minister, a trembling, shrinking woman begged money to save herself from a life of Slavery and further compulsory prostitution! One gentleman here arose and announced that the money should be forthcoming to "make her *free*," and that if necessary he would be personally responsible for the entire amount. This announcement was received with hearty and long-continued applause, the audience being no longer able to restrain their feelings, Mr. Beecher expressing his approval of the jubilant demonstration.

Sarah, the Slave-girl, had, up to this time, preserved a tolerable composure, but when the certainty was declared that she should not go back to a life of Slavery, she buried her face in her handkerchief and wept aloud. As, the collectors passed among the audience, the plates were actually heaped up with the tokens of substantial sympathy, one man took a breast-pin from his shirt-bosom and cast it into the fund. The amount collected and subscribed for on the spot was $784, which, besides completing the sum necessary for the purchase of Sarah, would also rescue her child, a boy of four years of age, who was then held in bondage by its own Father—the Father, too, of its unhappy Mother! The scene was one of the most remarkable and exciting ever enacted before a Religious congregation.

The *Washington* (D. C.) *Star*, the junior Organ of the Pierce Administration, of February 23, 1857, contains the following advertisement. We have no objection to advertise the goods and chattels of Mr. Francis Y. Naylor, levied upon by United States Marshal Hoover, President Pierce's escort to New Hampshire on his late visit, including " ventilators," " saucepans," and a " Woman !" Here it is:—

"*Marshal's Sale.*—In virtue of a writ of *fieri facias*, issued from the Clerk's Office of the Circuit Court for the County of Washington, in the District of Columbia, and to me directed, I shall expose to public sale, for cash, on Friday, the 27th day of February, 1857, commencing at 10 o'clock, A. M., at the Store-room of Francis Y. Naylor, on Pennsylvania Avenue, between 3d and 4½ streets, south side, the following goods and chattels, in part, to wit: One Woman; 2 bedsteads; 1 looking-glass; 1 ventilator; 1 saucepan; 1 dripping-pan; 1 ice-cream mould; and a lot of other household goods, seized and levied upon as the goods and chattels of Francis Y. Naylor, and will be sold to satisfy Judicial No. 1, to October term, 1856. "J. D. HOOVER,
"Marshal of the District of Columbia."

The correspondent of the *New York Tribune* says: "I attended the Auction Sale of the Woman, on Pennsylvania Avenue, yesterday. She was sold according to the terms of the advertisement. I have no story to tell. Tears rolled down the poor woman's cheeks, and she turned away her face and wept. And this is the Nineteenth Century, and this the Capitol of the 'great Republic' of modern days!"

The Hon. J. R. Giddings, in his Speech on the Slave question, delivered in the House of Representatives of the United States, December 10, 1856, said:—

"I never saw a panting fugitive flying from bondage that I did not pray God most earnestly to speed him in his flight, and to enable him to make good his escape. The whole sympathy of my nature is at once enlisted in his behalf. I always feel anxious that he may escape from the crushing power under which he has been borne down. And yet President Franklin Pierce assumes to lecture me because I choose to obey God rather than him. Why, sir, gentlemen may listen while I tell them that I have seen at one time nine fugitives dining in my own house—fathers, mothers, husbands, wives, and children, fleeing for their liberty, and, in spite of the President's censure, I obeyed the Divine mandate to feed the hungry and clothe the naked. I fed them, I clothed them. I gave them money for their journey to Canada, and sent them on their way. Was that treason? If so, make the most of it!

"Mr. BENNETT, of Mississippi.—I want to know if the Gentleman would not have gone one step further?

"Mr. GIDDINGS.—Yes, sir, I would have gone one step further. I would have driven the Slave-catcher who dared pursue them from my premises. I would have kicked him from my door-yard, if he had made his appearance there.

"Mr. BENNETT.—Would not the Gentleman have justified the taking of them by force or stealth in the first instance?

"Mr. GIDDINGS.—I would smite down the infamous Slave-catcher if he were to enter my door to arrest and enslave a brother man. I hope the President will feel no unhappiness at what I am saying. Mr. Speaker, I make these statements in order that the people of my native State of Ohio, the people of our Northern States, may express their Manhood, and not be held in silence by Executive insolence. *It is the duty of every man, it is a Christian duty, that we should speak out our honest sentiments in condemnation of those infamous crimes.* But I want to speak a little further. I do not mean to speak of Slavery as a mere crime. The Slaveholder controls the Slave by the lash. He scourges him into submission to his own will. But further than this, *no person is allowed to teach a Slave to read the Bible under a penalty of imprisonment. Ignorance is encouraged by legislative enactment.* Now, sir, further than this, whenever a 'Master' attempts to correct a Slave, and the Slave resists, the 'Master' is at liberty to shoot down such Slave. Thus, the 'Master' holds the power of life and death over his Slave, a tyranny which sets at defiance all antediluvian despotisms.

"Mr. Bennett.—I want the member from Ohio to draw the distinction between the Slaveholder bringing his Slave into subjection by the lash, and the Northern men bringing their poor people into subjection by starvation?

"Mr. Giddings.—The Gentleman understands that the 'wife' of a Slave held by the 'Master' is liable to his pollutions, and dare not resist her 'Master's' approaches. He sells her children—ay, his own offspring, born of his Slave—for paltry pelf. There is no such thing in our Northern code.

"Mr. Bennett.—I would ask the Gentleman from Ohio, if he is not aware that in a certain case of a separation of a child from its mother, by articles of separation, a Northern man was the purchaser of the child, and not a Southern man?

"Mr. Giddings.—I know not of the particular case referred to by the Gentleman, but here, in the City of Washington, as told you by that 'old man eloquent,' J. Q. Adams, twenty years ago, a Slave-dealer, reeking in iniquity, purchased a Mother and Child, up in Montgomery county, Md., and separated them from the husband and father and other children imprisoned them in that hell which once existed at the corner of Seventh street and Maryland avenue. There the Mother, with no eye but that of her God upon her contemplating the past, and looking forward to the horrid future, saw the doom to which she and her children were condemned, and when her soul was wrought up with frenzy, she took the life of her offspring, and then severed the thread of her own existence, and rushed to the presence of her God, and there made her appeal against those who uphold and apologize for Slavery. In Covington, Kentucky, a Father and Mother, shut up in a Slave-dungeon and doomed to a Southern Slave-Market, when there was no eye to pity and no arm to save, by mutual agreement, sent the souls of their children to Heaven rather than have them descend to the hell of Slavery, and then committed suicide, and rushed into the presence of God, and made their appeal against those who now sustain crimes which rise to Heaven and call for vengeance upon our guilty land.

"Mr. Bennett.—I desire to call the Gentleman's attention to another fact. I understand the Gentleman to take the position that there is no authority in the Constitution for surrendering up those who are held to service who flee from one State into another.

"Mr. Giddings.—I do; and whenever a Slave sets foot upon free soil, if I had the power, I would make him as free as the air which he breathes.

"Mr. Bennett.—I would ask the Gentleman if he is prepared to violate an express provision of the Constitution?

"Mr. Giddings.—No, Sir. I understand the Constitution of the United States; and I know that those who formed it never intended to degrade me or my fellow Republicans, by making us the bloodhounds to chase the panting fugitive. Sir, I repudiate and detest such doctrine. It never was the doctrine of the Constitution, and never will be.

"MR. BENNETT.—Another question. I ask the Gentleman to draw a distinction between the provision of the Constitution which requires the rendition of Slaves, and that provision of the Constitution which in the Electoral vote, gives a three-fifths Representation to Slaves. The words used are identically the same. In the one instance it provides for the rendition of those who are bound to Service; and, in the other, in fixing the rates of representation, it uses the words, 'those bound to service.' And although the same words are used, the Gentleman says, one means Slaves and the other Apprentices.

"MR. GIDDINGS.—If the Gentleman will propound questions to me pertinent to the subject under consideration, I will listen to them until my hour expires, but I am unwilling that he should occupy my time with such interrogatories as that now proposed. It has no relation to the remarks I was making.

"MR. BENNETT.—I desire to propound a question to the Gentleman. The provision of the Constitution which the Gentleman denies to be of binding force, uses identically the same language as that contained in the provision giving three-fifths representation. It says that persons escaping from service shall be rendered, upon application, to him to whom that service is due. The same language is used in the other clause of the Constitution to which I referred.

"MR. GIDDINGS.—I will always hear Gentlemen courteously who propound questions which are directed to the subject which I am discussing; but I can not be led off into the field which the Gentleman now asks, but he must not abuse my courtesy, by misrepresenting me as denying any part of the Constitution, when I distinctly informed him that I hold to that instrument and will obey it. I was speaking of the right of the people of the North to utter their sentiments upon this question of returning fugitive Slaves.

"Mr. BENNETT. — I desire the Gentleman to answer the question which I have propounded.

"Mr. GIDDINGS. — It takes the Gentleman from Mississippi quite too long to propound questions. He has abused my courtesy and transgressed all bounds of propriety. I will not suffer him longer to encroach upon my brief hour. I was about to proceed with remarks upon the opinions of the President and his usurpation and attempted tyranny, in thus endeavoring to exercise a supervision over the people who have made him, politically, what he is. But as I have but a minute left, I will, without going further into that subject, remark, that in what I have said touching the President, I have felt no spirit of unkindness. I feel a pity, a sympathy for him. He is somewhat advanced in life, and now cast off by his former friends. In his old age, the South — having got all the advantage they can make out of him, used him, body, and soul, and intellect — have now repudiated him; and, now that he is about to retire to private life, I would not add a single pang to his remorse."

A correspondent of the *New York Evangelist*, writing from Richmond, Virginia, says: "In my ramble through this City I passed a dismal-looking place, which, on inquiry, I found to be appropriated to the buying and selling of Men, Women, and Children. Curiosity prompted me to go in, and the scene I witnessed will never be forgotten. It was painfully impressive, and I suppose the great mass of the people of the '*free* States' would have felt just as I did. There I saw one feature of Slavery, an awfully abhorrent one. The weather was unpleasant, and the number of Slaves brought in for sale did not exceed twenty. I looked round upon them, and did not wonder that the Nations of Europe should point the finger at us, for our utter inconsistency in proclaiming 'Liberty,' while we tolerate the abominable traffic in Men, Women, and Children. All these were there. One young Woman, about twenty years of age, attracted my special attention. She was remarkably well proportioned, possessed a fine open countenance, and, in spite of all her ignorance and degradation, was vastly superior to her brutal 'Master.' I was shocked at the revolting manner in which the 'gentlemen Buyers' examined her, to see how much muscle and power of endurance she possessed. Says one, 'Open your mouth;' and then the wretch made his observation, as he would into the mouth of a horse. She held in her arms a Child about two years old, as I judged. I said to her, 'How old is your Child?' The reply I shall never forget, coming from one who was treated worse than a brute: 'He will be two years old, Sir, on the 11th day of next February.' What a burning indignation I felt, that my country should be so disgraced in the eyes of the civilized world, by such a spectacle!

"At length she was ordered to take the stand. The bidding was spirited, and soon she was run up to $1,175. At this point, the Auctioneer was about striking her down. Her brutal 'owner' perceiving it, called out, '*She shall not go at that price; I would sooner take her back to North Carolina. So fine a Woman has not been in the Market for twelve months.*' And took her from the stand. Much as I detested him, I talked a little with him about her good qualities. He told me what an amount of labor she could perform — how many rails she could split in a day, and remarked, '*She left one Child at home. I was sorry for it, but I could not help it.*' I tell you, my friend, my blood got almost to the boiling-point. But it was well that I exercised a little prudence. I could not have helped the poor Woman, and should have been lynched. I saw and heard things, that filled me with the direst apprehensions with regard to the Slavery issue."

A correspondent of *The Free Presbyterian*, writing from Augusta County, Virginia, says: " Observing in one of the daily papers of this place that a Sale of Slaves was to take place at Hill's Auction-rooms, I went down to see it. When I arrived there, I found the room nearly filled with men who had assembled to speculate in the flesh and blood of their fellows; and observing a crowd in one corner, between which and the street-door a screen was placed, I stepped up, when I saw a young Man, stripped entirely naked, and, amid the jeers of Traders, examined in a manner too revolting to rehearse, except it were in Newspapers published in a community where such things are permitted. In these examinations Sex forms no barrier. The Auctioneer announcing that the hour of Sale had arrived, a fine-looking Man, aged about twenty, was placed upon the stand. The Auctioneer commenced with enumerating his good qualities, and asked for a bid. $1,000 was the first offer, and soon run up to $1,300, and then to $1,350. He was now ordered to get down and walk across the room and back again; and several came up, asking questions and examining his teeth, &c. He again mounted the stand, and bidding continued until $1,375 was offered. He was again ordered down, and a similar course of examination took place. He was finally knocked off at $1,550. Next came a Boy, fifteen years of age. The same process was gone through as with the Man, and he was knocked off at $1,050. Next came a beautiful girl, about eighteen years of age, the same routine of exhibition and examination gone through with, and knocked off at $1,725.

" I left the Slave shambles with a sad sickened heart. But a few days previous, I had seen two men leaving their homes in the morning in perfect health; and before the sun had sunk behind the tall mountains, I had witnessed their mangled corpses disentombed from beneath the mountain rock, that had fallen upon and buried them. I had heard the shrieks and witnessed the tears of the wife, the parents, brothers, and sisters of the deceased; and I hope never to pass through such another scene. But what I witnessed at Hill's Auction-rooms was more horrible still. For my own part, I would infinitely rather bury every friend I have, than see them put on the Auction-block; and I would have declared the same to every Man in the room, were I not well assured by persons who could have no motive for misrepresentation, that it is but too notorious that *many here Sell their own flesh and blood. In fact, not only Sell their own Daughters but the Children of these Daughters, and of which they are also, not unfrequently, the Fathers.* Such is the polluting, soul-withering influence of Slavery."

The following letter, from a gentleman travelling in the Slave States, embodies a fair, unprejudiced, and impartial account of a regular Human cattle Sale in Virginia: "I came here from Washington, D. C., on the 14th of April last, without stopping in Fredericksburgh, as I intended. Richmond is the Capital of Virginia, and has about 35,000 inhabitants. * * * * * * * In this City one can have a better opportunity of observing the 'Peculiar Institution' than he could in Baltimore or Washington. Yesterday, I visited two Auction Sales of Slaves. I saw eleven sold, seven Men and Boys and four Girls. There was one lot, apparently a Family, of fine, healthy, sprightly Boys with their Sister. The Auctioneer told me that they were brought there by a Man, who was said to be their Father. The Girl was, I should judge, about 18 years of age, and the Boys say 13, 14, 15, 16, and 17. The youngest Boy was Sold first, and brought $750; the others from $875 to $1,325. The purchasers would feel their arms, legs, &c., poke them in the ribs, look into their mouths, examine their hair, and ask them all manner of questions about themselves. They were taken — male and female — behind a muslin screen, stripped naked, 'thoroughly examined,' and then made to 'show their paces,' by walking backward and forward on the long floor.

"One of the most beautiful young Women I ever saw in my life now mounted the stand. The Auctioneer's assistant, a Slave, exposed the victim's person, to show the 'muscles,' &c. The Auctioneer then told the wretched girl to 'look up,' and began :—

"'Gentlemen: This is a very choice specimen — a very likely Girl, warranted sound, in every respect, and the title is perfect ! — she's a tip-top Seamstress and threatens to become magnificently prolific ! What will you give for her, how much ? Do I hear, $1,000 ? $1,000 I'm only bid for this superb piece of property ! [Here one of the 'gentlemen' in a distant part of the room cried out, 'Send her this way,' and the Auctioneer stopped while the merchandise was told to 'walk out there, step lively now !' The 'gentleman' then turned the Girl round and round, told her to 'grin,' to show her teeth, and pushed her lips aside with his fingers, and then examined her person, from head to foot, asked her several questions about herself, and sent her back to the stand; the Sale then went on.] $1,100 — $1,200 — $1,300, and going at $1,300 ! Why, gentlemen, I'm really astonished at your backwardness ! This Girl is none of your every-day Niggers ! She's a specimen that some of your Abolitionists would give almost any price for; but they shan't have her! — no we've looked out for that. The man that buys her must give bonds never to let her go North again. $1,350 — $1,375 I'm only bid, and going at $1,375, once, $1,375, twice, $1,375 — going — going, gone to Cash for $1,375.'"

A young gentleman of New York, on his "first Southern tour," and not yet Cottonized by the new influences surrounding him, in a letter to the Editor of the *New York Tribune*, said : "Since I left home, I have seen the original ' Declaration of Independence,' and I have seen it 'illustrated' in this City of Richmond, Virginia. O my God ! O my Country ! I have been an eye-witness this morning" (March 3, 1853) "to scenes such as have never been described, and never can. I was told by some of my Pro-Slavery friends at the North, that the evils of Slavery were 'exaggerated.' But

SOLD TO GO SOUTH. (*See page* 178.)

they have not been half told. I have neither the ability nor the heart to describe the scenes I have this moment come from witnessing. I have spent two hours at the Public Sales of Men, Women, and Children. There are four of these Man-Markets, and all in the same street, not more than two blocks from the Exchange Hotel, where I am staying. These Slave Depots are in one of the most frequented streets of the City, and the Sales are conducted in the building on the first floor, and within full View of the passers-by. There are small screens, behind which the Women of mature years were taken for inspection, but the Men and Boys were publicly examined in the open room, before an audience of over one hundred persons. These examinations were carried on by the various parties interested, and were, I should think, enough to shock the feelings of the most hardened vagabond on earth. You really can not conceive that beings in Human shape could conduct themselves so brutally; each scar or mark was dwelt upon with great minuteness — its cause, its general effect upon the health, &c., &c. I saw full twenty Men and Women stripped this morning, and only three of them had what the Traders termed 'clean backs,' and some of them — I should think full one quarter of them — were scarred with the Whip to such an extent as to present a frightful appearance; one in particular was so cut up that I am sure you could not lay your finger on any part of his back, without coming in contact with a scar. The scars were mostly from the Whip or Cowhide, and were from two inches to one foot in length. The marks damaged his sale; although but 40 years old, he only brought $675; but for the scars, he would have brought $1,000. I saw several Children sold. The handsomest Girls brought the largest prices. Girls, from 12 to 18 years of age, brought from $575 to $1,530.

"One of the Slave-mothers attracted my attention. She was a beautiful-looking Woman, about 25 years of age, with three

Children that would have done honor to any Lady in Christendom. Her Children, as well as herself, were neatly dressed. I took my stand near her to learn answers to the various questions put to her by the Traders. One of them asked her what was the matter with her eyes? Wiping away the tears, she replied, 'I s'pose I have been crying.' 'Why do you cry?' 'Because I have left my husband behind, and his Master won't let him come along.' 'Oh, if I buy you, I will furnish you with a better husband than your old one.' 'I don't want any better, and won't have any other as long as he lives.' 'Oh, but you will, though, if I buy you.' 'No, massa, God helping me, I never will.' The most indecent questions were put to her, all of which, after a little hesitation, she answered. But when asked if she thought she could 'turn out a chattel a year,' she replied, 'No, massa, I will never have more, and I am sorry I got these.' She was then ordered to 'take the stand,' and the Sale commenced:—

"'Gentlemen, said the Auctioneer, look at this Girl! Did you ever see a more likely Nigger?—what will you give for her, how much? $1,000 is offered—$1,200—$1,300—$1,400 is offered for this magnificent article—something that no respectable man can do without!—a superb piece of property going off at a sacrifice!—going off at a dead loss!—how much am I bid?—that's it!—I see you, Sir—$1,500 is bid—$1,550—couldn't think of selling such a beautiful Nigger at such a rate!—did you say $1,600?—never mind speaking if you don't like—a nod will do for me—$1,650—$1,700, shall I say? $1,700 it is!—$1,700—that looks something like business—go it, gentlemen! and see who'll get tired first, you or me—keep at her!—nothing like progress—this is an age of progress—what have you got up over there?—'$1,725'—$1,750, did I hear? $1,750 it is!—go on!—you see, gentlemen, I'm getting excited! Come, go on!—never mind that fellow at the other stand!—our side for ever! $1,775, do I hear?—$1,775 it is!—that's it!—encourage true merit—don't be looking over there, Sir—if you don't mind what you're about, you'll lose your chance!—you'll let her slip through your fingers! Do I hear, $1,800?—$1,800 is offered, and going at $1,800—$1,825—$1,850, go it!—$1,875!—that's the ticket!—$1,875, that's well nigh prime cost!

$1,875, and going at $1,875, once, $1,875, twice, $1,875, going — going, gone to Cash for $1,875.'"

A correspondent of the New York *Independent*, in a letter to that journal, says: "While travelling not long ago in one of the Southwestern counties of Virginia, the following incident took place. Starting in the stage-coach, soon after breakfast, the morning being a delightful one in the latter part of the month of May, I took my seat on the box by the side of the driver, and behind me, on the top, was seated a bright, intelligent-looking mulatto boy apparently of 18 or 19 years of age. After being on the road a few minutes, I turned about and asked him where he was going. He replied he was 'going down a few miles to live with Master ———,' who kept the stagehouse at the west stand; that he had lived with him the last summer, and that his owner had sent him down to live with him the coming season. Turning from the boy, the driver remarked to me in an under tone, 'The boy is deceived; I am taking him down to the Slave-pen, a few miles on, where Slaves are kept preparatory to being sent to Louisiana; this deception is practised to get him from his home and mother without creating a disturbance on the place.'

"Shortly after we drew near to the place where the boy supposed he was to stop; he began to gather up, preparatory to leaving the stage, the few articles he had brought away from his home. The driver said to him in a decided tone of voice, 'You are not to get off the stage here.' The boy, in astonishment, replied: 'Yes, I is; I'se got a letter for Master — I'se going to live there this summer.' By this time we had reached the house, and 'Master' ——— making his appearance, John (for that was the name of the boy) delivered his letter and appealed to 'Master' ——— to be delivered from the command of the driver. The 'Master' made no reply, as this kind of deception was no new thing to him. After reading the letter and folding it up, he was about putting it in his pocket, when it flashed on the mind of the boy that he was sold and was bound for the Slave-pen. He exclaimed, in agony, 'Tell me, Master, if I'se sold!' No reply was made. He exclaimed, again, 'Tell me if I'se sold!' This last appeal brought the response: 'Yes, John, you are sold.' The boy threw himself back on the top of the stage, and rolling in agony, sent up such a wail of wo as no one in the stage could endure; even the Hotel-keeper walked away in shame, and the driver hurried into his box and drove off in haste, to drown the noise of his cry. The passengers were all deeply moved by the distress of the boy, and tried in various ways to soothe his crushed spirit, but his agony was beyond the reach of sympathy.

"When his agony had somewhat abated, he exclaimed: 'Oh, if they had only let me bid my Mother good-by. They have lied to me! They have lied to me! If they had a' told me I was sold and I could a' bid my Mother good-by, I'd a gone without making them trouble, hard as it is.' By this time we had passed on some two or three miles since leaving the stand; when drawing near to a pretty thick wood the boy became tranquil. Waiting till we had entered the wood a few rods he jumped from the top of the stage and ran into the wood, as agile as a deer, no doubt with the feeling that it was for his life. The driver instantly dropped his reins and pursued the boy. Proving himself no match, he returned, exclaiming: 'You see, I have done what I could to catch him.' He mounted his box and drove on a mile or so, when he reined up his horses to a house, and calling to the keeper, asked, 'Where are your sons?' He replied, 'They left home this morning, with the Hounds, to hunt a Nigger, and would not be home before night.' The driver said to him Mr. —— had sent his boy, John, on the stage that morning to be delivered at the pen, and that he had jumped from the top of the stage and taken to the woods. His reply was: 'We will hunt him for you to-morrow.' The driver said he wished only to notify him of being in the woods.

"As we drove on, I made the inquiry, 'How long have you driven a Stage on this road?' He replied, 'About fifteen years.' 'Do you frequently take Negroes down to the Slave-pen?' 'Yes, frequently.' 'What will become of this boy, John?' He replied, 'He will skulk about the woods until he is nearly starved, and will some night make his way up to his Master's house, and in about two weeks, I shall bring him down again to the Slave-pen in hand-cuffs.' After a pause, even this driver feeling his degradation in being the instrument of such misery, broke out into the exclamation: 'This is a cursed business; but in this case this is not the worse feature of it. The man who sold him is his own father!'"

Dr. C. G. Parsons, of Boston, Massachusetts, the Author of a Book on Slavery, entitled "A Tour among the Planters," in 1852, says: "The female Slaves can not be otherwise than degraded. Subjected at all times to the passions of the whites, chastity and refinement are out of the question. They are stripped entirely naked to be punished, not only on the Plantations, but by the city marshals in the cities, to whom the Slaveholders or 'Masters' send them for this purpose." (See chaps. i. and ii., of Part III.) "And often they are exposed in Public for Sale, in the same condition. Let the Northern tourist visit the Slave-Market, or the Whipping-post, and he will frequently behold scenes at which the most degraded African ever imported, would hang his head in shame. Only think of a Woman, entirely naked, surrounded by a profane vulgar crowd, while she writhes under the Lash, or is offered, for purposes of Prostitution, to the highest bidder! Such is the 'Christianizing influences' of which Northern Drs. of Divinity so loudly boast."

Dr. Ellwood Harvey, in a letter dated December 25, says: "I attended a 'Sale of Land and other Property,' near Petersburg, Virginia, and unexpectedly saw a great number of Slaves sold at Auction. The wretched creatures were told they would not be sold, and were collected in front of the quarters, gazing on the assembled multitude. The land being sold, the Auctioneer's loud voice was heard, 'Bring up the Niggers!' A shade of astonishment and affright passed over their faces, as they stared first at each other, and then at the crowd of purchasers, whose attention was now directed to them. When the horrible truth was revealed to their minds that they were to be sold, and nearest relations and friends parted for ever, the effect was indescribably agonizing. Women snatched up their Babes, and ran about the place screaming. Children hid behind their distracted Mothers, and Husbands, Fathers, and Brothers, stood in mute despair. The Auctioneer stood on the portico of the house, and the 'Men and Boys' were ranging in the yard for inspection. It was announced that 'no warranty of soundness' would be given, and 'Persons intending to Purchase must examine the Niggers for themselves.' A few decrepit old Men were Sold at prices from fifteen to thirty dollars, and it was painful to see the poor creatures, bowed down with years of toil and suffering, stand up to be the jest of brutal tyrants, and to hear them tell of their disease and worthlessness, fearing that they would be bought by the Traders and taken 'down the river.'

"A white Boy, about fifteen years of age, was now placed on the stand. His hair was brown and straight, his skin exactly the same hue as that of other white persons and no discernible trace of Negro features in his countenance. Some vulgar jests were passed on his 'color,' and $750 was bid for him; but the Auctioneer said that was 'not enough to begin on for such a likely young Nigger.' (Here a Slaveholder, said to be the Father of the Boy, said to me, in a sneering way, that it was 'wrong to Sell white Niggers.') Just before the Boy was bid off, his Mother, a fine-looking Woman, and as white as nine tenths of the Ladies of New England, rushed from the yard upon the portico, crying in frantic grief, 'My dear Son!—Oh, my poor Boy!—they will take away my dear—' Here her voice was lost, as she was rudely pushed back and the door closed. The Sale was not for a moment interrupted, and none of the crowd appeared to be in the least affected by the scene. The poor Boy, afraid to cry before so many strangers, who showed no signs of sympathy or pity, trembled and wiped the tears from his cheeks with his sleeves. During the Sale, the place resounded with cries and lamentations that made my heart ache.

"'Oh, I pity the poor little slave,
　Who labors hard through all the day,
　　And has no one,
　　When day is done,
　To teach his youthful heart to pray.

"'No words of love, no fond embrace,
　No smiles from parents, kind and dear;
　　No tears are shed
　　Around his bed
　When fevers rage and death is near.

"'None feel for him when heavy chains
　Are fastened to his tender limbs;
　　No pitying eyes,
　　No sympathies,
　No prayers are raised to Heaven for him.'

"A Woman was next called by name. She gave her infant one wild embrace before leaving it with an old Woman, and hastened mechanically to obey the call; but stopped, threw up her hands, screamed and was unable to move. One of my companions touched my shoulder and said, 'Come, let us leave here, I can bear no more.' We left the ground."

What keeps down the consciences of these traffickers in the Children of the Slave States? It is the "Public sentiment" of the community where they live; and that " Public sentiment" is made by what are called " Evangelical Ministers and Members of the Churches of Jesus Christ," North and South. The Slaveholder sees plainly enough that, if " Slavery is sanctioned by God," and it is right to set it up in new territory, it is right to take means to do this; and, as Slaves do not grow on bushes in Texas, Kansas, Nebraska, Utah, New Mexico, &c., it is necessary that there should be traders to gather up coffles and carry them there; and as they can not always take whole families, it is necessary that they should part them; and, as Slaves will not go by moral suasion, it is necessary that they should be forced; and, as gentle force will not do, they must whip and torture. Hence come gags, thumbscrews, cowhides, blood—all necessary measures for carrying out what the "evangelical Churches" say God sanctions.

A correspondent of *The Brooklyn* (N. Y.) *Times*, writing from Petersburg, Friday, March 21, 1856, says: " Gentlemen, one of your friends while in Richmond yesterday, attended an 'Auction Sale of Negroes,' and it being an entirely new scene to him, he thought some account of it would interest you. The Sale was in progress when I got there. On the block or stand was a large and powerful Man in the prime of life; after several biddings he was knocked down at $1,350. I counted fourteen Women, and about the same number of Men, beside several small Children, all waiting their turn to be sold. Most of the Men were from 20 to 35 years of age; they brought from $900 to $1,150; and Women, aged from 14 to 30 years of age, brought from $700 to $1,850. A smart little Boy, apparently about 8 years of age, brought $500; and some girls, aged about 12, were sold at from $700 to $850.

" The Auctioneer had a 'Nigger' to assist him, whose business was to bring his fellow-Slaves to the stand and exercise them, in order to display their 'points' to the bidders, that they might judge of their value; and accordingly, as soon as one was sold, the poor fellow would go and bring up another. 'Now, gentlemen,' said the Auctioneer, standing near the victim, 'here is a fine Boy' (Men generally are called 'Boys,' and Women 'Girls,' regardless of age), 'and warranted sound, clear title, and is sold for no fault.' In the meantime the assistant made the man pull off his coat and vest, roll up his shirt-sleeves, take off his shoes and stockings, and pull up his pantaloons, that the audience might see his limbs. 'Hold up your head! Stand up straight; open your mouth, and show the *gentlemen* your teeth,' said the Slave-assistant. 'Gentlemen, how much am I offered?' asked the Auctioneer—'$600, $650, $700, $725, $750'—and, bids beginning to drag, 'Gentlemen,' said the Slave-assistant, 'you do not see this Boy.' (Auctioneer meanwhile stops.) 'Come down here,' said the assistant, and he walked him up and down the room. 'Walk fast; hold up your head; now get up there again.' The Auctioneer then went on—$750, $775, $800, $825.' 'Bring that Nigger here,' called out one of the bidders from the back part of the room, which the assistant did. The gentlemen traffickers examined him closely, looked at his teeth and limbs, asked him various questions, and back he went to the stand again, and was finally sold for $1,125, and taken off to make room for the next.

"'Here, gentlemen, is a young lady for you,' said the assistant, as he led along a beautiful Girl, of 16 or 17 years of age. The Auctioneer began again, assistant rolling up her sleeves; all her limbs being more or less shown by him, and examined by the 'gentlemen traders,' and she went through the walking exercise, which was done in every case. 'There, gentlemen,' said the Auctioneer, as another Girl was put upon the stand, 'is as handsome a piece of furniture as can be produced in our glorious Republic,' and she was a fine-looking Woman, neatly dressed. 'Bring that Nigger here,' said a man near me; the examination, and the questions he asked, I may as well omit. I remained in the room long enough to see from 25 to 30 sold. All were knocked down singly, except in one case, where a 'Brother and Sister' were sold together. Among the groups to be disposed of were a 'Man and *his* Wife,' with a Child some six months old; and opposite them sat a Woman with a Child about three years of age."

The Staunton (Va.) *Spectator*, speaking of the late "pressure in the Money-market," says it did not seem to affect the price of Slaves:

"On New-Year's day, the Slaves belonging to the estate of John Frazier, deceased, were Sold at Public Sale in this place, at prices which show that Money can not be very scarce, notwithstanding the 'hard times.' A gang of Men, Women, and Children, varying from 3 months to 45 years old, averaged $900 each."

At a Sale of "Slaves, Horses, and other Cattle," in Abingdon, Va., in front of the Court-House, on the 25th of December, "very high prices were obtained." A large concourse of persons were present and the bidding was extremely spirited. "Good breeders were much sought after." At a Commissioner's Sale, in Danville, a Man sold for $1,270, and a Woman with a Child 5 months old, for $1,315. The rest of the "gang" sold for proportionately high prices.

The Slave population of Virginia, in 1830, as shown by the Census of that year, was 469,757. In the ten years following that Census, the Slave population of the United States increased to within a fraction of 24 per cent. According to this the Slave population of Virginia, in 1840, would have been 581,559, had there been in the meantime no deportation of Slaves. In the next ten years (viz.: from 1840 to 1850) the Slave population of the Union increased 28 per cent. At that rate of Natural increase, the Slave population of Virginia, in 1850, without any deportation in the meantime, would have been 749,106. But the actual Slave population of Virginia, in 1850, as shown by the Census, was only 472,528. The difference of 276,578 is to be accounted for by the deportation of Slaves. In other words, this difference is the result of the Virginia Slave trade.

This then is the fact which we commend to the attention of all, who ignore the hideous atrocity of the American "Domestic Slave Trade," and who in that willing ignorance affirm that "the Sale of a Converted Slave, except by the Slave's own Consent, is an almost unheard-of occurrence." The denial of this fact by mercenary scribblers may deceive persons at a distance, but it can impose upon no one in the Slave States. In separating a "Husband and Wife," or "Parent and Child," the trader or "owner" violates no "Law" of the State — neither Statute nor "Common Law." He buys or sells at auction or privately that which the "Majesty of the Law" has declared to be "property." The natural increase of Slaves in Virginia has been diminished by deportation at the rate of 15,828 Souls every year, for the twenty years preceding the Census of 1850. Those dry tables of the Census, with all the pains-taking of the Government to prevent any information about "Slavery" and "The Slave Trade" getting into them, have, nevertheless, a terrible testimony to give upon a careful Cross-examination.

The New York *Journal of Commerce* (an inveterate Pro-Slavery journal), of October 12th, 1835, contains a letter from a Virginian, whom the Editor calls "a very good and sensible man," asserting that 20,000 Slaves had been driven to the South from Virginia that year, but little more than three fourths of which had then elapsed. *The Virginia Times* (a weekly newspaper, published in Wheeling) estimated, that in the year 1836, the number of Slaves exported for Sale from Virginia alone, during "the twelve months preceding," at 40,000 souls; the aggregate value of whom may be computed at $35,000,000. Since 1836, the Trade has greatly increased.

Thomas J. Randolph, in a Speech in the Virginia House of Delegates, in 1832, said: "How can an honorable mind and a lover of his country bear to see this 'ancient Dominion,' rendered illustrious by the noble devotion and patriotism of her Sons in the cause of Liberty, converted into one grand Menagerie, where Men and Women are reared for the Market, like oxen or hogs for the shambles?" Is it better, is it not worse than the African Slave Trade; that trade which enlisted the labor of the good and wise of every civilized nation of the world to abolish? The Pirate-captain receives the stolen Man, a stranger in language, aspect, and manners, from the Merchant-kidnapper who has brought him from the interior. The ties of father, mother, husband, and child, have all been rent in twain; before he receives him, his soul has become callous. But here in Virginia, Sir, individuals whom the 'Master' has known from infancy, whom he has seen 'sporting in the innocent gambols of childhood,' who have been 'accustomed to look to him for protection,' he tears from the Mother's arms, and sells into a strange country, among strange people, subject to cruel taskmasters. It has been attempted to justify Slavery here, because it once existed in 'heathen lands.' Upon the same principle, the upholders of this withering system could justify Mahometanism, with its plurality of wives, petty wars for plunder, robbery, and murder, or any of the abominations and enormities committed in our midst—by the Christian Churches? Does Slavery exist in any part of Europe? No, Sir, in no part of it."

The New York Herald, of January 21, 1857, says: "The *Warrenton* (Va.) *Whig* was informed by Messrs. Dickinson, Hill, & Co., Auctioneers, of Richmond, that the gross amount of their Sales of men, Women, and Children, in 1856, reached $2,000,000. The entire Sales of houses in Richmond alone would make the amount go over $4,000,000, and still the business is increasing. 'We ourselves,' says the *Whig*, 'witnessed the Sale of thirty-five Slaves at an average value of $700. Girls, not ten years of age, sold for $800. A Carpenter, nearly forty years of age, brought $1,615. In Williamsburg, last week, Mr. R. Saunders, executor of the estate of the late *Rev. S. Jones*, exposed for sale twenty Slaves, all of whom commanded a most excellent price.'"

The Richmond (Va.) *Dispatch* says: "There has been a greater demand for Slaves in this city than ever known before, and they have commanded better prices. Prime field hands (Men) now bring from $1,250 to $1,500; and Women, from $900 to $1,100. Not long since a likely Girl sold in this city at private sale for $1,700. A large number of Men, Women, and Children, are bought on speculation, and probably there is not less than $2,000,000 in town now seeking investure in such *property*."

The Hon. Charles Sumner thus alludes to his tour in the Slave States, and to what fell under his personal observation: "It has been my fortune latterly to see Slavery face to face in its own home, in the Slave States; and I take this early opportunity" (December 2, 1855) "to offer my testimony to the open barbarism which it sanctions. I have seen a Human being knocked off at Auction on the steps of the Court-House, and, as the sale went on, compelled to open his mouth and show his teeth like a horse. I have been detained in a Stage-coach that our driver might, in the phrase of the country, 'help lick a Nigger;' and I have been constrained, at a public table, to witness the revolting spectacle of a poor Slave, yet a child, felled to the floor by a blow on the head from a clenched fist. Such incidents were not calculated to shake my original convictions. The distant Slaveholder who, in 'generous solicitude' for the Truth which makes for Freedom feared that like a certain Doctor of Divinity" (Nehemiah Adams), "I might, under the influence of 'personal kindness' be hastily swayed from these convictions, may be assured that I saw nothing to change them in one tittle, but to confirm them, while I was entirely satisfied that here in Massachusetts, where all read, the true character of Slavery is better known than in the Slave States themselves, where ignorance and prejudice close the avenues of knowledge."

CHAPTER II.

"We should transmit to posterity our abhorrence of Slavery."
PATRICK HENRY.

THE Hon. J. K. Paulding, late Secretary of the United States Navy, gives the following picture of a scene he witnessed in Virginia:—

"The sun was shining out very hot, and in turning an angle of the road, we encountered the following group: first, a little cart drawn by one horse, in which five or six half-naked colored children were tumbled like pigs together. The cart had no covering, and they seemed to have been actually broiled to sleep. Behind the cart marched three colored women, with head, neck, and breasts, uncovered, and without shoes or stockings; next came three men, bareheaded, half-naked, and fastened together with an ox-chain. Last of all came a white man on horseback, carrying a brace of pistols in his belt, and who, as we passed him, had the impudence to look us in the face without blushing. I should like to have seen him hunted by bloodhounds. At a house where we stopped, a little further on, we learned that he had bought these miserable beings in Maryland, and was marching them in this manner to some of the more Southern markets. Shame on the State of Maryland! I say—and shame on the State of Virginia! and every State through which this wretched cavalcade was permitted to pass. Do they expect that such exhibitions will not disgrace them in the eyes of strangers, however they may be reconciled to them by education and habit?"

The Washington correspondent of the New York *Independent*, in a letter to that Journal in July, 1856, spoke of a case of peculiar hardship in that city, growing out of the atrocious Slave system. The sequel of the case has recently transpired, and we give it to illustrate the working of the "institution":—

A noble specimen of colored manhood was born in Virginia, of a Slave mother. On the demise of his "owner" he was manumitted. The heirs-at-law broke the Will, and Charles was remanded to servitude again. Through the influence of some Quakers in the vicinity who knew the man, a nominal price of five hundred dollars was set upon his head, which, with the aid of his friends, he promptly met, and rejoiced in the possession and full ownership of his own body and soul. But the sad part of the story was, that "*his* wife and three children" were still doomed "to grind in the prison-house," and their descendants after them for ever. By the solicitations of the neighbors and friends, a man in the vicinity purchased the family for six hundred dollars, and offered the husband and father a "bill of sale" of his household when he should be able to refund that amount. This man was, and is, a member of the *Methodist Episcopal Church, and the head Steward of that Church in his vicinity. The "boy" Charles was a Member of the same Church, and for years communed at the same altar.*

Twelve years had gone by, and the family of Charles had toiled faithfully for the "owner." He himself had early gone to Washington (D. C.) to labor, and, if possible, raise the required sum to free his little household, and gather them around an humble altar which he could call his own. He had visited "*his* family" four times a year, sometimes taking down clothing, and such little things as a "husband and father," in such circumstances, would be prompted by affection to carry. In the meantime, the "family" had increased to six children. When the case was made known to a "Friend" by Charles himself, this "Friend" offered to see that the six hundred dollars was forthcoming, and he could, at the first opportunity, seek an interview, with the "owner" of "*his* family," and make all necessary preparations for their liberty. He sorrowfully told his "Friend" that a generous man in Washington had made him the offer of assistance previously, but from certain indications he had observed, he did not believe this professed Christian steward would comply with his promise. However, he tried, and his fears were fully realized, when this old sinner, of seventy years, coolly asked "four thousand dollars for the family." The man! all the man, in the freed and noble father and husband rose at this wanton and wilful violation of all decency, Christianity, and honor. He attempted to reason, basing his claims upon the God-given conjugal and parental affections supposed to have a lodgment in the person of the "owner" of another man's wife and children, but was peremptorily ordered to hold his tongue, and to mention the subject no more! The sequel is as follows: Within three months, Charles visited his family in Virginia, and went up to the "Master's house," as usual. He again introduced the subject of the purchase of his family, and the steward of the stony heart persisted in his demand of four thousand dollars. His offer was accepted, and he was asked to give a writing to that effect, specifying that upon payment of that sum the "*wife* and children" should be free. This also he refused to do.

The next day, he himself went to the nearest town and made a complaint against Charles, on a trumped-up story, that he was engaged in running off Slaves, and had the officers out in pursuit of him. It is sufficient to say, that due notice was given the victim, and the officers of the law did not succeed in finding his "brother communicant." The son and heir-at-law of the gray-headed steward, not being fully initiated into his father's duplicity, took sides against the officers, and in favor of Charles, stating that he was well known in that vicinity, and was respectable and strictly honest. The officers, not relishing the business, or the denunciations, informed the son as to who made the complaint, and a small family scene ensued. Of course, a hasty retreat had been beaten by the poor sufferer, and wearied, foot-sore, and broken-hearted, he entered again Washington city, after travelling on foot fifty miles without daring to stop and rest himself.

The *Savannah* (Ga.) *Republican*, speaking of the "flourishing condition" of the Markets of the South, in December, 1856, says: "On Monday last, at Warrenton, Va., many Slaves were sold at Auction, and brought extremely high prices. A boy, about eighteen years of age, sold for $1,245, and another boy, not over ten, for $799. A little girl sold for upward of $600. At a recent sale of the estate of Zeph. Turner, deceased, Rappahannock county, eighty Slaves, ranging from twelve to thirty-seven years of age, averaged $1,115."

In November, 1855, a Slaveholder with a family of his chattels, consisting of "husband, wife, and several children," took passage at Louisville, Kentucky, for Memphis, Tennessee, where he intended to take all except the husband ashore. The latter was hand-cuffed, and although his "Master" said nothing of his intention, the poor fellow made up his mind from appearances, as well as from the remarks of those around him, that he was destined for the Southern market. The Steamer reached Memphis during the night, and while within sight of the city, the heart-broken man caused "*his* wife" to divide their things, as though resigned to the separation, and then taking a moment, when his "owner's" back was turned, ran forward and jumped into the river. He sank, and his "Master" was $1,500 poorer than a moment before.

"COMMISSIONER'S SALE OF SLAVES. — As Commissioner, under a Decree of the Bourbon County Court, at the March Term, in the case of Alpheus Lewis and Margaret his wife, I will expose to Public Sale, at the Court-House door in Paris, on the 2d day of April next, County Court day for said County, on a credit of four months, two valuable Slaves, to wit: a Woman aged about twenty-five, and a Girl about twelve. Persons wishing to purchase, can see said Slaves by calling on J. Porter. Bond, with approved security, will be required, having the force and effect of a replevy bond.

"THOMAS A. TAYLOR, Commissioner.
"Paris (Ky.), *March* 22, 1855."

The younger of the two Slaves above spoken of, was found, "upon close examination," to have been cruelly treated. She showed burns that evidently were made with hot-irons upon her neck, hands, under both arms, and between her legs, both behind and before; besides bruises upon her head, and bleeding at the ears. It was also made known by white men in Mr. Lewis's employ, that Sally, the oldest Slave and the Mother of several Children, had been stripped, by Mrs. Lewis's direction, entirely naked, and her feet tied to a tree, about four feet from the ground. She then made a Woman force the pump, and another direct the hose so as to drench poor Sally with water, while she would stand off a pace and pelt her with stones, and then take to her more favored method of torture, the hot-iron. Sally had old scars upon her back and legs that could scarcely be covered with the palm of the hand. Both Slaves had suffered dreadfully from hunger and cold.

Mr. Alpheus Lewis is the son of Alpheus Lewis, of Clarke County, Ky. Mr. Lewis, senior, is a Member of the Baptist Church, a man of wealth, and reputed to be of one of the "best families" in the State. Mrs. Lewis's maiden name was Scott, daughter of Robert Scott.

A Committee of the Synod of the Presbyterian Church, of Kentucky, who had been appointed to make a Report on the condition of the Slaves in that State, said: "After making all allowances, the 'colored' population of the State, bond and free, can be considered, at the most, but semi-heathen. As to their temporal estate—Brutal stripes, and all the various kinds of personal indignities, are not the only species of cruelty which Slavery licenses. The law does not recognise the family relations of the Slave, and extends to him no protection in the enjoyment of domestic endearments. The members of a Slave family may be forcibly separated, so that they shall never more meet until the final judgment. Brothers and Sisters, Parents and Children, Husbands and Wives, are torn asunder never more to meet on earth. *Those acts are daily occurring in the midst of us.* The shrieks and the agony often witnessed on such occasions proclaim with trumpet-tongue the iniquity and cruelty of the 'Institution.' There is not a neighborhood where these heart-rending scenes are not displayed. There is not a village or road that does not behold the sad procession of manacled outcasts, whose chains and mournful countenances tell that they are exiled by force from all that their hearts hold dear. Our Church, years ago, raised its voice of solemn warning against this flagrant violation of every principle of mercy, justice, and humanity. Yet, we blush to announce to the world that this warning has been disregarded, even by those who hold to our communion. Professors of the Religion of mercy have torn the Mother from her Children and sent her into merciless and returnless exile. Yet acts of Church discipline have never followed such conduct."

The Rev. James H. Dickey, speaking of the horrors of Slavery in Kentucky, says: "As I was returning with my family from a visit to the barrens of Kentucky, I witnessed a scene such as I never witnessed before, and such as I hope never to witness again. Having passed through Paris, in Bourbon county, Ky., the sound of music (beyond a little rising ground) attracted my attention. I looked forward, and saw the Flag of my Country waving. Supposing that I was about to meet a Military parade, I drove hastily to the side of the road, and having gained the ascent, I discovered about forty Men, all chained together after the following manner: each of them was hand-cuffed, and they were arranged in rank-and-file. A chain was stretched between the two ranks, to which short chains were joined, which connected with the hand-cuffs. Behind them were about thirty Women, in double rank, the couples tied hand to hand. A solemn sadness sat on every countenance, and the dismal silence of this march of despair was interrupted only by the sound of two Violins, yes, as if to add insult to injury, the foremost couple were furnished with a Violin a-piece; the second couple were ornamented with Cockades, while near the centre waved the 'Star-Spangled Banner.'—the Flag of the 'Model Republic,' carried literally in chains! I could not forbear, as I drove by, exclaiming, in the words of Whittier, to the blear-eyed monster-captain of the gang :—

"'What, ho! our countrymen in chains!
    The whip on woman's shrinking flesh!
Our soil yet reddening with the stains,
    Caught from her scourging, warm and fresh!
What! mothers from their children riven!
    What! God's own image bought and sold!
Americans to market driven, and bartered as the brute for gold!'

"Heaven will curse that man who engages in such a traffic, and the Government that protects him in it. I pursued my journey until evening, and put up for the night, when I mentioned the scene I had witnessed. 'Ah!' cried my landlady, 'that is my brother!' From her I learned that his name is Stone, of Bourbon county, Kentucky, in partnership with one Cunningham, of Paris; and that a few days before he had purchased a Woman from a man in Nicholas county. She refused to go with him; he attempted to compel her, but she defended herself. Without further ceremony, he stepped back, and by a blow on the side of her head with the butt of his whip, brought her to the ground; he then tied her, put her on a cart, and drove off. I learned further, that there were 'about seventy Niggers,' besides the drove I had seen, shut up in the Paris prison for safe-keeping, to be added to the gang, and that they were designed for the New Orleans market."

The following letter, the publication of which caused Mr. J. Brady, a New England Schoolmaster, to be Lynched, at Lexington, Kentucky, by the "free and enlightened Democrats" of that place, will help the reader to a more correct knowledge of the workings of the "*heaven*-born institution" of the Republic:

"LEXINGTON, KY., *Tuesday, December 25, 1855.*

"MR. EDITOR: Christmas has come around again. It is a great day here" (perhaps I should say week), "especially for two classes — Slaves and School-children. Most of the former have that day as a holiday; the latter in most places in this State, have a week, sometimes including New Year's Day. Christmas is regarded as a great occasion, and was celebrated in the Episcopal and Catholic Churches. I have just returned from attending the service of the former. Both these Churches regard the day with much veneration, and well they may, being the Anniversary of the birth of our Saviour — of him 'who spake as man never spake,' whose wisdom and righteousness was above that of all men, and who gave himself a sacrifice for the sins of guilty humanity, so that all who would come unto him might have eternal life. To hear of this Saviour we assembled. Although it was so great an Anniversary, and the expected presence of the Bishop was announced, yet but a few persons were scattered over the Church. Notwithstanding the small attendance, all the ceremonies of that denomination were faithfully rehearsed. These were followed by a short but very eloquent discourse on the birth, life, and death of our Saviour. The prophecies in relation to his coming into the world, his holy life, and victorious death, were repeated; the actual verification of these prophecies in his real life and character was dwelt upon; and the noble sentiments which he had uttered, and the rules of conduct which he laid down for the observance of his followers, were made the subject of comment. In conclusion, the minister, on behalf of himself and congregation, in loud strains, thanked our Father in Heaven, that he had given to the World his Only Begotten Son to die for sinners; that he had cast our lots in a 'Christian land;' and especially, that he had cast them 'in the most enlightened community in all the earth, where peace, liberty, happiness, and Christian privileges, are vouchsafed to all.'

"We listened attentively, wondered that so few were present, and regretted that more were not in attendance to learn the extent of our blessings, and to receive upon their minds a still more forcible impression of the beauty and excellence of the sentiments uttered by the second person of the adorable Trinity, An invocation to the Father, Son, and Holy Spirit, that their blessings might rest upon us, closed the exercises, and we went forth in thoughtful mood, reflecting on that maxim of our Saviour. '*Whatsoever ye would that men should do to you, do ye even so to them,*' which is said to contain the essence of all our duties to our fellow-men, and on those two commandments, 'hang all the law and the prophets.' Scarcely had we proceeded two squares ere our footsteps were arrested by a crowd of men on the sidewalk, so dense that ladies could not pass, but were compelled to cross to the next sidewalk, pass round and recross beyond them. Curiosity at beholding a crowd so much denser than at the Church attracted my attention, and led me to halt a moment, when lo! there came to my ears the hoarse notes of the Auctioneer selling a fellow-creature, a Human being to the highest bidder! Never were my feelings so much shocked. Though I had before witnessed the horrid spectacle of the sale of a Human being, yet, upon this day, commemorative of such an event as can never be known again on earth — the birth of the immaculate and only Son of God — and after such a discourse as that to which we had listened, to witness a deed so revolting at any time to the feelings of any one in the least degree imbued with Christian philanthropy, and so contradictory to every precept of Him for whom the day has been named, was shocking beyond description. The Auctioneer was crying with stentorian voice:—

"'Only $1,285 is bid for this Boy — a fine, likely Nigger going at $1,285 — must be sold to the highest bidder — $1,300 — $1,325, and going at $1,325, once, $1,325, twice, and going at $1,325 — going, gone to Cash for $1,325.'

"Oh! what a contrast was this scene, almost at the door of the Church, to what we might have expected of that 'community' of which we had just heard so favorable an account. If this scene was thought to be in accordance with the Christian character, and the minister had such scene in view when speaking in such high terms of the 'community' (as he must have had), *I wondered, as the hour suited, after the Sermon, and before the Benediction, they had not held the Sale at the Church, the Minister being Auctioneer.* Perhaps, however, they knew that they could not get such a crowd there as they wanted, and, therefore, they came to the way leading up to the Temple of Justice. Oh! how I wished for a Paul to stand up before them, at the entrance of this Temple, and 'reason to them as to Felix, of righteousness, of temperance, and of judgment to come.' Like Felix, they must have 'trembled' at his reasoning; but like him, those who could be guilty of such an act of inhumanity, with all the lights of the Nineteenth century beaming upon them, would probably answer, '*Go thy way for this time; when I have no more Niggers to sell I will call for thee.*'"—(See chapters i. and ii. of Part III.)

A correspondent of the *New York Tribune*, writing from Cleveland, Ohio, under date August 9, 1856, says: "During the past winter and summer I have been travelling through Western Missouri and Kansas, and on the 21st of February last I was in Lexington, Missouri. On the morning of that day I was, for the first time in my life, a spectator of the Sale of Slaves. Two young men, and a girl, about eighteen years of age, were placed upon the block, surrounded by forty or fifty Slaveholders. The first put up was a 'Nigger' of great beauty and fine form. The Auctioneer commenced by exhorting the farmers to remember that the hemp was all down — hands were scarce — Niggers had taken a rise; and told them that there stood one of the best-looking 'Niggers' in the Republic; that he was sound — had good teeth and eyes. In short, was an 'excellent Nigger.' The bidding proceeded until $1,250 was reached. During the sale the Auctioneer, and others, indulged in witticisms and puns upon the boy, which set the crowd to laughing; but the Slave did not laugh. Not a smile did I notice during the whole time. His expression was that of deep despondency. Being called away, I did not see the other two sold."

A woman and several children were sold at Goldsboro', North Carolina, a short time since, at prices ranging from $710 to $827. *The Goldsboro' Patriot* says:—

"They were the children of a free Negro by the name of Adam Wynne, who had purchased their Mother, his wife, previous to their birth. They were, consequently, his Slaves; and he having become involved, they were sold for his debts."

We have seen many phases of the workings of Slavery presented, but none more revolting than the above. Here is a Man who has shown a most devoted attachment to one who afterward became his "Wife"— having purchased her freedom for that purpose! She was thus raised to equality with himself; and after years have passed of domestic happiness, she and her children are seized by the remorseless Demon-power of Slavery, and sold from the husband and father into life-long servitude, to appease the inexorable demands of the creditors of this unhappy Man! Ever since the days of Shakespeare, the name of Shylock has been held in abhorrence; but the exaction of the pound of flesh, of the Merchant of Venice, as "nominated in the bond" was merciful when compared to that of these Slaveholding fiends in human shape. Yet this is Slavery as it exists by "Law" in more than one half of the States and Territories of the "Model Republic"— which has been declared by the Presbyterian General Assembly to be "no bar to Christian communion."

"100 *Slaves for Sale.*—I shall offer at Public Sale, on the premises, commencing on the 22d day of February next, 100 Slaves, comprising some excellent Mechanics, such as Carpenters, brick and stone Masons, and the best Field-hands, many of whom have been, for the last few years, employed in the cultivation of Cotton on my plantation in the South; several excellent House-servants, Cooks, Washers, Ironers, &c. All of these *Negroes* were either raised *by myself or purchased, for my own use,* and I hazard nothing in saying, comprise altogether, the likeliest lot of Slaves ever before offered for Sale in this Republic, almost all of them being young, and consisting, chiefly, of able-bodied Men, Boys, and Girls. At the same time and place, I shall hire out 15 or 20 likely female Slaves to the highest bidders, some of them excellent House-servants. "N. T. GREEN, *Warren County, N. C.*"

In South Carolina, the "Market is firm." The demand for "Good breeders" is active. "The arrivals are below the wants of the trade"— and "the tendency is still upward." "A moderate business has been done in Women and Children for export."

The Columbia (S. C.) *Times,* speaking of the "happy condition of things" in that place, says:—

"There was a large amount of *property* sold yesterday (January 1), which we can not enumerate in full. Mr. A. R. Phillips sold an immense number of Men, Women, and Children. We subjoin some of the prices: One ordinary Man, 22 years of age, $1,085; 1 ordinary

Woman, 20 years of age, $1,070; 1 Boy, 15 years of age, $780; 1 Woman, 36 years, and Son, 4 years, $1,175; 1 Woman, 30 years, and 3 Children, $1,750; 1 Woman, and 5 Children, $1,960; 1 Woman, 32 years, and two Children, $1,380; 1 Girl, $580. For Commissioner in Equity: 1 Woman and 1 Child, $1,776."

A *friend* writing from Columbia (S. C.), says: "Never having seen a Slave-Auction, I determined to be a witness to one. Accordingly, about fifteen minutes before the appointed hour, I left my Hotel, and while yet within some distance of the Court-House, I heard the voice of the Auctioneer, as he appraised his Human chattels, and rattled out—'$750—no more than $750 for this likely Nigger fellow—$775,' &c. This was early on Monday morning. Scarcely had the echoes of the high anthem that pealed from the Episcopal organ and choir, a few hours before, yet died away. Hardly had the swell of the tune that rose from Dr. Palmer's Presbyterian Church yet murmured to the stars; and the loud Psalm-shout that ascended from the throats of a thousand Baptists the preceding Sabbath evening had as yet hardly time (if time it takes) to 'mingle with the triumphal and eternal chorus of the harps of heaven.' Having so lately heard all these, with what harsh and grating discord did the horrid voice of the Man-seller shake the heavens and strike upon my ear.

> "'Is it, O man, with such discordant noises,
> With such accursed instruments as these,
> Thou drownest nature's sweet and kindly voices,
> And jarrest the celestial harmonies?'

"The Sale took place on the steps of the 'Court of Justice' (ironically so called). Of the seventy-five or one hundred persons that composed the bidders, such a collection is never seen in a civilized community. There were groups of petty Merchants of the town, hard, close-fisted, money-loving, mean-looking men. There were a number of the poor Clay-eaters, from the Sand-hills, who were easily distinguishable by their cadaverous, ashen-white and half-human appearance. There were the gross, vulgar, and lecherous youths of the town. And (must I tell it, or shall I go backward and hide the shame?) there was a professed 'minister of the Gospel of Jesus Christ,' with the badge of his order round his throat, and who but a sun previous, had offered 'salvation and heaven' to all. Bidding was tolerably brisk, and competition keen. The first offered was a middle-aged Man, of, I should judge, about forty years of age, whose care-worn, broken-down, and dispirited countenance and deeply-wrinkled brow, intimated that the toil and trouble of at least twice forty years had been compressed into his brief existence. He sold for $875. Another Man sold for $1,345. A middle-aged Woman then took the stand. She had a vacant, careless look, and as the Auctioneer praised up her qualities, a malignant-like grin would now and then flit across her countenance. He declaimed about her, and continued repeating her praises as, '*This splendid Seamstress and Cutter. As a sewer and cutter, I am told Lucretia has no equal — besides being a valuable Housekeeper,*' &c. She was sold to a man who I learned was going to keep a Tavern. The next victim was a young Woman, who (her 'owner' and the Auctioneer said) was 'just eighteen years of age;' she was of an Olive-color, and had a pleasing countenance and mild, lustrous eyes. Her 'owner' (who was said to be her Father) took off her hood, to show her countenance, and, when she replaced it, again took it off; and in appraising her, by word and action, *appealed to the lowest and basest passions of the assembled crowd.* She clasped to her bosom a light-colored, blue-eyed child only three months old, and who, young as it was, cast a mournful look upon its Father, the 'owner' of its unhappy Mother, as much as to say, 'O father! O father!' The Sale now commenced :—

"'Gentlemen,' said the Auctioneer,' (taking off her hood), 'did you ever see such a Face and Head, and Form as that? Look at this!'

(pulling up her clothes and showing her limbs,) 'she's only eighteen years of age, and already has a child — a Male child — three months old, and will, consequently, make a valuable piece of property for some one. She's a splendid Housekeeper and Seamstress. Gentlemen, you have only to look at her and you will behold the most lovely Nigger you ever saw! That's a fact, Sir, and I'll put you down at $1,500! You say you didn't say anything — well, if you didn't, you smiled, and nobody has a right to smile at this stand unless they mean something! Smile again, Sir, if you please — that's it — $1,600 — $1,650 — don't mind the fifties — go it by hundreds! You all know what Shakespeare says about beautiful Niggers — don't damn him, Sir — and he's good authority — $1,700 — $1,800, did you say, Sir? $1,800 then! I don't want to make any reflections on the character and standing of the 'highly respectable gentlemen' before me, but you must all be aware that nothing improves a man's taste so much as the study of the works of nature — don't damn them, Sir, and by buying this magnificent specimen you will have an opportunity of indulging it to the fullest extent! Come, gentlemen, how much more am I bid for this splendid Nigger — how much — how much? Why, gentlemen, the speech I am making upon her is worth the money alone — how much for her with the Child — how much? $1,900 — $1,925 — $1,950 — $1,975 — that's it! — go ahead! — $1,975, I'm only bid for these remarkable specimens of humanity! — $1,975. Gentlemen, you're not going to let me be beat by that fellow at the Northern stand there, are you? — no, I am sure you won't — see how he looks at me, as much as to say, 'You can't come it!' — come now, bid up for the credit of our side of the Republic! — it will never do to let me be beat by that Northerner — I know you're all friends and will stand by my side of the Union — that's it! — $2,000 — that's the way to fetch me up! $2,000 — our side of the Republic for ever! — they can't hold a candle to us! $2,000, and going at $2,000, once — $2,000, twice — going, gone to Brother Foster, for $2,000.'

"The tears stood glittering in the poor Girl's eyes, and at every licentious allusion, she cast a look of pity and of wo at the Auctioneer, and at the crowd — which was responded to only by a brutal laugh. She was knocked down to 'Brother Foster,' a beastly-looking fellow about sixty-five years of age. She descended from the Court-House steps, looked at the audience, looked fondly into her Child's face, pressed it warmly to her bosom, with the Auctioneer's hard-hearted remark ringing in her ears, that 'that Child won't trouble her purchaser long.' I made my way to my temporary home, overpowered with a chaos of horrors. And when I entered the hall of the house, the merry glee and loud laugh of the female inmates too plainly announced to me the fact that the 'colored' daughters of 'the golden-rivered land of the plantain' find but few on earth who will shed for their sorrows a sisterly tear."

Surely the Virgins of the Heavenly land will descend at times to comfort their woful hearts — while God himself will "gather their tears in his bottle." He whose heart was so tender that he wept at the grave of Lazarus, over a sorrow that he was so soon to turn into joy — what does he think of this constant heart-breaking anguish?

"*By permission of the Court of Ordinary*, on the first Tuesday in January next, will be Sold at the Court-House in Gillisonville, Beaufort District (S. C.), fifteen Slaves, belonging to the Estate of William H. Mangin, deceased, and sold for the benefit of said estate. Terms Cash.
"J. J. STONY, *Executor*.

"N. B.—In connection with the above, will be Sold, in addition, ten Slaves, the *property* of John Stoddard, comprising the Families of the foregoing."

Now look at the cruelty of the above advertisement. First are to be sold the Parents, separately, or in the lot, as purchasers may incline. Then follow the Children, "comprising the Families of the foregoing"—a stroke of the Auctioneer's hammer settling the question whether the Parents go in one direction, and the Children in another.

"*On Tuesday next*, will be Sold at the North of the Exchange, at 10 o'clock, A. M., a prime gang of Negroes, accustomed to the culture of Cotton and Provisions, owned by 'The Independent Church,' in Christ Church Parish. "THOMAS N. GADSDEN, *Auctioneer*."

A correspondent of the New York *Evening Post*, writing from Charleston, says: "I have just seen a family of Slaves sold at Auction at noon-day, in the Public Square of this City.

They were placed on a cart as if for punishment. A red Flag was hoisted at their side — fit emblem of Crime and Slavery. The Auctioneer (Thomas N. Gadsden), who, I was told, was 'well received in Society,' praised the qualities of a poor Slave as 'very intelligent, and first-rate gardener.' The purchasers went up to the Men, Women, and Children, opened their mouths, and examined their teeth, limbs, &c., &c. The bidding then commenced, and the bargains were struck off. Twenty steps off, precisely in the same manner, they were Selling an Ass and an old Man. The ass sold for $71, and the Man for $69 — $2 less than the ass!"

"*For Sale.*—A Girl, about 29 years of age, raised in Virginia, and her two female children, one two and the other one year. The girl never had a day's sickness, with the exception of the *small*-pox, in her life. The children are fine and healthy. She is very prolific in her generating qualities, and affords a magnificent opportunity to any man who wishes to raise a family of healthy Niggers for his own use. Any man wishing to purchase will please leave his address at this office."—*Charleston* (S. C.) *Mercury.*

A Slave-mother, "belonging to Dempsey Weaver, Esq.," of Nashville, Tennessee, having committed some fault, Weaver threatened to sell her next day to a Mississippi trader. But she determined not to be sold or separated from her child, and jumped into the river with her babe in her arms, and were both drowned.

A young gentleman, who, like many other foolish young men, went South "for the benefit of his health," writing from New Orleans, says: "While at Tyrel Springs, twenty miles from Nashville, Tennessee, on the border of Kentucky, my hostess said, one day, 'Yonder comes a Gang of Slaves, chained.' I counted them and observed their position. They were divided by three one-horse wagons, each containing a 'driver,' armed to the teeth, and so posted as to command the whole gang. The old Men and Women were unchained; sixty were chained in two companies, thirty in each, the right hand of one to the left hand of the opposite one, making fifteen each side of a large ox-chain, to which the hands were fastened, and necessarily compelled to hold up—Men and Women promiscuously, and about in equal proportions, all young people. No Children here, except a few in a wagon behind, which were the only Children in the four gangs. I said to a mulatto-Woman in the house, 'Is it true that the Negro-traders take Mothers from their Babies?'—'Massa, it is true; for here, last week, such a Girl' (naming her), 'who lives about a mile off, was taken after dinner—knew nothing of it in the morning—sold, put into the gang, and her Baby taken away. She was a beautiful young Woman, and brought a high price.'"

The Savannah Georgian, of the 7th January, 1856, has the following Market intelligence: "Tuesday last was General Sales-Day throughout many of the States of the Republic—a day when Sheriffs, &c., offer *property* at Public Sale; to satisfy Executions, to close Estates, &c. We notice, from reported Sales in various localities that Men, Women, and Children, generally brought good prices—affording gratifying evidence that the times are not as hard as has been supposed. We need no better evidences than are thus afforded that the Money pressure is by no means of a general or serious character. As we have already said, the country is Solvent, and business affairs will soon regulate themselves. In short, Stock-raising" (that is to say, Slave-breeding) "was never in a more flourishing or glorious condition."

The Georgia Annual Conference of the Methodist Episcopal Church resolved as follows: "*Resolved, That the testimony of colored Members of the Churches shall not be taken against a white person.*" In the Day of Judgment "Nigger" testimony will be received, and there will then be heard the voices of the "evangelical" traffickers in Human flesh saying to the mountains and the rocks, "Fall on us and hide us from the face of Him that sitteth on the throne, and from the wrath of the Lamb." Think of it!

The *Augusta* (Ga.) *Sentinel*, speaking of the "property" of Ulm & Walker, which was advertised in its columns, says: " The Slaves averaged $499 per head, although there were among them a large number of Children, several at the breast, old Men and old Women, two superannuated, and one old fellow *dead*. The mules and jackasses averaged $148 per head. We are glad to see the *property* of our friends selling so well." What under the sun could have induced any "living man" to pay $499 for a "dead Nigger?"—

"'T'was not meat for a Christian you'll own;
'T'was plenty of skin — with a good deal of bone."

What respect can a community in which such things are done and reported so coolly, have for Human nature? The man or woman who would sell the "Dead" at Public Auction, and the people who would "Sanction" such infamy, would not hesitate to sell the body of our Saviour — were it in their clutches. Why is it that "the People" do such things? Is it because they "live in a land of Bibles and Protestant privileges?" Why is it that "heathen nations" never commit such deeds? Is it because they are not "blessed" with such "privileges?" Why is it that all the efforts of the Pro-Slavery Churches in "heathen lands" have, thus far, done no good but positive evil?

The *New York Dispatch* (a Pro-Slavery Journal), of March 20, 1856, says: " The Hawaiian nation which seventy years ago was estimated variously at 150,000 to 200,000, now only counts 72,000, a decrease within this period of at least two thirds. Vast tracts of land once under cultivation, are left to the rule of grass and weeds. The island of Kaui, remarkable for the productiveness of its soil, and able to sustain a population of 100,000 souls, contains a population of 6,000. '*It is* not to cruel and devastating wars that is attributed this unparalleled falling off in so short a time, but to the social contact with civilized man.' So writes one who is thoroughly acquainted with the history of the Sandwich Islands. And yet this same Hawaiian nation is constantly pointed at by the American Foreign Missionary Society as the evidence of their work. 'We have civilized and Christianized that people,' say they, 'by the untiring efforts of our Missionaries have the inhabitants of those islands been brought to a saving knowledge of the Gospel!' With truth they could add: 'It is true, they were a happy though a rude people, before our teachers went among their garden islands, once well populated and well cultivated; and, save a few incidental complaints, which native herbs could remove, they were tolerably ignorant of *small*-pox and other loathsome diseases — diseases which have since tainted the blood of every Hawaiian, and fearfully reduced their number; but then we have taught them the value of rum, tobacco, silver coin, and Christianity.' There will not be a thousand Kenackers alive twenty years hence; their doom is sealed, but have they not been 'saved'?— saved by the words of our Missionaries, backed by our Bible and New England rum."

Dr. C. G. Parsons, of Boston, Massachusetts, in his "Tour among the Planters," speaking of an Auction Sale of Slaves he witnessed in Georgia, says: "The doomed 'fathers and mothers' were standing with their arms around the necks of their 'wives and husbands,' from whom they were the next moment to be torn. These mothers were to become the mothers of yet more unfortunate children in Louisiana. The sale over, the Slaves were ordered to take their departure. They broke away from their 'wives and husbands' at the sound of the whip and started for that City of the Graveyard — New Orleans. One of them — whose name was Robinson — bounded back and gave 'his wife' a 'last kiss' of affection, and was then pushed on board. The heart-broken 'wife' had a present tied up, in an old handkerchief, which she designed to give her 'husband' as the last token of her love for him. But in the more than mortal agony of parting she had forgotten the present until the cars had started; and then she ran — screaming — as she threw the bundle toward the car; 'Oh, here, Robinson! I meant to give you this!' But instead of reaching him, it fell to the ground through the space between the cars, and such a shriek as that Woman gave, when she saw that solitary emblem of love for her 'husband' fail to reach him. Her heart was breaking! She could no longer suppress her grief, and for some distance after the cars started, the air was rent with her bitter lamentations."

A Slave-mother was hung lately at Cedartown, Georgia. Her "owner" told her that he had sold her four Children to a man, to whom they were to be delivered next day. The purchaser was known through the neighborhood as a tyrant and miser, who not only half-starved his Slaves, but beat them brutally at every opportunity. The mother, who tenderly loved her Children, was overcome with grief at the thought of having them sold to such a monster. She begged her "Master," on her knees, to keep the Children, or if they must be sold, to let them go to a more humane "Master." But all her efforts proving vain, and being driven to desperation, she, on the following night murdered the Children. This was the crime for which she was hung. (See chap. I. of Part V.)

At the Sale of the *property* of the late Edwin Townsend, of Huntsville, Georgia, the Slaves, 285 in number, all Field-hands, and a large proportion of them Children, sold for $207,195, being an average of $727. A young "man and wife," having no children — but thought to be "good breeding stock," sold for $3,005. Many boys and girls, from 16 to 22 years of age, brought from $1,300 to $1,750. Two twin-brothers, 15 years of age, sold for $2,350; a sister of these twins, 16 years of age, sold for $1,796, and a twin-sister for $1,630. The entire amount of the sale was within a fraction of $330,000.

"My poor Children," said a Slave-mother, "We are going to be Sold to-morrow, and we will never see one another again; when you are far away from your poor mother, remember that I shall see the same Moon and Stars that you look at, and when we die, we shall go to Heaven and be evermore with Jesus! O my Saviour! O my Children! O my Saviour! O my poor Children!"

"*For Sale.*—The Executors of the late Col. John H. M'Intosh, offer for Sale, and are ready to receive applications for the Purchase of all his real and personal *property*, consisting of mules, hogs, plantation implements, and *about* 221 Slaves, &c., all of which are on the plantation called 'Burlington,' Duval County, Florida."

By a refinement of contemptuous cruelty, the mules, hogs, and the very implements of toil, receive precedence of the despised Slaves. The Auctioneer is not even sure of their number—"about" and the "&c." are full of meaning. *They tell of Slaves unborn, who will open their eyes on nothing but Slavery, but whose advertised existence, as yet unconscious to themselves,* may screw some dollars additional out of the hard fist of the thin-lipped, ashen-faced Trader, or the unpitying-featured Yankee "admirer" of the "*heaven*-born Institution."

The National Intelligencer, published at Washington, D. C., and "renowned for its taste and talent," informs us that there "Will be Sold at Auction, at Bank's Arcade, on Magazine street, in the City of New Orleans, at 12 o'clock, on Tuesday, January 16, 1855, the Slaves (*about* 385 in number) of the late H. B. W. Hill, including choice Plantation Slaves, accustomed to the culture of Sugar and Cotton, and considered to be one of the most likely gangs in the South, and comprising all the requisite Mechanics, such as Sugar-Makers, Engineers, Blacksmiths, Coopers, Carpenters, Bricklayers, choice House-Servants, Cooks, and Field-Hands, and are to be Sold in

Families, and Singly, by a descriptive Catalogue. The Slaves are guarantied in title only."

Who and what was this "Hill"—dead or alive—that Human beings—skilled Mechanics—belonged to him? By what right, beyond that rewarded with the gallows in civilized communities, did he own them, and by what right were they conveyed to Executors?

"*For Sale.*—Twelve Slaves, Men, Women, and Children; a small Schooner, a Ferry-Boat; some Cows, Calves, Heifers, Bulls, Sheep, and four Philadelphia Hogs; a lot of Furniture; the contents of a Grocery Store, consisting of Hardware, Crockery-Ware, Groceries, Dry-Goods, a Boar-Pig," &c. [New Orleans *Bee.*]

A correspondent, writing from New Orleans, on the 18th of January last, says: "I have just returned from a Slave Auction, the most hideous exhibition of human depravity on earth. I as little dreamed, two hours ago, of attending a 'Nigger Auction,' as I did of taking a trip to the Cannibal Islands, or to the Kingdom of Siam. Let me tell you how it came about: I was sauntering along St. Louis street, when I observed a gang of Slaves, composed of Men, Women, and Children, marching, under the escort of a mean-looking Irishman, toward the St. Louis Hotel. A moment afterward, I observed another gang going in the same direction, and soon after a third. I had the curiosity to follow them, and as I entered the rotunda of the Hotel, observed, I should presume, no less than two hundred and fifty Slaves ranged in front of the different Auctioneers' stands. 'Operations' had not yet commenced. 'Fresh lots of Niggers' were constantly coming in, and the various 'dealers' were making examinations of the different 'articles' on exhibition. The immense Rotunda—an elegant and fashionable affair—was thronged with speculators, buyers, dealers, and lookers-on. Some were smoking their Havanas—some were taking their toddies—some were chattering on politics, the money-market, and the weather.

The laugh — the smile — the cordial greeting of friends — the courteous Auctioneers — the elegant hall — the flash of fashion, and the atmosphere of gentility pervading the gay throng — how unlike the horrors of my gloomy imaginings. Yet, what amazing callousness!

"The clock struck 12! A change came over the spirit of the scene. The batons of the Auctioneers, brought down against the solid marble, acted with the potency of magic upon the babbling throng. Four Auctioneers, in several sections of the Rotunda, hammered away with frightful gesticulation at four several parcels of Human 'chattels.' The four '*gentlemen* Auctioneers' shouting at the top of their voices, as if each made a point of striving to drown the voices of the others. But the 'gentleman' on my right seemed to carry off the honors, both as respected strength of lungs and rapidity of utterance. I wish you were standing near me, for I can give you but a very indifferent Daguerreotype of the efforts of this popular orator. Having ordered a Woman, with a sad, sickly countenance, to the stand, he informed the spectators that 'this Girl' (she was not under forty) 'is always pretending to be sick,' and did 'not, therefore, warrant her.' He sold her, however, for $645, and the next instant her place was supplied by a fine-looking, bright-eyed, young mulatto Woman, with an Infant, perfectly white, in her arms. He informed his patrons that 'this Girl is named Ann, aged twenty-two, and free from the diseases and vices designated by law,' and proceeded after the following fashion:

"'Gentlemen, look at this Girl! Good nurse and seamstress. Do I hear $1,000? — $1,100 — $1,200 — $1,250 — $1,275 — $1,300 — $1,325 — $1,350, and going at $1,350 — going — going, gone to Cash for $1,350.'

"The next victim, a Plantation-hand, named Onesimus, was bought by a man who gave his name as Nehemiah Adams, at which everybody laughed, and some strange allusions were made to the condition of the Churches in Boston, calling the Roll at Bunker Hill, &c. For a few moments the Sale flagged, and many stood on tip-toe to get a look at the last Buyer, whom they supposed to be the veritable Author of the 'South-Side View.' The next chattel, a girl about eighteen years of age, was sold to John H. Hopkins, for $1,776. The crowd again stared, and those near the purchaser eyed him from head to foot; some asking him questions about the state of the Markets in Vermont, &c. Our eloquent friend having disposed of his entire 'stock,' proceeded with hardly a moment's interruption, to sell a 'lot of real estate.' The three other 'gentlemen Auctioneers' were driving on an equally flourishing, though not quite so rapid a trade. One of them — a very handsome young-looking man — was devoting himself exclusively to the sale of young mulatto Women. On the block, at the time I approached his stand, was one of the most beautiful young Women I ever saw. She was aged about sixteen years, was dressed in a cheap striped woollen gown, and bare-headed. I could not discover a single trace of the African about her features. She was much whiter than the average of white New England women; her form was graceful in the extreme, and she carried a pair of eyes that pierced one through and through. Unlike many of her fellow-captives, she seemed fully sensible of her degraded position, and shrank with true maiden timidity from the stare of the hard-featured throng about her. She was struck off for $1,725, to one of the most lecherous-looking old brutes I ever set eyes on.

>"'Oh, how my very heart fills with sadness and grief,
>   As I think of that poor girl's fate!—
> Not a friend to protect or shield her from crime,
>   Nor lift from her spirit the weight.
>
>"'That vile Slavery's curse must evermove bind
>   On all who are held in its thrall;

Poor delicate, sensitive, heart-bowed quadroon,
    You must bear the rudeness of all.

"'You stand on that block to be sold for a sum
    That to you is nothing at all;
The one who bids highest will claim as his own
    Your body, your spirit, your all.

"'How sad and how hopeless your young life must be!
    How hard to endure its rough blast!
Oh, may you but hear of the Saviour's kind power,
    And on Jesus your sorrows all cast.'

"But I was destined a moment after to witness a far-sadder, more heart-rending scene. A noble-looking mulatto Woman was sitting upon a bench holding in her arms two little Children — one an Infant, and the other a beautiful bright-eyed little Boy of some seven or eight years. Her face wore a troubled and frightened look, as if she was conscious that some great evil was about to befall her. When her turn to be sold came, she ascended the platform, the Babe in her arms, and the little Boy clinging to her skirts. The Auctioneer offered to "sell the lot together," but no bids having been made, the Mother and the Children were put up separately, and sold to separate parties — the Mother going to Texas and the Children to Georgia. The final separation of the Mother and her children took place a few minutes afterward. I shall never forget the horror and agony of that parting. The poor frantic Mother implored 'Massa' to 'buy the children too' (and I will do him the justice to say that he was much moved by her appeals), and when she found that her efforts were in vain, she burst forth into the most frantic wails that ever despair gave utterance to. At last Mother and Children were forcibly separated and hurried off, to see each other no more.

"I asked a noble-looking Man, nearly white, who was on the point of being sold, if he had a family. 'Yes, massa,' he said, 'a Wife and three Children, two Boys and a Girl. One of my Boys was sold on Thursday last, to a Dealer from Mississippi; the other to a man from Georgia; and my poor Daughter, over there' (pointing to a beautiful Girl, of fifteen or sixteen years of age) 'has just been purchased by that big red-headed Irishman, and my Wife is now on her way to Kansas.' The allusion to his family seemed too much for him, for his frame quivered, and the tears began to flow.

"The Hotel, above and around this mart for the sale of Human flesh was filled with 'wealth and beauty,' and the music of piano and guitar were blending with the 'still sweeter music of glad voices.' Above the hoarser din of the mart below, was heard the loud laugh and 'heartful glee' of many of the Slaveholding nobility of the Sunny South. Gay equipages were drawing up before the stately pile and 'fair women and brave men' were proudly disappearing through its portals to swell the throng. Within the 'sumptuous halls'—amid that gay and gleeful throng—amid the 'flash of beauty, fashion, and wealth,' where so many splendors were gathered—who would dream that, under the same broad dome, and in the effulgence of the same 'golden sun-light'—crime, sin, and despair, were holding high revel? Who would dream that the former drew their sustenance from the latter?"

The New Orleans Delta, of the 24th of February last, has among the cold facts and speculations of its "Money-article," the following statement:—

"Within the last six weeks, upward of $1,000,000 in value of Men, Women, and Children, have been thrown upon the Market, and the means to pay for them have been extracted from the floating capital of the place. This amount, in the various ramifications through which it has gone, has liquidated a much larger amount of indebtedness, but as it has merely wiped out an amount which was unnatural and redundant, the benefit is rather of the negative sort, in preventing embarrassment, than of the kind which positively aids, by going into new channels and *fertilizing* new fields."

There is something worthy the arch-fiend himself in this mode of speaking of liquidating "indebtedness" to the amount of a million of dollars. Whoever heard of a Slaveholder "fertilizing" the soil? Slavery disgraces labor by making the laborer a brute — a "chattel," while it makes the Slaveholder the immediate rival of the free laborer in all the markets of the world. Hence Tiberius Gracchus, one of the greatest of Roman citizens, early saw that in a State where Slaveholders at the same time monopolized and disgraced labor, there would necessarily be a vast demoralized population, who would demand support of the State, and be ready for the service of the demagogue, who is always the tyrant. Gracchus was killed, but the issue proved the prophet. The canker which Rome cherished in her bosom ate out her heart, and the Empire whose splendor flashed over the whole world, fell like a blighted tree. Not until Slavery had barbarized the great mass of "the People" did Rome fall.

Slavery annihilates the conditions of human progress. Its necessary result is the destruction of humanity; and this not only directly upon the Slave, but indirectly by its effect upon the "Master." In the one it destroys the self-respect which is the basis of manhood, and is thus a capital crime against humanity. In the other it fosters pride, indolence, luxury, and licentiousness, which equally imbrute the human being. Therefore in Slave States there is no literature, no art, no progressive civilization. Manners are fantastic and fierce; brute force supplants moral principle; freedom of speech is suppressed because the natural speech of man condemns Slavery; a sensitive vanity is called "honor," and cowardly swagger, "chivalry;" real respect for Woman is destroyed by universal licentiousness; lazy indifference is called "gallantry," and an impudent familiarity, "cordiality."

PART THIRD.

SLAVE LIFE ON THE PLANTATION.

CHAPTER I.

"Avarice alone can drive, as it does, this infernal traffic, and the wretched victims of it, like so many post-horses whipped to death in a mail-coach. Ambition has its cover-sluts in the pride, pomp, and circumstance of 'glorious war;' but where are the trophies of avarice, the hand-cuff, the manacle, the blood-stained cowhide?" RANDOLPH.

IT used to be thought that Christianity was the religion of brotherly love, which had virtually annulled distinctions of race among men, by the revelation of their common fatherhood in God; but the Slaveholders, and their allies, insist that this is a lamentable mistake. Christianity, according to them, means the right of one man to appropriate the faculties and labors of another, the right to reduce him to the level of the brute — to deny him education and the means of spiritual growth — to control his most sacred domestic relations, and to buy and sell and scourge him, under no other restraint than simple self-interest. In excuse of this robbery, it has been pretended by the Slaveholders, and their abettors, that though indeed these children of the " cursed seed of *Ham*" are torn by fraud and violence from their homes, yet, " they thereby become the happier, and their condition the more eligible." They assure us that the Slaves are " well fed," " well clothed," and as " happy as kings." In fact, " perfectly contented !" Of course they are contented! do not the "misguided runaways" sing, nightly, to admiring audiences, "Oh, carry me home to Tennessee!"

Do they not clamor to be taken home to the arms of the loving "patriarchs" whom, in a moment of hasty ill-judgment, they have forsaken? Do they not mourn over their ingratitude in running away from "cottage, food, and raiment"?

In Baltimore, Maryland, a Slave was killed a short time since by his "Master," and "without any adequate provocation," as was proven. The deceased was esteemed by all who knew him as an honest, industrious, and inoffensive man. This man's "wife," on hearing of the death of her "husband," jumped out of the window of the place in which her beastly "owner" had confined her, and immediately took the nearest route to throw herself into the river. She was rescued, but begged the bystanders to let her drown herself, saying: "*I would sooner be dead, than go back again to be beaten, and otherwise abused, as I have been.*"

A friend, writing from Baltimore, states that the Slave of a Farmer in Jefferson County, having been jumped upon and stamped by his "Master," with spurs on so as to cruelly lacerate his face as well as his body, was found, next morning, in an adjacent pond, having tied a stone to his own neck and plunged in, under feelings of desperation, caused by the fiendish treatment of his "owner."

At a fire which recently took place in the Eastern section of the City, the firemen found a beautiful girl tied in the garret of a house, and bearing the marks of improper chastisement. She stated that she had been kept in that condition for nearly four weeks, and with scarcely a sufficiency of food to sustain life. As soon as she was loosed from her prison-house, she escaped and sought refuge in the house of an acquaintance in the Western part of the City. There was another woman, of a darker complexion—found in the same house, who had received the most barbarous treatment at the hands of the same parties. Her back, face, and limbs, were most horribly mutilated, while there was a severe contusion on her head, and it was thought that the skull was fractured. This poor girl was sent to the Infirmary, where her wounds could receive proper treatment.

A male Slave, belonging to a "lady" residing in Baltimore, and moving in the "first circles," died in the winter of 1855, at the Hospital in that City. He was her Coachman. During the severest weather he used to be kept sitting on the carriage-box, opposite to the *lady's* window, half clad, and, as was well known to be the case with this woman's Slaves, half starved. In this condition the man suffered, and eventually froze. The poor fellow becoming thus disabled and wholly unfit for service, a physician was sent for, who, after examining him, declared that he was frost-bitten from head to foot and could not live. He was sent to the Infirmary, where both his feet were amputated, and he shortly afterward died. A few years previous this same man's "wife," who also belonged to his Mistress, was so badly treated that she ran away and prevailed upon old Slater, the Slave-dealer, to buy her out of her Mistress' clutches. He did so; and she was ever after prohibited all intercourse with her "husband," who was kept from his "wife" to be treated in the manner we have described. This woman, on hearing that her "husband" was at the Infirmary, went to inquire after him. She was informed that he was dead, whereupon she fell on the floor in a fit and died.

Another female Slave, belonging to this woman, also ran away. Her son, a young man, was sent in pursuit of the fugitive. She was found at Cockeysville, 18 miles from Baltimore. He seized her, tied her to his buggy, and in that way drove her into the City at a rapid rate, with the woman running by the side of the vehicle. It was stated by some who witnessed the scene that it was hard to tell which was whipped most on the road, the horse or the Woman. Another female Slave belonging to the same fiend-woman fell from the third story of her Mistress' house, while engaged in washing the windows, and was taken up a cripple for life. It turned out that her Mistress, by way of punishment, had deprived her of sleep by compelling her to pass the night standing by her side, and that thus she fell asleep, which circumstance caused the fall.

"In Virginia," says the Hon. Alexander Smythe, "the Slaves are ill-fed. They are doomed to scarcity and hunger. They get only two meals a day; breakfast from 10 to 11 o'clock, A.M., and supper from 7 to 9 or 10 at night, as the season and crops may be." Another Virginian, Mr. William Leftwitch, says: "The Slaves generally take their meals without knife, dish, or spoon. They have neither beds nor bedsteads." The Hon. T. T. Bouldin, of Virginia, in a Speech in Congress, said he knew "that many Slaves had died from exposure to the weather;" and added, "The Slaves are clad in a flimsy fabric, which will turn neither wind nor weather." The Rev. C. S. Renshaw, speaking of the shocking condition of the Slaves in Virginia, says: "I have seen Men and Women at work in the fields, more than half naked." In the South generally Men and Women have scarce clothes enough to hide their nakedness, and the boys and girls, eight and ten years of age, are often entirely naked among their Master's non-colored children."

In the "Will" of John Randolph, distinguished as a "kind Master," we find the following clause: "*To my old and faithful Servants Essex and his wife Hetty, I give and bequeath a pair of strong shoes, a suit of clothes, and a blanket each, to be paid them annually; also a hat annually to Essex.*" No socks, stockings, bonnets, cloaks, handkerchiefs, or towels—no change either of outside or inner garments. And a solemn "Last Will and Testament" was deemed necessary to secure to them even the articles specified!

"Slavery," we are told, "is remarkably mild in Virginia;" but the following specimens explain what is meant by the phrase: On the 1st day of September, 1849, Simeon Souther, a Slaveholder of Virginia, tied his Slave Sam to a tree, and then whipped him with switches, and afterward with a cowhide; and, when fatigued with the labor of whipping, he called upon another Slave to cob Sam with a paddle.* He also called upon Sam's "wife" to cob him. And, after cobbing and whipping, he applied fire to * * * * * * and other parts of his person. He then caused him to be washed down with warm water, in which pods of red pepper had been steeped. After this tying, whipping, cobbing, burning, and washing, he kicked, stamped upon, and otherwise tortured, his wretched victim, until he died.†

On the 18th of July, 1854, a Slave, a young Man in the prime of life, was stripped, tied, strung up, and whipped in the most shocking manner, by an Overseer, in the neighborhood of Richmond. He was whipped for a very trifling offence. When so exhausted that he fainted, he was washed with brine; then whipped again. This was repeated several times. He was tied up early in the morning, and was released about one o'clock, and sent out to work. He fainted in the field. A shower came up, and he contrived to get into the barn, where he died. While the Overseer was beating him, he begged him to shoot him; while he could speak, he kept moaning, "Oh, pray, Massa! Oh, my Saviour! Oh, pray, Massa! Oh, my Saviour! Oh, pray, Massa!" The murderer moved about as if he had done nothing uncommon.

"Some people" have thought, and still think, that Legree

---

* The "paddle" is a thin shingle-like piece of wood, in which many holes are bored; when a blow is struck, these holes, from the rush and partial exhaustion of air in them, act like diminutive cups.

† "Souther *vs.* The Commonwealth," Grattan's Reports, vol. vii., p. 673, 1851.

was too great a fiend to be natural. We, however, sometimes see a symptom of his un-Christian spirit even among "gentlemen moving in the highest ranks of society." For instance, a "*free* Negro," named Fleming, had a dispute with a Mr. and Mrs. Poe about a small sum of money due him, and becoming excited, told his debtors what he thought of them. They had him arrested, and the Mayor directed that he should have "thirty-nine stripes, well laid on," on that day, and "thirty-nine more" the next, and then ordered his commitment "for twelve months in default of $500 security to keep the peace and be of good behavior," &c. *The Richmond Republican*, in its Report of the case, said:—

"Our only regret is, that the Mayor did not assess the punishment at three hundred lashes, well laid on with a hot iron-rod, to be repeated twice a week for twelve months. Such an impudent Nigger should no more be permitted to go at large than a mad dog."

On examining the Police reports of a single number of this "highly respectable journal," we find that "Jordan Goode, Slave of Haxall and Brother, was caged on Sunday night for not having his pass endorsed. The Mayor let him off, but for the next offence, won't he catch it?"—"Isaac Allen, a gentleman of *color*, Slave to Goode & *Allen*, received a part of his holiday suit yesterday, by order of the Mayor, for failing to have his Pass endorsed, and running from the watchman."—"Felix Harwood, Slave to George Turner, was caught by the watch when stealing a stick of firewood, on Sunday night last, and was caged. The Court ordered him a warm jacket, that his system might be heated by additional dressing. A striped jacket must have felt fine yesterday, as cold as the wind blowed."—"Joe Shieaway says he is a '*free* Nigger,' but as he was without a register to prove it, and no one felt disposed to take his word for it, the Mayor directed his delivery into the kind keeping of the old Commodore."—"Thomas Jefferson—what a big name for a Nigger!—was brought before

The Lash. (*See page 203.*)

the Mayor yesterday, and ordered thirty-nine lashes for firing pop-crackers in Carey street, on Saturday evening last. A lady of *color* was caged and condemned by the Mayor to receive thirty-nine lashes for being found without papers, and assaulting Elizabeth King, and endeavoring to make her escape from the City, attired as a Man."

If the word diabolical does not apply to the malicious delight in suffering and utter heartlessness of the foregoing, it should be discharged from the dictionary as useless. Think of talking of a torture which savages would be ashamed to inflict, as a " holiday suit," or a " warm jacket," and notice the offences for which poor creatures were flogged!

The following facts, gleaned from the examination of John Capheart, in one of the rescue trials, at Boston, Massachusetts, throws some light upon this " deeply interesting subject":—

"*Question.* Mr. Capheart, is it a part of your duty, as a Policeman, to take up colored persons who are out after hours in the streets?

"*Answer.* Yes, sir.

" *Q.* What is done with them?

"*A.* We put them in the lock-up, and in the morning they are brought into Court and ordered to be punished—those that are to be punished.

" *Q.* What punishment do they get?

"*A.* Not exceeding thirty-nine lashes.

" *Q.* Who gives them these lashes?

"*A.* Any of the Officers. I do, sometimes.

" *Q.* Are you paid *extra* for this? How much?

"*A.* Fifty cents a head. It used to be sixty-two cents. Now, it is only fifty. Fifty cents for each one we arrest, and fifty more for each one we flog.

" *Q.* Are these persons you flog Men and Boys only, or are they Women and Girls also?

"*A.* Men, Women, Boys, and Girls, just as it happens."

[Here the Government interfered, and tried to prevent any further examination; and said, among other things, that he "only performed his duty as Police-Officer under the Law." After some discussion, Judge Curtis allowed it to proceed.]

"Q. Is your flogging confined to these cases? Do you not flog Slaves at the request of their Masters?*

"A. Sometimes I do. Certainly, when I am called upon.

"Q. In these cases of private flogging, are the Negroes sent to you? Have you a place for flogging?

"A. No; I go round, as I am sent for.

"Q. Is this part of your duty as an Officer?

"A. No, sir.

* Hence such advertisements as the following:—

"Committed to jail as a runaway, a negro woman named Martha, 17 or 18 years of age, has numerous scars of the whip on her back."—*Nashville Banner.*

"Ten dollars reward for my woman Sally, very much scarred about the neck and ears by whipping."—*Mobile Com. Adv.*

"Lodged in jail, a mulatto boy, having large marks of the whip on his shoulders and other parts of his body."—*Milledgeville Standard of the Union.*

"Committed to jail, a mulatto fellow—his back shows lasting impressions of the whip, and leaves no doubt of his BEING A SLAVE."—*Fayetteville Observer.*

"Was committed, a negro boy named Tom; is much marked with the whip."—*Charleston Courier.*

"Ran away, a negro man named Johnson—he has a great many marks of the whip on his back."—*Augusta Chronicle.*

"Ran away, a mulatto boy named Quash; considerably marked on the back and other places with the lash."—*N. O. Bulletin.*

"One hundred dollars reward for my negro Glasgow, and Kate, his wife. Glasgow is 24 years old—has marks of the whip on his back. Kate is 26—has a scar on her cheek, and several marks of the whip."—*Macon Messenger.*

"Ran away, a negro fellow named Dick—has many scars on his back from being whipped."—*Vicksburg Sentinel.*

"Brought to jail, a negro man named George—he has a great many scars from the lash."—*Milledgeville Journal.*

"*Q.* In these cases of private flogging, do you inquire into the circumstances to see what the fault has been, or if there is any?

"*A.* That's none of my business. I do as I am bid. The Master is responsible.

"*Q.* In these cases, too, I suppose you flog Women and Girls, as well as Men?

"*A.* Women and Men.

"*Q.* Mr. Capheart, how long have you been engaged in this business?

"*A.* Ever since 1836.

"*Q.* How many Negroes do you suppose you have flogged, in all, Women and Children included?

"*A.* (Looking calmly round the room.) I don't know how many Niggers you have got here in Massachusetts, but I should think I had flogged as many as you've got in the State."

The same man testified that he was often employed to pursue fugitive Slaves. His reply to the question was, "I never refuse a good job in that line."

"*Q.* Don't they sometimes turn out bad jobs?

"*A.* Never, if I can help it.

"*Q.* Are they not sometimes discharged after you get them?

"*A.* Not often. I don't know that they ever are."

Hon. John P. Hale: "Why, gentlemen, he sells agony! Torture is his stock-in-trade! He is a walking scourge? He hawks, peddles, retails, groans and tears about the streets of Norfolk!"

The obligations of Marriage can not be performed by a Slave. The "husband" promises to protect *his* "wife" and provide for her. The "wife" promises to be the help-mate of *her* "husband." They mutually promise to live with and cherish each other till parted by death. But what can such promises by Slaves mean? The legal relation of "Master" and Slave renders them utterly void. It forbids the Slave-"husband" to protect even himself. It clothes his "Master" with authority to bid him inflict deadly blows on the Woman he has sworn to protect. It prohibits his possession of any property wherewith to sustain her. The labor of his hands it takes from him. It bids the Woman to assist, not *her* "husband," but her "owner." Nay, it gives him unlimited control and full possession of her person, and forbids her, on pain of death, to resist him. The following is a case in point:

A Slaveholder, named Richard Dudley, having been "refused" by a young Slave-"wife," and being urged thereto by her Slave-"husband," ordered two stakes or posts to be driven deep into the earth in his barn-yard. Two of the strongest Slaves on the plantation were compelled to perform this task. When the stakes were well driven, he commanded George and Caroline, "man and wife," to be tied fast, one to each stake. The stakes were about five feet apart and six feet high. The victims had their hands tied together fast to the top of the post, so that they stood on tip-toe, and their feet were tied fast to the stake just above the ground. In this way their bodies were exposed to the keen lash of the whipper, a poor white vagabond, called Robinson. The barn-yard was filled with sad and unwilling spectators of the infamous scene; some slowly sauntering about, others looking gloomily on, and others still turning their faces away. While the preparations were being made for the execution of the sentence, the Slaveholder continued to curse and upbraid Caroline with her obstinacy and disobedience in not acceding to his lustful desires. "I'll put an end to your fun," said he; "I'll make it a dear job for you both," he continued.

Meanwhile, poor Caroline was overcome with terror. Every now and then her unhappy "husband" would address her, in an undertone, in words of consolation and encouragement; but

SLAVE LIFE ON THE PLANTATION.

he dared not so speak as to be heard by his "Master," else his sympathy would but excite his rage still more. Caroline — who was as white and good-looking as any Woman in the State — was strung up high against the post, with her back to the whipper. Her chemise, a light cotton one, afforded no protection to the heavy blows of the whip. "Begin now!" shouted the Slaveholder, while he stood back some yards, placing his arms akimbo, and leisurely taking a survey of the scene. Robinson stepped up, took his stand at the requisite distance from his victims, raised his whip, swung the long and heavy lash scientifically around him several times, and brought it down with such force upon the back of poor Caroline, that it seemed to jar and shatter her whole frame. Instantly the blow extorted from her a loud and long scream of agony, which rent the air, and appalled every listener; and she writhed in intense pain. But Robinson was well used to such things. Her awful scream did not engross his attention for an instant, and he returned to repeat the exploit upon the more vigorous frame of his other victim. He cut and carved his broad back and shoulders scientifically, and exerted his utmost strength to make the blow tell upon him. George did not move. Yet he could not but utter one deep groan of suffering, forced from him by the pain which the blow inflicted. Next came Caroline's turn. The same blow, and the same scream, so heart-rending and affecting, were repeated. But Robinson paused not in his work. He had no time to lose. It would be night before his task was ended, and he had to hurry himself. Fast and thick the blows fell upon the two young Slaves. George gave but little proof of his sufferings. Caroline, long before a hundred blows had been dealt her, had ceased to scream, or to wail; but hung insensible by her hands to the post which sustained her lacerated body. And long before her "two hundred and fifty lashes" had been given, not only her chemise had been cut to pieces by the thong of Robinson's whip, but her whole back was cut into deep gashes; blood flowed plentifully down her person, and every time the lash touched her body it sank deeply into the soft, mashed, and lacerated flesh.

Caroline had already ceased to feel. She was for a few moments beyond the power of her " Master's" rage. She had fainted. By the Slaveholder's orders she was untied from the stake, and several of the elder Slaves carried her insensible body back to the hut, where they left her to recover as best she might, as they were afraid to offer her any assistance, lest they themselves might excite the wrath of their " Master." George still remained tied to the stake. He had yet one hundred and fifty blows to endure. As Robinson resumed his bloody task, the poor wretch could endure it no longer, and broke out into earnest supplication, "Oh, Master Richard, don't, don't whip me any more. I'm most gone!" said he, frantically. "Lay it on the scoundrel, lay it on," Richard peremptorily commanded Robinson, who obeyed him with alacrity. The body of George was by this time covered with scars, and cuts, and welts. The blood flowed freely. His sobs and groans alternated with the heavy blows of Robinson's whip. By the time his allotted four hundred lashes had been inflicted, the flesh hung in stripes from his bones. George, too, had fainted. His nature, strong and vigorous as it was, had sunk beneath the agony of that fierce struggle between fiendish wrath on the one hand, and enduring constancy on the other.

The four hundred lashes had been told, and Robinson's execrable work was done. George's body was covered with blood. The Slaveholder approached him and examined his wounds, while Robinson stepped back to sit down upon a log and rest himself. The Slaveholder seeing the loose flesh hanging in stripes from George's lacerated back, *took his jack-knife from his pocket, and amid the screams of his victim, just returning again to consciousness, cut off the stripes of flesh, and threw the pieces to the hogs in the barn-yard, which ate them with avidity.* He then commanded George to be untied. The poor wretch fell immediately to the earth. He could not stand, and moaning in his great agony, he, too, was carried to his quarters among the Slave-huts.

Mr. George A. Avery, of Rochester, N. Y., says: "I know a local Methodist minister in Virginia, a man of talents, and popular as a preacher, who took one of his party-colored Girls into the barn to whip her, and she was brought out a corpse." Mr. Avery states further, that the friends of this "minister" seemed to think it of no importance to his ministerial standing. He was not indicted. Mr. Avery also says, that he knew a young Man in Virginia who had been out hunting, and returning with some of his friends, seeing a Slave in the road, at a little distance, deliberately drew up his rifle and shot him dead. This was done without the slightest provocation, or a word passing. Another wretch killed a Woman with an axe-helve, for stealing a little salt. No notice was taken of the affair.

Lillburn Lewis (nephew of Thomas Jefferson, the penman of the Declaration of Independence), of Livingston county, Kentucky, was the owner of "about" fifty Slaves, whom he drove constantly, fed sparingly, and lashed severely. The consequence was, that some of them were in the habit of running away. This gave Lewis great anxieties until he found them, or until they had starved out and returned. Among the rest was a boy named George, about seventeen years of age, who, having just returned, was sent to a spring for water, and let fall a pitcher breaking it. This was the occasion. It was night. Lewis then collected all the Slaves into an out-house, and ordered a rousing fire to be made. When the door was secured, that none might escape, either through fear or sympathy, Lewis opened the design of the meeting, namely, that they might be effectually taught to stay at home and obey his orders. All things being now in train, he called up George, who approached his "Master" with the most unreserved submission. *He bound him with cords, and laid him on a meat-block, and seizing a broad axe, proceeded to chop him into pieces, commencing at the ankles.*

In vain did the unhappy victim call upon his "Master" to forgive him. In vain did he scream. Not a Slave durst interfere. Casting the feet into the fire, he lectured the Slaves at some length. He then chopped off below the knees, and admonished them again, throwing the legs into the fire. He then chopped off above the knees, tossing the joints into the fire, lecturing as he proceeded. The next two or three strokes severed the thighs from the body. These were also committed to the flames. And so were the arms, head and trunk, until all was in the fire. Still protracting the intervals with lectures, and threatenings of like punishment, in case of disobedience and running away. The Slaves were then permitted to disperse.

When the monster returned to his house, Mrs. Lewis exclaimed, "*Oh! Mr. Lewis where have you been, and what have you done!*" She had heard a strange pounding, and dreadful screams, and had smelled something like fresh meat burning! He replied that he had never enjoyed himself at a ball so well as he had enjoyed himself that evening.

John Randolph, speaking of the wretched condition of the Slaves, said: "When the measure of their tears is full, when their groans have involved heaven itself in darkness, doubtless a God of justice will listen to their distress." And when that day of retribution comes it will be the more terrible from this long delay, and the attempts to deceive the people and defraud them of their rights. On another occasion, in a Speech in Congress, he said: "What man is worse received in society for being a hard master? Who denies the hand of a sister or a daughter to such a monster?"

Had Mr. Randolph lived in these times, and put forth such sentiments, he would have been denounced by the whole pack of Administration followers, who train under the desecrated name of Democracy, as an " abolition fanatic," an " enemy to the Constitution," and a " treasonable sectionalist."

The Rev. James A. Thome, a native of Kentucky, and the son of a Slaveholder, says : " Slavery in the American Republic is the parent of more suffering than has flowed from all other sources since the days of Sodom and Gomorrah. Such sufferings too ! Sufferings inconceivable and innumerable; unmingled wretchedness from the ties of nature rudely broken and destroyed; the acutest bodily tortures, groans, tears, and blood; lying for ever in weariness and painfulness, in watchings, in hunger and in thirst, in cold and in nakedness."

" The poor Slave," says the Hon. C. M. Clay, of Kentucky, " rolls himself in his blanket about midnight, and is called up between three and four o'clock to commence another day's work."

Those who know anything about Slavery in the Southern States, agree that whipping Men and Women to death does frequently occur, but all will not believe that any one for conscience's sake, has died by the lash in "*free* America," but this is a mistake. One afternoon, while passing a Church in Walnut street, in Louisville, we heard the voices of the congregation singing. A clergyman who was with us, said it was a congregation of Methodists, and assured us that he had once dropped in and heard a sermon he liked. We went in and took a seat. A plain-looking elderly man preached in the style usual for Methodist preachers in country places — all about religion — its comforts in life and triumphs in death. Like Uncle Tom, he insisted, with great earnestness, that it was a great thing to be a Christian. Religion — it made the weak strong, and the meanest most honorable. To illustrate this grand truth, he told an anecdote as something coming

9*

within the range of his own knowledge, of an old Slave who had "got religion." His "Master" was kind, but irreligious and reckless, and was, withal, much impressed by the earnestness of his Slaves' prayers and exhortations. But one day, one evil day, on the Sabbath, too, this same "kind Master" was drinking and playing cards with a visiter, when the conversation turned upon the "religion of Slaves." The visiter boasted that he could "whip the religion out of any Nigger in the State in half an hour." The "Master," proud of possessing a rare specimen, boasted that he had one out of whom the religion could not be whipped. A bet was laid, and the martyr summoned. A fearful oath of recantation, and blasphemous denial of his Saviour, was required of the poor Slave, upon pain of being whipped to death. The answer was — "Bress de Lord, Massa, I can't."

Threats, oaths, and entreaties, were tried, but he fell on his knees, and holding up his hands, pleaded, "Bress de Lord, Massa, I can't! Jesus, he die for poor Nigger! Massa, please, Massa, I can't." The executioner summoned his aids, the old man was tied up, and the whipping commenced; but the shrieks for mercy were all intermingled with prayer and praises — prayers for his own soul and those of his murderers. When fainting and revived, the terms of future freedom from punishment were offered again, and again he put them away with the continued exclamation, "Jesus, he die for me! Bress de Lord, Massa, I can't."

The bet was to the full value of the "property" endangered. The men were flushed with wine, and the experimenter on "Nigger religion" insisted on "trying it out." Honor demanded he should have a fair chance to win his bet, and the wretched victim died under the lash, blessing the Lord, that Jesus had died for him. The preacher gave his recital with many tears, and before he was done, we do not think there was a dry eye, except our own, in the house. Our pulses all stood still with horror, but the speaker did not appear to dream that his story had any bearing against the "Institution" with which he was surrounded. He gave us this story of "suffering for conscience's sake" of a member of his own Church, to show what a good thing religion was. Of those who heard it, and the many persons there to whom we related it, we found not one who appeared to doubt it. Any indignation felt and expressed was against the individual actors in the tragedy.

On Saturday, July 8, 1854, the Rev. Joel Lambert, of Hendersonville, was seen to knock down one of his "colored" Boys several times with a loaded whip, and give him more than one hundred lashes. The wretched creature died in a few hours. The Coroner, Mr. James Rouse, held an inquest over the body, and the verdict was, that the Slave came to his death by "overbeating and imprudent whipping."

Mrs. Nancy Lowry, a native of Kentucky, gives us an account of the deaths of three Slaves, named John, Ned, and James, "caused by severe whipping." Mr. Long, the inflictor and "owner," was "a strict professor of the Christian religion."

The Rev. Francis Hawley, of Kentucky, states that a son of a Slaveholder "took the wife of one of the Slaves. The poor husband felt himself greatly injured, and expostulated with him. The wretch drew a pistol and deliberately shot him dead."

The "owner" of a girl (said to be his own daughter), a Methodist Class-Leader, proposed criminal intercourse with her; she refused. He sent her to the Overseer of his plantation to be flogged. Again he made advances—again she refused, and again she was flogged. Afterward she was compelled to yield.

The Cincinnati (Ohio) *Commercial*, of the 28th December, 1855, says that two Slaveholders (Dobyns and Bacon), of Maysville, Kentucky, had, the day before, murdered one of the waiters at the Parker House, in that place. The poor fellow, having been kept up until a very late hour, was so overcome with fatigue that he fell into a "deep sleep." The Slave-breeders concluded they would set fire to him, to awaken him. With this view they took a Camphene lamp and poured the fluid over his face, neck, and chest, which became instantly wrapped in an intense blaze. The sufferings of the victim were dreadful in the extreme. No refinement of torture could have produced more excruciating misery. But strange to say, death did not release him from torment till after the lapse of two weeks. The poor creature was the Slave of Mr. Ball, proprietor of the Parker House, who says that "no human suffering could exceed that of the Boy" (said to be his own son) "during the fortnight that he lived after the burning." The Slave-breeders are young men and wealthy. They compromised the matter "by paying to Mr. Ball $1,200 for the loss of his Boy." No movement has been made toward a legal investigation of the matter.

The Presbyterian Synod of Kentucky, speaking of the horrible condition of the Sons and Daughters of the "cursed seed of *Ham*" in that State, say: "The poor creatures suffer all that can be inflicted by wanton caprice, by grasping avarice, by brutal lust, by malignant spite, and by insane anger. Their happiness is the sport of every whim, the prey of every passion that may occasionally infest the Master's bosom."

The *New York Tribune*, of May 9, 1857, contains the following paragraph, copied from *The Cincinnati* (Ohio) *Gazette:* "A man in Pulaski County, a few days since, whipped one of his Slaves to such an extent that he died. He punished him six mornings in succession, and on the seventh day the Slave died. The poor fellow desired to see *his* 'wife,' who was owned by and lived with another party. The 'Master' refused permission; the Slave disobeyed, and visited *his* 'wife' in the evening, returning early next morning. For this the unfortunate man was whipped to death."

The Missouri Express has an account of the death of a Slave, in June, 1855, at the hands of his "Master," Josephus Hicklin, from which we make the following extract:—

"The only fault alleged against the Negro was that he was dissatisfied with his Master, and wanted to be sold. For this alleged offence he was put to the torture. It would be difficult to find any case that, in point of cruelty, affords a parallel to this. The gag, the lash, fire, gouging out of eyes, beating over the head, and rubbing of cayenne pepper and tobacco-juice into his eyes, wounds, &c., were some of the appliances used, not for a single hour, a single day, or a single week, but every day for more than three weeks, until he died."

A German family emigrated to the United States, in May, 1853, and on the passage out the Father died. Subsequently, and after arriving in St. Louis, Missouri, the Mother died, leaving a small Boy, who, being entirely destitute, was picked up by a man named Christopher Herbert, then living in St. Louis. Herbert moved to a farm in Jefferson County, taking the boy with him and treating him with severity. Occasionally the boy would be sent into the woods to search for the cattle, and if he either got lost himself or failed to find them, was invariably beaten inhumanly. At length, the treatment became so harsh that the boy could no longer stand it, but would often pass night after night in the woods; but upon returning for something to eat would only receive severer punishment. It seems that the lad, thus intimidated, remained out several nights, and was seeking some food in the evening late, when he was caught by Herbert, tied with a rope, the flesh stripped almost from his body with a Slaveholder's cowhide, and then tied and thrown into an outhouse, where he remained twenty-four hours. When released he again escaped, and endeavored to sustain life by going into the orchard at night and plucking fruit; but Herbert, it seems, suspecting this also, lay in wait for him, and again caught him. The punishment then inflicted is too inhuman for repetition. It is sufficient to add that the next morning the boy endeavored to crawl to a neighbor's house, but failed to do so, and lay exhausted in an adjoining field for two days before he was found. *When discovered, his back was a mass of putrid flesh; he was fly-blown and covered with vermin, and evidently beyond the hope of recovery.* The person who discovered him carried him in his arms to Herbert, the nearest place, and it is said that the moment Herbert saw his victim it was with difficulty he was prevented from again punishing his " runaway Slave," as he called him. Death, however, soon put an end to his miseries. The body was then thrust into an old boot-box, without clothing, and unceremoniously buried in a " mud-hole," dug by Herbert.

A correspondent of the *New York Tribune*, writing from Lexington, Missouri, under date August 11, 1856, says: "On Friday" (February 8, 1856), " a scene was presented in the Court-House of this place which almost beggars description. Sheriff Withers, having a 'Nigger Woman,' who, on the previous day, had been neglectful of her task-work, sent for a blacksmith to come and chastise her. He came, bolted the door, tied the woman's hands together, and lashed them over her head to the ceiling, and commenced whipping. The screams of the woman brought her 'husband' to the rescue. He broke open the door, and with a butcher's knife in his hand rushed forward to cut *his* ' wife' loose. The Slave and blacksmith encountered each other, and in the affray the latter got his arm cut. The Slave finally surrendered, and was led away to Jail, while the woman received a double whipping. News of this 'horrible outrage' was soon circulated, and the excitement became intense. One leading man was heard to say, ' I'll be hanged if I don't put a stop to this Slave rebellion, if I can only get three men to join with me.' When asked how he would do it, he said, ' I will take this Slave and that other one in Jail, and hang them both upon the same tree, and let them hang there a month!' 'Three men came forward to assist him, and the hour of four o'clock that afternoon was agreed upon for the execution. The excitement grew, waxing wilder and fiercer every hour, until such a storm of passion raged as was fearful to behold.

"At four o'clock, the mob, numbering about three hundred, moved toward the Court-House. The 'boy,' a quadroon, of about 40 years of age, was brought into the building and placed within the bar. Col. Reed was called upon to preside, and Col. Walton explained the object of the meeting. He said: 'A great crime has been committed — an outrage upon one of our citizens by a Nigger. We have come together not to imbrue our hands in the blood of innocence, but rebellion of Slaves is becoming common. Something must be done to put a stop to it, to protect *our* Wives, *our* Children, and *our* Sacred homes.' A member of the Legislature earnestly remonstrated against mob law, and recommended that a day be appointed to whip the Slave, and have all the Slaves in the County present. He was not heard through, for the speech did not suit the mob. A Committee of twelve was appointed to decide immediately what punishment the Slave should receive. That Committee retired, but soon returned, with Col. Reed at their head, who read the following announcement:

"'Your Committee have decided that the Slave shall receive one thousand lashes on his bare back, two hundred to be administered this evening, and the remaining eight hundred from time to time, as in the judgment of the Committee his physical nature can bear under it. Also, we advise that a Committee of three Citizens be chosen to whip him. Also, that the person whose arm was cut by the Slave have the *privilege* of giving him the last two hundred lashes.'

"The whipping commenced. More than a hundred heads were peering in to get a sight of their victim. But before a dozen lashes had been administered, the Slave fell to the floor, bleeding and writhing in agony. The whipper struck the harder, and ordered him to get up. Some one declared that he could never stand a thousand such lashes. Another cried out: '988 yet to come,' and the whipping was resumed. Lash upon lash was inflicted, until one hundred had been given, when his whole back, from the top of his shoulders down to his feet, was a mass of blood and mangled flesh. The whipping was continued without cessation amidst the most piteous and beseeching wails and cries, such as: 'O gentlemen, O gentlemen, have mercy!' 'O Lord! O Lord, come down in mercy!' 'O gentlemen! O Lord! O Lord!' until they became fainter and died away upon the ear.

"When they commenced giving him the second hundred, I left the room in anguish of spirit, exclaiming to myself: '*Oh that I were a dog, that I might not call man my brother!*'. He was not permitted to rise until the two hundred lashes were given. He was taken out the next day, but it was decided he was too sore to whip. On the third day he was taken out and whipped again in the presence of a large crowd; but when they had given him twenty, his strength completely failed him. Whether the whole of the thousand lashes were administered or whether he gave out before receiving the complete penalty, I have no means of knowing; but I do know that some of the leading Slaveholders pledged themselves to each other to carry it through, despite the indignation of a portion of the community and of the entreaties of his 'Master,' although at first the 'Master' had given him up to the mob heartily, and was even willing they should hang him. He also acquiesced in the judgment of the Committee.

"On the next evening (Saturday, Feb. 9, 1856), after the 200 lashes had been inflicted upon the Slave, Gov. Shannon arrived *en route* for Kansas Territory. A grand reception supper, costing some $300, was got up for him. The Governor was largely toasted, and replied in a speech, boasting of the power he had received from President Franklin Pierce, and how he would 'compel submission to the laws.'"

CHAPTER II.

IN North Carolina the greater part of the Slaves go half-starved most of the time. The breakfast is generally from 10 to 11 o'clock, A. M., and the dinner from 7 to 11, P. M. In the pine-tree country, the Slaves are employed in manufacturing turpentine. The allowance of the "turpentine hands" varies. The Slaves in the rural districts receive one peck of Indian meal per week. On the turpentine plantations some "bosses" allow, in addition, one quart of molasses. On many plantations the Slaves are allowed only one peck of meal a week, without any other provisions. Several who received no pork, or only two pounds a fortnight, complained that "we's not fed 'nuf, Massa, for the work they takes out on us," and others said the sameness of the diet was sickening.

The Manchester and Wilmington Railroad hands sleep in miserable shanties along the line. Their bed, a board — nothing softer. Their covering, a blanket. This road runs through the most desolate-looking country in the Union. Nothing but pine-trees can be seen from Wilmington until you enter South Carolina. Poor fellows, in that dreary section of country, they seldom see a woman from Christmas to Christmas. If they are "married" Men, they are tantalized with the thought that *their* "Wives" are performing for others those services that would gladden their weary life. They have still sadder reflections.

A "minister of the Gospel" in South Carolina, had a "Sabbath appointment" to preach, about eight miles from his residence. He was in the habit of riding thither in his "gig," with a swift trotting horse, which he always drove briskly. Behind him ran one of his party-colored boys on foot, who was required to be at the place of appointment as soon as his "reverend Master," to take care of his horse. Sometimes he could not keep up, and kept his "Master," waiting for him a few minutes, for which he was always punished. On one occasion of this kind, after sermon, the "reverend gentleman" told the Slave that he would this time take care to have him keep up with him, going home. So he tied him by the wrists, with a halter, to his gig, behind, and drove rapidly home. The result was that, about two or three miles from home, the Slave's feet and legs failed him, and he was dragged on the ground the rest of the way! Whether the "Master" knew it or not till he reached home is not certain; but on alighting and looking around, he exclaimed, "Well! I thought you would keep up with me this time!" so saying, he coolly walked into the house. Some of the Slaves came out and took up the poor sufferer for dead. After a time he revived a little, lingered for a day or two, and died. These facts were known all over the neighborhood, but nothing was done about it! The "reverend gentleman" continued preaching as before.

There really appears to be no end to the crimes against the Slaves committed by men living under the garb of a "Christian profession."

In a public address, recently delivered at Cincinnati, Ohio, by the Rev. Edward Smith, of Pittsburgh, Pa., he stated that a certain D. D. of his acquaintance, a Slaveholder, and a severe one, too, often, with his own hands, applied the cowhide to the naked backs of his Slaves. "On one occasion, a Woman that served in the house, committed, on Sabbath morning, some slight offence, but which was considered of too great magnitude to go unpunished until Monday morning. The Dr.

took his Woman into the cellar, and as is usual in such cases, stripped her, and then applied the lash. The woman writhed under each stroke, and cried, 'O Lord! O Lord!! O Lord!!!' The Doctor stopped, and his hands fell to his sides as though struck with palsy, gazed on the Woman with astonishment, and thus addressed her (the congregation must pardon me for repeating his words), 'Hush, you * * * * * * b——h, will you take the name of the Lord in vain on the Sabbath day?' When he had stopped the Woman from the gross profanity of crying to God on the Sabbath day, he finished whipping her, and then went and essayed to preach that Gospel to his congregation which proclaims liberty to the captive, and the opening of the prison-doors to them who are bound."

Recently, at a meeting of the Planters in South Carolina, the question was seriously discussed, "whether the Slave is more profitable to the owners, if well fed, well clothed, and moderately worked; or, made the most of at once, and exhausted in some five or six years." The decision was in favor of the last alternative!

The Southern Cultivator, for May, 1855, has the following hideous announcement, copied from *The Edgefield* (S. C.) *Advertiser*, and which *The Cultivator* strongly recommends "to other Masters and employers:"—

"*Overseers, Read This!*—It will be remembered by the Overseers of Edgefield, that Col. M. Frazier has offered a fine Watch as a reward to the Overseer (working not less than ten Slaves) who will report the best-managed plantation, largest crop per hand of cotton, corn, wheat, and pork for the present year. Col. Frazier has just returned from the North and laid before us this elegant prize. It is a fine English lever Watch, encased in a heavy silver hunting-case upon the back of which is beautifully engraved '*Presented by M. Frazier, Edgefield, S. C., as a reward of Merit.*' We assure those who are contestants for this valuable prize that it is eminently worthy of the donor and calculated to call forth the utmost energy and skill of which the candidates may be possessed.

Remember, then, that the prize is now fairly upon the stake, and that the longest pole knocks down the persimmon. Whip! whip!! Hurrah!!!"

Here we have an appeal to avarice and cruelty of the worst sort. Lest the work of the Overseer, however, should not be complete under the ordinary incentives of their power, here we have a reward offered for blood and sweat extortions — prizes for inhumanity — couched in saintly phraseology.*

"The smack of the whip," says Dr. J. Edwards, "is all day long in the ears of those who are on the plantation, or in the vicinity; and it is used with such dexterity and severity as not only to lacerate the skin, but to tear out small portions of the flesh at almost every stroke. This is the general treatment of the Slaves. But many suffer still more severely. Many are knocked down; some have their eyes beaten out; some have an arm or a leg broken, or chopped off: and many, for a very small, or for no crime at all, have been beaten to death."

At a Planter's dinner-table, one day, a guest — a Dry-Goods Jobber from Philadelphia — remarked upon the "hypocrisy of all religious Slaves." The planter dissented. He was the

---

* "Were it not for the din and clamor of Northern invectives against Slavery, we should hear more distinctly the candid expressions of our Southern friends with regard to the evils of the system. They tell us — and, indeed, every one *sees* it — that Slave labor in many cases is oppressively expensive, and the more so in proportion to the *conscientiousness* of the owners. It takes more hands to do the same amount of work than with us" (in New England); "the Slaves are hearty, and great consumers, frequently costing more for their food than the rest of the family."—"*A South-side View of Slavery,*" &c., "*By Nehemiah Adams, D. D.,*" p. 90. And, pray, at whose expense did "the rest of the family" get their living? Dr. Adams reasons like a man who has stolen an estate which belongs to a family of orphans. Out of its munificent revenues, he gives the orphans "food and clothing," while he retains the rest for his own use, declaring that he is thus rendering to them that which is just and equal.

"owner" of one who would rather die than deny Christ. This was ridiculed. The Slave was brought in and put to the test. He was ordered to deny his belief in Christ. He refused; was terribly whipped; retained his integrity; the whipping was repeated, and he died in consequence.

"In Tennessee," says the Rev. John Rankin, "thousands of the Slaves are pressed with the gnawings of hunger; and suffer extremely both while they labor and when they sleep, for want of clothing to keep them warm." *The Maryville* (Tenn.) *Intelligencer* says of the Slaves of the South and West, generally, that "*their condition through time will be second only to that of the wretched creatures in hell.*"

Recently, one of the Slaves of Matthew Raynor ran away. He pursued the fugitive and apprehended him in Memphis, and took him home. The next day Raynor commenced his cruel and fiend-like punishment, and after inflicting upon the poor fellow hundreds of lashes, and washing him down with brine, finished by cutting off both his ears, close to his head.

In Georgia the allowance of food is not adequate to the support of a laboring man. The corn is ground in a hand-mill, by the Slave, after his task is done. Generally there is but one mill on a plantation, and as but one can grind at a time, the mill is going sometimes very late at night.

Any person of "color," bond or free, is forbidden to occupy any tenement except a kitchen or outhouse, under penalty of from twenty to fifty lashes. Some of these laws are applicable only to particular cities, towns, or counties; others to several counties. The huts are generally put up without a nail, and contain neither chairs, table, nor bedstead. On the cold ground they must lie without covering, and shiver while they slumber.

The best possible testimony as to the condition of the Slaves, is that of the Slaveholders themselves, when given incidentally. They certainly can have no motive to represent their condition as worse than it is, and they have abundant means of knowing. We take the following from "A Detail of a Plan for the Moral Improvement of Negroes on Plantations," by Thomas Clay, a Slaveholder, and one of the most prominent men in the State. He says, on p. 13: "A subject, not less important, presents itself in the dwellings of the Slaves, and until greater attention is paid to this subject, it will be impossible to inculcate and maintain that regard for decency, which is so essential to good morals. Our physical habits have a vast influence on our moral; neither can they be entirely separated. Man is a physical, as well a moral being; and this fact must always be kept in view, in our endeavors to give elevation to the character. Should we fail to do this, the subjects of our philanthropy will point out the inconsistency, and distrust our sincerity. These reflections are strikingly applicable to the evils obviously arising from the mode of lodging in Slave-houses. Too many individuals of different sexes are crowded into the house, and the proper separation of apartments can not be observed. *That they are familiar with these inconveniences, and insensible to the evils arising from them, does not, in the least, lessen the unhappy consequences in which they result.*"

The Slaves have often been spoken harshly of in consequence of their "thievish habits." "In walking in the vicinity of Augusta, Georgia, one day," says John Ball, jr., "I came up to a Slave, who was carrying a bag of provisions from town to his owner's plantation. We talked a long time about the 'patriarchal Institution.' He said that plantation Slaves in this vicinity generally received one peck of meal and from one to two and a half pounds of pork a week. He knew one planter who gave a very 'short' allowance of meat:

"'So you see, Mass'r, his Slaves steal whatever they can lay their hands on. He's constant a whippin' 'em; but it does n't stop 'em. My 'Boss' gives us two and a half pounds, and so we never takes anything; we's above it.'

"'Are you a married man?'

"'Yes, Mass'r.'

"'Were you married by a clergyman?'

"'No, Mass'r; I was married by the blanket!'

"'How's that?'

"'Wall, Mass'r, we comes together into the same cabin; and she brings her blanket and lays it down beside mine; and we gets married that-a-way.'

"'How many suits of clothes are you allowed a year?'

"'Two, Mass'r.'

"'How many shirts?'

"'Two, Mass'r; only one at a time.'

"'How do you get it washed?'

"'I washes it at night, and sleeps naked till it's dry.'

"'Do preachers never marry you?'

"'Yes, Mass'r, sometimes; but not often. Mass'r, has you got a chaw o' 'bacco?'

"This question has been asked me dozens of times by Slaves—in fact, every time that I have gone into the country. *Negroes*, with an humble air and with hand touching hat, have asked me for it. 'A chaw o' 'bacco' has seldom failed to be the 'instrument' of conveying Republican ideas."

Dr. C. G. Parsons, of Boston, Massachusetts, speaking of his "Tour among the Planters," in 1853, says: "A few weeks before I left Savannah, I boarded at the Marshall House. A friend of mine who boarded at the same house for several years, and who had become an advocate of Slavery, not having witnessed much of the privations and sufferings of the Slaves, inquired of me if the Slaves in that city did not appear to be in better condition than the '*free* Negroes of the North.' And I was constrained to admit that, so far as I had been able to judge from what I had seen, the Slaves were 'cared for.' But before I left that house, some facts came to my knowledge in relation to the treatment of Slaves at public boarding-houses, which astonished some of my brother Yankees, who had been there for years. Mr. L., of Maine, contracted with Mr. Johnson, proprietor of the Marshall House, for a lease of the premises for several years. The keys were put into his hands on the third morning of January, 1853. When Mr. L. opened the bar-room door, *he found three male-slaves sleeping on narrow boards placed on chairs, the floor being sanded, without a pillow or blanket.* He opened the boot-room, and there found two of the boot-blacks in a place *too short* for them to lie down at full length, with nothing but boots for pillows. In the kitchen there were *five female-cooks sleeping on the solid brick hearth.* Mr. L. inquired of Mr. Johnson, if there were no beds furnished, and sleeping apartments appropriated to the Slaves? 'No,' replied Mr. J., 'Niggers never sleep on beds in the public houses in this State.' This being mentioned to a gentleman who was boarding at the Pulaski House, he said, 'Mr. Johnson is a brute not to furnish his Negroes with beds, for they have to work very hard.' The gentleman was then asked, 'Do they have beds at your house?' 'Of course they do,' was the reply. 'Are you sure? Because Mr. Johnson says they never have beds at the taverns.'

"The next day the gentleman asked Captain W., the proprietor of the Pulaski House, what kind of beds were furnished for his Slaves. '*Beds!*' *exclaimed Captain W.*, '*don't you know that Niggers never sleep on beds? Put one of my Niggers on the best bed there is in the house, and he won't lie there half-an-hour. Niggers prefer sleeping on the floor.*'"

The frightful spectacle of "burning a Nigger alive," took place in Sumter County, on the 28th of May, 1855. The pyre was composed of several cords of light dry wood, in the centre of which was a green willow stake, selected in consequence of its indestructibility by fire. On the top of the pile the "Nigger Dave" was placed, and securely chained to the stake. The match was then applied, and in a few moments the devouring flames were enveloping the doomed Man; his fearful cries resounded through the air, while the surrounding Slaves who witnessed his dreadful agony and horrible contortions sent up an involuntary howl of horror. His sufferings were excruciating; in a few minutes the flames had enveloped him entirely, revealing now and then, as they fitfully swayed hither and thither, his black and burning carcass, like a demon of the fire, grinning as if in triumph at his tormentors. Soon all was over, nothing was left but the burning flesh and charred skeleton. The heavens were reeking with the stench.

Had a white man committed similar crimes to those for which " Dave" suffered, upon the Wife or Daughter of a Slave, he would have got clear on the payment of the " assessed Money value" of such Slave to the " owner." Had the " owner" himself committed such a crime, it would have been simply a " loss of property."

A Slaveholder in Stewart County, had two fine young Men, brothers, for whom he was offered $1,350 and $1,500, for some cause or other he had entertained a dislike to them, and was constantly punishing them for the most trivial offences. He had them laid on the ground, and successively paddled them from the neck to the heels. *He then, with the flat part of a handsaw, broke all the blisters caused by the holes which had been bored in the paddle. He then bathed their backs in a solution of red pepper and salt brine.* Such were the torments inflicted on these poor suffering sons of humanity, that they determined upon absconding. The day following they were absent. He, fearing they had made their way northward, got up a party of his neighbors, armed to the teeth, and with a pack of bloodhounds went in pursuit. After a long search they came up with them on Flint River. When they heard the hounds baying (that is, the moment the dogs came close upon their prey, they utter a most hideous and mournful howl), *the runaways plunged into the river. In went the hounds after* them, some at one Slave, and some at the other. They bit them on the necks, arms, backs, and tried to pull them under the water. The poor fellows fought as long as they could, but got paralyzed, and not being able to swim and contend with the dogs at the same time, they appeared to resign themselves to their fate. A few gurgling sounds ascended to heaven, and their spirits had fled to Christ.

Another Slaveholder had a woman who was in the habit of smoking a pipe in the field; the overseer cautioned her several times not to do so — however, one day she clandestinely carried some fire to the field, and was lighting her pipe. All of a sudden, the Overseer made his appearance. He said, "I thought I told you the next time I saw you smoke, I would blow your brains out," and immediately shot her dead.

Another Slaveholder had a "Nigger" who ran away. The day he was brought home, he had a dog die of the distemper; he called the "cook," and desired her to cut off the hind leg, skin, hair and all, and slice it up, this he had fried in fat, and made the captured runaway eat it.

"In Georgia," says William Savery, Minister of the Friends' Society, "we rode through many rice swamps, where the Slaves were numerous — working up to the middle in water, Men and Women nearly naked." John Parrish, Minister of the Friends' Society, says: "In the rural districts, both male and female go without clothing until the age of eight or ten years."

In Alabama the Slaves are, as a general thing, wretchedly provided for. Thousands have hardly a rag of clothing on them. Generally the only bedding is a blanket, and that of the poorest manufacture.

Mr. Nero Geldersleve, of Georgia, formerly an elder in a Presbyterian Church at Wilkesbarre, Pennsylvania, describing the flogging of a Slave, in which one hundred lashes were inflicted on his naked body, says: "I stood by and witnessed the whole without feeling the least compassion; so hardening is the influence of Slavery." Such an admission does Mr. Geldersleve no credit. Cold-blooded selfish natures, like his, are very rarely, if ever, troubled with "compassion." Show a man of Mr. G.'s ilk a glittering bait, and he would do the work of Satan.

The Rev. Robert Jones, of Chambers county, a preacher of the Methodist denomination, lately stripped and tied one of his Boys to a tree, and whipped him to death. The account of this barbarity is given in *The Alabama Herald*. A neighboring clergyman, to whom a friend mentioned this case, said there was "nothing in the act contrary to the Book of Discipline. The man had a perfect right to do what he pleased with his own property."

The mutilation and murder of Slaves are thought to be so slight or unimportant matters, that not more than one case in twenty or thirty is ever reported in the papers at all. In fact, the Editors dare not do it.

A Slaveholder, near Courland, of the name of Thompson, recently shot a beautiful Slave girl, because she refused to comply with a proposition he had made to her. He buried her in an old log heap.

Two men found a fine-looking "colored man" at Dandridge's Quarter, without a "pass," and flogged him so that he died in two or three hours. They were not punished. Colonel Blocker's overseer attempted to flog one of the Slaves. He refused to be flogged, whereupon the overseer seized an axe and split his head open down to the neck. The Colonel justified it. One Jones whipped a half-starved Woman to death for grabbing a few potatoes.

An overseer of another Plantation came up to a Woman who was rather lagging behind. Naming her, he said: "I say, I thought I told you to mend your gait."—"Well, Mass'r," she replied, with tears trickling down her wo-begone face, "I'se so sick, I can hardly drag one foot after the other."

The monster laid down his lash, and took up a pine-root and made a blow at her head. The wretched creature tried to avoid the blow and received the weight of it on her neck. Her "husband" was obliged to stand aside to let her fall. She was taken up insensible and lingered till the following day.

The *New York Tribune*, of April 9, 1856, says: "Burning at the stake for heresies and crimes no longer exists in Europe, not even in Turkey. Roasting martyrs and evil-doers alive is a system which belongs there to the past. And yet Europe is almost entirely Monarchical. Saving Switzerland, the hereditary system of privilege is practically acknowledged in every European State. But, notwithstanding that such is the mitigation of the old severities there, *here in Democratic America, the flames roar around the criminal, for if a Slave, he may be burned alive. It is false to call us civilized; we are not so.* Some five millions of human beings are held in abject submission and ignorance, and hence habitually tending to commit violent crimes in the same proportion; and accordingly the necessities of the barbarous society which so debases them, cause the kind of punishment of which we are treating. We admire, therefore, the consistency of the local Southern press in despatching the matchless horrors of burning a Man to death in three lines, which we copy from *The Montgomery Journal*, published at the capital of Alabama, one of the sovereign States of the Union. That paper, on the 3d instant" (April 3, 1856), "made the following statement:—

"'*Burning of a Negro.*—We learn that the Negro who murdered Mr. Capheart'" (see p. 193) "'was burned to death yesterday at Mount Meigs. He acknowledged himself guilty.'

"This is at least consistent. A state of society essentially barbarous causes the 'burning of a Negro;' and such inflammatory procedures must multiply with the mental improvement of the Slave, and his increased restlessness. So, burn away, 'brother Democrat,' but no sentiment, if you please, thereupon!"

In Mississippi the Slaves are half-starved. They receive two wretched meals a day. Breakfast about eleven o'clock, A. M.; the other meal during the evening. The Rev. H. B. Abbott, of Augusta, Maine, says: "I am acquainted with a Baptist preacher in Mississippi, who compelled his Slaves, men, women, and children, to labor on the Sabbath, and justified himself under the plea that if they were not at work they would be roving about the fields, thereby desecrating the Lord's day more than by laboring under an overseer."

A young man, who went South in the hope of "bettering" his condition, stopped at a village in Mississippi, and obtained employment in the largest and most influential house in the place, as book-keeper. "A Slaveholder," writes this young man, "residing near the village, a bachelor, thirty years of age, became embarrassed, and executed a mortgage to my employer on a noble-looking Slave. He was quick-witted, active, obedient, and remarkably faithful, trusty, and honest — so much so that he was held up as an example. He had a 'wife' that he loved. His owner cast his eyes upon her, and she became his paramour. The poor 'husband' remonstrated with his owner, and told him that he tried faithfully to perform his every duty, that he was a good and faithful Nigger to him, and it was cruel, after he had toiled hard all day, and till ten or eleven o'clock at night, without wages, for him to have the 'wife' of his heart taken from him, and his domestic relations broken up. The white man denied the charge. One night the heart-broken 'husband' came home earlier than usual. It was a wet dismal night; he made a fire in his cabin, went to get his supper, and found ocular demonstration of the guilt of his owner. He became enraged, as any man would, seized a knife and cut his owner's throat, stabbed his 'wife' in over twenty places, and came to the village and knocked at the

Office door. I told him to come in. He did so, and asked for my employer. I called him. The man then told him that he had killed his owner, and his 'wife,' and what for? My employer locked him up, and he and a doctor and myself went to the house of the old bachelor, and found him dead, and the wretched 'wife' nearly so.

"My employer and myself returned to the village, watched the 'husband' until about sunrise, left him locked up, and went to get our breakfasts, intending to take him to jail (as it was my employer's interest, if possible, to save him, having $1,000 at stake in him), but while we were at breakfast, some persons, who had heard of the murder, broke open the door, seized the poor fellow, put a long chain round his neck, *and started him for the woods at the point of the bayonet*, marching by where we were eating with a great deal of noise. My employer hearing it, ran out, and rescued the man. The mob again broke in, and took him, and marched him out of town. My employer begged them not to disgrace their town in such a manner; but to appoint a jury of twelve men, to decide what should be done; whereupon twelve of the mob stepped forward and said he must be hanged. They then tied a rope round his neck, and set him on a horse. He made a speech to the mob, which I at the time thought, if it had come from some Senator, would have been received with rounds of applause; and withal, he was more calm than I am now in writing this. And after he had told all about the deed, and its cause, kicked the horse out from under him,- and was launched into eternity. My employer has often remarked, that he never saw anything more noble in his life, than the conduct of that poor Slave."

A shocking murder of an inoffensive Slave-mother was recently committed by John Manning, an Overseer on a Cotton plantation near Natchez, Mississippi. The Slaves, men and women, were "hoeing" each their "row" of Cotton, and about twenty yards from a fence, when suddenly the Babe of one of the Women began to scream as though its little heart-strings would break. No Slave being allowed to leave off work without permission from the Overseer, the state of the poor Mother's mind may well be imagined; but in this case, the maternal feelings got beyond the fear of orders, and she rushed to the rescue of her Child, which was struggling with a huge snake. Manning cried out, "*Stick to your work, your b—h, or I'll cut you in pieces.*" But the poor trembling Mother kept on her maternal errand of mercy, snatched up the little one with the snake wound around it; the Overseer followed close upon her heels with curses and imprecations for leaving her work without orders. He stripped her as naked as the day she was born, fastened a rope upon her wrists, and ordered two Slaves to climb a tree with the other end of the rope, and pull her up so that her feet would be about two feet from the ground. This done, Manning whipped her until he literally cut her in pieces, as he said he would. She screamed as the lash went into her flesh, in these words: "*Pray, massa! Pray, massa! O pray, massa! Snake bite chile, massa! O massa, forgive me, massa! Snake bite chile, massa! Lord make massa have a little feeling for poor Nigger! O massa, forgive me, massa! Snake bite chile, massa! O Jesus, pity me! pity me! Massa, forgive me! forgive me! Snake bite chile.*"

Her voice became more and more faint, till the faculty of speech was whipped out of her, so that she hung without any motion whatever. Rousing herself for a single moment she glanced in the direction of her child, and murmured—"Jesus—heaven—chile, come—co—" and her spirit took flight to a happier world.

"O massa, let me stay, to catch
My baby's sobbing breath;
His little glassy eye to watch,
And smooth his limbs in death,

> And cover him with grass and leaf,
> Beneath the plantain tree!
> It is not sullenness, but grief—
> O Massa, pity me!".

The condition of Solomon Northrop, during the nine years that he was in the hands of Eppes, was of a character nearly approaching that described by Mrs. H. B. Stowe, as the condition of "Uncle Tom," while in Mississippi. During that whole period poor Northrop's hut contained neither a floor, nor a chair, nor a bed, nor a mattress, nor anything for him to lie upon except a board about twelve inches wide, with a block of wood for his pillow, and with a single blanket to cover him, while the walls of his hut did not by any means protect him from the inclemency of the weather. He was sometimes compelled to perform acts revolting to humanity, and outrageous in the highest degree. On one occasion, a party-colored girl belonging to Eppes, about 17 years of age, went one Sunday, without the permission of her "Master," to the nearest plantation, about half a mile distant, to visit another girl of her acquaintance. She returned in the course of two or three hours, and for that offence she was called up for punishment, which Solomon was required to inflict. Eppes compelled him to drive four stakes into the ground at such distances that the hands and ankles of the girl might be tied to them, as she lay with her face upon the ground; and having thus fastened her down, he compelled him, while standing by himself, to inflict one hundred lashes upon her bare flesh, she being stripped entirely naked. Having inflicted one hundred blows, Solomon refused to proceed any further. Eppes tried to compel him to go on, but he absolutely set him at defiance; and refused to murder the girl. Eppes then seized the whip and applied it until he was too weary to continue it. Blood flowed from her neck to her feet, and in this condition she was compelled the next day to go into the field to work.

On the 21st of March, 1853, while at dinner in a Public House, at Wablack, Miss., a man was telling of having his saddle-girth cut; and said he got out his dogs (blood-hounds), and put them on the track, and followed to a hut, where they seized a Slave by the throat, whom they took to his "Master" to whip him. The owner contended that the dog-testimony was not evidence, and that the man should not be whipped on the strength of it. But his captor, who had two friends with him, told the owner they were determined to whip him. Accordingly, they commenced whipping him by turns, till they had given him three hundred lashes. His owner then asked him, "Did you cut it?" "Yes, massa, I did." His owner then beat him to death.

James Clark, a well-known citizen of Clark county, made an assault upon one of his Slave women, for an object which need not be stated. He then ordered her into a corner of the room, and commenced pitching his knife at her, point foremost. *As the knife would enter her flesh, he would compel his victim to draw it forth, and return it to him.* This demoniacal amusement was continued until the poor Slave was covered with some fifty bleeding gashes! The same day he whipped his own wife, cut her all over the head with his knife, in a mass of cruel and painful punctures. He also *cut off her eyelids!* This drama wound up on the following day by the commission of murder. Clark ordered his wife to go and call Lewis, a Slave belonging to the family. She obeyed, but the Slave refused to come, through a dread of his enraged "Master." Mrs. Clark returned, and was whipped by her husband for not bringing the Slave. Five times was she sent up on this capricious mission, five times was it fruitless, *and each time she was whipped for her failure.* Clark then called to Lewis, informing him that he would shoot him next morning. The Slave, it seems, did not heed the warning, for while splitting rails the next day, he was deliberately shot by Clark. The wound was fatal; poor Lewis ran two or three hundred yards, and fell in mortal agony. Clark confessed that he had committed these crimes, but justified his conduct by quoting Scripture, saying, "*the Bible commands Wives and other Servants to obey their Owners, and if they will not, the Master should make them.*"

The Rev. J. A. Lyon, Pastor of the Presbyterian Church, in Columbus, in a lecture delivered in that City, and published in Mississippi, in June, 1855, says: " The reckless manner in which the sixth Commandment, which forbids murder, is disregarded in this community, is truly alarming, and should excite the well-grounded fears of every friend of morality and good order. *An army is slain every year by the hands of violence in our country, boasting of more intelligence, freedom, and civilization, than any other upon the globe!* We find that of the murdered host, only thirty-two fell in the six New England States, only one hundred and six in the Middle States, including the largest States and Cities in the Union. The blood of all the rest was spilt in the South and West. Three hundred and forty-six have been slaughtered in the South alone; that is, in the Southern States proper, not including Missouri, Kansas, or California. I am sorry to say that as many as thirty-two have been slaughtered in Mississippi."

Mr. Lyon does not appear to have kept a record of more than one murder in every seven committed.

In Louisiana there is a great deal of suffering among the Slaves from hunger. Thousands perish every winter for want of proper food and clothing. Until recently the Sugar planters usually found it necessary to employ twice the amount of labor during the "boiling season" that was required during the season of raising, but can now, *by excessive driving, day and night,* during the boiling season, accomplish the whole labor with "one set of hands." By pursuing this plan they can "afford to sacrifice one set of hands once in seven years."

The late Mr. Samuel Blackwell, of Jersey City (N. J.), visited many of the Sugar plantations in Louisiana, and said: "The planters generally declared to me that they were *obliged* to so overwork their Slaves, during the Sugar-making season" (from ten to twelve weeks), "as to use them up in five or six years; for, said they, 'after the process is commenced, it must be pushed without cessation, night and day, and we can not *afford* to keep a sufficient number of Slaves to do the extra work at the time of Sugar-making, as we could not *profitably* employ them the rest of the year.'"

The late Hon. Henry Clay, of Kentucky (himself a Slaveholder), in a conversation with James G. Birney, said that, Outerbridge Horsey—formerly a Senator in Congress, and the owner of a Sugar plantation in Louisiana—declared to him that his Overseer worked his hands so closely that *one of the Women brought forth a Child while engaged in the labors of the field.* Also, that he was at a brick-yard in the environs of New Orleans, in which one hundred hands were employed; among them were from twenty to thirty young Women, in the prime of life. He was told by the proprietor that there had not been a Child born among them for the last two or three years, although they all had "husbands."

When a Child is a week old the Mother is considered to be "in working "order."

One of the most revolting deeds, for the benefit of Slavery, ever witnessed in a "Christian community," took place at Alexandria (La.), in September, 1855. It was the public execution of a lad not quite ten years of age, and, strange to say, "Christian men and women" rode forty miles to see it. As an evidence of how mere a child he was, some gentlemen who called to see him the day before his execution, found him playing with marbles in his cell. On telling him that he was to be hung the next morning, and asking him what he thought of it and why he did not pray, he answered that it was nothing, adding that he had been hung many a time. He was playing all the time in jail, never once realizing the dreadful fate that awaited him. When brought out to die, and seeing the preparations that had been made for his execution, for the first time he began to have some idea of what was before him. He then asked that he might be allowed to pray, after doing which he began to cry, and in the midst of his childish wailings was sent out of the world.

The secret of this affair is, that he belonged to the "race of *Africa*" or "cursed seed of *Ham*," and was executed for giving his tyrannical owner, the Rev. J. J. Weems, a knock on the head. For the purpose of "*impressing the surrounding Slave population*," a boy of ten years of age was just as good as an adult who had arrived to years of moral responsibility, and possibly better.

The Pro-Slavery Pulpits and the Pro-Slavery Presses, protest against Uncle Tom's Cabin, on the ground that its incidents are "exaggerated," in fact, "a stupendous lie," although the accomplished writer, in her "Key to Uncle Tom," has justified every event and circumstance which it describes, by citing parallel facts. But if the Key had never been prepared, the columns of the Southern journals themselves would have furnished ample evidence of the substantial truth of Mrs. Stowe's representations. No one of her incidents, for instance, has created more remark than the death of Uncle Tom by means of the violence of Legree, and it has been said that no such wretch as he is represented to be could exist in a "Christian country," and that no such event as the murder of an old, faithful, and pious Slave by his owner, was likely to occur. Yet read the following paragraph from *The Carrollton* (La.) *Star*:—

"We grieve to have to record an outrage practised on the body of an old Negro of this place, named Johnson, the Slave of Charles Hines, by Hines himself, which resulted in death. The Negro was nearly *ninety* years of age, and venerated for his honesty, as well as for his Revolutionary reminiscences. The Master, taking umbrage at some petty offence, deliberately whipped, stamped, and kicked him to death. Persons who witnessed poor Johnson's sufferings, say that the sight was extremely sickening — his whole back cut and bruised into jelly, and the lower part of his person kicked to pieces."

Only think of the hideous cruelty of murdering an old man who had reached the Patriarchal age of nearly ninety, and who appears to have served in the Revolutionary war!—deliberately whipped and kicked to death! Is there anything in any of the "Novels" that have been written to show the fiend-like influence of Slavery more clearly than this? Yet we are told that these "Novels" do Southern society the greatest injustice, and are libels upon the truth!

A Slave, little girl, named Louise, aged ten years, on the 7th of October, 1855, presented herself at the Police office of the Second district, New Orleans, seeking protection from the cruel treatment of her "Mistress," Madame E. Cruzelle. The Slave had been brutally beaten, her back, and other parts of her body, being literally cut to pieces. She stated that her owner had beaten her in this manner because she did not sell enough cakes, &c., to gratify her cupidity. She was placed in jail to await an investigation of the matter.

Society in New Orleans appears to be resolving itself into its pristine elements, and the community bounding onward to political chaos. Just look at the chronicle of the City for a single month, as recorded in *The True Delta;* and, as a private letter says, "*bad as it is, it does not include more than half of what has taken place:*" On November 1, there was an inquest upon the body of Joseph Steiner, and on the same day Joseph Damon snapped a pistol at a Slave named Long. On the 2d, a man named Cullen shot Daniel Hallem in a coffee-house, and Thomas Armstrong was arrested for wounding his sister with a Cotton-hook. On the 3d, Henry Kelter was charged with firing a pistol at Herman Baurichter, and two men named Fitzgerald were examined for murdering their sister; it was recorded, likewise, that Dr. Meighan was stabbed in several places at his own door. On the 4th, an unknown man was found drowned in a saw-mill pond; a record was made of the murder of Mike Anderson by George Thomas, in a coffee-house, and examination of James Coyle for stabbing John Reilly, with intent to kill, was postponed.

On the 5th, a German named Allemande was badly wounded, and Antoine Freiler killed; Major Blaize was shot at and wounded; E. S. White, the contractor, was slung-shotted; a tailor was stabbed, and a man named Patterson was knocked down and kicked severely; Joseph Nutter was shot in the leg; James Boyle and Edward Jones were shot at; a man was shot dead; James Peterson was stabbed, and Edward Evans was beaten so unmercifully that his life was despaired of. On the 6th, Dr. C. Sherener was shot at his own door and died, and Nicholas Gavin was stabbed. On the 7th, Watchman Tate was brutally beaten while discharging his duty. On the 8th, Mr. A. B. Bacon, a lawyer, was badly beaten at the polls with a slung-shot. On the 9th, a grocer named McCogga knocked down Joseph Goddard, and further maimed him by biting off his nose and two fingers. On the 10th, a German named Krost had several fingers bitten off; an engineer on the railroad was stabbed; Alderman Dural was knocked down with a pair of brass knuckles; a Slave was prevented from shooting his owner; and a gang of rowdies beat Felix Bosquillon to death for refusing them liquor. On the 11th, one murder and five robberies were committed. On the 12th, Daniel Sullivan beat awfully and tried to kill his brother-in-law by firing a pistol.

On the 13th, A. H. Dobbins wounded Christian Shaffer with a drinking glass, and Charles Smelsey struck Jean Loze with a slung-shot. The 14th was a day of *rest*. On the 15th,

Jack Allen was arrested for murder; and a free colored man stabbed another. On the 16th, an application was made and refused on behalf of Charles Bell, charged with shooting murderously at his brother-in-law; Owen Marth stabbed Mrs. Burns, and her son, who interfered; Pierre Trousky assaulted John, a Slave, and attempted to shoot Clarissa, another Slave; Thomas Farris stabbed Michael Henly at the polls; and Captain Snow was arrested for cutting C. A. Clark. On the 21st, J. G. Cabore was fired at. On the 23d, John Feehan was badly cut by a police officer; and Samuel Smith badly wounded Andres Quitana. On the 25th, Martin Gray cut off the finger of Patrick Nolan. On the 26th, F. Barsicola, an Italian, was murdered. On the 27th, C. de la Torra died of intemperance; Thomas Hussey was badly cut; the body of a new-born infant was found—a case of infanticide; a woman and child were wounded in the streets, from the shot of parties fighting with double-barreled guns in a grocery; an English sailor was thrown down stairs, and had his skull fractured; James M'Gregor was thrown from a window, and died; and J. Dabill was stabbed by robbers.

On the 28th, Barletta Walker, a German woman, far gone in pregnancy, was brought to the Hospital, stabbed by her husband; and Major Blaze was assaulted by a man with intent to kill; John Graham died of his wounds, and Mrs. C. Howard was stabbed by Thomas Foley; and another woman and a man besides were stabbed. On the 29th, a German named Eczinger, was shot and wounded in three places; John Shaeffer and Moran Meinnich were stabbed; a Slave stabbed a free colored man; Patrick Brown was stabbed; a German named Dreyfuss was stabbed; Hayes, an Irishman, was stabbed; Charles Gavin slung-shotted and shot.

The (New Orleans) *True Delta*, of the 4th November, 1856, has the following paragraph: " The assassination of citizens has now become so common that the reporters of the daily press scarcely deem them worth an item. Literally and truly we have no laws. Equally literally and truly may it be said that we have no public opinion."*

These facts need no commentary. They show the horrible cruelty of the Slaveholding Democracy of the "Model Republic," and the unmitigated diabolism of a Slaveholding religion. What meaning can there be in the words *justice* or *mercy*, what significance in the doctrine of human brotherhood, or what force in the precepts, " Love thy neighbor as thyself," " Remember them that are in bonds," &c. In every Slave-consuming State see the " Receiving-houses," whither these poor wrecks and remnants of families are constantly borne ! Who preaches the Gospel to the Slave-coffles ? Who preaches the Gospel in the Slave-prisons ? Is it not mockery to pray, " Thy Kingdom come," and refuse to engage in labors like these ? If the work of elevating depressed humanity be Christ's work, should not the " undoing of the heavy burthens," and " letting the oppressed go free," be the work of Christians, the mission of the Church of Christ ? If you turn away indifferent from this cause — " if you forbear to deliver them that are drawn unto death, and those that be ready to be slain ; if thou sayest, Behold, we knew it not, doth not He that pondereth the Heart consider it, and He that keepeth the soul, doth He not know it, shall He not render to every man according to his works ?"

The bodily tortures endured by the Slaves are, indeed, enough to awaken profound sympathy and excite an intense indignation ; but, oh ! how much more appalling is the violence done to those higher faculties, through which they are allied to God, and made heirs to an immortal life !

* A correspondent of one of the "evangelical" Pro-Slavery journals of New York, writing from the interior of Turkey, enlarges upon the "barbarous habits of the people," and states, as an appalling fact, that "in the course of a year, one man has been killed in public, and three brutally beaten." The "interior of Turkey" must try again.

PART FOURTH.

EDUCATION AND RELIGIOUS INSTRUCTION OF "SERVANTS," AND OTHER NEGROES.

CHAPTER I.

"We should march up to the very verge of the Constitution to destroy the traffic in Human flesh."—FRANKLIN.

THE Slave Power goes further. It lays its deadly grasp on the very souls of its victims. It subjects all the " religious privileges" of the Slave—we beg the reader's pardon, of the " Servant"— to the absolute will of the " Master," whether he be " Christian" or infidel. It does more, it prohibits the " Master" from teaching his Slaves to read, even the Word of God, and thus cuts off the unfortunate creature from one of the greatest privileges which God has ever bestowed on man. It aims to keep the mind in abject ignorance and degradation, lest the enslaved should grow dissatisfied, and claim the inalienable rights of humanity.

Nor is the non-Slaveholding white portion of the population scarcely in a better condition. Ignorance is an "Institution" in the Slaveholding States. It is a political necessity, and is as much provided for by legislation and by " public sentiment," and guarded by enactments, as intelligence is in the "*free* States." It must be. The restrictions which keep it from the Slaves keep it from the "*free* whites," excepting, always, the few who live at the top. There can not be an atmosphere of intelligence. Slaves would be in danger of breathing that. "Knowledge is Power," not only, but Powder, putting the South in the risk of being blown up, by careless handling and too great abundance.

The self-preservation of the Slaveholders, requires that Negroes, bond and *free*, should be treated worse than asses — beaten, and cruelly tortured, or murdered if refractory. In consonance with this "opinion," we deem such resolutions as the following, passed a short time since at a public meeting in Upper Marlboro', Prince George county, Maryland, absolutely necessary:

"*Resolved*, That, in a Slaveholding community like this, it is unwise, inexpedient, and dangerous, to allow large bodies of Slaves or *free* Negroes to assemble at night for any purpose whatever, whether it be Religious, Social, or Moral; such assemblages are sure to beget feelings of Physical superiority, in regard to numbers of the white race,.and, even when unaccompanied by tumult, have always a natural tendency to engender discontent and insubordination on the part of the colored race.

"*Resolved*, That this meeting is animated by no feelings of Political or Religious excitement whatever, but as Slaveholders alone, *regardful of their own personal rights and safety*, they have met together to express their unqualified disapprobation of such night meetings of their Slaves."

In Virginia, it is enacted "that all meetings or assemblages of Slaves, *free* Negroes, or mulattoes mixing and associating with such Slaves at any Meeting-house or houses, &c., in the night; or at any school or schools for teaching them reading or writing, either in the day or night, under whatsoever pretext, shall be deemed and considered an unlawful assemblage." —" Corporal punishment may be inflicted on the offender or offenders, at the discretion of any Justice of the Peace, not exceeding twenty lashes. If a Postmaster, or deputy Postmaster, know that any book or other writing has been received at his office in the mail, *he shall give notice thereof to some Justice, who shall inquire into the circumstances and have such book or writing burned in his presence;* if it appear to him that the person to whom it was directed subscribed therefor, knowing its character, or agreed to receive it for circulation to aid the purpose of Abolitionists, the Justice shall commit such person to Jail. If any Postmaster, or deputy Postmaster, violate this section, he shall be fined not exceeding two hundred dollars."—(Revised Code, p. 434.)

The Richmond Enquirer (a leading Buchanan journal), of August 29, 1856, says: "Every school and college in the South should teach that *Slave society is the common, natural, rightful, and normal state of society.* Any doctrine short of this contains Abolition in the germ; for, if it be not the rightful and natural form of society, it can not last, and we should prepare for its gradual but ultimate Abolition. They should also teach that *no other form of society is, in the general, right or expedient.* There are exceptional cases, such as desert or mountainous countries, where the small patches of fertile land are inadequate to support a larger family than husband, wife, and children — such as Lapland, Sweden, Norway, Switzerland, and parts of Africa — such, also, as New England, and Eastern New York, and Eastern Pennsylvania, which, though admirably adapted for commerce, manufactures, and fishing, are little fitted for Cotton or Sugar raising. Our schools should also teach that the Slaves should be a different race or nation from the Master, and the wider the distinction the better, as in such case the Slave is less apt to be degraded, or wish to assert his freedom and equality. To teach such doctrines we must have Southern teachers. *It is from the school that public opinion proceeds, and the schools should be set right.* No teacher should be employed in a private family or public schools at the South, who is not ready to teach these doctrines. Parents, trustees, and visiters, should look to this thing."

The citizens of Caroline county, held a mass meeting in September, 1855, to consider the proper course to be pursued with regard to "*free Negroes*" in their midst, when the following pregnant preamble and resolutions, reported by a Committee of twenty prominent citizens appointed at a former meeting, were unanimously adopted:—

"All Governments restrict and diminish the liberties of the People, in order to promote the happiness and well-being of society. They who are governed can not be free. Various forms and degrees of government have ever existed in society, each answering equally well for all nations and individuals endowed with various degrees of self-control, morality, and civilization. The least degree of government to which men most civilized, moral, and enlightened, can be subjected, consistently with good order and security, is that of being governed by laws made by representatives chosen by themselves. But this degree of liberty can be safely given but to a small fraction of individuals, even in the best and purest society. The children must be governed by parents and guardians; the apprentices by Masters" (that is, Slaveholders); "the soldiers and sailors by superior officers; wives must be subjected to husbands; lunatics and idiots to trustees and committees, and criminals be confined in jails and penitentiaries. *In all cases, it is not the law of the land that governs, but the will of a Master*" (that is, a Slaveholder). "All experience, all history, shows that man is only fitted for the government of mere law when he has become so highly civilized, prudent, and moral, *as to regard liberty in its broad and common sense as a thing to be avoided as an evil, rather than as a good to be sought after*. With the whites, we carefully adapt the mode and degree of government to the wants of the governed. Let us adopt *the same wise and just rule with our Servants*. Let us not attempt to govern those by mere law, who when adults, require, as much as white children between sixteen and twenty-one, to be governed by the will of another. Call that other 'guardian,' 'Committee,' 'captain,' or 'Master,' 'tis but a different name—the mode of government is the same. The strong and stringent measures adopted by many of the '*free* States' to exclude '*free* Negroes' from their territories, *justify our present course, and rebuke our past tardiness*, because the reasons and necessity for their exclusion exist in tenfold greater intensity with us than with them.

"A. S. BROADUS, *Chairman.*

"BROKENBROUGH PEYTON, *Secretary.*"

The Constitution and Statutes of "*free* States" debarring their "*free* colored Citizens" from eligibility to Office, and from equal access to the Ballot-box, are among the most marked and mischievous specimens of injury to the colored race. This greatly encourages and sustains the Slave States in their oppression of both the bond and the *free.*

"Virginia," says *The Richmond Argus,* of March 24, 1854, "is a very great State — very great! Virginia in this confederacy is the Impersonation of the Well-born, Well-educated, Well-bred Aristocrat." *Well-born,* indeed, while the Children of Jefferson and the only Children of Madison are a "connecting link between the human and brute creation;" *Well-educated,* with 25 per cent. of her White adults unable to read the vote they cast against the unalienable rights of man; *Well-bred,* when her great product for exportation is — the Children of her own loins! Slavery is a "patriarchal institution;" the democratic Abrahams of Virginia do not "Offer up" their Isaacs to the Lord; that would be a "Sacrifice of *property.*" They only sell them. Virginia is, indeed, "a very *great* State," so far as this article of export is concerned, for she Sells $25,000,000 worth of her Sons and Daughters every year.

At the Sunday School Convention, which was held in Lynchburg, in June, 1855, a Committee of twelve Clergymen and Laymen representing the "*evangelical*" denominations in the town, was appointed to prepare an Address in behalf of Christian education in Southwestern Virginia. It has been published and presents some suggestive statistics. According to the Census of 1850, the entire white population of the State was 971,770. Of these there are over 20 years of age, 452,832; of whom there are who can not read, 86,183. That is nearly one in five of the grown whites of the State. Where will these adults learn to read, if not in the Sunday School? They are too old, or too poor, or too proud, to attend any other. But again, there were in 1855, in Virginia, 379,845 young persons between 5 and 20 years of age, of whom there were at school or college only 111,327; leaving as attending no school at all 268,416; that is, for every young person in the State between 5 and 20 years of age receiving instruction, there are two who receive none! In other words, *two thirds of that portion of population who are to become Citizens within the next fifteen years, are, in these most precious years of their history, going totally untaught.*

To the questions, "What can be done to change this sad prospect?" "How is light to be poured upon the darkness which is thus settling all around the people?" "How are the blessings of general, and especially of Christian instruction to be here diffused?" the Report answers as follows:—

"The best hope, we have no hesitation in answering, is in that admirable institution of our age, which is peculiarly conformed to the spirit of Christianity, the Sunday School. This agency, whether conducted on individual responsibility, or under denominational direction, we cordially recommend as eminently beneficial in tendency. But there is one great Sunday School organization of which we would especially speak as peculiarly adapted to the wants of the land — The American Sunday School Union. This is a great National association of *good* men, belonging to the leading *evangelical* denominations of the country," &c.

These facts are startling. One in five of the grown white persons of Virginia — the "Old Dominion" — unable to read! An education is due to them, such as will enable them to understand their duties and their rights. But will even these simple suggestions be carried out? Of course not. The people in twenty-six counties even, of a State which will tax its downtrodden "*free* Negroes" $50,000 for sending the aforesaid "*free* Negroes" — who don't want to go — to *Africa*, and then steal the money and throw it into the Treasury for State purposes, as Virginia has lately done, will raise no money by taxing themselves for Sunday Schools, or any other schools, to educate their own ignorant whites, so long as they can thrust an arm into the vaults of a Northern Sunday School Union for such an object.

The Washington Star, in reference to some observations made by the *New York Tribune*, in January, 1856, on the shocking condition of the poor whites of the Slave States and Territories of the Union, put the following question:—

"The theory is that the existence of Slavery in a community degrades free labor therein. Now, throughout the Slaveholding States *no others are more emphatic enemies of Abolitionists and Abolitionism than our workingmen, in all callings. Far more free to do and say as they please, than those who live by the employment of the Capital of others at the North, not an Abolitionist is to be found among them!* If they are degraded, why is it that they do not show something like restiveness under their condition? Why do they, the *freest*, most independent, and *self*-willed laborers on the face of the globe, who have been living since the formation of the Government in this alleged degraded condition, *hate and despise Abolitionism with unanimity and heartiness such as was never before exhibited on any other subject by any other people in our country?* Here is a nut to crack."

Unfortunately the great bulk of the poor whites of the Slave States and Territories are altogether too ignorant to have any precise idea of the extent of their degradation, and still less of the causes of it, and of the means of its removal. The enmity of the whites, and especially of that most degraded class of them, the inhabitants of villages and towns, to Abolitionists and Abolitionism, is very easily explained. Degraded as they are, they still have the consolation of seeing *beneath* them a class, and a large class, still *more* degraded in the eye of the law. What a consolation to that pride so innate in the human heart, and one of the mainsprings of human action, for the most worthless, idle, pauper vagabond of a white man still to be able to set himself down as standing in the social scale *above* the great mass of the laboring population, and in the Slave States *above* the majority of the whole population!

The poor whites are able to see that the abolition of Slavery would deprive them of this "glorious advantage;" that if Slavery were abolished, capacity and industry would *then become the test, and that in order to keep in advance of the Slave population, it would be necessary to surpass them in labor, intelligence, usefulness, and productive skill.* They see plainly enough what they would lose; they are not able to see what they might gain. *Never having known a state of society different from that in which they live,* they have no means of conceiving of the advantages which Freedom gives to the intelligent and industrious laborer, and their Slaveholding neighbors make it a point to do their best to prevent anybody from giving them the needed information. The Slaveholder knows very well that when you have taught a man what are his natural rights, he will begin to inquire why he is deprived of them. He reads in his Bible that God has given the earth to the children of men; he knows himself to be a man's child, and he therefore asks, "Where is my portion of the Earth?" He perceives he has no interest in the soil, and has nothing which he can call his own; that he is a Slave, not the Slave of a particular individual, but of the State.

The Hon. Cassius M. Clay, of Kentucky, himself formerly an extensive "owner" of Slaves, whom he had emancipated, in an address to the Slaveholders of his native State, said:—

"No! it is you who repress Education and Moral instruction — who dare deny the Holy Scriptures to the poor Slaves and all the non-Slaveholding White Millions of this accursed South — who sear the conscience and imbrute men to violate female innocence and murder infants! The fact is on record, in divers places, that you have been the cause of the committal of those crimes upon the Wives and Daughters of the friends of the poor Slave and caused the perpetrators to run off." Again: "Under your infamous Statute, 2d and 3d Sections, the liberty of over 700,000 of the native White population of the State is insidiously endangered. Whenever a man is true enough to the instincts of nature to refuse to become your watch-dog, some one of your number — and you are not wanting in that virtue — has only to swear that he *suspects* him of an intent to induce a Slave to runaway, and the poor devil is thrown into prison to die, or forced to sign the warrant of his own exile from his native land." Again: "Shall the poor man have no home? *Shall*

FLOGGING THE NEGRO. (See page 206.)

the Sanctity of the Bedchamber and the Hearthstone be known only to the wealthy Slaveholder? Shall the laborer's Wife and Children have no resting-place where brutal intruders dare not come? Where are the sons of the Boones and the Kentons? Does no rusty rifle rest upon the rack, to teach our tyrants that, among freemen, the cabin and the palace are alike inviolable."

Mr. Clay, in a Lecture on the "Despotism of Slavery," delivered in the Tabernacle, New York, said: "Citizens of New York, where are your rights South of Mason and Dixon's Line?" (that is, South of the State of Delaware.) "Where is your right to petition? Does the Senate at this day respect it and give you a hearing? Has not the Postoffice been violated, and letters of friendship and affection rudely broken open *by those who are in search of information against the lovers of liberty and haters of oppression.*"

Judge Hall, at the opening of the United States Circuit Court, Canandaigua, New York, in June, 1855, in his remarks to the Grand Inquest, alluded to this infamous practice, and charged that no man, whether in the employ of the Government or not, had any right whatever except in case of "dead letters," to open a letter intrusted to the Mail, or to detain such letter. Judge Hall was at the head of the Postoffice Department during the Administration of Millard Fillmore. The same infamous practice was pursued during the Administration of Franklin Pierce, and will be continued under the Administration of James Buchanan.

The *New York Tribune*, in June, 1855, said: "The United States Government, as the reader is aware, has an army of employées called 'Mail Agents,' who travel with the mails on our leading thoroughfares. The Mails go under their guardianship, and it has heretofore been supposed that the people were gaining something by the arrangement in the way of security to their communications. But this appears to be an entire mistake. These Mail Agents have free access to the mails; and not only so, but it seems they take the liberty of *opening letters whenever they see fit to do it.* If Mail Agents are in the habit of opening letters, may they not sometimes *pocket the contents?* They may as well do it as to break open a letter and copy it."

A few days later (June 23, 1855) the *Tribune* said: "There is certainly an immense number of letters mailed which never reach their destination ; scarcely a day passes that we do not at this office obtain letters stating that money has been remitted to us which we have never received. A business firm writes us from Illinois : ' We consider the management of the Postoffice past all endurance. Our own losses from stolen letters during the last year amount to $2,685.'"

Every Postmaster acts as a Spy and a Judge Lynch on every document that comes into his hands. Nor is this system confined to the Slave States and Territories. You will find it, as we have, to our great cost and injury, in New Jersey, Pennsylvania, Indiana, Illinois, and other States of the "*free* North." But the worst of all the "*free* States" is New Jersey, because the most Pro-Slavery.

In the city of Louisville, when, on a recent occasion, an attempt was made to assert the "rights" of the working-classes of Kentucky, the men who made the attempt were met with the Revolver and Bowie-knife.

The "people" of Kentucky, if permitted to breathe free air, would be brave and generous ; but Slavery has broken their spirit, and they now wink at crimes and outrages which would make savages stare with astonishment.

When Mr. Brady, the Lexington schoolmaster, was surrounded — in December, 1855 — by a gang of ferocious poor whites, all burning with a desire to "taste the blood of an Abolitionist," and peering through the windows to see that he did not escape, there were in the same apartment with him, the School Committee, four Members of the City Council, the City Marshal, and the Mayor. They urged him to sneak out of the back-door! He asked them whether it was not their business, in such a case, to protect him? They shrank from the task, and replied, that "it would cost them their lives if they did;" in other words, it would be dangerous to do their duty! Mr. Brady bravely, nobly, manfully told them, that he scorned to fly when he had committed no crime; so he went forth to meet the mob; and the mob, taking advantage of his defenceless condition, wreaked their cowardly vengeance upon him. The "chivalrous" officers did sneak out of the back door; but the "trembling Abolitionist" fearlessly confronted the mob. What a contrast does this present! Alas for Kentucky! (See p. 166.)

It having been reported that the Abolitionists of New England intended to establish an Anti-Slavery paper at Lexington, on account of the outrage on Brady, the Louisville *Times*, the leading "Democratic paper" of the place, replied as follows:—

"Those that commence the paper had better get all the hair taken off their heads, so that the Lexington people will only have the trouble of taking off their skin."

Barbarians have a natural antipathy to a stranger. Should one by chance come among them, he is looked upon as a "natural enemy" and killed, perhaps cooked, without further ceremony. There is some sense in the custom, if it be admitted that barbarism is a good thing, and worth keeping in repair. Strange eyes and "foreign tongues" are bad for abuses of any kind. So that those who thrive by them, or think they do, may well be jealous of such prying intrusions. The Slaveholding Democracy of the Slave States and Territories share to a considerable degree in this suspiciousness. They don't like spies about them, and there are thousands of instances of their dealing with lookers-on who had unpleasantly excited their notice, in a way that would have done no discredit to a Feejee Islander.

In North Carolina, to teach a Slave to read or write, is punished with thirty-nine lashes or imprisonment, if the offender be a "*free* Negro;" but if a white man, then with a fine of $200. The reason for this " law," assigned in its preamble, is, that teaching Slaves to read and write "*tends to dissatisfaction in their minds, and to produce insurrection and rebellion.*" The patrols search every hut for books or prints of any kind. Bibles and Hymn-books are looked upon as "most dangerous to the welfare and happiness of the domestic institutions" (Slavery and Polygamy) " of the South."

In 1853, the Mechanics of Concord, Cahawus county, without consulting the Slaveholders of the place, held a meeting to discuss their own business, and consult on matters of mutual interest; to discover particularly what their position was in relation to the colored and party-colored population about them. Their great complaint was that wealthy men, who had "*Slave mechanics,*" *were in the habit of underbidding them on contracts, and that "free Negroes" who bound their own bodies, to be security to white men for Money loaned, came into the county and took away business that belonged to the white laborers.* The principal speaker at the meeting was a young man of more than ordinary intelligence, to which he united the irascibility of his countrymen. He spoke in favor of resolutions to employ no Slaves or " free Negroes" as journeymen while whites could be had. This young man was unmarried but supported an aged Mother.

The next day the meeting was discussed by the " influential" men. The speeches and resolutions were condemned. Mark this, *by men who were not mechanics, and who had no interest in common with mechanics.* The leader in this movement was a fiery fellow, entirely unworthy the confidence of the community — a " Nigger speckylator," illiterate and unreasonable — as an evidence of which we mention the fact that about that time he nearly killed with a knife, while in a passion, his brother-in-law, whom he cut severely many times before he could be made to comprehend that he had hold of the wrong man, and that his antagonist had escaped. This person advised to send the chief speaker out of the country— he was a dangerous man to have about. This course was agreed upon, and one of "the *freest*, most independent, *self-willed* laborers on the face of the globe" had to leave his home on the demand of a "Nigger-driver," because he dared talk as if he had "rights."

In South Carolina, it is declared that " having Slaves taught to write, or suffering them to be employed in writing, may be attended with great inconveniences." It is therefore enacted that " all and every person or persons whatsoever, who shall teach or cause any Slave or Slaves to be taught to write, or shall use or employ any Slave as a scribe, in any manner of writing whatsoever, hereafter taught to write, every such person or persons shall for every such offence, forfeit the sum of $500." (*Brevard's Digest*, p. 243.) Again: "All assemblies of Slaves, free Negroes, Mulattoes, and Mestizoes" (mixtures of white and Indian), "whether composed all of any such description of persons, or of all or any of the same, and of a portion of white persons *met together for the purpose of mental instruction,* are declared to be an unlawful meeting, and the Officers dispersing such unlawful assemblage may inflict such corporal punishment, not exceeding thirty-nine lashes, as they may judge necessary. It shall not be lawful for any number of Slaves, free Negroes, Mulattoes, or Mestizoes, even in company with white persons, to meet together for the purpose of mental instruction, either before the rising of the sun, or after the going down of the same."—(*Brevard's Digest*, p. 254.)

The Southern Presbyterian, published at Charleston, S. C., thinks that "if Slaves are taught to read the Bible, they may read other books; and then they may rebel; and *our* Wives and *our* Daughters may fall victims to *their* vengeance." Where did the party-colored population of the Slaveholding States come from?

A short time since the Methodist Conference of South Carolina appointed a Missionary to "labor among the colored people," but it was soon "suppressed by the citizens." A Committee was appointed, who addressed a letter to the Missionary requesting him to desist. This was backed up by a remonstrance to the same effect, signed by James S. Pope and 76 others. The document argued at length the incompatibility of Slavery with the "mental and religious instruction of Slaves." Hear them:

"Verbal instruction," said they, "will increase the desire of the Slave population to learn. We know of upward of a dozen *Negroes* in the neighborhood of Cambridge (S. C.), who can now read, some of whom are members of your societies at Mount Lebanon and New Salem. Of course, they will supply themselves with Bibles, Hymn-books, and Catechisms. Open the Missionary sluice, and the current will swell in its gradual onward advance. We thus expect that a progressive system of improvement will be introduced, or will follow, from the nature and force of circumstances, and, if not checked — though they may be shrouded in sophistry and disguise — will ultimately revolutionize our Civil institutions."

The document referred to the "Laws of the State," and hoped that "South Carolina is yet true to her *vital* interests." The missionary enterprise was at once relinquished.

The Editors of *The Mountaineer*, published at Greenville, said: "The opposition to the late Home Missionary among us comprised the great body of our most respectable citizens."

In Georgia, if a white man teach a *free* Negro or Slave to read or write, he is fined $500, and imprisoned at the discretion of the Court. If the offender be a "colored" man, bond or *free*, he may be fined or whipped, at the discretion of the Court. Of course, a father may be flogged for teaching his own child. "No congregation, or company of Negroes, shall, under any *pretence of divine worship*, assemble themselves, contrary to the act regulating patrols." (*Prince's Digest*, p. 342.)

No poor white laborer dare show any sympathy with Anti-Slavery sentiments; if suspected of having a pitiful heart toward the Slave, he is marked and doomed; there is no rest for him till he finds it in a "*free* State." And as the majority of that class can not readily command the means to move their families into a "land of freedom," the condition of remaining where they are is silence on the subject of Emancipation and opposition to all forms of Anti-Slavery.

We have known of Northern men strongly opposed to Slavery, whose business called them temporarily to the South, who have bought one or more Slaves, in order to quiet the suspicions and gain the confidence of the oppressors who give "character and tone" to Society. Northern Anti-Slavery clergymen become Slaveholders with the design, apparently, of disproving the sincerity of their former opinions.

It is well known to those who know the South that Slaveholders resort to various tyrannical methods to free their neighborhoods of poor whites, especially if they show any discontent with Slavery. If they can not buy the little property owned by those poor people, they often set up false claims to it, or find some pretended ground of legal action against them; and as the Courts always favor the Slaveholder, the result is always disastrous to the helpless and friendless non-Slaveholder. Instead of being, as *The Washington Star* affirms, "the *freest*, most independent, and *self*-willed laborers on the face of the globe," they are the most dependent and obsequious white men in the world, and as much the objects of pity as the Slaves themselves. They are too ignorant and too poor to escape from their degradation, and remain quietly where they are only by loving and hating what the fierce, unreasoning Slaveholder loves and hates.

The Rev. Charles C. Jones, of Georgia, addressing "Masters," says: "You have the power to open the kingdom of Heaven or to shut it, to your Slaves." (*Religious Instruction of the Negroes*, p. 158.)

The Georgia, a prominent journal of the State, commenting on the deplorable condition of the non-Slaveholding white population, says: " By reference to the last Census, it will be seen that between 1840 and 1850 the rate of increase of the entire white population was a little under 28 per cent. During the same time the rate of increase of the number of adult Citizens in the State, unable to read, was over 34½ per cent. It is only by distinctly observing this rapid increase that we see the facts in their appalling magnitude. This vast army of ignoramuses *will be more than doubled in thirty years!* At the rate of the increase shown by the Census, it will have within its ranks, in the year 1900, *one hundred and seventy thousand* of the citizens of Georgia. This is the rigid result yielded by the figures. The boy of to-day, who may live to old age, will see the time when this host of unlettered, uncared-for multitude in our State will have grown to over *two hundred thousand*, unless an entirely new and effective effort be made to drive this sore evil from the land."

The nature and value of *that* " liberty" which a community enjoys in conjunction with Slavery, is thus frequently illustrated by the Slaveholders themselves, but seldom more forcibly than in the recent outbreak at Mobile, Alabama. Here is one of the Slaveholding mob's own version of the affair and its provocation:

"MOBILE, *Saturday, August* 16, 1856.

" There has been great excitement here to day, which had its origin in the sale of Abolition books by a stationery firm in this city. The name of the firm in question is *Strickland & Co.;* the individual members being Wm. Strickland and Edwin Upson. The only charge against them was the selling of books that were regarded as of an incendiary character, *inasmuch as they favored the freedom of the Slave.* This, however, was more than our people could submit to, and a Committee of Five of our Citizens was accordingly formed, who waited upon the individuals above alluded to, and ordered them to leave the city in five days. As soon as the action of the Committee became generally known, the excitement rapidly increased, and the parties, for fear of more desperate measures against them, fled the City in the most secret manner possible. The firm was in the enjoyment of a large business, and have heretofore been liberally patronized by our Citizens."

It is not pretended that these booksellers had violated any law; if they had, there was no need of a "Committee of Five" to "order them to leave the city in five days." On the contrary, they would have been prosecuted, arrested, and held to answer for their offence. They were only charged with "selling books that were regarded as of an incendiary character, inasmuch as they favored the freedom of the Slave." Jefferson's Notes on Virginia, might suffice to sustain this allegation. It was charged that they sold such books to Slaves, nor even to "*free* Negroes." Of course, they only sold to such Citizens as wanted books of that character; had there been no buyers, there would have been no sale. And for thus supplying "*free* Citizens of Alabama" with such books as they desired and chose to read, in violation of no law and no right, these booksellers were hunted like wolves from Alabama, and had their business broken up.

The Mobile Tribune, of August 17, 1856, gives the following list of "gentlemen" present at the meeting: "Dr. J. C. Nott, the Hon. John Bragg, the *Rev. W. Hawthorne*, Dr. J. H. Woodcock, Dr. H. S. Leverett, Wm. F. Cleaveland, A. Brooks, Joseph Sewell, the Hon. A. P. Bagby (Minister to Russia, in 1848), A. G. Humphreys, the Hon. J. W. Lesesne, Dr. G. A. Ketchum, Wm. Boyles, Esq., J. H. Daughdrill, John Scott, Jacob Magee, the *Rev. Dr. F. A. Ross*, Joseph E. Murrill, R. C. Macy, the Hon. E. S. Dargan, Wm. Harris, John Hall, Goddard Bailey, S. C. Stramler, John Mann.

"The examining Committee was composed of the following gentlemen: The Hon. J. W. Lesesne, Dr. J. C. Nott, the

Hon. John Bragg, Dr. J. H. Woodcock, J. S. Secor, Esq. The Committee who were appointed to wait on Messrs. Strickland & Co., were Dr. J. C. Nott, Dr. H. S. Leverett, W. F. Cleveland, Esq."

To the *Rev. W. Hawthorne,* Messrs. Strickland & Upson are indebted for the loss of their business, he having acted the spy and informer. A pretty "follower of Christ," to be sure!

The night following that on which Strickland & Upson were examined, immense columns of smoke were seen issuing from the chimneys of several of the bookstores.

CHAPTER II.

IN Louisiana, the law declares, that using language in any public discourse, from the bar, bench, stage, or pulpit, or in any other place, or in any private conversation, or making use of any signs or actions having a tendency to produce discontent among the *free* colored population, or among the Slaves, or who shall be knowingly instrumental in bringing into the State any paper, book, or pamphlet, having the like tendency, shall, on conviction, be punished with imprisonment or death, at the discretion of the Court.

The Pro-Slavery Churches, North, "fear" that if Emancipation of the Slaves took place it would be followed up by Amalgamation! just as if Slaveholders would be getting married to "*black* girls." This argument is certainly paying a fine compliment to "black women" and a very poor one to white ones. "Amalgamation!"— why, a Slaveholder would no sooner give up amalgamation than he would his life. There is no adjunct of Slavery that he so much fancies as amalgamation. Where did the party-colored population of the Slave States come from? The various shades of complexion everywhere tell the story. The very first "Act" of Slavery was to abolish the Marriage relation, and the result is that we dare not reveal the horrors of that infamous concern, called the "Peculiar Institution."

The slang about amalgamation generally proceeds from men who have its odor strong upon them. Whoever needs any confirmation of its truth has only to trace out the origin of a half dozen of the "colored" sons of the "cursed seed of *Ham*" nearest him. Of the whole class, now in the United States, there is no man who doubts that ninety-nine of every hundred of the white fathers are Slaveholders, or at least vehemently hostile to Abolition. Every city in the Slaveholding States and Territories is checkered with half-bleached and three-quarters-bleached "Niggers," while the birth of one in an Anti-Slavery community is as rare as that of an Albino.

It is common to suppose that the creeds of the Slaveholding Churches are "derived from the Bible," that this is a "symbolical book." No mistake could be greater. They are founded in the Slaveholder; he is the hope of these Churches, North and South, and Slavery is "translated out of the original tongues" and "appointed to be read in the Churches."

The word "Servant" is a most convenient term in the "religious instruction" of Slaves, as it brings them within all the Scriptural injunctions respecting Servants, and by keeping out of view Human chattelization, it adroitly places, as we shall see, the Slave *on the same level with every Man who receives Wages or a salary*. Thus, in one of the Sermons composed by Bishop Meade, of the Episcopal Church, for Slaves—"to be read to them," and "preached to them," they are told, "You must let your light shine as *Servants*. Some of us must always be *Servants*. The richest and best man among us must be a *Servant* to some one. Every clerk in a store is a *Servant*. Every lawyer is a *Servant* to the men who employ him. Every minister of the Gospel is a *Servant* to his people, and every physician a *Servant* to his patient."

Little, indeed, can the Slave be raised above idiocy, if he does not perceive and despise such contemptible sophistry. His grievance is, not that he works for another, but that, unlike the lawyer, the physician, and the preacher himself, he works *without pay* and under the lash.

The abhorred word "Slave" is rarely mentioned by the preachers. Circumlocution is resorted to. They seek to escape a guilty confession; they call it by the reputable name of "Servant," instead of the accursed word "Slave." As the Syrian queen, about to perpetrate a deed which would consign her character to infamy, called it by the sacred name of "marriage" and committed it, so the "ministers of the Gospel of Jesus Christ," speaking of the most guilty and cruel of all relations between man and man, seek to avert their eyes from the act, and to pacify the remonstrances of conscience against every participation in the atrocious crime, by hiding under the reputable word "Servant;" but the day is coming when God will lay bare their hypocrisy.

"Now," continues this precious Doctor of Divinity, "when correction is given you, you either deserve it, or you do not deserve it. But whether you really deserve it or not, it is your duty, and Almighty God requires, that you bear it patiently. You may, perhaps, think this is hard doctrine; but if you consider it rightly, you must needs think otherwise of it. Suppose, then, that you deserve correction, you can not but say that it is just and right you should have it. Suppose you do not, or, at least, if you do not deserve so much or so severe a correction for the fault you have committed, you, perhaps, have escaped a great many more, and are at last paid for all. Or, suppose you are quite innocent of what is laid to your charge, and suffer wrongfully in that particular thing, is it not possible you may have done some other bad thing which was never discovered, and that Almighty God, who saw you doing it, would not let you escape without punishment one time or another? And ought you not in such a case to give glory to Him, and be thankful that he would rather punish you in this life for *your* wickedness than destroy *your* souls for it in the next life?"

The preacher seems doubtful whether it will satisfy his

"colored brother," writhing under the lash, or sinking under his labor, to be told that he is only a "Servant," like the richest and the best man in the country; hence the "power of religious faith" is called in to produce passive obedience, and he is told again that *God* has made him what he is — that *God* has placed him where he is. Hear him:

> "All things whatsoever ye would that men should do unto you, do ye even so unto them; that is, do by all mankind just as you would desire they should do by you, if you were in their place, and they in yours. Now, to suit the rule to your particular circumstances, suppose you were Masters and Mistresses, and had *Servants* under you, would you not desire that your *Servants* should do their business faithfully and honestly, as well when your back was turned as while you were looking over them? Would you not expect that they should take notice of what you said to them? that they should behave themselves with respect toward you and yours, and be as careful of everything belonging to you as you would be yourselves? You are *Servants:* do, therefore, as you would wish to be done by, and you will be both good *Servants* to your Masters and to *God*, who requires this of you, and will reward you well for it, if you do it for the sake of conscience, in obedience to His commands. Take care that you do not fret or murmur, grumble or repine at your condition, for this would not only make your life uneasy, but would greatly offend *God*. Consider that it is not yourselves, it is not the people that own you, it is not the men that have brought you to it, but it is the will of *God*, who hath by his providence made you *Servants*, because, no doubt, he knew that condition would be best for you in this world, *and help you the better toward Heaven*, if you would but do your duty in it. So that any discontent at your not being free, or rich, or great, as you see some others, is quarrelling with your heavenly Master, and finding fault with God himself, *who hath made you what you are*. If others will run the hazard of their souls, they have a chance of getting wealth and power, of heaping up riches, and enjoying all the ease, luxury, and pleasure, their hearts long after. But you can have none of these things; so that, if you sell your souls for the sake of what poor matters you can get in this world, you have made a very foolish bargain indeed. Brethren, beware of temptation."

We find the South Corolina Episcopal Church declaring, through Bishop Freeman's Tract, that "Slavery, as it exists at the present day, is agreeable to the order of Divine Providence." And Slavery of the present day virtually denies the Bible to 4,500,000 of the colored and party-colored natives of the country. But let them be comforted, their want of the Bible is a matter of no consequence. Listen to the consoling words of the preacher :

"The sun is sometimes shut up behind a cloud, so that you can not see it : you can not point where it is. Yet you can see all around you light enough to answer your purposes. *You work by that light"* (that is, a Pro-Slavery Christianity). *"You enjoy that light, and for all common things"* (that is, Niggers) *" it answers just as well as if there was no cloud,* and the sun was pouring down upon you. It is just so about the Bible. You can not read. The Bible is hid from *you* just like the sun behind the cloud."

Surely there are Bibles enough in New York, Boston, Philadelphia, Cincinnati, and the other Union-saving Cities of the Republic, to give light behind the cloud. Let the Bible Societies cease to waste the people's money in printing more. It is sickening to see men styling themselves " ministers of the Gospel of Jesus Christ," instead of sympathizing with the poor Slave and condemning his grievous wrongs, resorting to all sorts of tricks, and sophisms, and falsehoods, to make him believe that his privations and sufferings proceed not from cruel laws and wicked men, but from *God* himself, and that " religious privileges," which are deemed of " inestimable value" to white men, are not needed by the Slaves and "*free* blacks."

Mrs. Douglas, a pious lady of Norfolk, Virginia, not embracing this " doctrine" about the Bible shining behind the cloud, undertook to teach some "*free* colored children" to read, and was committed to Jail. As *God* enslaves the "race of *Africa*," or " cursed seed of *Ham*," so, perhaps, *He* imprisoned this lady, and therefore her imprisonment was, like Slavery, " just and holy." Mrs. Douglas suffered imprisonment, not because it was actually a crime to teach a "*free* colored child" to read, *but because intelligence is dangerous to Slavery.* It was deemed necessary to make an example of her to deter all future offenders. Judge Baker, in vindication of the "justice of the sentence," said:

> "In *good sense* and *sound morality*, my discretionary power to imprison for six months or less does not authorize a mere minimum punishment. Your guilt is beyond a doubt, and there are many aggravating circumstances. Therefore, as a terror to those who acknowledge no rule of action but their own *evil* will and pleasure, and in vindication of the *justness* of the laws, the judgment of the Court is, that you be imprisoned for a period of one Month in the City Jail."

On the imprisonment of Mrs. Douglas every Anti-Slavery heart in the "*free* States" cried "Shame!" "Shame!!" "Shame!!!" The Slaveholders then offered to release her on condition that she would leave the State, &c. This, with true nobility of soul, she utterly refused to do, preferring to suffer the full penalty of the "law," though her jailers hoped she would leave the city. It was then (February 9, 1854) that *The Norfolk Argus* said: "On this refusal becoming known all sympathy departed, and in the breast of every one rose a *righteous* indignation toward a person who would throw contempt in the face of the laws, and brave the imprisonment for the 'cause of humanity.'"

Such a burlesque of all that is truly enlightened and just can not be improved by any comment. It is an admirable illustration of the significance attached to that clause in the Declaration of Independence which guaranties "life, liberty, and the pursuit of happiness" to every American citizen, whether applied to Mrs. Douglas or the "*free* colored children." It explains the fact that of the 971,770 white or non-"colored" sons and daughters of Virginia, there are 86,180 adults who can not read.

We have another Sermon about the Bible, and a queer one it is. How could that be morally right which renders obedience to Divine command Impossible? How could Slaves and "*free* blacks," forbidden to read, search the Scriptures? The late Rev. C. K. Nelson, of North Carolina (see chap. iii. of Part I., p. 78), answers the question. Taking the Bull by the horns, he has published a Sermon to Slaves, on the command itself! After showing the necessity of the Bible, its great excellency and the goodness of God in giving it, he comes to the passage—" Search the Scriptures." But they can not read; no matter, God does not command impossibilities. Hear him:

> "Brethren, it is not necessary you should know how to read to search the Scriptures. Don't your Master or Mistress read this book every morning and evening at prayers? Don't your minister read it at Church every Sunday? Can't you go there and search the Scriptures? Have you no young Master or Mistress who would read the Bible to you? Have you ever asked them? Brethren, God tells you to 'Search the Scriptures,' and God would not tell you to do so unless you could."

In the whole range of Pro-Slavery Theology, it would be difficult to match the cool impudence of this Sermon. In his last days, Mr. Nelson appeared to have an instinctive dread of the future, and hence his remarks, given at page 78. If the Sermons and Catechisms "prepared for Slaves" and "*free* blacks," are wretchedly adapted to win their faith to a religion which, instead of condemning, approves and sanctifies their wrongs, still less are the men who minister to the Slaves and "*free* blacks," fitted to attract their confidence and affection. With very rare exceptions, they are themselves dealers in Human flesh, and identified in feeling and interest with their brother Slaveholders.

Bishop Polk, brother of Ex-President James K. Polk, was lately lauded in *The New York Observer* for the excellent management of his plantation. The Hon. Erastus Brooks, the principal Editor and proprietor of the *New York Express*, visited, in 1853, the plantation of this "eminent Churchman," and was so much delighted with its management, that we can scarcely avoid wishing that, instead of laboring as an Editor to strengthen and extend Slavery, he could personally experience its pleasures under Episcopal sway. The Bishop, it would seem, "*prefers raising his Stock to buying it.*" He had, according to Mr. Brooks, "*ninety children under ten years of age.*" For these lambs of his flock the Bishop established no school in which they could be taught to read the word of God. No spelling-books, no hymn-books, no Sunday-school books, were theirs. But, says Mr. Brooks, "The young ones eat hominy and possum-fat, sweetened with sugar, *plentifully* supplied, and, with an appetite that one might envy."

That the Bishop's lambs are well-fattened for Market, there can be no doubt. "*Eighteen Children had been born upon the plantation in less than a year, and a Child twenty-four hours old is worth* $100." A crop of Babies, in less than a year, worth $1,800 is rather a novel source of revenue for "a Servant of Jesus Christ," but it fully warrants a *liberal* supply of hominy and sugar, especially as these *black* lambs, under ten years old, "are worth about $12 per pound."

The Rev. Prelate is too good a manager to let his Mothers waste their time in taking care of *their* Children: "The Children have their Nurseries, where the *very old* take care of the *very young*, while the Mothers are at work on the plantation." Thus the Slaves who can not labor are turned to account as Nurses, while the Mothers are sent to the field. "The Bishop's Slaves, *about* 340 in number," Mr. Brooks assures us, "fare sumptuously."

> "Oh, 'tis den we are so happy, when we all sit a watchin'
> As de last piece go from de bones ob de possum."

Bishop Polk, according to *The New York Observer*, "rules his Slaves in obedience to Christ's command." The Right Reverend Father *in* God, Leonidas Polk, Bishop of the Protestant Episcopal Church of Louisiana, therefore, "is a

Servant of Christ." The Bishop of course, breeds and fattens them for the Market, in pursuance of a command from the same authority. Happy is it when "religious duty" coincides with "pecuniary interests." Who can fail to see and feel what powerful influence in *hastening* the Abolition of Slavery in Louisiana the Gospel must exert, when preached as it is throughout the State by a Right Rev. Father *in* God, holding "about 340" of his fellow-immortals in abject bondage, and deriving an annual addition to his wealth of $1,800 from his crop of Babies, in addition to the unpaid labor of *their* Parents?

With no exceptions worthy of consideration, the Churches, "ministers and people," are banded together in maintaining the Satanic traffic. Yes, the "servants *of* Christ," and the servants of Satan are united, heart and soul, in spreading the horrors and abominations of Slavery. Thus we find the "religious Press" urging the establishment of Slavery in Kansas.

The "evangelical" Stock-raisers forego, for "a week," the services of their "colored sisters in Christ," and permit them to become Mothers, and then, instead of knocking them on the head, "mercifully raise the helpless and Infant offspring," and are rewarded for their *benevolence* by the value of the "property" thus acquired.

What estimate can a true disciple of Christ have of the piety of a teacher, however "venerable" he may be in years, who would torture the truths of Revelation to support open Robbery and universal Prostitution?

The House of Bishops, of the Episcopal Church, now, January 1, 1857, consists of the following Doctors of Divinity. The stars attached indicate Slave States and Territories:—

    The Right Rev. Dr. Brownell, of Connecticut,
      Right Rev. Dr. Meade, of Virginia,*
      Right Rev. Dr. H. U. Onderdonk, of Pennsylvania,
      Right Rev. Dr. B. T. Onderdonk, of New York,

Right Rev. Dr. John Henry Hopkins, of Vermont,
Right Rev. Dr. Smith, of Kentucky,*
Right Rev. Dr. M'Ilvane, of Ohio,
Right Rev. Dr. Doane, of New Jersey,
Right Rev. Dr. Otey, of Tennessee,*
Right Rev. Dr. Kemper, of Wisconsin,
Right Rev. Dr. M'Coskry, of Michigan,
Right Rev. Dr. Leonidas Polk, of Louisiana,*
Right Rev. Dr. Delancy, of Western New York,
Right Rev. Dr. Whittingham, of Maryland,*
Right Rev. Dr. Elliot, of Georgia,*
Right Rev. Dr. Lee, of Delaware,*
Right Rev. Dr. Johns, of Virginia,*
Right Rev. Dr. Eastburn, of Massachusetts,
Right Rev. Dr. Chase, of New Hampshire,
Right Rev. Dr. Clark, of Rhode Island,
Right Rev. Dr. Cobb, of Alabama,*
Right Rev. Dr. Hawks, of Missouri,*
Right Rev. Dr. Freeman, of Texas,*
Right Rev. Dr. Boone, Missionary Bishop,
Right Rev. Dr. Southgate, Missionary Bishop,
Right Rev. Dr. Potter, of Pennsylvania,
Right Rev. Dr. Burgess, of Maine,
Right Rev. Dr. Upfold, of Indiana,
Right Rev. Dr. Green, of Mississippi,*
Right Rev. Dr. Payne, Missionary Bishop,
Right Rev. Dr. Rutledge, of Florida,*
Right Rev. Dr. Williams, of Connecticut,
Right Rev. Dr. Whitehouse, of Illinois,
Right Rev. Dr. Davis, of South Carolina,*
Right Rev. Dr. Atkinson, of North Carolina,*
Right Rev. Dr. Kipp, of California,
Right Rev. Dr. Scott, of Oregon,
Right Rev. Dr. Lee, of Iowa,
Right Rev. Dr. H. Potter, of New York.

The Right Reverend Father of the North echoes the sentiments of the Right Reverend Father of the South. While Leonidas of Louisiana raises providentially accursed children of an inferior race, on his plantation, John Henry of Vermont exerts himself, in his diocese, to keep up the value thereof. The principal undertaking of Bishop Hopkins' book, "The American Citizen, his Rights and Duties," is to prove that it is the duty of each citizen to assist in returning fugitive slaves; and Bishop Polk writes to his fellow Bishops of the South, on the necessity of adopting more stringent measures against the "Abolitionists or infidels of the *North*."

Piety is, as a general thing, proportionate to the number of Slaves held by the "elect" brethren. If a saint in crape be twice a saint in lawn, a saint with a hundred Slaves may well take precedence in the path to *Heaven* of one that only owns fifty; and if a confessor rise to the possession of three hundred Slaves, the halo that irradiates his brow is enough to illuminate a whole Church, not to say a presbytery or a diocese. Nor must it be supposed that the "evangelical" Slaveholding "Churches of Jesus Christ" are only for the purity of the faith that hath been committed unto them. They exercise, also, a strict surveillance over the lives and conversations of Clergymen and Professors, and either correct gently lapses from "*pure* morality," or else cut off the offending member and cast it from them—as was done in the case of the "gross heresy and immorality" of the Rev. Mr. Boardman, by which he had shocked the saints of Beaufort, S. C.

The crime of dancing hath more than once exercised their anxious thoughts, and the offence of "profane stage-plays" is one that weigheth heavily on their hearts. "The posture suitable to be used in prayer" is another question which hath powerfully agitated their souls, and hath not been entirely set at rest yet. It is true that some of the more material of the discussions to which these "vital" matters have given rise have been held in the Northern States. But it has been generally on the frontier, where the "Southern brethren" are in strong force, and greatly influence, if they do not entirely control, the assembly of the good. There is plenty of mint, anise, and cummin tithed everywhere, as is well known to all; but we think the more zealous of the exactors of the tenths of these herbs will be found among the "Southern Christians" and their "South-side" brethren farther North.

An important question has lately been settled by the Lutheran Synod of Missouri. It touched a matter no less "vital" than the mode of distributing the "Sacramental-loaf" among the believers. The Godly were divided in opinion as to the point whether it were more orthodox to cut it or to break it. Grave doubts hung over that portion of the Vineyard, and there was a danger of schism and a divided Zion. The dispute was finally settled,—Slaveholder-like—in favor of the knife, on the ground that "breaking the bread was connected with the Popish Doctrine of the Real presence;" and this, although it was admitted that *breaking*, and not cutting, was the example set by Christ and the Apostles. We do not perceive, ourselves, the precise pertinency of the argument on which the decision was made, but we feel that we can leave this important matter in no better hands than those of the "eminent" Divines and "pious" Laymen, North and South, who have undertaken the "holy cause" of perpetuating the cancers of Slavery and Polygamy by hallowing them with the sanctions of Religion.

William Aiken, an Irish-American, of South Carolina, one of the present Members of Congress, and who came within two Votes of being elected Speaker of the House of Representatives, goes ahead of Bishop Polk as a trafficker in his fellowmen. He owns "about 1,300" of the unfortunate sons and daughters of the "race of *Africa*," or "cursed seed of *Ham*." They are "valued at $1,300,000." What a commentary on Republican institutions! So it is. The Irish-American traffickers in Men, Women, and Children, occupy seats in Congress, and make laws for "freemen." It is such glaring inconsistencies as this that induces "outside barbarians" to mock at the Republic. They can not see how supporters of the most shocking system of iniquity on the face of the earth can be honest in their "patriotic" speeches for freedom.

The Rev. Robert Fair, of Abbeville, South Carolina, argues in favor of giving the Bible to Slaves, as the best means of convincing them of the Divine authority of the institution of Human bondage. Hear him:—

"There is enough between the lids of the Bible upon the subject, fully impressed upon the mind and heart of the Slave by human and divine instrumentalities, to guaranty the stability and perpetuity of the institution of Slavery, without one line of legislation upon our part, looking to the accomplishment of such an end. So rooted and grounded are we in the faith of the entire Scriptural propriety of Slavery, from the fullness of the Bible upon the subject, we can not discard from the mind the belief, that it is by means of the teachings of his Word, in justification of the institution, operating by divine influence upon the heart of the Slave, and we may say of the Master too, the Almighty intended to secure its perpetuation; and we should trust him for the accomplishment of His purposes, and look alone to these means in hopes of maintaining the institution; for it is by them alone that it can be maintained."

We advise the "Rev. Robert *Fair*" to lose no time in procuring a copy of a little work published by M. W. Dodd, Broadway, near Broome Street, New York, entitled, "The Converted Murderer." By Rev. William Blood. (*See Revelation*, xxii. 15.)

In a Report from a Committee of the Synod of South Carolina and Georgia, printed in Charleston, we have the following opinion of Slave piety:—

"From long-continued and close observation, we believe that the Moral character and Religious condition of the Slaves is such that they may be justly considered the Heathen of this *Christian* country. * * * * * * * The influence of the *Negroes* upon the Moral and Religious interests of the whites is destructive in the extreme. We can not" (dare not) "go into detail. It is unnecessary. We make our appeal to universal experience. We are chained to a putrid Carcase; it Sickens and Destroys us. We have a millstone hanging about the neck of our Society to sink us deep in the Sea of Vice. *Our children are corrupted from their infancy; nor can we prevent it.* Many an anxious parent wishes that his children could be brought up beyond the reach of these corrupting influences. Nor are these influences confined to mere childhood. If that were all, it would be tremendous; but it follows us into youth, into manhood, and into old age."

What else could be expected, when we find that this same "Synod of South Carolina and Georgia" were, and are, traffickers in the blood and bones of their fellow-men? Here is the proof from *The Savannah* (Ga.) *Republican*, of the 23d March, 1855:—

"Also, at the same time and place, the following Slaves, to wit: Charles, Peggy, Antonet, Davy, September, Maria, Jenny, Isaac, &c., levied on as the property of Henry T. Hall, to satisfy a mortgage *fi. fa.*, issued out of the Supreme Court, in favor of the Board of Directors of the Theological Seminary of the Synod of South Carolina and Georgia, *vs.* said Henry T. Hall. Conditions, Cash. "C. O'NEAL, *Sheriff*."

An article of the creed of this very Committee, of the Synod it represents, and indeed of all the Soul-destroying and Child-corrupting Churches of the Slaveholding States, is, that "the Institution is of Divine appointment," and, as Bishop Freeman asserts, and the Churches respond, "No man is entitled to pronounce it wrong!" But it will be said, "This 'putrid carcase' consists of the *heathen*, not of the '*Christian* Slaves'—not those who have been 'baptized' and 'confirmed' and 'received the communion,' and 'committed to memory' the 'Catechism for Slaves.'" Then hear the Committee once more:—

"The offences of colored communicants against Christian character and Church order are very numerous, and frequently heinous. The discipline is difficult, wearisome, and unpleasant."

These "revelations," be it remembered, are not the "ravings of fanatical Abolitionists," but the solemn asseverations of Southern "evangelical" Clergymen and Laymen of the City of Charleston, South Carolina, the very hotbed and focus of Slavery propagandism and Cotton divinity; made by men who are themselves engaged in defending and upholding the accursed system and blessing it "in Name of the Father, the Son, and the Holy Ghost." They dread and deplore the contamination of *their* " white children," but show no compassion for *their* party-colored children, deprived by law of all conjugal and parental rights. They are zealous in sending Bibles to black, blackish-brown, brown, and peach-blossom colored "foreign heathen," but to the yellow, ashy-pale, and French-white heathen at home, the Bible is as a Sun hid behind a Cloud, and they need not its bright effulgence.

"There are," we are told, "very pious men indeed among the Southern clergy," but their piety seems never to prompt them to remove the "putrid carcase" from among them. They love the corpse; they behold it with delight; they hug and kiss it!—it is their cow, their bread, and their butter.* They acknowledge it to be " a Gift from *heaven*." They are anxious to transmit it to their white children, and fly into a passion with those who would fain relieve them of it. But it does, they admit, smell very bad, and injures their white children's health; and hence they go to work, not like sensible men, to bury it, but like a party of midnight conjurers, to disinfect it by certain religious incantations and strange Catechisms, and equally repugnant to common sense and the glorious Gospel of Jesus Christ.

Thomas Jefferson (the immortal penman of the Declaration of Independence), in a letter to M. Warville, Paris, February, 1788, speaking of the intercourse between "Master" and Slave, says: "The parent storms, the child looks on, catches

---

* Dr. Bowring, in his "Manners in China," says : " A dead body is an object of so little concern that it is sometimes not thought worth while to remove it from the spot where it putrifies on the surface of the earth. Often have I seen a corpse under the table of gamblers — often have I trod over a putrid body at the threshold of a door."

the lineaments of wrath, puts on the same airs in the circle of smaller Slaves" (see Engraving at the head of chap. i., of this Part) "gives loose to his worst passions; and, thus *nursed, educated, and daily exercised in tyranny, can not but be stamped by it with odious peculiarities.*"

The Hon. Lewis Summers, Judge of the General Court of Virginia, and a Slaveholder, said in a Speech before the Virginia Legislature, in 1832: " Lisping infancy learns the vocabulary of abusive epithets, and struts the embryo tyrant of its domain. The consciousness of '*superior* destiny' takes possession of his mind at its earliest dawning, and love of power and rule ' grows with his growth and strengthens with his strength.' Unless enabled to rise above the operation of those powerful causes, *he enters the world with miserable notions of self-importance, and under the government of an unbridled temper.*"

What a state of society that must be to afford opportunity to escape from the influence of which "gentlemen" send their children to foreign lands to be educated!

Well has it been said by *The True American*, published at Trenton, New Jersey, that " the greatest impediment to the success of the Anti-Slavery cause is the opposition to it by those men who profess to have been commissioned by heaven to go abroad and use their efforts for the mitigation of human wrong. This assertion, which appears so monstrous, will not surprise any one who lives among Slaveholders. Our conviction of its truth has been confirmed by extensive observation, North and South."

Sunday after Sunday, Church-members meet to listen to the garbled presentation of God's word, members of one Church, claiming one God as their Father, one Heaven, to which there is, according to Jesus Christ — but one strait and narrow way of entrance; yet here in the visible Church, divided, *black* from *white*, by a wooden fence, and on Sacrament days, after the white members had partaken of the "bread and wine," the party-colored members crawled through a little gate, left open only on that day, and came forward, ten or twelve at a time, to take the bread and wine.* We have listened to one of these "ministers of the Gospel" read the "Discipline" and explain the clause forbidding to Church-members the traffic in Slaves, by remarking that it referred to the *African* Slave Trade, but had no allusion to American Slavery, or to the exchange of Slaves already in bondage, and then proceed to an harangue of an hour's length on the sin of wearing jewelry and artificial flowers.

" As in water face answereth to face," so will Southern and Northern Pro-Slavery piety, in all religious denominations answer this picture. And this religion, the very embodiment of Atheistic selfishness, cruelty, and oppression, baptizes itself (what astounding blasphemy!) in the name of Him who came to proclaim liberty to the captives and opening the prison to them that are bound!

The Cincinnati (Ohio) *Christian Press*, a journal which vaunts itself as the especial champion of "Evangelical" Orthodoxy, while it brands the friends of the Slave, as "infidels" with whom no Christian can associate without being defiled, says:—

---

* *The New York Tribune* of December 6, 1855, speaking of the Churches of that City, says: "Each congregation seems to enjoy and desire only the most exclusive attendance of its own members and pew-holders; they do not literally post up a notice at the holy gate, prohibiting visitors, or any species of outsiders, from the sacred fold, but they do morally, and quite as effectively, the same thing. He must indeed be bold who ventures, a stranger and alone, into a great Church in this City; his nerves need to be well-balanced, and his temper under steady control." Such Churches need another Christ to die for them. They are dying for lack of the poor in the midst of them. The real Church, it seems, even in the nineteenth century of the Christian era, is to be found among "publicans and sinners." Not only has a " Church of Christ" no right to withdraw its worship and ordinances from the lowly, but by so doing it utterly destroys its own vitality.

"The external forms of religion, a compliance with which costs no sacrifice, receive from a large majority of its professors far more attention than the practical godliness which affords the only true evidence of a saving union with Christ. There is not one in ten of the professed followers of Christ who maintain a consistent regard of his requirements, and are governed by the principles of his gospel. Probably not one in fifty of those who profess to love Christ, and the souls of their fellow-men, feel any real practical interest in the salvation of sinners, or put forth any adequate efforts for their conversion. There is not one in twenty of those who pretend to preach the Gospel who declare the whole counsel of God, and who do not seek the praise of men more than the praise of God. The amount of money expended in building and decorating Churches, not for the purer worship of God, but the gratification of pride, exceeds a hundred-fold the amount contributed to give the blessings of an uncorrupted Gospel to the destitute, and to those who are perishing in ignorance and sin. The amount of talent and money expended for the propagation and support of denominational interests— in other words, sectarianism — exceeds a hundred-fold the amount expended for the dissemination of the essential saving doctrines of the Gospel. The Churches, for many years, have put forth vastly more effort for the unity of the Churches *in* sin than for their purification *from* sin. This is especially true in regard to the enormous sin of Slavery. *It is admitted and declared by the leading teachers of Religion, that if the Churches would purify themselves from the sin of Slavery, there is no other power that could sustain that sin, and it would speedily be removed from the land;* yet many leading men in the Churches, those who have the pre-eminence, oppose to the utmost all efficient measures for the removal of Slavery from the Churches. Hence the sacerdotal robes of the Churches are stained with blood of millions of Men, Women, and Children, in bondage under the yoke of oppression."

Now the opponents of Slavery affirm that the Churches and Ministry, whose portraits are thus sketched, are not the Churches and Ministry of Him who came to preach deliverance to the oppressed, but an arrant imposture — synagogues of Satan. At this *The Christian Press* waxes indignant, and affirms that, notwithstanding their manifold corruptions, "*they* are the Official representatives of Christ, having in *their* hands His commission, which endows them with authority of which *they* can not divest themselves." Which of these parties exhibits the spirit of the Nazarene, and which that of the Pharisees?

The Slaveholding Churches boast, with regard to the "heathen of foreign lands," of the "peculiar" advantages they enjoy by means of what they are pleased to call "an express revelation from *heaven*," forgetting that *they themselves are, in effect, these very heathen;* for, with all their "superior light," they instil into those whom they call "benighted heathen," the most despicable opinion of Human nature. They, to the utmost of their power, weaken and dissolve the universal tie that binds and unites mankind. They sacrifice their reason, their humanity, their Christianity, to an unnatural sordid gain. How can Churches and Missionary Boards, who traffic in Human flesh — who are steeped to the eyelids in the pollutions of Slavery, dare to offer the Bible to "foreign heathen"? How are they to "give the Bible to all the nations," while consenting to the withholding of Bibles from 4,500,000 of their fellow-men at home? How teach Christian marriage abroad, while they consent to and assist in its abrogation at home? How teach that "the Polygamy of the Mormon Church is of Satan," while they constantly practise, sanction, and sanctify it in their own Churches. How call "foreign heathen to repentance" for "their barbarity, their injustice, their violations of human rights, their spirit and their usages of caste, their concubinage, impurity, and lust," while they quietly and complacently sit down at the "Communion Table" with the same sins at home?

The fact is the Slaveholding Churches have tinkered the "foreign heathen" quite long enough to prove their utter impotency—heavenward. These Churches have become so perfectly coated with "professional piety" that they are "like unto whited sepulchres, which indeed appear beautiful outward, but are within full of dead men's bones and all uncleanness."

It is easy to wear a long face and make long prayers, and eat bread, and drink wine in the name of a "crucified Saviour." This is done by the greatest robbers and oppressors the world ever saw — by men who fatten on the unpaid toil of the outcast and imbruted Slave, and sell him on the Auction-block to raise Money with which to convert the "foreign heathen;" compassing Sea and Land to make Proselytes, and leaving them fifty-fold more the children of Perdition than they were before, by teaching them, in addition to all other vices which fester and grow under a spurious Christianity —

"To break the bondman's heart for bread,
Pour out the bondman's blood for wine;"

in confirmation of the infinite love manifested in that sublime death on Calvary, 1800 years ago. Conversion to such a Religion, instead of indicating any progress in the cause of Justice, Freedom, and Christianity, or furnishing any occasion for congratulation, is a sure sign of Moral degeneracy, Judicial blindness, and Pharisaical malignity.

On the 29th of November, 1856, "Thanksgiving Day," the Rev. George B. Cheever (Editor of a Religious Family Newspaper, called "*The Independent*," published weekly, by Joseph H. Ladd, at No. 22 Beekman st., New York), delivered, before a large Congregation, a most interesting discourse, taking for his text the 14th verse of the 29th chapter of Proverbs:

"*The King that faithfully judgeth the poor, his throne shall be established for ever.*"

In the course of his Sermon, the worthy Doctor said, that although it was not stated in the text that a nation that oppressed its poor, or does not faithfully judge them should not at any time prosper, but on the contrary, in the Word of God, it was admitted that for a season, even by means of oppression, there might be great apparent power, luxury, and riches, yet God demonstrated to us that the end thereof was death, and that such a nation was on the high road to perdition; the most striking example of which was given in the history of the Jews. The most pointed and tremendous illustration of the text might be found in the 22d and 34th chapters of the Prophecy of Jeremiah. In regard to these people, they became so in love with power, and of such insatiable avarice in the desire of turning their "Men servants" and "Maid servants" into Slaves and articles of property, whom they could hold at their pleasure and exact their service without hire; that they combined to introduce and establish in place of the system of freedom and *paid labor* which God had appointed, the system of Slavery which he had forbidden. They concocted and completed this enormous crime under the reign and guidance of Zedekiah, *the last King of Judah, and they had no sooner done it than the sentence of God's wrath followed, from which there was no reprieve, and in only three years time Jerusalem was burned with fire, and the whole people were swept into captivity or destroyed with sword and famine.*

The 22d chapter of Ezekiel and 5th chapter of Jeremiah were also cited in illustration of the text. (At this point a prominent member of the Church left his seat and bustled out of the Church, slamming the door as he left the house.) " Now although," said the speaker, "some may wish that all reference to such a subject as that of Slavery could be avoided on every such occasion as this (and would to God there were no such thing as Slavery, so that there never need be any occasion to mention it), *yet all must be compelled to acknowledge that the view of that subject which we find in God's word is God's own view in regard to it, and is put there for his creatures' guidance; and it is neither wise nor safe for us to hide ourselves from God's judgment on that or any other subject.* And after all our circuitous political turnings and windings, we shall have to present ourselves at the bar of God's word. It must come to that, for God is the judge, and promotion cometh neither from the east nor from the west, nor from the south; but God is the judge—he putteth down one and setteth up another. And although this is a sore spot for us, and the whole region of the sore very tender to the touch, and easily irritated, yet I will not think so poorly of an audience in the Church of the Puritans as to deem any apology necessary for presenting any of God's messages, historical or perspective. *It is the selfish pursuit of wealth, prosperity, and power, as ends and not means, with the neglect at first, and afterward the oppression, of the poor, the weak, and the unprotected, that has brought nearly every great Nation of the globe in turn to destruction.* Slavery has always been one of the producing causes of national poverty, though it has been ranked among the sources of national wealth; but Slavery is ignorance and poverty combined, and oppression added. The Roman Empire fell by this cause—the selfish luxury of the wealthy, and the frightful ignorance of the poor."

The 82d Psalm, against unjust governors and judges, nogether with the 94th, 74th, and 72d, was consulted in illustration of the text. The provision appointed in the word of God—the speaker said the faithful judgment and right government of the poor requires and comprises their Education in Religious knowledge, which is at the bottom of everything else, and is the only security and pledge of perseverance in any and every effort of benevolence that can be resorted to.

If the pulpits of the Northern States were supplied with true men—with men who really cared for the oppressed, they would produce a revolution more sublime than any which the world has yet witnessed. American Slavery could not last a year under such preaching. Heaven speed the day when every Pro-Slavery pulpit in the "*free* States" shall be sent to quarantine, and kept there—until their "owner" calls for them.

"If there is in the world," says a writer in a late number

of the *Revue des Deux Mondes,* " a great nation which has need to turn back upon itself and to sound by reflection the dangers of the future concealed beneath present prosperity, it is surely the United States of America. The great increase of their population, the boldness of their enterprises, the progress of their wealth, may doubtless dazzle the traveller who runs through them, and may bewilder themselves. Of such illusions there are abundant examples. In the political order, the equality of men has been proclaimed as the absolute basis, and, as it were, special prerogative of this Republic. *Alone among nations it pretends to follow this principle to the end, and yet to-day not only the maintenance but the extension and consecration of Slavery has become the pivot of its entire political movement.* This so shameful question agitates the elections, absorbs the press, and floats as a flag at the head of a party; and this party, which wishes to keep in eternal Slavery a whole race of Men, is the preponderant party! Within, it controls the Administration; without, it makes conquests of Territories, for the sole purpose of legalizing Slavery there, in order that this crime may be represented in Congress by so many additional members that it may secure a perpetual majority, and may become the palladium of the sanctuary of equality.

"And to arrive at this end, this party does not fear to favor aggressions which touch not merely feeble neighbors, but which, to a certain degree, infringe upon the interests, the ideas, the honor, even of European nations; so that, under the actual circumstances, a European war against America, whatever might be the cause or pretext of it, *would be likely to take on the character of a Monarchical crusade for the rights of Man against a Republic which disregards and oppresses them!* If these fundamental contradictions of this internal anarchy do not develop themselves in some exterior discord, if this contest of principles does not tend to manifest itself in events, then

12*

America must be a part of the world where facts and thoughts have no connection with each other — a state of things even more lamentable than would be revolutions from which it is saved at such an expense.

"In consequence of not having listened to Jefferson, America still drags this chain, growing daily still and still heavier — herself the Slave of Slaves. She proceeds in a course opposite to that of other nations, and notwithstanding the prodigies of productive industry which she exhibits, *she runs, with all steam up, headlong toward barbarism. It is impossible that in this mad course she will not dash against some rock which God will put before her.* Heart-rending delineations of American Slavery, which, obliged to defend itself against universal repulsion by atrocious laws, corrupts the family of the Master, teaches ferocity to his children" (see Engraving at the head of chap. i. of this Part), " and unsexes the heart of his wife, have found readers even here. This will be the first instance of a Republic maintaining itself by perverting morality at its source, and in the face of the common idea that the strength of Republics is in their morality. This, too, will be the first time that a State has set itself to run counter to the movements of the whole world without being trodden under foot. May the voices, as yet but too few, which raise themselves in the United States against this scourge, grown now almost irresistible, be better listened to."

The French writer, quoted above, has missed the most alarming symptom in the case. It has insinuated itself into the heart's blood of the Churches, North and South. It has diffused its poisonous and disorganizing leaven through all the great institutions of benevolence. It subjects the religious books, tracts, and all other publications, to a Pro-Slavery censorship, and is constantly attempting to gag the few Pulpits whose occupants have the courage to speak "a seasonable word for freedom."

The preachers, with rare exceptions, refuse to say anything about Slavery or political wickedness. They complain that it makes them nervous and spoils their dinner. In their prayer-meetings the subject of *American* oppression is never alluded to, because they " never heard of such a thing as Slavery or oppression in the United States!" Ah, they did, indeed, sometimes in India, and the South Sea Islands, and other places in distant heathen regions, where the missionary work was going on, but not in " Christian America," for this was too near home, and too political. It is easy and popular to preach about idolatry and persecution, and distress among " the heathen of the *old* world," and speak about " breaking their chains," and they sing:

> " Go to many a tropic isle,
> In the bosom of the deep,
> Where the skies for ever smile,
> And the oppressed for ever weep."

This is very proper, but to talk about Slavery and idolatry, and the oppressed in the United States and Territories, only rouses up opposition and wrath, and makes " some people" nervous, and "grieves the Spirit of God, and prevents Revivals of Religion." So the iniquity is shielded, is concealed from exposure, and all mention of it is abhorred. The preachers do in effect make Christ the minister of sin; and in forbidding the manifestation of this fearful system of wickedness, as God's Word condemns it, and in exciting men's prejudices and aversion against all reference to it, they keep the people in the dark in regard to it, and thus prevent that repentance on account of it, on the part of the people, which would forbid its extension, procure God's forgiveness, and secure the country from ruin.

Every reason that demanded or made necessary God's vengeance against the Jews exists in full force against the people of the United States and Territories, and their iniquity being the same as theirs, what possible imagination can any man indulge, that whereas the Jews perished, the traffickers in Men, Women, and Children of "Christian America," shall escape; the Jews in the furnace of Divine wrath, "Young America" walking at large in the area of his exultant oppression unrebuked, unvisited; the Jews in the mire of the Nations, trodden under foot, begging for the privilege of selling "old clothes," Young America on the throne claiming international sanction for the breeding and trading of "property" in Human flesh, frequently the Children of his own loins!

How can any man but see, who believes in a God, and reflects at all, or has examined the record, that every attribute of Jehovah is pledged against the Churches, the Preachers, and the People, who uphold or connive at such an atrocious system of iniquity. The glory of His name, the majesty and purity of His law, the truth of His predictions, the Divine nature of His statutes, their wisdom and benevolence, requiring to be demonstrated against the blasphemous libel of their being a cover and shield of the most execrable avarice and oppression; the vindication of the New Testament, as well as the Old, and its religion of love, from such a burning odium as that of practically going against its own great law of *doing to others as we would they should do to us;* the vindication of Christianity against infidelity, and the rescuing of imprisoned souls *made infidel by the Churches enshrining oppression as a form of Christianity* — all these things compel the descent of God's curse upon the "evangelical" traffickers in their colored and party-colored fellow-men, and for whom, with us, Christ Jesus suffered, bled, and died.

PART FIFTH.

DOMESTIC AMUSEMENTS IN THE SLAVE STATES.

CHAPTER I.

"They all lie in wait for blood; they hunt every man his brother with a net. That they may do evil with both hands earnestly, the prince asketh, and the judge asketh for a reward; and the great man he uttereth his mischievous desire: so they wrap it up."

"It is really astonishing," said the Right Reverend Father *in* God, Leonidas Polk, D. D., LL. D., Bishop of the Protestant Episcopal Church of Louisiana, "how little our colored *Servants* appreciate the special blessings of their condition." (See chap. ii. of Part IV.) And yet, strange to say, to get out of it, one secretes himself in the hold of a vessel; another packs himself in a cask; a third threads woods and swamps in the dark, guided only by the North star; a fourth swims rivers and risks bloodhounds and rifle-bullets sooner than be taken; a fifth disguises himself and sets out for Canada without a penny in his pocket; a sixth plunges into the river, preferring drowning to capture. One day it is a boy that has run away, the next day a girl; then a man and *his* "wife;" then a mother and *her* children; then a superannuated old man. Last week we heard of six from Virginia, yesterday of eleven from Arkansas, to-day sixteen from Kentucky. One is half-naked, another has a scarred cheek, a third a branded forehead, a fourth a mangled back, a fifth a bullet in his leg, a sixth an arm broken, a seventh an ear cut off, an eighth an eye put out. Yet all these were "better fed, clothed, and treated," and more kindly "cared for in old age," we are expected to believe, "than the laborers of the New England States," &c.

If Slavery is so agreeable a condition to the Slaves; if they are so well nurtured and "cared for" under it, how comes it that Women are crazed by the thought of being returned to it? How comes it that they forget all the dictates of a Mother's heart, and condemn their Children to death by their own hands, rather than relinquish the possession of them to their pretended owners? How comes it that their companions, who are arrested as accomplices in this crime of murder, say that they would rather be tried for their lives, and afterward marched to the gallows, than be sent back to Slavery? They know what Slavery is, and they know what Death is, and, with many that have gone before them in this world, they cry, "Death before Slavery."

There is something in the heart of the poor Slave which whispers to him that the body is more than raiment, and the freedom of the soul infinitely greater than the comforts of the body. Like the rest of us, he yearns for Freedom, and having achieved freedom, though but for a few days, he welcomes the grave as the alternative to bondage. But in doing this he has in History some pertinent and illustrious examples. The annals of man are filled with similar incidents. There are names that have been rescued from that mortality which follows all human affairs, solely on the ground of such exhibitions as we have seen in Ohio and other sections of the "*free* North," not to mention the thousand occurrences in barbarian times — when fathers and brothers despairing of safety destroyed those who were most dear to them.

When Mithridates was defeated by Lucullus he ordered the

sacrifice of his wife and sister to prevent their falling into the hands of the enemy; and writers who relate the tale are accustomed to dilate upon the act as a proof of the dignity and grandeur of his soul. When Virginius, summoned by Appius' Claudius to surrender his daughter as a Slave, plunged the dagger into her bosom rather than yield to the demand, the pen of the historian warmed into eloquence as he described the heroic virtue of the Roman father, and the imaginations of the poets were kindled into tragic sublimity.

The finest of the Lays of Rome, written by Macaulay, is decidedly that which tells of the fate of the hapless Virginia; one of the most touching and effective of recent tragedies is founded upon the same subject. We have seen the latter, indeed, as enacted upon the stage, melt the eyes and stir the inmost depths of emotion in large audiences, in whose shuddering sympathy with the child was always mingled a lurking admiration for the stern heroism of the parent. Yet in what respect does the act of the Roman Virginius differ from that of the poor Slave-mother on the banks of the Ohio? In the one case the daughter was claimed as a Slave, under an infamous law of Rome, trumped up for the occasion, and the father, rather than submit to it, plunged his knife in the heart of his daughter. In the other case the child is claimed as a Slave, under an infamous "Law" of the United States of America, and the Mother, rather than yield to it, drew the knife across the throat of her child. In the former, however, the crime becomes classic; History celebrates it; Artists spread it on their canvass; poets embalm the memory of it in undying lines; and the world does not cease to admire it, while it shudders, as a manifestation of the sternness and grandeur of Roman courage. But, in the latter case, where there is even more to excuse the criminal aspect of the transaction, and more to heighten its pathetic interest, because the perpetrator is a Woman and a Mother, she is hurled to prison as a murderess, either to suffer the penalty of the "Law," in that character, or to be restored to a bondage which she regards as infinitely worse than Death.

"Oh, thou mother, maddened, frenzied, when the hunter's toils ensnared
Thee and thy brood of nestlings, till thy anguished spirit dared
Send to God, uncalled, one darling life that round thine own did twine—
Worthy of a Spartan mother was that fearful deed of thine!
Worthy of the Roman father, who sheathed deep his flashing knife
In the bosom of Virginia, in the current of her life!
Who, rather than his beauteous child should live a tyrant's Slave,
Opened the way to freedom through the portals of the grave!"

The New Bedford (Mass.) *Standard*, of September 5th, 1855, says: "Mrs. Peterson called upon us, yesterday morning, with two Slave children, of whom we before spoke as having been purchased in Washington, D. C., by the liberality of some of our Citizens and persons in Boston. The children are little girls, of the ages of *six* and *eight* years. They are bright, intelligent-looking and quite pretty, with a remarkable regularity of features. The most acute observer would not discover the slightest evidence that African blood flowed in their veins, and, the fact of their having been Slaves to the contrary, we can scarcely believe that they are not as pure Anglo-Saxon as any children in Massachusetts. There is not about either of them the first physical peculiarity indicating that they belong to the 'colored' race, and not one person in a hundred thousand would ever entertain a suspicion that such was the case. We trust that some one, if not all, our Daguerrean artists will take pictures of these little girls, and place them in their case of 'specimens' by the street side, so that the world may see what an American 'Nigger' is made of."

There are hundreds of thousands of just such instances of white children in bondage in the Slave States of the "Model Republic." That the "Niggers" are fast "bleaching out" is well known, and that thousands with the blood of Southern Statesmen and Northern "hirelings" in their veins are now in chains, can not be disputed. In a few years more there will scarcely be a "*black* Nigger" in Slavery.

A Southerner arrived in New York City in March, 1856, and made known to a confidential friend—a Cotton Broker, that he had come in pursuit of a "runaway Nigger," his own *property*, and from the fact of the Slave being "a beautiful female Nigger, about sixteen years of age, and perfectly white," he thought it advisable not to attempt to recover her by making application in any quarter where the fact of his pursuit would be likely to be made known to the public, as his object might thereby be frustrated. His friend advised him, therefore, to offer a reward of three hundred dollars, to some intelligent Police officer, for the arrest of the fugitive, and trust to his prudence and discretion. The advice was taken, and after a while a clue was got to the whereabouts of the "beautiful Nigger," but before she could be arrested she was "up and gone," the graceless girl, and away to Canada, and beyond the reach of her "legal owner."

There was nothing unusual or marvellous in all this, but it was discovered during the time that the search for the fugitive was being made, that the "beautiful Nigger" was his own daughter, and had escaped from a lecherous old wretch, to whom he had hired her for five years. Soon after her arrival in New York, she had captivated the heart of a white gentleman who married her. He did not suspect her origin. The husband having by some means or other got scent of the danger, instead of playing the part of Inkle to his Yarico, had the manliness to start with her to Canada.

Isaac Johnson and his wife, who recently escaped from Slavery, give a narrative of the hardships they endured, and from which we deduce the following facts. They were held as "property" in the State of Mississippi, a short time since.

and were the parents of an only child, which was about thirteen months old. A few days before they started on the hazardous voyage to Canada, the mother learned that she was sold to a Slave-trader, who intended to separate her from her "husband" and child, never more to see them on earth. But they resolved on running away with their child or perish. They succeeded in reaching what is called a "*free* State" (Indiana), with their child, where they were chased until it was sacrificed. On seeing that they were closely pursued, they broke and ran to a corn-field — the "wife" first got over the fence, and the "husband" handed her the child, with which she ran as fast as she could. She heard the pursuer saying, "stop, stop, or I'll shoot you down;" and before she had proceeded far, a gun was fired, and her child was shot dead from her back — and the ball, which passed through the child's neck, cut off one corner of the mother's ears. At this moment the poor mother fell down with her lifeless babe, when she was rushed upon by two men, who tried to tie her with cords; but when she cried for help, her "husband" came to her relief — the contest was desperate for a few moments; the "wife and husband" both fought until they brought down the murderer of their child, and his companion fled. The "husband and wife," fearing that they would soon be surrounded and overpowered, and seeing that their little one was dead, and that they could do it no good, reluctantly left it lying by the villain who shot it. Fortunately for them, they soon found a depot of the "underground railroad," and one of the conductors thereof was kind enough to put on an extra train, which soon landed them on Canadian soil.

On Sunday evening, October 5, 1856, about nine o'clock, the steamship Roanoke arrived at her dock, in New York, from Richmond, Virginia, and during the night, as they were discharging her cargo, one of the hands discovered a box, in which was secreted a Man, who being nearly suffocated for the want of air, had forced the lid, when it was discovered that he was a fugitive Slave. The Steamer was immediately sent from her dock, and anchored off Sandy Hook, and the Slave put on board one of the Richmond packets, to be taken back to "Old Virginia."

In September, 1851, a warrant was issued in Philadelphia, Pennsylvania, by Edward D. Ingraham, United States Marshal, authorizing the arrest of two party-colored Men, claimed to be the "property" of Edward Gorsuch, a prominent Member of the Methodist Episcopal Church, who with his two Sons, Dickinson and Joshua, and his nephew, Doctor Thomas Pierce, and several other persons, reached the place where the fugitives were harbored at daybreak, on the 11th of September, 1851. This was a two-story stone building on the farm of Levi Pownall, three miles from the village of Christiana, in the county of Lancaster. The Slaves were summoned to surrender, and the United States warrant read aloud by the Marshal. The owner of the house denied that the Slaves were in the house, although the hunters had seen them at the upper window, and called upon them to descend. Upon their refusal to do so, the Marshal attempted to ascend the stairs, whereupon an axe was hurled at him from above, and a gun fired from the window; the Marshal then fired a pistol, and his fire was returned by the Slaves. The Marshal and his party then withdrew from the house, and were again fired upon from the upper windows.

The Marshal again read aloud his warrant, and Mr. Gorsuch entreated his *property* to surrender. During this parley, two white men, Elijah Lewis and Castner Hanway, came up —a horn was blown, and several "colored men" rushed to the scene from the surrounding woods. Some of them were armed with guns and pistols, and others with scythes and corn-cutters. The Marshal and his posse requested Lewis and Hanway to aid in making the arrests, and exhibited and read the warrant.

But this they refused to do. Upon this encouragement, the party outside surrounded the Marshal and his men, shouted and fired upon them. Edward Gorsuch fell dead. Dickinson, his son, while running to his aid, was shot through the heart; and Joshua received a shot in the head. Dr. Pierce fought desperately. He was wounded in more than twenty places.

A most disgraceful and brutal occurrence took place at Wilkesbarre, on the 23d of September, 1853. About 7 o'clock, A. M., an attempt was made by "Deputy Marshal Wynkoop" (a brother to Colonel Wynkoop) and "Joe Jenkins," and three assistants from Virginia, to arrest, as a fugitive Slave, a waiter, in the Dining-room of the Phœnix Hotel. Immediately after receiving their breakfast at the hands of "Bill," the unsuspecting fugitive, who is a tall, noble-looking, remarkably intelligent, and active man, they suddenly, from behind, knocked him down, and partially shackled him; but, by a desperate effort, and after a most severe struggle, with the whole five upon him, he shook them off, and with the aid of his handcuffs, which were only fast upon his right hand, he inflicted wounds on the countenances of the hunters, the marks of which they will carry to their graves. But, notwithstanding the odds against him, he broke from their grasp, and, covered with blood, rushed from the Hotel, and plunged into the River close by, exclaiming, "*I will drown myself rather than be taken alive!*" His pursuers fired twice at him on his way, without checking his speed, and, on reaching the bank, they presented their revolvers, and called on the fugitive, who stood up to his neck in the water, to come out and surrender himself, or they would blow his brains out. He replied, "*There's no use — I'll never go back — I'll drown myself first!*" They then deliberately fired at him five times; the last ball was supposed to have wounded his head, for his face was instantly covered with blood, and the poor fellow shrieked out in agony, and no doubt would have sunk, but for the buoyancy of the water holding him up. The wretched, chicken-hearted Citizens, who had by this time collected in large numbers, were becoming excited, and could no longer refrain from crying out, "Shame, shame!" and which had the effect of causing the hunters to retire a short distance, in evident consultation.

The Slave, not seeing his pursuers, came to the shore; but not being able to support himself in the water, he lay down exhausted, and was supposed to be dying, on hearing which the Slave-catchers remarked that "dead Niggers were not worth taking South." A poor "*free* colored woman" brought a shirt and a pair of pantaloons and put them on the fugitive, who, in a few minutes, unexpectedly revived, and was walking off from the river, partly held up by the husband of this poor woman, whose name was Rex; on seeing which the hunters again headed him, and presented their revolvers, and called upon him to stop, threatening to shoot any one who assisted him. The white doughface friends of Rex instantly shouted, "Stand away! stand away, Rex! You'll get shot, too." This was bad advice, as it had the effect of encouraging the pirates, who kept advancing toward the fugitive, and at the same time intimidated Rex, who drew back, exclaiming to the Slave: "Away, Bill, to the water again; don't be taken alive!"

The poor fellow, seeing himself deserted (for there was a general drawback of the doughfaces, on the Revolvers being presented), turned, and plunged into the river, and this time swam out of the range of pistol-shot, where he remained upward of an hour, covered with blood, and in full view of hundreds of *things* called "white men," who lined the banks of the river. His pursuers dared not follow him into the water, for, as he afterward remarked, "*I would have died contented could I but have carried two or three of them down with me.*" In the meantime, some few "Men" had arrived, who were determined to have the hunters arrested. Judge Collins questioned them as to their names and authority, to which they replied: "You act more like a lunatic than a Judge," &c. They, however, saw the sentiment was strong against them, and drove off before an officer could be found to arrest them. A telegraphic despatch to the constable in Hazleton caused their detention there; but he was overawed by such pompous United States officers, and they were allowed to go.

After the departure of the pirates, the poor fugitive, afraid to come out there again, swam some distance up stream, and got out above, and was found by some " colored women," flat on his face in a corn-field ! These Christian women carried him to a place of safety, dressed his wounds, and at night he was so far recovered as to be able to start for Canada.

There was a general dread of the pirates, who bullied and browbeat any one who ventured to speak above his breath, exclaiming, occasionally: " Gentlemen, you can have him for $1,500 ; but we are United States Officers ; resist us at your peril."

On the 18th September, 1854, at 4 P. M., a suspicious-looking carriage-full of white men was seen near Byberry; they lurked about in the neighborhood until nightfall, when they drove up and rushed into a house and seized a " colored man," in the presence of his wife and another woman, threatening to shoot them if they interfered, and dragged him out, beating him over the head at the same time. The poor fellow continued to scream for help, but they forced him into their carriage and drove off, before any assistance could be offered. The neighborhood is cut up by several roads, leading in various directions, which facilitated their diabolical deed, making it impossible, under cover of the night, to tell which road they had taken. The kidnapped man had resided several months in Byberry, previous to which he had lived in New Jersey. Whether he had ever been a Slave or not, none could tell.

He had gained the respect of the people of Byberry by his sober and industrious habits. He left a heart-broken wife and one child to mourn his loss.

Byberry is a Quaker neighborhood not more than fifteen miles from the Hall where the Declaration of Independence was signed on the fourth day of July, 1776.

The borough of Harrisburgh was thrown into a state of "considerable excitement" on the 23d of February, 1855, in consequence of a daring attempt to Kidnap George Clark, a "*free* colored boy." The circumstances of this case are briefly these: Clark had been lured from a dance-house, kept by a "colored man," under the pretext of being sent on an errand for brandy for the occasion. Two white men, Dr. Thompson and J. Jackson, accompanied him, and took him to Solomon Snyder's residence, in the lower section of the borough, and invited him up-stairs to get some "grog." Immediately after entering Snyder's room, the latter fastened the door and said: "Clark, I am going to take you back to your owner." A struggle ensued; the boy made for a window fronting on the depot of the Pennsylvania Railroad, broke the sash through— severely cutting his arm — and raised a cry of "Murder!" A number of people made for the spot, and found Clark hanging out of the window, some forty feet from the ground, head downward, and Snyder and his wife holding on to his legs. A party rushed up-stairs, and learned from the boy that he was "free;" that an attempt had been made to knock him down and gag him, and that his only refuge was to jump from the window.

Snyder, who stood like a felon detected in his wicked act, had nothing to say for himself, and was taken before a magistrate and thence to prison. Jackson was captured, but Thompson made his escape.

Judge Stroud, of Pennsylvania, in his "Sketch of Slavery," says: "Remote as in the City of Philadelphia from those of the Slaveholding States in which the introduction of Slaves from place to place within the United States is freely permitted, and where also the market is tempting, it has been ascertained that more than thirty free colored persons, mostly children, have been kidnapped here and carried away within the last two years.* Five of these, through the kind interposition of several humane gentlemen, have been restored to their friends, though not without great expense and difficulty. The others are still retained in bondage."

On the 13th of December, 1854, Mary E. Parker, a young woman, residing in Chester county, was seized, in the evening, by two kidnappers, and carried to Baltimore, sold, and transported to New Orleans. A fortnight later, December 30th, her sister, Rachael Parker, was forcibly taken from the house of Joseph C. Miller, by two men, who took her to Baltimore and sold her.

Mary Gilmore, of Philadelphia, claimed as a "runaway Slave," was proved to be the child of Irish parents, and had not a drop of African blood in her veins.

Another outrage, of this sort, was perpetrated on Sunday evening, July 1, 1855. The facts of the case are as follows: Benjamin Johnson, a lad 15 years of age, was on his way from the residence of his parents, near Evansburgh, to Samuel Jarrett's, near Jeffersonville, with whom he had been living.

---

* The *New York Tribune*, of the 7th of October, 1856, says: "It may surprise many of our readers to learn that from thirty to forty white Children are stolen every year in New York from their parents, and never heard of more. Yet such is the fact. A child is lost, search is made by the parents; days, weeks, months pass, but no tidings of their little one are ever heard. At last the search is given over, and the matter is forgotten until a similar calamity brings anguish into another family. The mystery is, what is done with them? Something ought to be done to preserve the children and save parents the anguish of losing them." The kidnappers invariably seize the handsomest children, nine out of ten being female children. Handsome "white Nigger girls" are "anxiously sought after"— in the Southern Markets.

THE BLOODHOUND BUSINESS. (See page 292.)

He was overtaken by a well-dressed, genteel-looking young man in a carriage, who asked him where he was going, and then told him that as he was going to Jeffersonville if he would get into the carriage he would take him there. The boy at first declined, but finally consented. The man then drove in the direction of Jeffersonville for about a mile, conversing with the boy meanwhile on various subjects. He then drove off at a rapid pace on another road. Night coming on, the boy became fearful that all was not right, and resolved, if possible to make his escape. He made an effort to spring from the carriage, when the villain caught him and drove off at full speed, and by threats and blows prevented him from making any alarm. He drove to the stone hills, fifteen miles from Jeffersonville, where, in consequence of his whole attention and strength being required to manage the horse, the boy succeeded in escaping from the carriage and making off, and reached his father's residence at sunrise next morning.

On Friday, July 9th, 1855, at an early hour in the morning, a white girl, fourteen years of age, the daughter of Samuel Godshall, residing within three miles of Downington, Chester county, was carried away by two men, in a close carriage, a distance of twelve miles from her home, toward the Maryland line. The girl had been with a neighbor for the past two or three weeks taking care of a sick child, and on the morning of Friday, while going along the road to drive a cow from the pasture-field, she was accosted by two men, very genteelly dressed, who were standing near a carriage. They asked her name, and where she lived, to which inquiries she gave answers without hesitation, supposing that they were friends or acquaintances of a gentleman residing in the neighborhood. Without any further conversation, one of them opened a tin box, and took therefrom what appeared to be a pitch-plaster, which he instantly clapped over her mouth, when both of them dragged her into the carriage and drove off, by an indirect route from the place, through Coatesville, three miles from her home. Here she managed to jump from the carriage and run into a wood.

The poor girl, faint and sick from mental excitement and terror, scarcely knew where she was or what to do, when she was met by two colored men, who assisted her and advised her as to her course homeward. She reached her home late in the evening. She stated that when her sobs and efforts to cry prevailed, the kidnappers threatened to knock her brains out.

Among the freight which passed through Pittsburgh recently, on the "Underground Railroad," was a daughter of "a wealthy and influential citizen" of Baton Rouge, Louisiana, a young lady of remarkable beauty and no mean supply of spirit and intelligence. She had been well brought up and kindly cared for by her father; but a creditor levied on her for debt. She was taken to New Orleans and placed in a calaboose for safe-keeping, and for the inspection of purchasers. Among those who thought of buying the article was one *gentleman*, who wished to learn if her bust was indebted to padding for its form; but the girl resented this pursuit after knowledge as a personal insult, whereupon the wretch drew a heavy whip and dealt her a blow, which she caught upon her right arm and shoulder. That night — the night before the sale — some one came into her prison, and gave her a suit of gentleman's clothing, bade her dress quickly, and follow. She did so, and was placed by the unknown friend on a Steamboat bound for Pittsburgh, where she arrived safely. Her arm and shoulder were disabled from the effects of the blow by her "chivalric" would-be purchaser, but she was thankful to have got off so cheaply; was hopeful for the future, and, with a considerable company of emigrants, was promptly forwarded to Canada.

We learn from *The Pittsburg* (Pa.) *Dispatch*, of the 6th of August, 1856, that a grand "Nigger-hunt" had just come off in Greene county, in which fifty armed white men were engaged in the pursuit of nine Slaves, who had runaway from Booth's Creek, Harrison county, Virginia (eight miles from Clarksburg), a few days before. The fugitives, three men and six children, escaped, and the Pennsylvania "Nigger-hunters" earned, not the reward they so anxiously sought, but the contempt of all honorable men. In one township half a dozen of them drew their Revolvers on a Woman, who had refused to allow them to search her house for the runaways.

The *New York Tribune*, of the 7th of August, 1856, says: "Two runaway Slaves from the northern part of Kentucky arrived in Erie (Pa.) on Saturday last. Some of their friends in town secreted them and arranged for their translation to Canada, which last stage in their journey was safely traversed, although the poor fellows were hotly pursued by a man who claimed to own them. He arrived in Erie in time to learn that they had evaded him."

Not long since a runaway Slave, from a plantation in Western Maryland, was captured and taken to Baltimore, half doubled up with the weight of irons around his neck, which the poor fellow said he had worn for nearly ten months. This iron-collar was so arranged as to have a bell in it behind his shoulders. When he was brought in, a crowd of the "poor whites" collected around him to know where he was from, and who he belonged to; and in the crowd was one more bold than the rest, who spoke, and said, "Take off his irons, take off his irons." But an old gray-headed man spoke up and said, "*Oh, no, no, I would not take off his irons; make the black rascal keep them on.*" And that same old man had, only the day before, received the "Holy Sacrament" at "Christ's Church," the Rev. Dr. Johns.

Mr. John H. Pope, of Frederick, Maryland, addressed a letter, in January, 1855, to the Editor of *The Montreal Gazette*, in relation to his proposed "Nigger-hunt" on British ground. It is so exquisitely "chivalric," so thoroughly indicative of the "great beauties of the Fugitive Slave Law of 1850;" and of the means proposed "to conquer the prejudices" (to quote from Daniel Webster's 7th March speech) of the people of free communities, that we can not refrain from copying it entire. Here it is:

"FREDERICK (Md.), *Jan.* 16, 1855.
"*To the Editor of the Montreal Gazette:*

"SIR: Properly to reply to the article in your paper, commenting on a letter received by the Sheriff of your City, would be impossible, as I have been unable, as yet, to obtain the article, and can only speak of it as I gather its import from *The Baltimore Sun.* The generous reception, and still more generous treatment which you promise, in anticipation of my coming, is fully appreciated, and is as much as could be expected from one of Her Majesty's 'most loyal subjects.' What a magnanimous people the Britons are! Why, Sir, with my dog 'Taylor,' named after 'old Zack,' and six good mounted riflemen, I would not hesitate to invade Canada, hang Her Majesty's sheriff, tar and feather Her loving editors, and place myself 'at the head of affairs.' Fear to enter Canada in pursuit of my runaway *property!* No, Sir; the wife of that German Prince will soon be compelled to relinquish her American possessions, and the least violence offered to a *free* and enlightened American Citizen would only anticipate the event. Her Majesty's 'black regiment,' composed mostly of runaway Niggers from Western Maryland, would likely be the first to yield the ground, as many of them are familiar with the bark, if not the bite of 'Taylor,' and Her Majesty's editor, whom we suppose either black or tinctured with the blood, had better not be in command, for fear that 'Taylor' might want his accustomed provisions.

"In conclusion, we have only to say that Her Majesty's editor and Her Majesty's sheriff have only to prepare against an invasion which involves more than runaway Niggers, and which, in result, will give freedom to Canadians, and a defeat to that power which has ruled the wave and the land for the last few years; save when General Jackson, with his forces, lick'd the devil out of 'em at New Orleans.* Now I have done with you, Mr. Editor, and have only to request that you will be

---

* Since which time he appears to have been the "particular patron" of the "good people" of Western Maryland.

honest, and give my sentiments to the world; then honest men may judge between us, and ascribe to each his proper share of praise.

"JOHN H. POPE."

Travellers, with Sun-burnt complexions, should be extremely cautious as to how they "circulate" themselves in Western Maryland.* But the Slaveholding States are not the only States where bloodhounds are kept to hunt down and destroy "the race of *Africa*" or "cursed seed of *Ham*." *The Cleveland* (Ohio) *Plaindealer*, says: "Ephraim Whitehead, son of Mr. R. Whitehead, who lives on Cedar street, was missing on Saturday (March 29, 1856), about 11 o'clock. After dinner the family became alarmed, and search was instituted for him. A nephew of Mr. Whitehead discovered the boy in a field, some twenty rods from the house, nearly dead, having been attacked and torn in a most shocking manner by a bloodhound slut. The poor little fellow lived only half an hour after he was found. When he was discovered, the question was asked if it was the bloodhound that had attacked him. He had barely strength enough to half articulate 'Yes.' The boy was about *eight years* of age, and was a general favorite with the family. The hound is of the same breed used by Slaveholders

---

* *The Philadelphia* (Pa.) *Bulletin*, of the 28th July, 1856, contains the following, which it gives as perfectly reliable: "It seems that in some of the border counties of Maryland there is a patrol established to prevent the escape of Slaves. A few days ago two men belonging to this patrol were walking along, when they met with a Slave whom they accosted, asking where he was from. He replied, naming a well-known place. One of the parties questioned him further, and for a reply the Slave suddenly drew a weapon, and, with a back-handed blow, severed his inquisitor's head from his body! The headless trunk dropped on the road. The surviving man's first impulse, after the shock, was to pursue the Slave, but he gave up the chase, and the Slave escaped. A bowie-knife and revolver were found upon the person of the dead man. The scene of this tragedy was in Cecil County, near the head of Sassafras river. The Maryland people have published nothing about it, as it is considered 'more prudent to keep quiet about all such things.'"

to hunt runaway Negroes. We hope that this sad event will teach and enforce the necessity of killing all Slaveholders' dogs, as it is dangerous to the safety of Women and Children to have such animals *in a thickly-populated City like ours.*"

Ohio is full of such animals. The Dry-goods Jobbers, &c., of the State have to look after the interests of those in Kentucky, Tennessee, and other Slave States, with whom they "do business."

The Cleveland Herald, of June 13th, 1856, has an article stating that great havoc had been committed by Slaveholders' bloodhounds among flocks of sheep *in different parts of the State.* One farmer had 90 killed in one night; another lost 30, and so on.

The following incident occurred in the Township of Orange: A Slaveholder's bloodhound kept by a Mr. Honeywell, rushed into a School-house among the children, biting them right and left. One little girl was dragged all around the School-room by the brute, and six children were bitten. One little girl had a large piece taken from her hip. The children sought refuge under the benches and wherever they could, to get out of the reach of the brute. A man came with an iron bar to the relief of the children and killed the monster.

The assertion has been frequently reiterated by the Pro-Slavery Doctors of Divinity and their allies, that the fugitives in Canada are incompetent to provide for themselves, that many persons consider it no act of kindness to aid them in their flight from bondage. Determined to ascertain their actual condition, a gentleman of the highest respectability, a resident of Cleveland, Ohio, who visited in Dec., 1855, parts of the Upper Province, in which a great many of them reside, says: " My efforts were both successful and highly satisfactory. Everything appertaining to this persecuted people I found had been misrepresented. Evidences in abundance were discovered to show that they are as competent to take care of themselves as the white folks of New England. Their Farms, Dwellings, Workshops, day and Sabbath schools, are as well managed as similar matters and things among our Yankee population. If you should travel from house to house, in any direction from Cleveland, among the New England Farmers, you would not find stronger evidences of advancement and comfortable living than were discoverable among an equal number of these colored Families. On the score of Kindness, Affability, and Good manners, it is feared the former would suffer by the comparison.

"It is evident that the present generation of colored men are rapidly accumulating wealth and power, and it requires no spirit of prophecy to predict that the ensuing generation will make its mark upon the page of history. The young, of both sexes, harbor a deadly hatred toward the South, and even against the whole Union. From infancy they have heard one constant narrative of wrongs suffered by their parents, and many of them expressed both an anxiety and determination to seek revenge whenever circumstances would permit. Without knowing how to read or write, many of them are sensible and judicious in their conversation and actions. The want of Education evidently stimulates them to furnish means for instructing their Children."

"*Ran away* from the subscriber, living near Upper Marlboro', Prince George's county, Maryland, on Monday, the 28th August, a Negro boy, who calls himself Allen West. He is about 20 years of age, *a bright light color, freckled face, straight red hair;* has a large scar on one of his wrists (caused by the bite of Mr. Pope's dog 'Taylor'); he is about 5 foot 6 inches in height. He has relations living in Washington City. He has also a brother belonging to Richard B. B. Chew, Esq., and a sister belonging to Thomas Talbert, Esq.; and *his* father belongs to Colonel William D. Bowie, and stays at his 'Bellfield plantation.' I have reason to believe he is endeavoring to pass himself off as a white boy! I will give $300 reward for his apprehension, if taken in a *free*

State, or $100, if taken elsewhere, provided he is brought to me or secured in some jail so that I can get him.

"CHARLES CLAGETT."

"$100 *Reward*.—The above reward will be paid for the apprehension of my Slave man William. *He is of a very light color, and has straight yellowish hair.* I have no doubt he will change his name, and try to pass himself for a *white* man, which he may be able to do, unless to a very close observer. "T. S. PITCHARD."

The staple argument in favor of Slavery is based on the inferiority of the *African* blood, but as in more than half the States of the Republic three fourths or more of the blood is mixed with the blood of the "first families," such advertisements as the above are of every-day occurrence. Fathers advertise for, and hunt down with bloodhounds, their runaway Sons and Daughters, and Grandchildren, and catching them, sell them into Slavery. If a Slave can "*pass himself off for white*," he is essentially white; and the "Nigger argument" falls to the ground.

Notwithstanding the constant boastings by the champions of Slavery of the "kind indulgence extended to the Negro race in Slaveholding communities," how uniformly do facts disprove the truth of such boastings, and hold up to scorn the heartless exercise of power by the fearful and, consequently, cruel oppressors of their fellow-men. A short time since one of the Washington Newspapers contained an account of the arrest of a dozen or more "*free* men of color," who had, as was proved, assembled in a room, at night (the only time they probably could have taken), for the purpose of raising a sufficient fund, out of their own means, in good part, to purchase the freedom of a young woman whom they wished to befriend; and of their being detained in the watch-house all night, and in the morning compelled to pay, to the Corporation of Washington, fines exceeding in the aggregate the amount of the fund they had collected for the noble purpose they had in view!

DOMESTIC AMUSEMENTS IN THE SLAVE STATES. 297

"*Ran Away* from the plantation of James Surgett, the following *Negroes:* Randall —— has one ear cropped; Bob —— has lost one eye; Kentucky Tom —— has one jaw broken."—*Southern Telegraph,* Washington, D. C.

"$300 *Reward*.—Ran away from the subscriber on 'Difficult Run,' near George W. Hunter's Mill, Fairfax county, Va., on Sunday, the 13th inst., a *Negro* woman, having with her a child six months of age, *almost white.* The said woman is delicately made, of a very light color, is five feet two inches in height, and is supposed to be in the neighborhood of Georgetown, D. C. The above reward will be given if she be taken in Georgetown or Washington, or the adjoining counties, and secured so that I can get her. "CHAS. W. ADAMS."
Washington Star, Jan. 18, 1856.

There can be no difficulty in deducing from facts like these the moral and religious condition of the people of the District of Columbia. Evils, crimes, and purposes like these, can only spring from a public sentiment utterly corrupted, no matter what may be the Religious pretensions and professions of the people. "By their fruits shall ye know them."

To run away from Slavery has been declared to run away from God. The "evangelical" Slaveholding "Church of Jesus Christ at Union, Farquier county, Virginia," has pronounced excommunication against one of its members for running away from his "evangelical" owner, a member of the same establishment, and "seeking freedom in the North." This "Nigger" (see Engraving at the head of this chapter) "who so disobeyed the laws of God and man," in the language of that Church, was caught, and by the active endeavors of President Franklin Pierce and his Agents, and the Agents of Cotton and Doughfacery, was restored to "Christian Society," and the "pious owner" who bewailed his Slave's backsliding into Massachusetts. After a season of repentance, under the exhortations of the "blood-stained cow-hide" and the Rev. John Clark, this member of the blood-stained menagerie was bought out of Slavery by the Abolitionists of Boston,

13*

Massachusetts, and presented to himself. Taking the gift, he straightway went to Oberlin, Ohio, to Educate it for the ministry. Arrived there, he, Child-like, wrote back to Union, to his old Pastor, for a letter of dismission from the Church he so wickedly ran away from when he ran away from Slavery. The Pastor, the Rev. John Clark, made the following answer:

"THE CHURCH OF JESUS CHRIST, AT UNION, FAUQUIER CO., VA.:
" *To all whom it may concern.*
"*Whereas,* Anthony Burns, a member of the Church, has made application to us by letter to our Pastor, for a letter of dismission in fellowship, in order that he may unite with another Church *of the same faith and order;* and, *Whereas,* it has been satisfactorily established before us that the said Anthony Burns, absconded from the service of his owner, and refused to return voluntarily, *thereby disobeying both the laws of God and man,* although he subsequently obtained his freedom by purchase, yet we have *now* to consider him only as a fugitive from labor (as he was before his arrest and restoration to his owner), have, therefore, *Resolved,* unanimously, that he be excommunicated from the Communion and Fellowship of the Church of Jesus Christ— Done by order of the Church, in regular Church-meeting, this 20th of October, 1855.
"W. W. WEST, *Clerk.*"

With this "evangelical" Slave-breeders' "Bull" of excommunication went a letter from the Pastor, which "pitched into Burns" in a fashion which would be called "diabolically vicious" if it did not proceed from an "evangelical minister of the Gospel." He convicts him, "logically and from the Holy Scriptures," of having denied the *Christian* character in seeking Freedom while his owner wanted him to remain a Slave —recommends him when licensed to preach, to select for his field of labor the North bank of the Ohio River, and taking the text about Onesimus, to exhort therefrom all "runaway Niggers" from Virginia to run straight back to their owners. "By so doing," adds this precious Slave-breeding Saint, "you may measurably make amends to Jesus Christ for stealing yourself away from your legal owner."

The fate of Anthony Burns is indeed a warning to all slippery and slipping sinners of his slippery class. He now knows what he has lost by his perverseness in allowing the rebellious old Adam to harden his heart. He thought it hard to work for another man for nothing, and to be beaten with stripes to boot. He yielded to the promptings of his own carnal nature, and now what is his condition? Cut off from "the Church," denied the sympathies and prayers of its members, shut out from the ordinances of Religion, the door of Heaven slammed in his face, and he given over to be buffeted by the great Adversary of Mankind! Poor Anthony! Much as we blame him, we can not but feel some natural yearnings of compassion toward him. Indeed, he is as Touchstone said to Corin, "in a parlous state."

If the Church, at Union, Fauquier county, Virginia, is losing members by what the "evangelical" Pro-Slavery Doctors of Divinity call the "Infidel love of Freedom," is it not "largely growing in grace?"

"*The Richmond* (Va.) *Enquirer*, of the 10th December, 1856, says: "Every day develops some fresh scheme of revolt among the Slaves of the Western and more Southern States. To those already reported in our Columns, we have to add another prepared plan of insurrection just detected and defeated in South Carolina. Occurring at the same time in so many separate localities, these discoveries suggest the suspicion of a very general spirit of insubordination among the Slave population. Why should this State alone be exempt from the danger which impends over nearly the entire Southern community? In Montgomery county and in the Vicinity of Williamsburg, facts have been brought to light which warrant the apprehension of an outbreak, and justify the owners in the most summary measures of suppression. It is a remarkable circumstance in all these schemes of meditated insurrection that Christmas was selected as the day of their accomplishment. Now observing so wide-spread a spirit of revolt among the Slaves, perceiving that the same incendiary causes operate in full vigor in this State, and seeing, indeed, that indications of intended outbreak have been detected in more than one County in Virginia, we venture, at the hazard of even exciting unnecessary apprehension, to inquire if it is not the duty of the authorities and of the people to provide every possible precaution against any demonstration of violence among our own Slaves? Shall we not be admonished by timely discoveries in other States? Or, shall we neglect our own security until we too, are exposed to extreme alarm, if not to actual peril?

" The military system of Virginia is in utter dilapidation. Out of the cities we have no organized means of protection against a sudden emergency. Every consideration, then, suggests the necessity of adopting immediate measures of prevention. Obviously the best thing to be done under the circumstances, is to appoint patrols for the counties, and to stimulate the police of the towns to more rigor and vigilance. It is especially important that the counties should be thoroughly patrolled, so as to interrupt extensive communications among the Slaves, and to prevent them from assembling in large numbers."

" *Ran Away* from the subscriber, living in the County of Rappahannock, on Tuesday last, Daniel, about 5 feet 8 inches high, about 35 years old, very intelligent, has been a wagoner for several years, and is pretty well acquainted from Richmond to Alexandria. He calls himself Daniel Turner; *his hair curls, without showing black blood, or wool;* he has a scar on one cheek, and his left hand has been injured by a pistol-shot, and he was shabbily dressed, when last seen. I will give $25 reward if taken out of the county, and secured in jail, so that I can get him, or $10, if taken in the county. "A. M. WILLIS.

" RAPPAHANNOCK CO., VA., Nov. 29."

" $100 *Reward* will be given for the apprehension of my Negro, Edward Kenney. He has straight hair, and complexion so white that it

is believed a stranger would suppose there was no African blood in him. He was with my boy Dick a short time since in Norfolk, and offered him for Sale, and was apprehended, but escaped under *pretence* of being a white man! "ANDERSON BOWLES."
Richmond (Va.) *Whig.*

A colored man who had obtained his freedom, by placing the Ohio river between him and his "Master," a liberty which he, however, held by a precarious title, though it was previous to the enactment of the Fugitive law, was compelled to leave his "wife" behind him in bondage. He did not, however, forget her. Freedom without her was but half enjoyed, while the thought of what she was suffering embittered his days. He meditated many a scheme for her deliverance, which, however, he was unable to put into execution. Her "owner" was a Presbyterian clergyman "in good standing" with his Church in Louisville, Kentucky. He, however, had no inclination to practise that portion of the Gospel which proclaims "deliverance to the captive," and the enslaved "wife" was held, like hundreds of thousands of her fellow-Slaves, in forcible separation from her "husband," by one who professed to be a "follower of Christ."

The "husband" of this woman was brave and determined, and he had a brother, of a spirit like unto his own, who was also a fugitive from Slavery. The two concerted a plan for the deliverance of the "wife." Inasmuch as the brother was unknown to the "owner," and would therefore be less likely to be intercepted in his enterprise, it was determined that he should cross the river, visit the plantation, and attempt her rescue. The "husband," meanwhile, was to prepare himself, and meet them at the Ferry on the Kentucky side of the river. Late on Saturday night the brother reached the Plantation of the clergyman, and on Sabbath morning, just before the time for service, it was ascertained that one of the preacher's Slave women had fled. The first impulse of the Rev. Doctor was to make instant pursuit himself, but remembering his pulpit duties, he mounted his horse, and having given the alarm, and started some "well-armed brethren" on the track, he applied himself to the duties of the day, preaching in person and hunting Slaves by proxy. The fugitives had the advantage of the night travel, but the pursuers were mounted, and at the very instant when the brother met, and congratulated his "wife" and brother on the bank of the river, the "evangelical" horsemen in pursuit dashed down to the Ferry, and sprung from their horses to secure their prey. They at once remonstrated with the Slaves, and spoke of the *wickedness* of stealing themselves from a "minister of Christ." To this the brothers replied with a contemptuous laugh.

Large promises of better treatment were made, but this made no impression. The hunters enraged, drew their revolvers; the "husband" and brother coolly presented theirs also, and told them they were also ready to shoot. They stood close by a small skiff used at the Ferry, its bows just clinging to the shore. The Slaves facing their pursuers, and with pistols presented, with the "wife" behind them, marched backward to the boat. The woman and brother seated themselves, and the "husband" stepped in and shoved off. The water was shallow, and a Kentuckian rushed forward and seized her bow, and attempted to drag it back to the shore, but a bullet from the brother's pistol grazing the top of his head, stunned him for an instant; he seized once more the boat, when the "husband" shot him through the breast, and he fell, while the boat was shoved rapidly into the river, in the midst of a volley of shots.

The wounded hunter was placed in a house near the Ferry, and seemed to be rapidly approaching his end. The next morning the reverend trafficker in human flesh hurried to the scene. He found that his Slave had, indeed, escaped, and that his hired pursuer was mortally wounded. Finding that nothing could be accomplished by remaining, he gave his friend some "excellent counsel" about "life's uncertainties," and departed. The Slave hunter, of course, went to heaven, the final abode of all good Slave catchers, and their defenders. Had he not obeyed the Lord's will in carrying out, to the utmost of his ability, the duty to curse the wretched seed of Ham? Had he not spent the Sabbath in this holy business of fulfilling prophecy? Did he not depart in expectation that the Slaveholder, Abraham, would reach out his arms and welcome him to glory? No Abolitionists in heaven! No Nigger-stealers in Abraham's bosom!

"Thou shalt not deliver unto his master the servant which is escaped from his master unto thee: he shall dwell with thee, even among you, in that place which he shall choose in one of thy gates, where it liketh him best: thou shalt not oppress him."

A party of men, three of whom were Kentuckians from Mason and Fleming counties, recently passed through New Petersburg, Ohio, in pursuit of three Slaves, the "property" of one of the hunters, named Pierce, and another "owner." It seems that they had information from a Pro-Slavery Doctor of Divinity in Ohio, which put them "on the track," and led them to believe that the Slaves were on the route through New Petersburg to Greenfield, but they had not yet crossed Rattlesnake Creek, which runs about a mile east of Petersburg. From Petersburg there are two roads leading to Greenfield, one of which crosses the creek over a bridge, and the other by a ford half a mile further up. Three of the hunters stationed themselves at the bridge, and two at the ford, and awaited the coming of the Slaves. The hunters at the bridge had not waited long, when the Slaves, two men and a woman, made their appearance, escorted by a white man and a boy, as guides. As soon as they were fairly within the bridge, which is a covered one, the Kentuckians sprang upon them and a desperate fight ensued. The fugitives were armed with guns, pistols, and knives, and fought with the utmost energy and desperation. The battle lasted for nearly an hour. The result was, that one of the Slaves was captured, after being shot and cut up in a most shocking manner. The others escaped. Pierce, the "owner" of the captured Slave, was "done up brown." The desperate character of the affray may be judged from the fact that the broken britch of a gun and pistol was found on the spot, and the place was covered with blood.

The Editor of *The Oberlin* (Ohio) *Times,* speaking of the death and burial of a fugitive Child, which occurred a short time since in that village, says: "We were present last Sabbath afternoon at one of the most affecting scenes that has ever occurred in our town. Many of our friends were not, and perhaps a brief sketch of the exercises may not be uninteresting to many, although it can not convey the impression made upon the minds of eye-witnesses. The audience, as usual, was large, numbering, at a low estimate, two thousand souls. After an able and truly eloquent sermon from Prof. Thome, founded on the words, 'Jesus wept,' it was announced to the congregation that the Funeral exercise of *a little slave boy* would take place after service, and those of the congregation who chose to remain in the Church could do so. The entire audience remained. The Corpse was then brought in, and the mourners took their seats in front of the pulpit. *They consisted of the gentleman and his wife at whose house the little one had died the day before, and also a young lady— 'Dorcas'—who had watched over the little sufferer with a tenderness and self-forgetfulness that we fear is thought less of on earth than in Heaven.* Prof. Peck, who took charge of the funeral, then remarked :

"'My friends, we meet this afternoon under 'peculiar' circumstances, to pay our respects to the lifeless form of what, according to the Laws of the United States is, at most, a 'chattel.' The brief history of this little Child is simply this. He was the son of his 'Master,' his mother being a Slave. Two years since, when the little one was three years old, his mother dying, left him to the care of a fellow Slave. The 'husband' of this caretaker was sold South, and she then determined to flee. A few weeks since she left her hut in Kentucky, and took with her seven of her children, *but forgot not the promise made to the dying one! She folded it to her bosom and gave it protection with her own.* The weather was damp and cold, the travelling was bad, and close at hand and hard after, was the 'Master,' the father of the little boy, in hot pursuit, to drag back to the prison-house his own offspring. The poor woman, with her precious charge, arrived here, and escaped the clutches of the Slaveholder, but fatigue and cold had done its work upon the little boy, and he was left to die among strangers. After a week's suffering he has gone to a Court that knows no 'Compromise Measures,' or 'Fugitive Slave Law.' What a commentary on the 'institution' of Slavery is this. *A father hunting his own son to doom him to the prison-house of Slavery!* Can anything be more abominable? Look at the corpse of this little one! I thank God that seven hundred young people are assembled in this place to be instructed, and may we not hope that *all* of you will be found on the side of Justice and Humanity — that no one of you will yield to the 'Slave-power,' and thus degrade your nature? Cursed be the hand that shall be raised to help the miserable wretch who comes to tear away the poor and stricken ones from all life holds dear and sacred, and consign them to the awful doom of Slavery.'

"At this point in the Doctor's address our pencil would not write — our heart was in the Coffin with the little fellow, or it had gone (on a fool's errand in the 'Model Republic') to seek an altar to Liberty to renew its vows to her.

"Professor Thome, following, said : 'My friends there is more than ordinary interest connected with this case. I feel, as I have observed my brethren feel, a sentiment struggling in my breast for utterance, a sentiment that I can not fully express. A motherless babe is left with us to be unwept — a victim of that atrocious system of 'chattel' Slavery. And yet it is not in view of this single case alone that our sympathies are drawn out. It is for the millions of helpless sufferers that this one comes to represent. It conjures them up before us! They hover around us! They ask us to remember their wrongs — the wrongs of two hundred and fifty years inflicted upon their race by American 'Democrats!' and to look along down the dark future, and weep for the woes of millions — yet unborn. My young friends, no better occasion could be furnished you, than is granted you to-day in the Sanctuary of the Religion of Jesus Christ, to gather around this Coffin and swear eternal allegiance to the interests of Humanity, and ceaseless hostility to Slavery!'

"His remarks to the friends who had taken care of the deceased were extremely affecting. We can not attempt to give them. He concluded: 'Let that Grave be a Sacred spot. Plant there the flower, to be watered by the tears of the future visiter. Erect a Monument to the Memory of the little Slave boy, bearing the inscription 'Resurgam!' and believe that as certainly as this little one shall rise again, so surely is it written on the 'institution' of Slavery, 'it shall fall!'"

"The day with its Sabbath stillness — the place, a Christian Church, sacred to Civil and Religious freedom — the large congregation of young people preparing for active public life — the effect of a Sermon representing so clearly the Son of God as identifying himself with Human suffering — the sweet innocence of the poor, hunted little boy — all contributed to make common words eloquent, and eloquent words almost divine. We could but wish, from our inmost heart, that the father of that little boy and every Slaveholder and trafficker in the flesh and blood of their fellow-men in the American Republic were present.

"After the exercises at the Church, a large company went to the Grave and gave the little fugitive a permanent home. Then by its side — poor Child! were sung the following verses, composed by a heart that loves and feels for the crushed and bleeding race:—

> "'Shielded by an Almighty arm,
> Thy griefs and sufferings now are o'er;
> Beyond the reach of tyrant's harm,
> Freed spirit, rest for evermore!
>
> "'Lone little wanderer, now no more
> 'Mid stranger hearts to seek for love,
> Thou'st gained thy home, thy native shore
> And boundless love thy bliss will prove.
>
> "'Thy Father called thee, suffering one,
> He knew and felt thy untold grief,
> To him *complexions all are one*,
> He died alike for their relief.
>
> "'Thy Angel-mother waits her child,
> Without a pang she'll bless thee now;
> She fears no scenes of danger wild,
> There's heavenly calmness on her brow.'"

On the 1st of August, 1855, there arrived in Delaware, Ohio, six runaway Slaves — a man and his "wife" and four children. They were taken to Church and placed behind a screen. During the service, a clergyman made some eloquent and touching remarks on the horrors of Slavery, and then drew the curtain, not only in language, but in reality. "There," said he, "is a specimen of the fruits of the infernal system of Slavery, as practised in the 'great Republic.'" The audience were surprised and horror-stricken. Eyes were filled with tears, and money was at once contributed to pay their way, by the "Underground Railroad," to Canada.

The Cincinnati Gazette, of the 29th of January, 1856, says:

"A party of seventeen Slaves escaped from Boone and Kenton counties" (sixteen miles from the Ohio river), "Kentucky, on Sunday night last, and taking with them two horses and a sled, drove that night to the Ohio river, opposite Western Row, in this City. Leaving the horses and sled standing there, they crossed the river on foot on the ice. Five of them were the Slaves of Archibald K. Gaines, three of John Marshall, both living in Boone county, a short distance beyond Florence, and six of 'Misther L. F. Dougherty,' of Kenton county. We have not learned who claims the other three. About seven o'clock this morning the owners and agents arrived in pursuit. They swore out a warrant before J. L. Pendery, United States Commissioner, which was put into the hands of Deputy United States Marshal Geo. S. Bennet, who obtained information that they were in a house belonging to a son of Joe Kite, the third house beyond Mill-creek. The son of Kite was formerly owned in the neighborhood from which they had escaped, and was bought from Slavery by his father.

"About ten o'clock the Deputy United States Marshal proceeded there with his posse, including the Slave-owners and their agents and 'Misther Murphy,' an extensive Slaveholder. On the Slaves being ordered to surrender, a firm and decided negative was the response. The officers, backed by a large crowd of Cotton-Brokers, Dry-Goods Jobbers, Sugar and Tobacco dealers, and other persons, 'doing business with the Slave States,' then made a descent. Breaking open the doors, they were assailed by the Slaves with pistols and cudgels. Several shots were fired, but only one took effect, so far as we could ascertain. A bullet struck a man named John Patterson, one of the Marshal's Deputies, cutting off a finger of his right hand, and dislocating several of his teeth.

"On looking around, horrible was the sight which met our eyes. In one corner of the room was a Slave-child bleeding to death. His throat was cut from ear to ear, and the blood was spouting out profusely, showing that the deed was but recently committed. Scarcely was this fact noticed, when a scream issuing from an adjoining room drew attention thither. A glance into the apartment revealed a Slave-mother holding in her hand a knife literally dripping with gore, over the heads of two of her children, who were crouched to the floor and uttering the cries whose agonized peals had first startled them. Quickly the knife was wrenched from the hand of the mother, and a more close investigation instituted as to the condition of the children. They were discovered to be cut in several places and the blood trickled down their backs and upon their sleeves.

"The woman avowed herself the Mother of the children, and said she had killed one, and would like to kill the other three, rather than see them returned to Slavery. On being asked whether she would rather go back to bondage or be tried for murder, with a chance of being hanged, she said:

"'Rather than go back to Slavery, I would go Dancing to the Gallows.'

"To the inquiry if she was not excited almost to madness when she committed the act: 'No,' she replied, '*I was as cool as I now am; and would much rather kill them at once, and thus end their sufferings, than have them taken back to Slavery, and be murdered by piecemeal.*'"

But this poor heart-broken Mother did not have an opportunity to "go Dancing to the Gallows." The United States Judge (Leavitt) decided that if a runaway Slave commits a murder in the State of Ohio, the *Slaveholder's claim takes precedence over Ohio law*, and the murderer must be delivered up into bondage, and the Laws of Ohio trodden under the hoof of the Slave-Power!

John Joliffe, Esq., of Cincinnati, defended the Slave-mother through the arduous struggle, without the slightest hope of reward. Several citizens, however, of Cincinnati, appreciating such noble conduct, contributed a handsome sum, and presented it to him as a Testimonial of regard for his humane efforts, with an appropriate letter. Among the names of the Committee, signing this letter, was that of *Samuel Straight*, a member of the house of Straight, Demming & Co., wholesale grocers. Hereupon some " dear lover of the Union," and of "good customers," marked the letter in *The Cincinnati Gazette*, and sent it to sundry Southern firms dealing with Cincinnati, whence it elicited the following response:—

"NASHVILLE, *March* 6, 1856.
" *To Messrs. Straight, Demming & Co., Cincinnati* :—
"GENTLEMEN: We notice in *The Cincinnati Gazette*, of the 1st inst., a letter addressed to Mr. John Joliffe, tendering him sympathy, and remunerating him, pecuniarily, for his defence of fugitive Slaves, to which we observe the name of S. Straight attached. From our former pleasant business correspondence with you, we feel at liberty to ask you if this Mr. S. Straight is a member of your firm, and if his name was placed to that letter by his own free will and accord, and if that letter expresses his views upon the subjects therein discussed. A prompt reply is respectfully solicited. Yours, respectfully,
"HART, MACRAE & CO., "S. N. HOLLINGSWORTH,
"B. LANIER & CO., "MERRIT S. PITCHER,
"B. W. MACRAE & CO., "LANIER & PHILLIPS,
"ROBB & SMITH."

To this inquiry, Mr. Straight very courteously replied, admitting that he was a signer of the letter in question, but explaining that its phraseology was not chosen by him, and did not precisely express his views, and trusting that " *the free expression of views conscientiously cherished*" would not be deemed offensive by his Southern customers. But this " soft answer" did not turn away the wrath of the Nashvillians. Hear them :—

"NASHVILLE, *March* 24, 1856.
" *S. Straight, Esq.*, Cincinnati : ***** You say you are unable to divine the objects of our favor of the 6th inst. One of our objects was

to afford you a fair opportunity to *disclaim, excuse, or justify your participancy in the presentation letter to Mr. Joliffe.* Some of us have been in pleasant business correspondence with you for several years, in which position we could not *conscientiously* remain, provided you answered our questions in the affirmative; and as you have done so, we here take occasion to say, that though we grant you the fullest privilege in regard to freedom of thought and expression of cherished views, we, as Southern merchants, possessing the same *free* privileges as yourself, can not longer contribute to sustain by our patronage a merchant, however correct as such he may be, who entertains views so hostile to institutions which we cherish" (that is, Slavery and Polygamy), "and have been reared up from childhood to look upon *as the most sacred rights guarantied by the Constitution of the United States.*"

A "new beauty" of the infamous Fugitive Slave Law, of 1850, was developed in the trial of this Slave-mother: that while the Government, at Washington, will pay the fees of witnesses who testify in favor of the kidnappers, it is its practice to refuse compensation to all witnesses who testify in behalf of the freedom of the alleged Slave.

The *Cincinnati* (Ohio) *Freeman,* of the 7th August, 1856, says: "On Monday last, a mother and a son, haggard with long travel, crossed the river, *en route* for Canada. The bloodhounds, two-legged and four-legged, were after them. The boy was remarkably handsome; his mild, bright eyes were full of intelligence, his head was finely shaped, and the curling ringlets of auburn hair that clustered about his brow were extremely beautiful. The mother was a woman somewhat darker than her son, of great intelligence and energy. She was a Christian mother flying, with her child, from the demon of Slavery."

"Wicked laws," says the Rev. George B. Cheever, "are no excuse for personal wickedness, nor any apology for disobedience to God. They are not to be obeyed, but, on the contrary, denounced and rejected; and only by being thus faithful to God can a people keep their freedom. And while it shows that a people are on the high road to ruin who will suffer and obey wicked Statutes, it also shows the terrific responsibility and wickedness of those who concoct and endeavor to enforce such Statutes, and who set the example of such iniquity. *If there be a lower pit in hell than any other, such men will, beyond all question, occupy it, along with those who have put out or concealed the lights of God's Word, and have put up false lights to lure men to perdition.* It is such as these, whom God gives judicially over to a reprobate mind, to be filled with all unrighteousness, who, knowing the judgment of God, that they who commit such things are worthy of death, not only do the same, but have pleasure in them that do them.

"Nothing can go beyond this wickedness. It is a fountain sin, *a germinating sin, an accumulating and multiplying sin, a sin that causes others to sin, a sin that enlarges from generation to generation all the way into the eternal world.* If it brings a million of souls under its power this year, it may bring two millions the next; this generation ten, the next generation twenty, the next forty. 'Cursed be he that maketh the blind to wander out of the way, and all the people shall say, Amen!' But he that strikes out the eyesight of a whole nation, that obliterates the law of justice and humanity, and sets in its place Statutes of injustice and inhumanity, and thus compels a nation, so blinded, to wander in iniquity, what shall be said of such a monster? What curse is heavy enough for such an incarnation of malignity, or what curse can measure in retribution the dreadful consequences of such crime?"

CHAPTER II.

"This is a people robbed and spoiled; they are all of them snared in Holes, and they are hid in Prison-houses; they are for a prey, and none delivereth; for a spoil, and none saith, Restore."

"The glorious tree of American liberty," says *The Columbia* (S. C.) *Telegraph*, "is springing up everywhere, and the benighted Nations of Europe will recline — one of these days — in its shade. Our example is contagious."

In another column, of the same number of *The Telegraph*, the Editor says: "Let us declare that Slavery shall not be open for discussion; that the system is too deep-rooted among us, and must remain for ever; that the moment anybody attempts to lecture us upon its immoralities — in the same moment *his or her tongue shall be cut out and cast upon the dunghill*. Let us, with the friends of *freedom* and *justice* everywhere, make common cause against all disorganizing influences, isms, and invasions of the glorious principles of the Constitution of our highly-favored country."

Nothing could be more fitted to create contempt for a Republican form of Government, than such barefaced and shameless inconsistency. The Roman Republic feared death from the advance of barbarians; the North American Republic fears it from the retreat of "Niggers," ninety-nine in a hundred of whom are the Children of her own loins.

"*Ran away* from the subscriber, in November last, a *Negro* man, about 35 years of age; height about 5 feet 8 or 10 inches, has *blue eyes, yellow hair, very fair skin*, particularly under his clothes. Said *Negro* was raised in Columbia, S. C., and is well known by the name of Dick M. Frazier." (See p. 211.) "He was lately known to be working on the Railroad in Alabama, near Moore's Turnout, *and passed as a white man* by the name of Joseph Tears. I will give a reward of two hundred dollars for his delivery in any jail so that I can get him; and I will give five hundred dollars for sufficient proof to convict, in open court, any man who took him away "J. D. ALLEN."
"BARNWELL COURT-HOUSE, S. C."

The Montgomery (Ala.) *Advertiser*, of the 13th December, 1856, says: "Under our Telegraph head will be found the startling intelligence of a Slave insurrection in South Carolina. To what extent the insurrectionary spirit of the Slave population of the State extends, we are not apprized. We trust it is confined to a small extent of country, but our fears are for the worst. For years past Northern emissaries have been in our midst tampering with our Slaves. We have too often suffered them to depart unhung. Simply tarring and ejecting an Abolitionist is but a child's remedy; and so far from its having the effect to stop his mischief, it will only case-harden and make him worse. Hang them when you catch them in your midst. Your self-preservation, the security of yourselves and families, and the perpetuity of the institution itself, demand that the life of an Abolition emissary should pay the forfeit of his temerity. Wherever you catch an Abolitionist, there let him find his grave."

While Mr. Core, a planter, of Fayette county, South Carolina, was on his plantation, a short distance from his residence, he perceived, approaching him from the woods, a stout, able-bodied runaway Slave. Mr. Core awaited his approach, thinking he belonged to one of his neighbors, and had been sent upon some errand. He came boldly up to Mr. C., and accosted him thus: "Your name is Core; I am a runaway and have long wished to have a conversation with you. I do not fear being apprehended — I am well armed" (exhibiting a brace of Pistols and a Bowie-knife) — " but I have long wanted to see you."

Mr. Core, doubting the propriety of attempting to arrest him, as he was alone, concluded he would question him about two runaways, who had been gone some time, and asked him if he knew them, and when he had seen them. The fugitive promptly replied, that he did know them, and volunteered to assist Mr. C. in arresting them, and told him, " if he would meet him alone, at the same place, the next day, he would carry him where he could arrest both, as they had been very troublesome to him, and he wanted to get rid of them." Mr. Core promised to meet him at the place and time appointed; but, instead of going alone, he took with him his Overseer, and another man, and secreted them, armed with double-barrelled guns, in the vicinity of the place of meeting.

At the appointed time the fugitive made his appearance, but instead of finding Mr. C. alone, found the two men with their guns levelled upon him. He at once surrendered, and gave up his weapons, begging them not to hand-cuff or tie him, as he wanted to be taken, and was tired of staying out, having been in the woods long enough; and he belonged to a man in Alabama, and that he would still go with them and show them the two runaways as he had promised. They concluded to trust him, and all four proceeded in company to an old deserted cabin close by. Upon approaching it he informed his captors that their runaway " property" was in it — that if they would suffer him to approach the cabin first, as soon as they entered the door he might close it up, and thus capture them with his assistance. They agreed to this plan, and he proceeded cautiously toward the cabin, and as he entered the door beckoned to them to rush up. They did so; but lo and behold! they perceived a back window, through which their prisoner had jumped, and mounting Mr. Core's horse, made good his escape.*

The Rev. Edward Mathews, an agent of the American Free Mission Society, recently visited Richmond, Madison County, Kentucky, and took occasion to advocate from the pulpit Anti-Slavery sentiments, after which he was assailed by a mob, and driven from the town. Returning in a short time, he left a communication respecting the transaction at the office of *The Richmond Chronicle*, and again departed, but had not gone far before he was overtaken by four men, who seized him, and led him to an out-of-the-way place, where they consulted as to what they should do with him. They resolved to duck him, ascertaining first that he could swim. Two of them took him

---

* The Macon "Telegraph" gives us a description of an underground den in which such runaways hide:—

"A runaway's den was discovered on Sunday near the Washington Spring, in a little patch of woods, where it had been for several months, so artfully concealed under ground that it was detected only by accident, though in sight of two or three houses, and near the road and fields where there has been constant passing. The entrance was concealed by a pile of pine straw, representing a hog-bed—which being removed, discovered a trap-door and steps that led to a room about six feet square, comfortably ceiled with plank, containing a small fireplace, the flue of which was ingeniously concealed in the straw. The inmates took the alarm and made their escape; but Mr. Adams and his excellent dogs, being put upon the trail, soon ran down and secured one of them, which proved to be a negro fellow who had been out about a year."

Hurrah for the "excellent dogs" of the excellent Mr. Adams!

Doubtless some people say, "What a fool the nigger was, to live in such a miserable place, when he might have had 'enough and to spare' if he had stayed with his master!" So he might; but it is a noteworthy fact that some other people are so fond of liberty as to take it under any circumstances they can get it. We are told in the eleventh chapter of the Epistle to the Hebrews, that some excellent persons, "of whom the world was not worthy," lived in "dens and caves of the earth."

and threw him into a pond, as far as they could, and on his rising on the surface, bade him come out. He did so, and on his refusing to promise never to come to Richmond, they threw him in again. This operation was repeated four times, when he yielded. They next demanded of him a promise that he would leave Kentucky, and never return again. He refused to give it, and they threw him in the water again, when, his strength failing, and they threatening to shoot him, he gave the pledge required, and left the State.

On the 16th of June, 1855, evidence was obtained that a Mr. Pullam, of Garrard county, had induced some Slaves to runaway. Accordingly a warrant was issued by a Magistrate of Bryantsville for his arrest. The constable, with five assistants, went to the field where he was working and arrested him. They started to return, but after progressing a short distance the prisoner broke away. He outran the officer and his posse, and the constable seeing his prize about to escape, fired a pistol, hitting him on the back. He instantly fell, screaming with pain, but just as the pursuing party came up, he arose and fled toward the river. Coming to a high cliff he fell first about seven feet, then ten, and finally over a precipiece thirty feet high, making the fall altogether forty-seven feet.

Pullam seemed endowed with more than mortal vigor, and rising, plunged into the river. Nothing has been seen or heard of him since. The poor fellow merited a more fortunate end. His blood will be found, at the Day of Judgment, on the skirts of the Pro-Slavery Churches.

"RAN AWAY from the subscriber, at the Galt House, Louisville, a *Negro* Woman named Polly, aged about forty years. She has *long auburn hair*, and a blemish on her right hand, caused by a burn, which stiffens her fingers. She has a quantity of good clothing, and most of the time dresses in black. *Her general appearance is modest and genteel.* I will give $250 reward for her if taken out of Kentucky, or $100 if in this city or State, and secured so that I can get her.

"MRS. ELLEN A. JARVIS."

Long auburn hair, well dressed, modest, and genteel. That will do very well.

Miss Mary Gibson, another "beautiful Slave girl," escaped recently from Marysville, and succeeded in reaching Canada. Miss Gibson is as white as any woman in the United States. Unless informed of the fact, no one would have the remotest suspicion that she had a drop of "colored" blood in her veins. *Her eyes are blue, her hair brown, her complexion fair and clear.* She is very intelligent, and her appearance exceedingly prepossessing. The name of the "high-born aristocrat" who owned Miss Mary Gibson is not given. The man who would keep such a fair chattel should be known, but in default of such knowledge, let us imagine a public dinner, and the company, with that "chivalrous" man present, and the proceedings, at Toast No. 13 :

"Woman !" (Nine cheers.)

> "O, woman ! in our hours of ease,
> Uncertain, coy, and hard to please,"
> &c., &c., &c.

(Immense applause, the whole company rising and using their glasses, some breaking them.)

The gallant Colonel Fitz, of Kentucky, being called upon to respond to this toast, rises and speaks as follows :

"MR. CHAIRMAN AND GENTLEMEN : It is a time-honored custom to toast 'Woman' at public dinners ; and, what is more, to reserve the toast till the close of the feast, when our hearts are warmest, and, under the inspiration of jolly Bacchus, our feelings mellowest." (Cheers and laughter.) "Woman ! what shall not be said in her favor ? When too young to know love or gratitude, who nurtured us at her breast, and soothed our helplessness and infant sorrows ?"

A VOICE—" Yer Mother !" (Cheers.)

> "Who ran to help me when I stumbled ?
> Who raised me gently when I tumbled ?
> Who flogged me soundly when I grumbled ?"

A Voice — "Yer Mother!" (Laughter.)

"When a little older, the first beam of divine feeling comes from the rainbow of undefined passion which overarches our existence, even in the dawn of youth." (Applause and disorder.) "Then in our days of ripened passion, what makes the stars shine, the floweret perfume, the grove vocal — what makes life worth the toil of existence but the love of woman!

"Who sewed the buttons on my shirt?"

A Voice — "Yer Wife!" (Cheers and laughter.)

"O how poor, how mean is our boasted ambition, our public honors, our private labors, without her smile!" (Applause and hiccoughs.) "But how doubly, trebly, quadruply blest, are we in this 'land of liberty,' where alone Woman is respected and protected by the law! Look at Europe, and you find her ever and everywhere doomed to the coarsest toils. War's greatest martyrs, and the shame of Peace! She plows, digs, delves, carries loads, plays scavenger, and is habitually prostituted. But in our glorious country — the 'land of the free and the home of the brave' — Woman first finds a place due her honor, nobility, and tenderness. Here she is respected. Free as virtue can render her, respected, beloved, venerated — this is her paradise." (Cheering and hiccoughing *ad libitum*.) "Go where you will in the thirty-one States, and the Territories (including the District of Columbia) of our glorious Republic, and a halo of idolatry encircles her fair brow!" (A *gentleman* who hiccoughs, "All except Niggers.") "The gentleman need not correct me — I said *fair* brow." (Great cheering and laughter.) "Woman, Mr. Chairman and gentlemen, now and for ever — God bless her!"

Need we add that, beyond doubt, the gallant Colonel sat down amid loud applause, long continued, and that in spite of his speech, Miss Mary Gibson found it necessary to run away from his proprietorship.

"$100 REWARD. — Ran away from James Hyhart, Paris, Ky., the boy Norton. Would be taken for *a white boy, if not very closely examined. His hair is black and straight.*"

The Indianapolis (Ind.) *Journal* gives an account of the capture of two fugitive Slaves by John Mancourt, conductor on the Madison and Indianapolis Railroad, and William Munroe, Adams & Co.'s Express Agent. It seems that the poor Slaves had been *hunted by bloodhounds on the Kentucky side of the river, but had in a desperate fight killed the animals with knives.* They then crossed the river and were wandering from Sunday night till Friday without provisions. Worn-out, ragged, and foot-sore, having had nothing to eat but what the orchards and forest trees provided, they despaired of escape, and hailed the cars. They were taken on board and carried to Vernon to the United States Commissioner, and before sundown were again in Slavery in Kentucky.

A native or citizen of a "*free* State," who would thus volunteer to restore a fellow-man to bondage, is no better than a pirate.

The Rev. T. B. M'Cormick, of this State (Indiana), was suspended in October, 1855, from the functions of the "Gospel ministry," on *suspicion* of having been concerned in the "underground railroad"— helping poor fugitives from Slavery, on their way to Canada. For this he was compelled to flee from his family, and from the "*free* State" of which he is a citizen, to escape arrest under a warrant of *Gov. Wright of Indiana*, issued in compliance with a requision of *Gov. Powell of Kentucky*.

If there are heights of tyranny or depths of servility not yet reached by the Slaveocrats and their cringing sycophants, we are becoming curious to learn what they can be. Here is a Citizen of a "*free* State" suspected of no crime but that of assisting some of his fellow-men to "secure the blessings of liberty," by sending them to Canada. This Christian minister, for this "un-Christian conduct," or rather on mere suspicion of it, is gravely arraigned and authoritatively "suspended from the functions of the Gospel ministry!" This otherwise blameless citizen, suspected only of assisting his fellow-citizens to "secure the blessing of liberty," is placed under the ban of a "*free State*" and hunted from off its soil as a felon!

The statement of such a case appears more like fiction than like reality. A writer even of romance should be criticised when his narratives, by being overdrawn, do violence to that innate instinct of probability, so necessary to invest fiction with the interest of imagined fact. An effort will be required in the reader before he can fully realize that the facts of this case are facts. He will wish to see, as we have seen, the man himself, and have the attestation from his own lips. He will wish to see and handle, as we have done, the Official document, under the Seal of the State of Indiana, and signed by her Secretary, the attested copy of the indictment of the Kentucky grand jury, and the requisition of the Kentucky Governor. The significancy of an event like this awaits a full revelation afterward. Judge Kane and Passmore Williamson, Gov. Wright and T. B. M'Cormick — names long to be pondered — letters of an alphabet yet to be mastered, wherewith seeing eyes may divine nameless and yet shapeless things. The elements of a future — the cypher of a coming American history may be in process of development in these dim beginnings. There is much yet to be learned, much yet to be attempted, much yet to be achieved. A great nation is to be delivered from the fangs of the "evangelical" Pro-Slavery Churches.

In October, sixteen Slaves, Men, Women, and Children, arrived in Chicago, Illinois, worn down with fatigue, and sickened by the exposure which they had undergone in travelling. They were not only poor, but destitute, and sought not only bread and meat, but that protection and support which they had a right to expect from people who profess to be followers "of the meek and lowly Jesus," and which neither Turk nor Algerine has ever refused to give to weary strangers who cast themselves upon their hospitality. Several of these persons had long passed the meridian of life. Four of them were fathers, the same number were mothers, and they all possessed those earnest affections which are alone developed by that circumstance, and which would entitle them to honor and respect even among heathens. Two were young men, with strong arms and hearts, that throbbed for "liberty." Two also were young girls just in the bud of womanhood. Four were little babes, not taken from their mothers' breasts, and entirely oblivious to the deep emotion which stirred the fountains whence they drew their life. Poor things! how little did they know that the tears which trickled down upon them, and the cold and hunger which those mothers had endured for many long weary days and nights, were that they should not be torn from their hearts and trained up in physical and spiritual prostitution.

If the angels of Heaven who had never heard of the Pro-Slavery Churches or the "lower law" D. D.s and LL. D.s, could have looked on this little group, how their hearts would have exulted in the expectations of seeing the thousands of professing "Christian people" who dwell in the city meet them as they entered it, and welcome them to their protection and hospitality—each one striving to perform those little offices of kindness which Christ blessed, saying, "*Inasmuch as ye did it unto the least of these ye did it unto me.*" But no! they came into the city when it was dark—when the Churches of Cotton-divinity or "lower law" were fast asleep, so that they might not be seen by those who were ready to let loose upon them the bloodhounds of "the law." Their arrival was not heralded abroad but whispered from one to another, as if it were a fearful responsibility to know of their presence, and involving one still more fearful to tender them the aid which their destitute condition demanded. But their presence did become known. The bloodhounds, in human shape, were upon their tracks. The Governor of the State, from his high place, had commanded the Military Companies to get ready, with swords drawn, bayonets set, and cartridges rammed down, to aid the bloodhound minions of a bastard Democracy to take and bind these helpless way-worn and sick fugitives, and send them — where, and what for? The men and fathers, who had toiled, early and late, all their lives for their self-constituted "Masters," were wanted to toil more. The mothers who had scrubbed, washed, baked, and drudged from infancy, and who had given birth to children that had been taken from them and sold at Auction in order to fill their "Masters'" pockets, were wanted to scrub and drudge the remainder of their days, and to give birth to more babes to sell to the Mississippi, Louisiana, and Nebraska speculators in Human cattle, or to the libertine, just as the demands of the one or the other preponderated.

The young men were also "wanted" for Slaves that their "Master's" cupidity might be gratified. And the young women, with their full round forms, their bright orange-colored faces, deep black eyes, pouting lips, and gently curling tresses — what were the two-legged bloodhounds so anxious to take them for?* And those little babes — helpless little creatures, whom the Saviour requested might be permitted to come unto him, because of such was the Kingdom of Heaven — they, too, were "wanted," that they might be torn from their mothers' hearts, and turned over to the Auctioneer like so many pigs or

---

* The Author of the "*South-Side View of Slavery*" says, at p. 87, that "the only object of the Slaves in running away is to form *a new adulterous marriage.*" While laws exist to punish swindling in the sale of a bogus watch, we do not see why there should not be laws to punish the "getter-up" of a book intended to deceive. But so it is. The world has got into its head that laws to punish lying in the "evangelical" Pro-Slavery Churches are unnecessary.

calves for the butcher's shambles. And it was for this that the Governor of the "*free* State" of Illinois issued his mandate, and that the National Guards, commanded by a "good Democrat," one "Misther Thomas Shirely," paraded the streets of Chicago with the "Star-spangled Banner" flying, their bayonets set, and their muskets charged with powder and ball, ready to shoot down all persons who might dare to interfere between the ravisher and his victim! Brave men! voluntarily becoming parties to the ravishment that was sought to be accomplished! — standing by, with the United States flag flying, and swords drawn to compel the victim to submit!

We have not learned words that sufficiently express our detestation of the *men* — mankind, forgive the insult! — who thus lend themselves to the capture of Women and little Children, that they might be consigned to physical and moral prostitution. It was an act of meanness, so atrocious in every light by which it can be viewed, that it has no parallel in the history of the most brutish nation of the antediluvian world; and if men's spirits pervaded their bodies, the worms that feast and riot with luxury upon a dead dog would turn from the carcass of the Slave-breeder with loathing and disgust.

Had any person asserted that there was a single individual in Chicago *who would lend his aid, directly or indirectly, in hunting down modest young women, that they might be debauched by force*, or in tearing little babies from their mothers' breasts, to be sold — where, and to whom, God only knows — the citizens would have repelled it as the veriest libel that ever was perpetrated. But, alas! the National Guards — National? — God forbid — showed that they, like their brethren of Boston, Mass., in the case of Anthony Burns, were infinitely below the point we had thought poor weak humanity could reach.

"We have just met," says the Chicago *Free Press*, "with another white American Slave-mother. We could detect no trace of African characteristics about her. Her employment in South Carolina — the land of 'chivalry'— was that of a Field-hand. Her patience held out until her last child was sold to satisfy the claims of her 'Master's' creditors, when, to save herself from the like calamity, she set her face Canada-ward."

In December, 1855, an attempt was made by a Slaveholder, to bribe the Chief of Police of Montreal, Canada, to aid in enticing to " the other side of the river" an unfortunate " chattel" who had escaped from bondage. It seems that the ill success attending the efforts of this Southern specimen of humanity has not had the effect of deterring others from making similar ventures.

Mrs. Sylvia Young, a "colored" woman — now residing with Mr. Thomas, of the Shakespeare Restaurant, Stratford, Canada, was formerly the " property" of a *lady* of the name of Dustin. Mrs. Young is an excellent cook, and in the Slave States of the " Model Republic," where such "property" is an article of merchandise, would have sold for about $1,300. The woman, Dustin, got married to a fellow, named Stewart, and removed to Chicago. Stewart, like a " good Democrat," then thought of looking after his wife's runaway " property," and, putting their heads together, they hit upon what they, doubtless, conceived to be a cunningly-devised scheme, to be rewarded with success. Accordingly in pursuance of their plan, the wife addressed a letter to her runaway " chattel" or Human cow, of which the following is a copy:—

" CHICAGO, ILLINOIS, *December* 23, 1855.

" SYLVIA: You see, from the date of my letter, that I have changed my place of residence. We have been living here about four months; we like the place very much. I at first thought I would not answer your letter at all, but the *children seemed so anxious* to see you and hear from you again, that I have consented to write to you and make a proposition, and let your feelings and judgment decide for you. You say you are happy. I can not think one with your *strong feelings* can be happy so far from your *relations and native home*. Now, if you are disposed to come here — which is a short journey — and live with me, and serve me

faithfully two years, I will give you your free papers. Then you will be at liberty to settle among your *old friends,* and not be compelled to confine yourself to Canada. Write to me and let me know what you think of my proposal. Besides, Sylvia, you know you will, in a few years, at farthest, *inherit considerable from* your *father.* I do not wish to persuade you against your will; but, located in a strange place, I would be glad to have the services of one that understands my ways as well as you do. The *children* all send their *love.* " Your *friend,*
"E. G. DUSTIN."

On the same day that the above ingenious and *loving* letter arrived, Mr. Townsend, Chief-Constable of Stratford, received a very different communication from her husband, W. G. Stewart, proprietor of the Boone House, corner of Clarke and Jackson streets, Chicago, Illinois:—

" CHICAGO, ILLINOIS, *Monday, Dec.,* 24, 1855.
" CHIEF-CONSTABLE — SIR : I enclose you a letter from a runaway Slave, who belongs to my wife as well as myself, late residents of Louisville, Kentucky. You see what she says about going to Cincinnati. *I want to catch her there!* If you will put her into my possession there, or in the custody of the State Marshal in that city, so that I can secure her, *I will pay you the sum of* $200. Should you feel disposed to act in this matter, it would be necessary for my wife and self to be in Cincinnati at the time she would be there. You might follow her on to that city and trace her to where she would stop, and if you could notify me to be there, *I would do the rest,* and pay you the $200.
" W. G. STEWART."

Mr. Townsend, very properly, handed this letter to the magistrate of the town, and wrote Stewart an evasive reply, so as to induce him to visit Canada, in order to secure his missing " property." Had he done Stratford the honor of visiting it, he would have " caught" something which he would have had good cause for remembering to the last hour of his villanous life.

" BLOODHOUNDS ! I would respectfully inform the citizens of Missouri that I still have my Nigger Dogs, and that they are in prime training, and ready to attend to all calls of Hunting and Catching runaway Niggers, at the following rates: Hunting per day $5, or if I have to travel, every day will be charged for, in going and returning, as for hunting, and at the same rates. Not less than five dollars will be charged in any case where the Niggers come in before I reach the place. From $15 to $25 will be charged for catching; according to the trouble; if the Nigger has weapons, the charge will be made according to the difficulty had in taking him, or in case he kills some of the Dogs, the charge will not be governed by the above rates. I am explicit to prevent any misunderstanding. The owner of the Nigger to pay all expenses in all cases. I venture to suggest to any person having a Nigger runaway, that the better plan is to send for the Dogs forthwith when the Nigger goes off, if they intend sending at all, and let no other person go in the direction, if they know which way the runaway went; as many persons having other Niggers to hunt over the track, and failing of success, send for the Dogs, and then, perhaps, fail in consequence to catch their Nigger, and thus causelessly fault the Dogs. Terms cash. If the money is not paid at the time the Nigger hunted for is caught, he will be held bound for the money. I can be found at home at all times, five and a half miles east of Lexington, except when professionally engaged — in hunting with the Dogs. "JOHN LONG."

Lexington (Mo.) *Democratic Advocate*, Feb. 14, 1855.

In April, 1856, a female Slave of a Mr. Pond, living near Palmyra, Missouri, ran away, and, after several days' search, she was captured on the Ferryboat crossing from Missouri to Quincy, Illinois. She had been kept at the house of a Mr. Davids, a German, in Palmyra, for a few days, and brought from thence by a Mr. Scheible, another German, to the Ferryboat opposite Quincy. When she was taken back to Palmyra, both Germans were imprisoned. Upon the examination of Scheible, *he swore that he did not know the girl was a Slave, as she was as white as any woman in the State.* Several gentlemen were called on the witness stand, who testified that they had seen her while she was at Davids, and thought she was *a genuine white woman.* After a three days' trial Scheible was discharged, *on the ground of his ignorance of her being a Slave;* but " he found it necessary," said the *Palmyra*

Whig, "to leave the State forthwith." Davids, it was intimated, would be sent for five years to the Penitentiary.

This case presents the true features of the "peculiar institution" in a strong light. An honest German brings what he supposes to be a white woman in his carriage from Palmyra to Quincy. He is suddenly arrested, thrown into prison, held up to the community as a "Nigger-stealer," subjected to a trial, and would have been sent to the State-prison for five years had it not been for the fortunate circumstance that several gentlemen in Palmyra had seen the girl, and had the moral courage to come into court and testify that they believed her to be *a white woman!* And even after being discharged, the man, for fear of personal violence from the "poor whites" of Palmyra, had to leave the State, because he did not know that a white woman was a "Nigger"! After this, travellers in Missouri must be cautious whom they ride with. Before a man can safely admit a woman into his carriage he must insist upon seeing her "dockymints"—her "*free* papers," or have legal evidence that she is not a "Nigger."

The Missourians, not content with managing the affairs of Kansas, seem also to have undertaken a similar good office for the State of Illinois. We find in *The St. Louis Republican* the following rather singular notice :—

"RUNAWAY NOTICE.—Was taken up in Union County, in the State of *Illinois*, as a runaway Slave, on the 15th of October, 1855, a *Negro* man, who calls himself Nicholas, and says he belongs to Umprey White, in Onslow County, in the State of North Carolina. Said *Negro* is dark copper color, five feet five inches high, aged *about* 40 years, weighs *about* 150 pounds, and had on when taken up, a drab cloth coat, stripped worsted pants, cloth cap, and is blind in his right eye. The owner of said *Negro* is hereby required to come and prove said *property*, pay all charges incurred on account of said *Negro*, within three months, otherwise he will be sold on Saturday, the 7th day of March, 1857, at the Court-House in Jackson, Cape Girardeau County, State of Missouri, for ready Cash.

"JOHN F. BURNS,
"*Sheriff of Cape Girardeau County, Mo.*"

From this Advertisement, it would appear that the Missouri sheriffs of the border counties of that State, consider the adjacent counties of the bordering "*free* States" as falling within their respective bailiwicks, so far as the "colored population" are concerned. Or, is there a sort of private partnership between Sheriff Burns and certain residents of Union County, Illinois, by virtue of which they are to Kidnap and to convey to Missouri all the stray "Niggers" on which they can lay their hands, while the said sheriff is to sell them, for the joint benefit of the parties?

The Missouri Democrat, of the 4th of December, 1856, says: "In calling attention to the frequency and increase of the reported plots on the part of the Slave population within the past year, we design not so much to speak of the measures which have been found necessary for their repression, as to point to one great cause which has more than all else encouraged and instigated them, and that is the agitation of the Slavery question by every demagogue in the Slave States, who wishes to acquire transient notoriety. In Missouri, especially, have we felt the effect of this Slavery agitation and Slavery extension policy upon the part of the nullification faction, who have sought to float into power and office by continually exciting the passions of men, *and provoking discussion in regard to this theme;* and we venture to assert that in consequence thereof more Slaves have been induced to run away, more desperate resolutions having been put into their heads, and more general insecurity entailed upon that species of *property* within the past year, than during any five years preceding. The ferment excited in the minds of the Masters soon extended itself to the Slaves — for all who have lived in Slaveholding communities well know how eagerly every scrap of parlor conversation, every excited harangue on the stump, or loud-toned dispute in the streets, is treasured up by the Nigger, and made the burden of comment during the night."

"RAN AWAY from the subscriber, living near White's Store, Anson county, on the 3d of May last, *a bright boy,* named Robert. He is about five feet high, will weigh about 130 pounds; is about 22 years old, and has some beard on his upper lip. His left leg is somewhat shorter than his right, causing him to hobble in his walk; *has a very fine face, and will show color like a white man.* It is probable he has gone off with some wagoner or trader, or he may have free papers and be passing as a free white man. He has *straight hair.* I will give a reward of two hundred and twenty-five dollars for the delivery to me of said Nigger boy, or for his confinement in any jail, so that I can get him.

Newbern (N. C.) *Spectator.* "ADAM LOCKHART."

"$250 REWARD will be given for the apprehension and delivery to me of the following Slaves: Samuel and Judy, *his* wife, with *their* four children, belonging to the estate of Sacker *Dubberly,* deceased. I will give ten dollars for the apprehension of William *Dubberly,* a Slave belonging to the estate. William is about nineteen years of age, *quite white, and would not readily be taken for a Nigger.*

Newbern (N. C.) *Spectator.* "JOHN L. LANE."

The West Tennessee Democrat, edited by the Rev. Mr. Brownlow (commonly called " Parson Brownlow"), of Knoxville, is horrified at the impiety of Mrs. H. B. Stowe, whom the " pious Editor" sets down as a " dangerous infidel," and styles her book — Uncle Tom's Cabin — "a fling at the *Christian* religion in general, and Southern Methodism" (of which the Parson is a burnin' and shinin' light) " in particular." The " pious Editor" waxes wroth at the inhumanity of such a publication, but has no word of comment upon the following, which appears in the same number of his paper:—

"BLOODHOUNDS! I have two of the finest Dogs for catching runaway Niggers in the South-West. They can take a trail twelve hours after the Nigger has passed, and catch him with ease. I live just four miles south-west of Bolivar, on the road leading from Bolivar to Whitesville. I am ready at all times to catch runaway *property* of every description.

"BOLIVAR, West Tennessee." "DAVID TURNER.

This " Rev. gentleman," speaking of the " burning alive of a Nigger," for a crime that would have only sent a white

Southerner to jail for a week or two, if at all, says: "*We unhesitatingly affirm that the punishment was unequal to the crime. Had we been there, we would have taken a part, and even suggested the pinching of pieces out of him with red-hot pinchers — of cutting off of a limb at a time, and then burning them all in a heap.** The true-hearted Citizens of Tennessee and *property*-holders, ought to enter into a league, and whip black, and ride on a rail, irrespective of age, calling, or family associations, every Clergyman, Citizen, or Traveller, who dares to utter one word in opposition to our Domestic Institutions" (Slavery and Polygamy), "or who is found in possession of an Anti-Slavery document. These are our sentiments, and we are willing and ready to help others to carry them out."

"RAN AWAY from the subscriber on the 23d of June last, a bright mulatto Woman, named Julia, about twenty-five years of age. She is common size, *very nearly white, and very good-looking* — for a Nigger.

---

* What a difference between the Methodist John Wesley, and the Methodist Brownlow! Southern Methodists "swear by" Wesley, but indignantly insist that he never called slavery "the sum of all villainies." We need no further proof that it *is*, than to see how thoroughly it has imbued this good brother Brownlow with the spirit of the devil. Brownlow would be at home among the tortures of the Inquisition, and would clap his hands for joy, to see some poor mortal (provided he were a "nigger" mortal or an "abolitionist") broken alive upon the wheel. From all such preachers, and from all their preaching; from all who uphold them, and from all the hellish things by which they are upheld; from the smitings of their own conscience (if they have any conscience) here on earth, and from the eternal tortures of remorse in the world to come—worse than red-hot pincers and pinching, cutting and burning and mangling— may the Good Lord deliver us! There is every reason to believe that John Wesley was a good Christian; and that, with his clear convictions of gospel truth, and his stern views of church discipline, he would have turned Brother Brownlow out of meeting.

DOMESTIC AMUSEMENTS IN THE SLAVE STATES.

She is a good Seamstress, and reads a little. *She may attempt to pass for white:* dresses fine. She took with her Anna, her Child, eight years old. She once belonged to a Mr. Helm, of Columbia, Tennessee. I will give a reward of $50 for said Nigger and Child if delivered to me, or confined in any jail in Tennessee so I can get them, or $100 if taken in any other Slave State; and $200 if caught in any *free* State, and put in any good jail in Kentucky or Tennessee, so I can get them.

"A. W. JOHNSON."

Republican Banner and Nashville Whig.

"NOTICE TO PROPERTY-HOLDERS. — On the first of November last, I took up and committed to jail a runaway Nigger — *nearly white*, calling himself Ireneus Prime. He had on a large Neck-iron, with a huge pair of horns, and a band or clog of iron on his left leg. He lost his hat and bundle in a cane-brake while running from my Dogs. The owner of said Nigger is requested to prove *property*, pay charges, and take him away. The rascal says his father is a white man and lives in New York. "N. ROSS.

"RANDOLPH, Tipton county, Tennessee."

In March, 1855, we saw a poor heart-broken Slave pass through the streets of Nashville, who had been captured by a pack of four-legged and two-legged bloodhounds, belonging to a "gentleman" of that city. His coat, pantaloons, and shirt, were torn to pieces, and his person mangled in a most shocking manner; the blood was streaming from his face, hands, legs, &c.

When a wretched runaway is killed, either designedly or by accident, the Southern newspapers speak of it merely as a "loss of property." Nothing is ever said about the bereaved Widow, Children, or Parents of the deceased.

BLOODHOUNDS! "The undersigned, having purchased the well-known Nigger-Dogs of David Turner, formerly of this County, offers his services to the Citizens of this and adjoining Counties, for the purpose of Hunting and catching runaway Niggers. All who have Niggers in the woods will please give me a call. I live three miles north of Bolivar, on the Jackson road. "JAMES SMITH."

Bolivar (Tenn.) *Democrat,* May 9, 1855.

" $500 REWARD. — Ran away from the subscriber, on the 25th of May last, a Nigger boy, twenty-one years of age, named Washington. Said

Nigger, *without close observation, might pass himself for a white man, as he is light colored, has sandy hair, blue eyes, and a fine set of teeth.* He is an excellent bricklayer; but I have no idea that he will pursue his trade, for fear of detection. *Although he is like a white man in appearance,* he has the disposition of a *black* Nigger, and delights in comic songs and witty expressions. He is an excellent house servant, very handy about a hotel; tall and slender, and has rather a down look, especially when spoken to, and is sometimes inclined to be sulky. I have no doubt but he has been decoyed off by some Abolition scoundrel; and I will give the above reward for the apprehension of the boy and thief, if delivered at Chattanooga; or I will give $200 for the boy alone, or $100 if confined in any jail so that I can get him.

The Chattanooga (Tenn) *Gazette.* " GEORGE O. RAGLAND."

The leading Journal of the National Democratic Party—Pierce, Buchanan, & Co.'s " Own," speaking of the " deplorable condition of the down-trodden people of the Nations of the Old World" says:

"Ignorance of the real state of political parties in *this* Country, and the force and direction of *our* National currents, may naturally be expected among a class of men whose interests are all wrapped in *old* laws and customs. Being *foreigners,* they can not know *our* Character, or judge correctly of *our* Social, Moral, Religious, or Political condition; for *no* one can understand, thoroughly, the Opinions, Feelings, and Habits of Americans, who has not studied them on their own Soil, and at their own Firesides. Being *opposed* to a Republican form of Government, they are *naturally* prejudiced against us, are liable to be deceived, and are *pleased* when they can seize upon anything that can be twisted into an argument against a *free* and *happy* people. Our citizens" (that is, the genuine whites) "know that *their* arguments in favor of Monarchical and Despotic forms of Government are *not* supported by facts. Here the oppressed children of the *Old* World can bask in the sunshine of Civil and Religious *liberty,* and be *protected* in their *natural* rights. We must let *our* light shine."

The Persians have an old saying, to the effect, that it is well to aim at the Sun, for, although the arrow will not hit the mark, it will fly higher than if aimed at an object on the plane. There are, however, two sides to this " question," and the other view is given and illustrated by the veritable historian Æsop, in the fable of the Frog that attempted to blow himself up to the size of an Ox, and made a melancholy failure of it. It will be remembered that he not only fell far short of the dimensions of the Ox, but utterly blighted his career of usefulness as a Frog, by bursting himself into a great number of small speckled or party-colored fragments, each one of which impressively set forth the melancholy consequences of inordinate ambition. Sad as was the fate of the lamented batrachian gentleman, who not improbably left behind him a weeping widow and a large family of mourning tadpoles, all mortals do not take to heart the lesson, but are far more influenced in their actions by the "glittering generalities" of the Persian proverb, than by the mournful speciality of the *Phrygian* fable.

The National Democratic Party — Pierce, Buchanan, & Co.'s "Own" — have yet to learn the true signification of the parable of the Good Samaritan. (See Hebrews xiii. 3; Romans i. 14; and James ii. 4–9.)

CHAPTER III.

"When the measure of their tears is full, when their Groans have involved Heaven itself in darkness, doubtless a God of Justice will listen to their distress."—JEFFERSON.

The Savannah Republican, printed in a State which boasts a Senator, Robert Toombs, who says he will yet "call the roll" of his Slaves "at the foot of Bunker Hill monument," has in its impression of the 15th October, 1855, the following advertisement:—

"RAN AWAY from the subscriber, on the 22d ult., my Negro man, Albert Jock, who is twenty-seven years of age, *very white, so much so that he would not be suspected of being a Negro. He has blue eyes, and light hair.* Wore when he left, a long thin beard, and rode a sorrel horse. He is about 5 feet 8 inches high, weighs about 140 pounds, has an humble and meek appearance, can neither read nor write, and is a kind and amiable fellow, speaks much like a low country Negro. He has no doubt been led off by some infidel during my absence to New York. $50 reward will be paid for his delivery to me, or to Tison & Mackay, or for his apprehension and confinement in any jail where I can get at him.

"J. M. TISON.

"BETHEL, Glynn Co., Georgia."

"There was ne'er a loon in a' the toun like our little Jock,
There was ne'er a loon in a' the toun like our little Jock;
But since he became a member o' the Young Band o' Hope,
There's a wonderfu' improvement on our little Jock.
He wadna bide within the door, nor gang to kirk or schule—
He tore a suit o' claes to rags frae Whitsunday to Yule;
He ran through Winter's frost an' snaw without a shoe or sock,
Sic a hardy little customer was our little Jock."

DOMESTIC AMUSEMENTS IN THE SLAVE STATES.

Dr. C. G. Parsons, of Boston, Massachusetts, speaking of his "Tour among the Planters," gives us an account of a Slave-hunt he witnessed on Flint River. Having ascended a small hill, he saw a man coming up on the other side slowly, and almost naked. The instant the man saw Mr. Parsons, he threw up both hands, and exclaimed imploringly, "O Goddy, Massa!" Mr. Parsons supposing that the poor runaway thought he would betray him, said: "I will not betray you." But before he had time to inquire into his history, two blood-hounds came dashing over another hill, half a mile distant. The moment the baying of the dogs reached the ear of the Slave, he made for the river, jumped in, and swam a long distance under water toward the opposite bank; on reaching which, he ran to a large tree, got up into it, and seated himself on a limb. The hounds came following the track — and well they might, for the blood of the wretched fugitive was left in every footstep — keeping up a constant baying. They rushed up the hill, plunged into the river where the Slave did, swam across, and ran up to the tree baying in blood-thirsty tones in triumph of success. Soon two men came over the hill on horseback, and when they saw the Slave in the tree, and heard the hounds baying beneath it, they shouted and rode on at full speed.

"One day," says Dr. Parsons, "while I was in Macon, there was a cry of 'a Nigger in the river!' Besides the 'Nigger,' three bloodhounds were in the river also, endeavoring to catch him; but the poor fellow, being a good swimmer, every time the hounds came close upon him, would dive a long distance under water, so deep, that the hounds could not see the direction he took, but when he raised his head above the water to breathe, they swam toward him and seized his limbs and held on till he jerked them away, leaving his flesh in their teeth. Soon his two-legged bloodhound pursuers were seen coming from the woods, and perceiving that farther at-

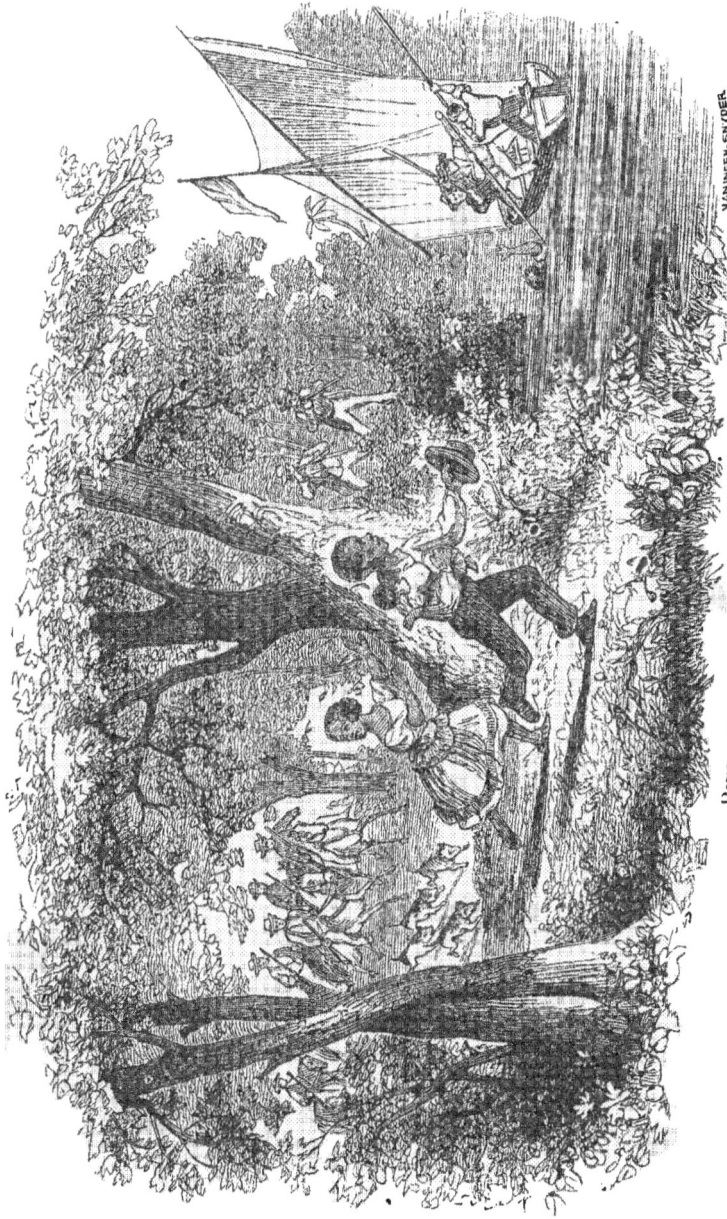

RUNNING AWAY. (See page 345.)

tempts to elude them were in vain, he told them if they would call off the dogs he would come out. This they did. Two of the hunters dismounted, and took him, one by either arm, to lead him over the bridge into the city, in the midst of hosts of the exulting 'poor whites.' No sympathy was manifested for the suffering Slave, whose naked limbs were horribly lacerated by the hounds. And what most shocked the feelings, as the two-legged hounds were leading him, was to hear the 'poor whites,' men and boys, tell the dogs to bite him — saying, 'Seek him!' 'Take hold of him!' — just as they would set the dogs on swine, and with as little pity."

The following letter was received lately in Oberlin, Ohio, from a prominent Member of the Methodist Episcopal Church Georgia. Its authenticity is guarantied by the Editor of *The Oberlin Evangelist:*

"DEAR SIR: I take my pen to write to you once more, though it is not I that write to you, but the *Lord* that writeth through me. Permit me to inform you that since I wrote you last I have come out and embraced the Religion of the Lord Jesus Christ, and am now living in the *light* and liberty of the children of God. We have had quite an interesting Church meeting here last week in relation to Deacon D——. It was thought by many that he would be disfellowshipped; but his case was set forth in such a vivid light by the influential members of the Church, our Pastor among the rest, that he was honorably discharged. *For fear you will think the case worse than it is,* I will just state the facts: The Deacon had an old Slave that had been in the habit of running away, but had always been caught, until finally about two weeks ago, he made another escape. No sooner was the old fellow missing than cousin H—— borrowed neighbor P——'s hounds and started in search of him. He had not proceeded far in the woods before he found the old man perched upon the limb of a large tree. He ordered him several times to come down, but the old fellow, stubborn as an ass, still maintained his position. The deacon then becoming excited, fired his gun at him. The ball passed through the old man's ankle, and mangled it in such a manner that it mortified and he died. But as I have before stated, our good Pastor (may the Lord prosper him) held for the justification of the Deacon in such a vivid, *heaven-*approving style, that he was discharged upon the

15

ground that he had a right to do what he pleased with his own *property* — a judgment that would have been passed by any righteous man. Your Uncle J—— died last week. We had the greatest kind of a time when he was a-dyin'— he went straight to glory, anyhow. His Niggers are a-goin' to be sold on Saturday next.

"I have partly bargained for fifty Niggers belonging to a neighbor. If I can get them as cheap as I expect to, I shall make a handsome profit on them, for I understand that the Orleans market is quite good now. I expect to send them down as soon as my Driver recovers; for in flogging one of my old Slaves the other day, he received a very severe wound from him, he having struck him with his hoe, whereupon the Driver instantly drew his pistol and shot him dead upon the spot, a fate which he justly merited. From his extreme age (being a little over 79 years), I consider his death a gain and not a loss to me.

"In your last letter you spoke of visiting us next year. If you come, I pray you to leave your Abolitionism behind, and show yourself a man. It is now time to go to Prayer-meeting, and I must close. My wife joins me in love to you."

It is a question which becomes the more hardened comparatively in iniquity — a nation or an individual? The individual has his moments of reflection, but the nation once on the downward slope appears to have neither brains nor bowels. There is a familiarity with evil which the Apostle calls being "dead in trespasses and sins." There is an awful paralysis of the Moral sense when deeds unholiest and crimes most fearful cease any longer to affect the nerve. The bloodhound, the emblem of cowardly distrust and brutal cupidity, is now a household word — a "domestic institution" of more than one half the States and Territories of the Union. He is as regularly advertised as the animal Man. Shame is no longer felt in this regard. Hear them:

"BLOODHOUNDS! The undersigned having a magnificent Pack of Hounds, for Trailing and Catching runaway Niggers, takes this method of informing his Friends and the Public, generally, that his prices are as follows: For each day employed in either Hunting or Trailing, $2.50; for catching each Slave, $10; for going over ten miles and catching a

Slave, $20. If sent for, the above prices will be expected, in Cash. The subscriber lives one mile and a half south of Dadeville.

Dadeville (Ala.) *Banner.*   "B. BLACK."

Was this the "Idea" which blazed and culminated on the lips of the "Sires of '76"? Was this the "Idea" which prompted that spirit of fraternal affection which produced the last great fruit of the Revolution — the Union of the States under a Constitution of confederated Republican Government? Was this the "Idea" of the men who penned the Declaration that "All men are born Free and Equal, and entitled to Life, Liberty, and the pursuit of — of — of — of — Happiness"?

"BLOODHOUNDS! The undersigned having purchased an entire Pack of Hounds, of the Hay and Allen Stock, he now purposes to Catch runaway Niggers, of every description. His charges will be $3 a day for Hunting, and $15 for Catching.

North Livingston (Ala.) *Whig.*   "WILLIAM GAMBREL."

"BLOODHOUNDS! The undersigned would respectfully inform the Citizens of Montgomery and the surrounding Country, that he is stationed one mile from the Court-House, on the South Plank Road, with the Well-known Pack of Hounds formerly owned by G. W. Edwards, and will attend to all calls he may be favored with. Terms of Hunting as follows: Catching, $10, if in or near the City, and charges in proportion to distance and trouble. Information by any person or persons of Niggers lying about their premises will be attended to, without charge, if they are not their own.*   "A. V. WORTHY.

"MONTGOMERY (Ala.), *May* 29, 1855."

The Christian reader shudders — and well he may — at the reading of such advertisements as these, but in Alabama, or any of the Slaveholding States and Territories, they excite no more attention than the reading of the ordinary advertisements

---

* *The New York Ledger*, of the 9th August, 1856, says: "A fugitive Slave, that was hunted with Dogs among the swamps of Alabama, a few days since, finding escape impossible, turned at bay, and after a desperate fight, was torn in pieces by the Hounds, but not until he had killed two of them and severely damaged three others." That "Nigger" deserved a better fate.

published in the towns and cities of the "*free* States." What, then, must be the "public sentiment" of such a people? — to what must it have sunk, when scenes like these can not only be advertised, but continually enacted, and the people meantime, instead of blushing for shame, at such abominations, boastingly declare themselves the "Model Republic," and invite all the people of Europe to institute similar Governments for themselves.

Did the eccentric imagination of Rabelais or the morbid misanthropy of Swift ever conjure up such grotesque monstrosities and incredible contradictions? What is the "American Idea" or "Machine" worth when the Press of Anglo-Saxondom enforces diabolism unknown, in the desperate meanness and cruelty of its details, to the scalping Savage? He at least scents out his victim and runs his mortal risk. But the Hunters with Bloodhounds of the poor shivering Slaves, sons of poverty and shame, what shall we say of them? Why, perdition itself has scarcely an adequate state of punishment for such wretches.

There are thousands of poor runaways whose story the world never hears. Their bones lie bleaching in the lone forests, in the dismal swamps, in the caves, and in the riverbeds, not only of the South and West, but of the "*free* North." Oh, if they could speak, they would tell us of the intolerable cruelties from which they fled, to encounter cold and heat, darkness and tempests, bears and wolves, nakedness and starvation, and bloodhounds, or their more brutal "Masters."

"RAN AWAY from the subscriber, working on the plantation of Col. H. Tinker, a boy, named Alfred. He is about eighteen years old, pretty well grown; *has blue eyes, light flaxen hair, and skin disposed to freckle.* He will try to pass as freeborn. "S. G. STEWART."
"GREENE COUNTY, Ala."

"WILL BE SOLD, in front of the Court-House, in this County, on the first Monday in November next, for cash, between the hours of 11, A. M., and 4, P. M., of said day, a Nigger woman, named Elizabeth Johnson, who says she is free, and that she is from Charleston, South Carolina. She is about 27 years of age, five feet six or seven inches high, *of very light copper complexion,* and has *very straight hair.* Said woman was committed to jail on the 5th of January, by Thomas Durden, a Justice of the Peace for Montgomery County, as a runaway Slave; and *her owner having failed to come forward, prove property, pay charges, and take her away,* she is, therefore, to be sold, in compliance with the Statute in such cases made and provided, to pay jail fees, &c.

"J. J. STEWART,
"*Sheriff of Montgomery County, Alabama.*"

"$100 REWARD.—Ran away from the subscriber, a bright mulatto man-Slave, named Sam. Light, sandy hair, blue eyes, and ruddy complexion—is so white as very easily to pass for a free white man.
"MOBILE, Ala." "EDWIN PECK."

Two runaway Slaves, from Alabama, sought protection in Billy Bowlegs' camp, in Mississippi. Repeated demands for their return to their "Master" had been denied by that Chief of the Seminoles. On the 4th of July, two of Billy's men, Toney and Simon, visited the United States troops. They were seized and heavily ironed, and placed in the custody of the Camp guard, to be held until Billy sent in the two runaway Slaves for their ransom. One of the Slaves was brought in and one of Billy's men demanded. To this demand, the Indian Agent refused to accede. The Slave was taken into custody and returned to his "owner."

The first treaty made with the Creek Indians, contained a provision for the return of fugitive Slaves. That treaty was violated. The Indian, debased as he was, could not return his flying brother into the horrors of Slavery. He had not been corrupted by Theological dissertations. To "teach" the poor Indians a "lesson," $125,000 due them were accordingly withheld, to pay the value of fifteen Slaves! Besides this, $150,000 were also "appropriated" to repay Slave-breeders for children not yet born.

"RAN AWAY.—A Nigger girl, called Mary Orville Dewey; has a scar over her left eye, a green patch over the other, a piece bitten out of her upper lip, and a good many teeth missing. The letters M. O. D. are branded with a hot iron on her forehead, cheeks, and the inside of her legs, half way between her knees and buttock."—*Natchez* (Miss.) *Courier.*

The practical illustration of the "peculiar institution" of the "Model Republic" has no limits; its honors swell into infinity. Human language can not describe its cruelties. No pencil can portray them; no statistics exhibit the sum total. The Slave Code is sufficiently horrible, but every syllable of it can be written, printed, and measured by pages.

"NOTICE TO PROPERTY OWNERS.—A Negro's head was picked up yesterday, which the Owner can have by calling at this Office, on paying for this advertisement."—*Natchez* (Miss.) *Free-Trader.*

"RAN AWAY, or stolen, from the subscriber, living near Aberdeen, Miss., *a light-colored Woman*, of small size, and about 23 years of age. She has *long, black, straight hair, and she usually keeps it in good order.* When she left she had on either a white dress, or a brown calico one with white spots or figures, and took with her a red handkerchief, and a red or pink sun-bonnet. *She generally dresses very neatly.* She calls herself Mary Ann Paine — can read — has some freckles on her face and hands — Shoes No. 4 — had two rings on her fingers. *She is very intelligent.* Fifty dollars reward will be given for her, if taken out of the State, and twenty-five, if taken within the State.
"U. M'ALLISTER."

"$25 REWARD will be given for the apprehension and confinement in any jail of the Slave-man Hardy, who ran away from the subscriber, residing at Lake St. John, near Rifle Point, Concordia parish, La., on the 9th of August last. Hardy is a remarkably likely Nigger, *entirely free from all marks, scars, or blemishes,* when he left. He is about six feet high, of light complexion, *fine countenance,* unusually smooth skin, good head of hair, *fine eyes and teeth.* Address the subscriber at Rifle Point, Concordia Parish, Louisiana. "ROBERT Y. JONES."
Daily Courier, Natchez, Miss.

"$25 REWARD.—Ran away from the undersigned, a Negro man by the name of Allen, about 23 years of age, near six feet high, of dark

mulatto color, *no mark, save one, and that caused by the bite of a dog;* had on, when he left, Lowell pants, and cotton shirt; reads imperfectly, can make a short calculation correctly, and can write some few words. Said boy has runaway heretofore, and when taken up was in possession of a free pass. He is quick-spoken, lively, and smiles when in conversation I will give the above reward to any one who will confine said Negro in any Jail, so that I can get him. "THOS. R. CHEATEM."
Natches (Miss.) *Free Trader.*

A Slave belonging to Captain Newport, of East Baton Rouge, Louisiana, while closely pursued by the bloodhounds of an Irish-American " Demmycrat," of the name of Roark, ascended a tree and hung himself. " Misther Roark," with Captain Newport's son-in-law and an Overseer, were in pursuit of a runaway Slave. They did not know this one was " out," and were surprised upon their arrival, a few minutes in the rear of their fellow-bloodhounds to find him suspended by his neck, with his feet dangling only a foot or two from the earth. Every effort was made to restore animation, but without success, although on their coming up the body was still warm. The act was one, it would seem, of resolute predetermination, as the Slave was well provided with cords, which he made use of to perpetrate his suicidal purpose. This " speaks volumes" for the " tender mercies" of the " *divine* institution."

The St. Francisville (La.) *Chronicle* has an account of a " Nigger-hunt," from which we learn that a *gentleman* of that Parish while out hunting runaways came upon three of them on Cat Island. He succeeded in arresting two, but the third made fight, and upon being shot in the shoulders fled to a sluice, where the hounds succeeded in drowning him before assistance could arrive.

"Bloodhounds! The undersigned would respectfully inform the Citizens of Ouachita and adjacent Parishes, that he has located about two miles east of Deacon John White's, on the road leading from Monroe to Bastrop, and that he has a superb Pack of Hounds for catching runaway Niggers, of every variety. Ladies or gentlemen wishing Nig-

gers caught will do well to give him a Call. He can always be found at his stand, when not professionally engaged. Terms as follows: $5 per day and found, when there is no track pointed out. When the track is shown, $25 will be charged for Catching. "M. C. GOFF."
Ouachita Register, Monroe, Louisiana.

Pardon Davis, a citizen of Berlin, Marquette county, Wisconsin, had been spending some time in Tensas Parish, La., engaged in business. In September, 1855, having settled up his business, he was upon the point of returning to the North, when he was met by Perkins and his bloodhounds, who drew a revolver and threatened to fire upon him in case he moved or made a noise. He was then handcuffed and brought before a Magistrate, who informed him that he was accused of "aiding Slaves to escape from their owners." The whole town was soon assembled, and in a high state of excitement. The citizens, fearing that the evidence against Mr. Davis would prove insufficient, formed themselves into a mob for the purpose of inflicting lynch-law, in case he should be acquitted. Some cried, "Hang him;" some, "Shoot him," others, "Give him a thousand lashes on the bare back." No one dared speak a word in his behalf, save a Mississippi lawyer, who informed the prisoner that the chances were against him — that if he had been charged with larceny or even murder, there might be hope, but little hope as the case was. He was conducted to jail, through a heavy rain, where he was handcuffed and his feet put in stocks. Mr. Davis, the prisoner, subsequently had his trial, and was sentenced to twenty years confinement in the State Prison of Louisiana, and is now in Baton Rouge, suffering this penalty.

The arrest of Mr. Davis was brought about in this way. A man in Mississippi having discovered a trail of runaway Slaves sent for Perkins to come, with his hounds, and catch them. Perkins went and caught them, after a chase of thirty-five miles. Upon overtaking them, they all ran to a tree, and got up into it. Perkins, with his four-legged bloodhounds, dashed up, drew his revolver, and asked the Slaves who they belonged to. They, poor fellows, gave a fictitious name, and presented their passes, which he read; but being, like all other cat's-paws of Slavery, North and South, a villain at heart—and wishing to show his employers the dangers he had to encounter—ordered them down, two at a time, and then set the hounds on them. The poor creatures, after being torn in a shocking manner, promised, if he would desist, they would tell the truth.* The hounds being called off, the wretched men made the following confession:

"We belong to Mr. Dunkin. The overseer, Mr. Higgins, whipped us nearly every night, because being new hands, we could not pick Cotton enough. We stood it as long as we could, and then ran away. We went to Mr. Davis's woodyard and told him our complaint. He let us hide in the wood and carried us bread and water until last Saturday night. He baked us some bread, gave one of us a pair of shoes, another a hat, another a shirt, three quilts, to sleep under, some money, these passes, and then took us across the river in a canoe, one at a time, and told us to go toward the sunrise, but, getting entangled in the swamp, we lost our way."

"Oh, if you could," said Mr. Davis, in a letter to his friends at Berlin, "be on the plantation near where I have lived, and, at night, when the Cotton is weighed, out of two hundred Slaves, not less than twelve are whipped every night—Oh! could you hear the shrieks, cries, groans, prayers to God, to Christ—yes, if you could hear all this, and see the victim on his knees praying with all the earnestness a man is capable of,

---

* "Stranger," said a two-legged bloodhound of St. Francisville, La., "if I can catch a cuss'd runaway Nigger without killing him, very good; though I generally let the Hounds punish him a little, and sometimes give him a load of squirrel-shot. If mild measures, like these, do not suffice, I use harsher punishment." The moment the hounds come close upon their prey, they utter a hideous and mournful howl. Then heaven pity the poor Slave.

to that brutal overseer, and promising to strain every nerve on the morrow to pick more Cotton—it would melt your hearts. Who can look on such scenes as these and not be moved to tears? I feel that my days are numbered. And now, my friends, *when you meet to pray for the 'heathen of foreign lands,' remember, Oh, remember, our own country.* Watch over the declining steps of my parents; 'tis the greatest boon I can ask, for I fear that this intelligence will bring the gray hairs of a loving father and an affectionate mother to the grave. Comfort them with the thought that we may meet in a happier world."

"RAN AWAY from the plantation of the undersigned, the Nigger Shadrach, a preacher, 5 feet 9 inches high, about 40 years of age; has the letters M. B. stamped on his breast, and both small toes cut off. He is of a very dark complexion, with eyes small but bright, and a look quite insolent. He dresses well, for a Nigger, and was taken up *as a runaway* at Donaldsville some three years ago. A reward of three hundred dollars will be paid for his arrest, by addressing Messrs. Armant, Brothers, St. James' parish, or A. Miltenberger & Co., 30 Carondelet st., New Orleans."

This is the loudest " call" for a preacher we have seen lately. Clergymen of the "right stripe," we are glad to learn, "are in great requisition." The fact indicates a pervading religious sentiment highly creditable to the "*free* and enlightened Democracy" of the "great Republic." But it is quite unusual to offer a reward for preachers who, for any cause, change their parish. Shadrach must have been a very "acceptable dispenser of the word" to have his return pressed so earnestly. But poor Shadrach succeeded in escaping the "tender mercies" of his "beloved brethren," North and South, and now keeps an eating-house at 72½ Notre Dame street, Montreal, Canada, and displays upon his show-board the words, "Uncle Tom's Cabin, by Shadrach."

The following case—the circumstances of which are a romance of themselves—show how inexorable the Slave law contends with the kind designs of the "Master:" Elisha Brazealle, a planter, was attacked with a loathsome disease. During his illness he was faithfully nursed, by a beautiful Slave girl, to whose assiduous attentions he felt that he owed his life. He was duly impressed by her devotion, and soon after his recovery took her to Ohio and had her educated. She was very intelligent, and improved her advantages so rapidly that when he visited her again he determined to marry her. He executed a deed for her emancipation, and had it recorded, and made her his wife. Mr. Brazealle returned with her, and in process of time had a son. After a few years he sickened and died, leaving a "Will," in which, after reciting the deed of emancipation, he declared his intention to ratify it, and devised all his property to his wife and son, acknowledging them in the will to be such. Some poor and distant relations in North Carolina, whom he did not know, and for whom he did not care, hearing of his death, came on, and claimed the property thus devised. They instituted a suit for its recovery, and the case (it is reported in Howard's Reports, vol. ii., p. 837) came before Judge Sharkey. He decided it, and in that decision declared the act of emancipation "an offence against morality, and pernicious and detestable as an example." He set aside the "Will," gave the property of Brazealle to his distant relations, condemned Brazealle's son, and his wife, that son's mother, again to bondage, and made them the Slaves of these North Carolina kinsmen, as part of the assets of the estate!

In March, 1818, three ships arrived at New Orleans bringing several hundred German emigrants from the province of Alsace on the lower Rhine. Among them was Daniel Muller and his two daughters, Dorothea and Salome, whose mother had died on the passage. Soon after his arrival at New Orleans, Muller, taking with him his two daughters, both young children, went up the river to Attakapas parish, to work on the plantation of John F. Miller. A few weeks later, his relatives, who had remained at New Orleans, learned that he had died of the fever of the country. They immediately sent for the two girls, but they had disappeared, and the relatives, notwithstanding repeated and persevering inquiries and researches, could find no traces of them. They were at length given up for dead. Dorothea was never again heard of, nor was anything known of Salome from 1818 till 1843. In the summer of that year, Madame Karl, a German woman, who had come over in the same ship with the Mullers, was passing through a street in New Orleans, and accidentally saw Salome in a wine-shop, belonging to Louis Belmonte, by whom she was held as a Slave. Madame Karl recognised her at once, and took her to the house of Mrs. Schubert, who was Salome's cousin and God-mother, who declared, the moment she saw her, " My God! here is the long-lost Salome Muller !"

"RAN AWAY from the plantation of Madame Fergus Duplantier, on or about the 27th of June last, a boy named Ned; he is stout-built, about five feet eleven inches high, and speaks English and French; he is about thirty-five years of age. He may try to pass himself for a white man, *as he is of a very clear color, and has sandy hair.* Twenty-five dollars reward will be paid to whoever will bring him to Madame Duplantier's plantation, Manchac, or lodge him in some jail, where he can be obtained."
New Orleans Picayune.

"RAN AWAY from a Gang, in February last, a boy, named Nehemiah Adams. He is about five feet three inches in height, with hazel eyes and brownish hair. He will not acknowledge that he is a Slave; says his father is a white man and lives somewhere in Boston, Massachusetts. He is an habitual runaway, and was shot in the ankle while endeavoring to escape from Baton Rouge Jail. A reward of $325 will be paid on his delivery to me, or for his apprehension and commitment to any jail from which I can get him." " A. L. BINGHAM."
New Orleans Delta.

The Cincinnati (Ohio) *Columbian,* says, that a legal gentleman of that City was called on in March, 1855, to write a deed of manumission to be given by a Louisiana planter to one of his Slaves, a young girl whom he had brought with him. As the description of the girl was somewhat curious, the Editor of *The Columbian* copied it from the deed: "*Said Sarah Maria is* 17 *years of age, medium height, and rather slim figure, very fair complexion, with straight light brown hair, and hazel eyes, with features of the Caucasian race.*"

"BLOODHOUNDS! The undersigned would respectfully inform his Friends and the Public generally, that he will keep in the County of Brazoria, the celebrated Pack of Hounds formerly owned by Deacon John Glascock. Price for Catching a runaway Nigger $25, or $5 per day. "J. PORTICE.
"BRAZORIA COUNTY, Texas."

"BLOODHOUNDS! The undersigned would respectfully inform his Friends and the Public generally, that he has just purchased Mr. Ruff Perry's famous Nigger Dogs, and will give his undivided attention to the business of Hunting and Catching runaway Niggers. His terms are $20 for Catching, or $3.50 per day. "JOHN DEVEREUX.
"MARSHALL, Texas."

In July, 1855, a fight took place between Sam Jones, a notorious desperado of Texas, and fifteen Lipau Indians. Jones was in a corn-field when the "Sons of the Forest" made their appearance, but managed to escape, with an old German, into his cabin. The Indians soon surrounded the house. Jones had but little ammunition, and was anxious that every shot should tell. When the Indians attempted to break in the door, he would shoot; and while he was loading, the German kept them at bay, by pointing an unloaded gun at them through the crevices of the house. They managed in this way till the outside of the house was bristling with arrows, aimed at them between the logs, and Jones' powder had given out. At this moment, the Indians retreated a short distance to hold a council of war. The besieged availed themselves of the chance to get the assistance of a dozen of bloodhounds that were confined in an outbuilding. Under cover of the two unloaded guns, Mrs. Jones liberated the dogs. Here was a reinforcement the Indians had not calculated upon, and, in the twinkling of an eye, five of them were torn to pieces. The others came to the rescue, and soon shot the remainder of their arrows into the hounds, and beat a retreat, leaving their dead and wounded. After the fight, the field exhibited seven dead Indians and five dogs, sundry pieces of buckskin, mingled with clotted masses of Indian flesh, and hundreds of arrows and pieces of bows.

"The origin of all Slavery on the Globe," says the Rev. George B. Cheever, "has been violence and theft. An unrighteous predatory war is theft. A man taken from his family and thrust into bondage is a stolen man, no matter whether ten men did the deed or ten thousand. The first gang of captives landed in Virginia, the origin of Slavery in the United States, were brought in as the prey of Kidnappers, Slave-traders, the most abandoned, degraded, infernal miscreants on the face of the earth, hovering on the coast, stealing up the creeks and rivers, prowling about the unguarded hamlets, and like vultures, grasping their victims in their talons, or with stratagems and lures, bribing others to entrap them. The Slave-ships and the Slave-pens, have been crowded, and are still, for still the accursed traffic rages, with such outraged and down-trodden human beings, bought and sold, and the 'Slave property,' so called, in the United States and Territories is the result of bloody violence and theft. Though the Slaveholder may tell as much as he pleases of his Slaves having been 'inherited,' or as having been the 'property' of his father, or grandfather, or great-grandfather, yet every increase from every ship's cargo ever landed in the United States, from the latest importation in this generation, back to the landing and enslavement of the very first gang, is piracy; and all the increase by natural propagation is the result of it, and the race is a stolen race.

"The quality of crime, the taint of theft, the essential element of man-stealing, is in the very title by which the Slaveholder claims his fellow-man as 'property.' It is a brand that no art can efface, no file of sophistry rasp out, no machinery of law erase. The brand of ignominy which he puts upon the man when he calls him a 'chattel,' and treats him as such, is the brand burned deeper in his bargain, in his complicity with robbery, in the immorality of his 'legal title,' and generation after generation can not eliminate it; can not so vulcanize it, but that the fires of the Judgment-Day will bring out its essence of oppression and iniquity.

"The sum of $100,000,000 might be paid for a man by a Slave-trader, but he would have no more right of 'property' in him, after he had paid that sum, than before, or than if he had paid but one farthing. The common law lays down this principle, even in regard to a horse, which, if it be stolen and sold forty times over, neither the selling, any more than the stealing, can take away the right of the lawful owner; but whenever, and wherever, he appears he can claim his property. Now a stolen man may have been passed through five hundred hands, and the five-hundredth may have paid more for him than all the four hundred and ninety-nine put together; but the last purchaser has no more rightful claim over him, no more right of 'property' in him, than the first stealer. And if he purchased him with the knowledge of his being originally stolen, he is himself also a thief, a conspirator, a pirate—on the principles of common law and righteousness. And if he had not that knowledge, but made the purchase ignorant of the original theft, his ignorance can not change right into wrong, can not take away the man's indefeasible and inalienable right of ownership over himself. The price of a world might have been paid for him, but he is still his own.

"The Slave holds, under God's own hand, a note against the robbers of his liberty, with compound interest, for the crime committed against his father; and when the Slaveholder lays his grasp upon his children, and takes them as his 'property,' the note is more than doubled against him, and the interest runs on." (See the Slave-Trade, Appendix C.)

Ah! there is a God in heaven that looks on, and his justice takes account of these atrocious transactions. Think of it! (See Matt. xxv. 34–46; Hebrews xiii. 3; Romans i. 14; and James ii. 4–9.) With nations, as with individuals, when the course of corruption begins, it is too often the principle—

"I am in blood
Steeped in so far, that, should I wade no more,
Returning were as tedious as go o'er."

PART SIXTH.

THE SLAVE POWER ADVANCING.

CHAPTER I.

"IT has often been observed by lawyers skilled in criminal jurisprudence," says the *New York Tribune*, "as well as by those who in civil practice have obtained a wide knowledge of human nature, that if you can get a rogue to write a series of letters, he is sure, while attempting to give plausibility to his falsehoods, to involve himself in such contradictions as can not fail to betray his real character and objects. Since the advent of Franklin Pierce's Administration" (on the 4th March, 1853), "in the only important cases which have arisen, the foreign policy of the country has been governed by one invariable rule. This rule may be stated, in brief, as simply to truckle to the strong, and bully the weak." What saith the historian?

And it came to pass after these things, that Isabella, the Spaniard, had an Island called Cuba, hard by the Model Republic of Uncle Sam, the Yankee; and Uncle Sam spake — through his servant, Soulé — unto Isabella, the Spaniard, saying, Give me thy Island, that I may have it for breeding Niggers, because it is near unto my dominions, and I will give thee the worth of it in money; or else, if it please thee, I will give thee another down the river — in the Mississippi. And Isabella, the Spaniard, said to Uncle Sam, the Yankee, The Lord forbid it me, that I should give the inheritance of my fathers unto thee. And Uncle Sam came into his

White House, heavy and displeased because of the words Isabella, the Spaniard, had spoken unto him, and he laid him down upon his bed, and turned away his face, and would eat no bread. But his servant, Marcy, said unto him, Why is thy spirit so sad, that thou eatest no bread? And he said unto him, Because I spake unto Isabella, the Spaniard, and said unto her, Give me Cuba, for money; or else, if it please thee, I will give thee another for it down the river — in the Mississippi; and she answered, The Lord forbid it me, that I should give the inheritance of my fathers unto thee. And his servant, Marcy, said unto him, Dost thou not now *govern* the Model Republic? arise, and eat bread, and let thine heart be merry: I will give thee the Island of Isabella, the Spaniard. So he wrote letters, in Uncle Sam's name, and sealed them with his seal, and sent the letters unto his fellow-servants, Soulé, Buchanan, and Mason; and he wrote in the letters, saying, You are hereby commanded to proceed, forthwith, to Ostend, in the Kingdom of Belgium, and there await further orders. (See 1 Kings xxi. 1-16.)

The Ostend correspondence reveals a most remarkable Executive, Administrative, and Diplomatic confusion. First, we have a Minister to Spain apparently selected because of his known fillibustering tendencies with reference to the fairest portion of Spain's territories — a selection most indecorous in itself, and involving conduct unworthy of a great power toward a weak one. To make the matter worse, that Minister made, on the very eve of his departure upon his Mission, a street harangue to a band of lawless persons, avowedly organized for the purpose of wresting that territory from Spain, in which he expressed sympathy with their design, and very broadly intimated that he was empowered to employ his official powers for that object. A mission thus begun could not be otherwise than unfortunate in its progress and conclusion. The whole business was a playing at cross purposes, the parties to the sharp practice being *Franklin Pierce*, the President of the United States — the greater the pity that it should have to be said — *William L. Marcy*, Secretary of State; *Pierre Soulé*, Minister to Spain; and a *Mr. Perry*, his

(Soulé's) Secretary. Each seems to have been chiefly aiming at outwitting the other.

The President consigned Mr. Soulé to Secretary Marcy for instructions, and Mr. Marcy gave them, in accordance, as he believed, with the views of the President. Mr. Soulé received them with all apparent respect, as though he designed in good faith to follow them. Then the President supplied him (Soulé) with a secretary (Perry), after, with seeming delicacy, consulting his wishes, and Mr. Soulé received him (Perry) into his confidence accordingly, and Mr. Perry appeared to work harmoniously in his subordinate capacity to the Minister. So far, each kept his secret and preserved the semblance of candor, harmony, and good faith. But it is proverbially difficult for two persons to act disingenuously toward each other for any length of time without a rupture; and the difficulty is more than quadrupled where four persons are playing at a game of cross purposes. The structure of disingenuousness gives way, and what an exposure follows!

President Pierce seems to bear the palm of disingenuousness, for it does not admit of a doubt that—while leaving his Secretary of State to suppose that, in virtue of his office, he had alone given Mr. Soulé instructions—secret, and superior orders, were received by the Minister from the President; and while the President virtually encouraged Mr. Soulé to place unlimited confidence in his secretary (Perry), he at the same time permitted, if he did not invite, that officer to act the part of a spy and informer upon his superior officer. Nor was this all. The President seduced the Minister, temporarily, from his post, on the pretence that he would highly value the joint council of himself and others on an important question; and during his absence at Ostend, his secretary (Perry) had abundant opportunity and leisure to peruse the records and correspondence of the legation, and make to his employer (President Pierce) a full report against his superior (Soulé). No one will say that in this matter the Chief Magistrate of the Model Republic appeared in a very dignified or favorable light.

Mr Perry having finished his work of espionage, Mr. Soulé returned to Madrid from Ostend, and a communication from the Secretary of State, in the President's name, opened his eyes to the fact that the Ostend Conference was but a trap, and that he must straightway undo and unsay all that he had done and said under his former instructions from the President and Secretary of State, and then he had been tripped up at his highest speed by his own confidential secretary (Perry) with the connivance of Pierce and Marcy!

There can be no doubt but that from the first the President was playing a double game with the Secretary of State, as well as with Mr. Soulé. But Mr. Marcy had more experience in political life than President Pierce, and is altogether a shrewder and abler man, and it is by no means improbable that Mr. Marcy appreciated the relative position of the President and Mr. Soulé, and comprehended from an early day the understanding that existed between them; but maintaining his seeming ignorance of such duplicity, skilfully manœuvred to lead the plot to its final development. That he has, by his adroitness and prudence, saved the country a needless and not reputable war with Spain, and with other powers, which embroilment was evidently the object of the President and Mr. Soulé's proceedings, is now beyond a doubt. But that does not exonerate Marcy from connivance at and encouragement of the clandestine correspondence of Mr. Perry and his espionage over his superior. Mr. Marcy partakes, equally with the President, in the disgrace of that complicity with a spy upon the actions of a gentleman in whom they both professed to have confidence, and whom they treated as though in correspondence with him alone.

While Mr. Marcy was deceiving Mr. Soulé, Mr. Soule was

deceiving Mr. Marcy (but preserving some degree of good faith with the President), for while pressing the acquisition of Cuba, in obedience to the President's instructions, he was purposely retarding the settlement of the "Black Warrior" claim by withholding from the Spanish Government communications made to him from the State Department by Marcy for the purpose of being laid before that Government. And he was himself deceived in turn by his secretary (Perry), who was making notes of his proceedings and passing his own comments upon them in a clandestine correspondence with the Government at Washington!

The conduct of Mr. Perry has been excused, on the ground that he saw that the interests of his country were being wilfully sacrificed by Mr. Soulé, and thought it his duty to acquaint his Government of the fact.

There is not a redeeming point of honor in the whole business. If the Executive is to stoop to these acts of duplicity and fickleness, what is to become of the "high character" of American diplomacy? What gentleman, what man, with a spark of self-respect, or innate sense of honor, will consent to wear the title of "American Minister" abroad, if it is to be understood that the President has placed a spy and informer at his elbow, to supervise his diplomacy and whisper secretly in the President's ear his own interpretation of his (the Minister's) acts, and that informer is his (the Minister's) subordinate, his own President appointed secretary? What security has Mr. Buchanan, late Minister to England, and now President of the United States, that Mr. Dan Sickles did not review his every act in secret correspondence with President Pierce? Or Mr. Mason, the Minister to France, or any other Minister, that his secretary does not clandestinely pursue the same course, with the President's approval and encouragement; and that a similar correspondence to Mr. Perry's awaits an opportunity to be used against him?

As to Mr. Soulé's successor, General C. A. Dodge, no one can pity him if he is betrayed, like his predecessor, for he accepted the mission with the same secretary (Perry) attached to it!

The country is deeply disgraced when its first Magistrate, and its Officials, stand before the world in the light of such revelations as these. Every citizen shares in the disgrace. This is no "party matter." It can not be made a party question. No party will be quite mean enough to attempt its defence. Just imagine how utterly suicidal it would be for any party — Whig, Democrat, Fusion, or Know-Nothing — to incorporate this plank into its platform:

"*Resolved*, That it is honorable to the man, and befitting to the Chief Magistrate of the United States, as well as delicate and proper toward the Ministers of this Republic, accredited at Foreign Courts, that a system of secret espionage shall be exercised over those Ministers by the President, and that their subordinates in office be employed for that purpose; for which end they shall open a clandestine correspondence with the President of this Republic, and cultivate the fullest confidence of their superiors. And the more honorably to fulfil this duty, the President shall occasionally send the leading Ministers on a fool's errand to Land's End, that their trusted secretaries may have opportunity and leisure to study the correspondence of the legation, and so make a better show of service to the Chief of the Spy Department at Washington, D. C."

The bombardment of Greytown, and the Sacking and burning of Lawrence and Osawattomie, are the "great achievements" of President Pierce's Administration. What a spectacle it was — a great power directing its force against a helpless little seaport of five hundred inhabitants, which had committed no offence, except that its territory was coveted by Slaveholders. In respect to Lawrence, the "free-State men" were able and ready to defend themselves from merely "border ruffian" attacks, but a "border ruffian" attack, led by United States officers, and instigated by President Pierce himself, was more than they could stand up against.

In the "sacking" of Lawrence, assassinations, robberies, and outrages of every description were freely practised. Other and still more infamous deeds were committed — deeds that should have aroused the "*free* States," from Maine to Iowa, as one man, and shaken the Nation to its centre.

At a "Mass Meeting of the Citizens of New York," held at the Tabernacle, in that City, on the 27th day of August, 1856, Ex-Governor Reeder, of Kansas Territory, said:

"The robbers, ravishers, and murderers of Kansas, have in their own hands the arms of the law, and they are made the ministers of this awful and horrible system of civil, political, and social oppression. I shall not undertake to give you a catalogue of the robberies, the house-burnings, the plunderings, the horse-stealings, the murders and outrages, that have been perpetrated upon the soil of Kansas; for, did I undertake such a task I should request you to camp here a week. It is beyond the limits assigned any speaker to present such an inventory. Should I undertake even to give you any portion of the details, where the acts of our oppressors were stained with blood, and with every attribute that could disgrace humanity, I should not know where to begin or end." * * * * * * "I have seen not long since, Representatives of the people, from the '*free* States,' whose conduct I could not explain or reconcile, except on the supposition that if the South should demand it of them, they would have Slavery among you in the North. And I believe there are men among you now, who, were the question raised, would be ready to introduce it into New York. At one time, I should have considered this idle talk; but that time has gone by, and the existence of this fact should put every man upon his guard, and make him exceedingly sensitive to public opinion upon this subject."

The Hartford (Ct.) *Press*, of August 30, 1856, contains what it calls "verbatim copy" of a Speech delivered at a "Kansas Aid Meeting," held in that city, on Friday, August 29, 1856, by a "runaway border ruffian," Mr. Selden C. Williams, formerly of Meriden, Ct. The Connecticut journals endorse Mr. Williams as "a reputable and reliable man." It would seem, according to Mr. Williams's account, that Buford's men are not only ruffians and murderers, but also partake somewhat of the character of cannibals:

"In one of the forays upon which we were sent, we came upon a small party of 'free-State men.' They resisted our taking away their property, and Buford's men left them dead upon the grass! When we were in the Shawnee Country, we were invited to call at one of the Mission Churches. As the doors opened before us, what a sight presented itself! Three Massachusetts men were hanging by the neck. For daring to say they were for 'free-Soil,' two had been shot and one stabbed to the heart, and they were hung up, to strike terror to the hearts of the people from the East. Four days after, one of Buford's men came into the camp, holding upon the point of a Bowie-knife a human heart! 'Boys,' said he, 'see here is the heart of a d——d Abolitionist; he told me he was an Abolitionist, and I up with my rifle and dropped him. I cut his heart out, and it ain't cold yet; and now I'll cut it open and see how it looks inside; then I shall fry it and see how the d——d thing tastes!'"

General J. H. Lane (Commander of the "free-State party"), in a letter to the New York journals, dated Fremont County, Iowa, September, 22, 1856, says:

"On my arrival in Kansas I found the border papers teeming with inflammatory denunciations of our citizens, and boldly proclaiming against them a war of extermination; and in response to their incitements, hordes of depraved, misguided desperadoes entered the country, many of them having inscribed on their hats, 'Death to Abolitionists, and no quarter.' A mother and her two daughters, in the absence of the husband and father, were violated by nearly one hundred fiendish men. The gifted Major Hoyt, who had gallantly served his country in the Mexican war, was brutally hacked to pieces, and a few sods thrown over him, leaving his arms and feet projecting from the earth, a prey for wolves. Prisoners were murdered in a manner exceeding the shocking barbarity of savage tribes, and afterward scalped. One man was scalped while alive, and who yet lives to exhibit his skinless head to an outraged world. Dwellings were burned over helpless women and screaming children."

The Sub. Committee, of the National Kansas Committee, in obedience to instructions, waited on President Pierce, on Saturday, the 30th August, 1856, and prayed his interposition against his border ruffian herds. The following is a summary of results. We give it without remark. Comment is not needed. The President said:

"While Government has been exhausting its Constitutional powers, to maintain *order*, Kansas Aid Societies have been actively stirring up rebellion. A factious spirit among the people of Kansas respecting institutions which they need not have concerned themselves about, and which would have all come right in time, originated the troubles. From the nature, habits, and *education* of the border-men, it was natural to find them excited at such an agitation. The sufferings of the settlers are of their own seeking, and the legitimate fruits of that gunpowder-Bible-preaching which they and their supporters at the North have advocated."

REPLY OF THE COMMITTEE.

"Mr. President, during the eighteen months or more that Executive power has been exerted, as is alleged, to preserve *peace* in Kansas, and vainly exerted, it would seem, from admissions here made, the disorders of that Territory have grown only worse. At this moment, they are more threatening than ever; a peaceful solution of its troubles seems still more uncertain than at any period of its former history. The President affirms that he has exhausted all his Constitutional powers. And yet 'order' is not restored. Under such circumstances, may it not be worth while to inquire *whether the germ of the evils is not to be found in the Territorial laws themselves?*"

President—"This question I do not propose to discuss, at the present time."

Committee—"From whatever source, then, sir, the difficulties in Kansas have originated, this one thing is patent to the country and the world: that notwithstanding all the *efforts* of the Government, disorders of the most frightful character have prevailed; disorders that would shame the worst despotism of the worst ages; disorders so wide-spread and so atrocious, so bloody and so infernal, so deeply damning and inhuman, that to escape them, the wretched inhabitants would make a gain if transferred to the most despotic Government that ever existed in the antediluvian world. During this dark reign of blood and terror; during this fearful tempest of violence and anarchy, these poor unshielded victims of plotted vengeance have broken no law and committed no crime. For hating Slavery, because they loved Liberty, all these things have come upon them. Such, Sir, is the nature and character of the events which have transpired in Kansas during the past eighteen months' policy of the Government. As representatives of the National Kansas Committee, we are here to-day to ask *whether any change in this policy of the Administration is to be expected?*"

President—"No, Sirs! There will be none!! the laws of the Territory must be obeyed!!!"

"Such, gentlemen of the National Kansas Committee, is the substance of our interview with President Franklin Pierce. The duty of commenting on the facts here stated we leave to you. Our mission is ended.

"Respectfully, etc.,
"THADDEUS HYATT,
"W. F. ARNY,
"EDWARD DANIELS,
New York, *Sept.* 1, 1856. "Sub. Com. of Nat. Kansas Com."

Reader, look for a moment, and see what those "laws" are which President Franklin Pierce says, "must be obeyed." Here is a specimen:—

"SECTION 1. Be it enacted, by the Governor and Legislative Assembly of the Territory of Kansas, That every person, bond or free, who shall be convicted of actually raising a rebellion, or insurrection of Slaves, free Negroes or mulattoes, in this Territory, shall suffer death.

"SEC. 2. Every free person, who shall aid and assist in any rebellion or insurrection of Slaves, free Negroes, or Mulattoes, or shall furnish Arms, or do any overt act in furtherance of such rebellion or insurrection, shall suffer death.

"SEC. 3. If any free person shall, by speaking, writing, or printing, advise, persuade, or induce any Slave to rebel, conspire against, or murder any Citizen of this Territory, or shall bring into, print, write, publish, or circulate, or cause to be brought into, printed, written, published, or circulated, or shall knowingly aid or assist in the bringing into, printing, writing, publishing, or circulating in this Territory, any book, paper, magazine, pamphlet, or circular, for the purpose of exciting insurrection on the part of the Slaves, free Negroes, or Mulattoes, against the Territory, or any part of them, such person shall be guilty of Felony and suffer death.

"SEC. 4. If any person shall entice, decoy, or carry away out of this Territory, any Slaves belonging to another, with the intent to deprive the *owner* thereof of the services of such Slaves, or with intent to effect or procure the freedom of such Slaves, he shall be adjudged guilty of grand larceny, and, on conviction thereof, shall suffer death, or be imprisoned at hard labor for not less than ten years."

SECTION I.

Be it enacted by our noble band
Of Border-Ruffians (bowie-knife in hand),
That should a sneaking Yankee from the East
Come here, and dare to meddle, in the least,
With any of our Niggers, and incite
Them to resist our *sacred* right;
Then, whether they be Niggers, black as night,
Or those in whom we've mix'd a little white,
Whether they wear the chains of Slavery,
Or have the sad misfortune to be free,
Any Missourian, happening to be here,
May cut that Yankee's throat from ear to ear.

SECTION II.

If Northern whites, pretending to be free,
Shall aid our Niggers to gain their liberty,
Or furnish rifle, cannon, shot, or shell,
To help them send their *owners* back to hell,
Then some good friend of order and of law,
Around the Traitor's necks the hemp shall draw.

SECTION III.

If any Yankee in this Territory,
Shall circulate an Abolition story,
That tends to make the happy, well-fed Slave
Begin to think his *owner* is a Knave,
And when he feels the lash, to snarl and pout,
Until, at length, he e'en presumes to doubt
Our right to trade in Human flesh and bones;
Then brave Stringfellow, or gallant Jones,
Or Atchison, or any man of note,
May cut his cuss'd Anti-Slavery throat.

SECTION IV.

If any notion-pedlar shall induce
A Nigger from his owner to cut loose,
And slope for Canada — shall aid his flight,
And thus deprive his *owner* of his right —
Shall coax the Nigger thus to flee,
With horrible intent to make him free,
He shall be guilty of Grand Larceny;
And, if we catch him, on a gallows high
Th' infernal Abolition cuss shall die,
Or toil ten years in prison with a throng
Of thieves and robbers, should he live so long.

Ex-Governor Robinson, of Kansas, in a Speech on the sufferings of the people of that Territory, at the Academy of Music, New York, Oct. 22, 1856, said:—

"But many will ask here to-night, 'Are not these things exaggerated?' 'Have the people of Kansas really suffered as it is said they have?' 'Are the Newspaper reports true?' *Now, I tell you that I have not the power to depict to you the outrages that have been committed there, and if I had the power, you could not believe them. I tell you that you can have no adequate conception of the outrages perpetrated there. No! the tongue of an angel could not show them.*"

The Providence (R. I.) *Journal*, contains a letter from General Pomeroy, to the Rev. S. Wolcott, dated Lawrence, Kansas, October 22, 1856, in which he says:—

" The prairie fires have spread over our rich, rolling grass-fields, and a terrible fire of war and passion has burned up every green thing in society and in our comforts, and our prospects are dark and dreary. There are men, women, and little children, who are reaping a harvest of sorrow from seeds sown by invaders from Missouri and the South. I visited, the other day, a family of six little girls. Their mother left them sorrowfully last spring, for 'that undiscovered country.' Their father, a noble man, is a prisoner at Lecompton; and for a month the oldest girl, of twelve years, had to support all the little ones by getting corn from the fields and grinding it upon a tin pan, punched full of holes with a nail, then making a cake and baking it in the ashes. I am unused to weeping, but I wept like a child at such a scene. I could only supply them temporarily, and commend them to the Great Shepherd 'who tempereth the wind to the shorn lamb.' *Oh, what a record of sorrow and crime stands charged to the Administration of Franklin Pierce! There are scores of men, unknown to fame, but whose record is on high, who lie sleeping in their bloody shrouds, uncoffined, without a stone to mark the place of their resting.* Day before yesterday we followed to the grave, Mr. Bowles, who died a prisoner at Lecompton. He came here from a Slave State, to get away from Slavery, and early identified himself with the bravest defenders of Freedom. His long marches, exposures, and night watches, brought on a fever, and after forty-eight hours of suffering, unattended by physician or relative, death, the despairing prisoner's friend, came to his release. There are over a hundred of our young men now in prison, and some are sick—all confined for acts and efforts which an angel might envy."

The Chicago (Illinois) *Tribune* has the following statement. We presume the informant of that journal is Governor Gorman of Minnesota Territory:—

"We are told by a Democrat of unquestioned faithfulness to his party, *himself a Governor,* that in a late conversation with Governor Geary, that gentleman stated that, *during a trip on a much frequented road, soon after his arrival in the Territory, he saw the bodies of twenty-six murdered Free-State men.* Some of these had been shot or brained, and thrown out by the roadside to rot under the burning sun. Others had been scalped as Indians scalp their victims. One was pinioned to a tree by a bowie-knife driven through his heart into the solid wood at his back; on his breast was fastened a written warning to all other "Abolitionists." Some were buried just beneath the prairie sod, their hands and arms left sticking out of the shallow holes into which they had been thrown. Upon others, the nameless mutilations of private parts had been committed. In all cases, brutality seemed to have exhausted itself in insulting what, among civilized men, whether friend or foe, are looked upon with respect — the bodies of the dead."

Even in this world, retribution sometimes follows hard upon the heels of sin. Franklin Pierce thought he had secured his renomination to the Presidency of the United States by pursuing the course we have described. But the Slaveholders demanded an exhibition of virtue even sterner than this; they demanded a larger sacrifice, and Mr. Pierce, like Mr. Douglas, gave himself away — "sold out."

There were some such apostles of Democracy in the days of old, and of one of these Jeremiah the prophet speaks thus:

"Therefore, thus saith the Lord concerning Jehoiakim, the son of Josiah, king of Judea: They shall not lament for him, saying, Ah, Ah, Lord! or Ah, his Glory! Ah, my brother! or Ah, my Sister! but he shall be buried with the burial of an ass."

There have been such funerals in all the "*free* States" of the Union, and there will be many more. (See the Doughface, Appendix B.)

CHAPTER II.

DURING the debates on the repeal of the "Missouri Compromise," in the United States House of Representatives, in 1854, the following language was addressed to the opponents of that "Measure" by Senator Alexander H. Stephens, of Georgia:

"Well, gentlemen, you make a great deal of clamor on the 'Nebraska Measure,' but it don't alarm us at all. We have got used to that kind of talk. You have threatened before but never performed. You have always caved in, and you will again. You are a mouthing, white-livered set! Of course you will oppose: we expect that, but we don't care for your opposition. You will rail, but we don't care for your railing. You are like the devils that were pitched over the battlements of heaven into hell! They set up a howl of discomfiture, and so will you! But their fate was sealed, *and so is yours!* You must submit to the yoke. But don't chafe. Gentlemen, *we have got you in our power.* You tried to drive us to the wall in 1850, *but times are changed.* You went a wooling and came home fleeced. Don't be so impudent as to complain. *You will only be slapped in the face.* Don't resist, *you will only be lashed into obedience.*"

On the 22d of May, 1856, while Senator Charles Sumner, of Massachusetts, was writing at his desk, in the United States Senate Chamber, he was violently assaulted by two men— Preston S. Brooks and Lawrence M. Keitt, members of the House of Representatives, from South Carolina. They had armed themselves with Revolvers and heavy Bludgeons, and approaching the Senator, while sitting at his desk, engaged in writing, Brooks struck him with his bludgeon a violent blow on the head, which brought him stunned to the floor, and Keitt, with his weapons, kept off the bystanders, while Brooks repeated the blows upon the head of the apparently lifeless victim.

The Richmond (Va.) *Whig*, speaking of this assault, ranted its joy after the following fashion : " A glorious deed ! a most glorious deed ! ! Mr. Brooks, of South Carolina, administered to Senator Sumner, the notorious Abolitionist, from Massachusetts, an effectual and *classical* caning. We are rejoiced. The only regret we feel is that Mr. Brooks did not employ a Slave-whip, instead of a stick. We trust the ball may be kept in motion. Seward and others should catch it next."

The Petersburg (Va.) *Intelligencer* said : " We entirely concur with The Richmond Whig, that if thrashing is the only remedy by which the Abolitionists can be controlled, that it will be well to give Senator William H. Seward a double dose at least every other day until it operates freely on his political bowels."

The Richmond (Va.) *Examiner*, one of the most blasphemous and "highly respectable" journals in the State, commenced thus : " Good ! — good ! ! — very good ! ! ! The Abolitionists have been suffered to run too long without collars. They must be lashed into submission. Sumner, in particular, ought to have nine-and-thirty early every morning. There is the blackguard, Senator Wilson, an ignorant Natick cobbler, swaggering in excess of muscle, and absolutely dying for a beating. Will not somebody take him in hand ? Senator Hale is another huge, red-faced, sweating scoundrel, whom some *gentleman* should kick and cuff until he abates something of his impudent talk. We trust other *gentlemen* will follow the example of Mr. Brooks, that a curb may be imposed upon the truculence and audacity of Abolition speakers. If need be, let us have a caning or cowhiding every day."

The Examiner-man but echoes the all-prevailing sentiment of the unhappy South, whose feverish writhings and contortions seem to indicate "the torments of the damned," and may appropriately exclaim in the language of Milton's Satan:

> "Me miserable! Whither shall I fly?
> Which way I turn is hell — myself am hell!"

The South Side (Va.) *Democrat* said: "The telegraph has recently announced no information more grateful to the feelings of the *chivalrous* sons of the South than the caning which this Abolitionist received in the United States Senate, on the 22d instant" (May 22d, 1856), "at the hands of the *chivalrous* Brooks, of South Carolina."

It is clear, that if Senators and Representatives from the "*free* States" can not enjoy the right of free speech or free discussion, without being liable to brutal assaults, they must, of necessity, arm themselves with Bowie-knives, Sword-canes, and Revolvers. To think of enduring quietly such attacks as that upon Mr. Sumner is craven and pusillanimous. The "chivalrous" champion traffickers in Human flesh will never learn to respect Northern men until a few of their number have rapiers thrust through their ribs or feel bullets in their throats. It is the only way to put a stop to their "classical" Slave-breeding nonsense. Once admit the idea of the predominance of brute force — of the right of individual appeal from words to blows — and human society becomes a state of war diversified by interludes of fitful and hollow truce. And they who, as legislators, editors, public speakers, or in whatever capacity, suggest apologies for ruffian assaults, or intimate that words can excuse them, make themselves partners in the crime and the infamy.

The New York Journal of Commerce apologized for the

brutality of Brooks and Keitt, by saying that Sumner was guilty of "wholesale denunciation and bitter personalities," and quoted what one of the Slaveholder's Organ, *The Washington* (D. C.) *Star*, said of the character of Mr. Sumner's speech. What the *Star* said was nothing to the purpose, the question is, what Mr. Sumner said, and as his speech was published prior to the publication of *The Journal's* article, the "pious editors" of that "highly respectable evangelical journal" should have placed it before their readers. They had, however, an eye to the "Southern department" of their business, and prudently kept the provocation out of sight.

Every press, North and South, in the employment of Satan and Slavery, has a thousand times iterated and reiterated the cry of "slander" and "falsehood," but no one has made a single specification. *They dare not make the attempt.* They know the charges are true, and that every villany Mr. Sumner charged them with they have committed. *It is, in very truth, because it is not false, that he has offended.* If his charges were false, all that was necessary to consign him to disgrace was to prove them so. But no number of canings or murders will ever prove these charges false. They are irrelevant testimony. They do not touch the case, or if they do, they only go to confirm the truth of Mr. Sumner's statement. He says that "Slaveholding is aggressive, insolent, and overbearing." Keitt says it is a "lie," and a "slander," and Brooks, to prove it a *lie* and a *slander*, clubs him for saying so. He does this "as a gentleman," and this the Slaveholders and their "white Niggers," North and South, consider conclusive proof that Sumner's charges are false!

In countries not essentially barbarous, when a man commits a murder, everybody has a right to speak of it. The criminal, instead of being permitted to kill, or to threaten to kill, like Brooks, those who speak of it, is shut up in jail and considered the culprit.

THE SLAVE POWER ADVANCING. 371

General James Watson Webb, Editor of *The New York Courier and Enquirer*, in a letter to his Journal, dated Washington, D. C., May 24, 1856, says:

"To attempt to describe the actual state of affairs here in the Capitol of the Nation, would be a hopeless task. *It would not be believed were one from Heaven to proclaim it trumpet-tongued through the land,* and yet no one can live here, as I have for the last six months, without feeling his blood boil at witnessing the *fears and apprehensions of fatal consequences, on the part of our Northern men,* if any one ventures openly and manfully to speak the truth in the bar-rooms, on the corners of the streets, and on the floor of Congress. And there is reason for these fears! This is a city in a Slave District, visiters are mostly from the Slave States, and a large majority of them (not the better portion of them), carry Revolvers and Bowie-knives; and what is more, they have both here, and elsewhere, proved that they will not hesitate, on occasion, freely to use them. *They are overbearing, threatening, and defiant in their manners, and our people have been overawed and cowed.* It is the right of Freemen boldly to express their sentiments here, as well as elsewhere; I tell them, in all sincerity, that the time has arrived when they must do so, courteously, and fearlessly, on all proper occasions, and in all proper places, *or we shall all, and speedily too, become as completely the Slaves of the Slave Power as are their plantation chattels; or, what is far more degrading, we shall become the same pliant, cringing, and sycophantic instruments of the Slaveocracy as are the Northern doughfaces*" (see Appendix B), "*who are made by the present Administration to discourse just such music as their Southern Masters may be pleased to dictate for the time being.*

"Aside from the favored few in the Slave States, nineteen twentieths of their population carry Arms, Bowie-knives, Revolvers, and Sword-canes. This is conclusive as regards the demoralizing tendencies of an 'institution' which the Administration, *acting under the dictation of the Slave Power, and aided by unscrupulous politicians of the North*, are endeavoring to force upon the free people of Kansas. To this end, the entire influence and patronage of the Government, its Civil, Military, and Moral power, are all directed; and alongside of these, prominent and threatening, stands the bullying of the Slaveocracy, boastingly pointing to the Bowie-knife, the Revolver, and the Bludgeon, and impudently taunting the entire North with cowardice! I can not blame them for their love of power and their desire to extend it; I do not quarrel with their ruder civilization, the natural offspring of their '.peculiar institution;' and I do not wonder at their believing that the doughfaces of the North, who so meekly do their behests, are but a type of our whole people, and that we can be bullied, whipped, or 'kicked' into any course of policy which they may please to dictate to us.

"Will the North—the *free*, and educated, and civilized, and peace-loving North—tamely submit to the impudence and the bullying of the Slave Power? This is the question which I desire to put, directly, to every law-abiding and Union-loving freeman of the North." (See Appendix B.) "I would have the entire North awaken to the attempt of the Slave-Power to extend the 'institution' into free Territory, and the means resorted to, to accomplish that nefarious purpose. I would have them feel that the time for action has arrived; and that not only must that action be prompt and efficient, if we would protect ourselves from the encroachments of Slavery, but that if we tamely submit to the bullying habitually resorted to here, in the Capital of the Nation, we shall very soon be taught that Liberty of Speech is a boon which we hold subject to the caprices of the Slave Power, and to indulge in it equally with themselves may, at any time, be visited by the discretionary application of the Revolver and the Bludgeon.

"Of the purposes of the Slave Power and its Northern allies in the coming Presidential Election" (November 4th, 1856), "there is no longer any doubt. It is openly declared by the Democratic press from Maine to Texas; and only this day, the Government organ" (*The Union*) "published in this City, boldly declares that '*whatever other question may enter into the coming contest, the Slavery issue, as included in the Kansas measure, must and will take precedence. In comparison with it, all other questions are of minor importance.*' And in allusion to Mr. Buchanan's past Federalism, and the suspicion only that it may cause him to prefer his country, and the rights of freedom, to mere party, it adds: '*We want no man whose record is not thoroughly Democratic.*'

"These declarations are significant; and richly will the people of the North have merited the outrages and contumely which are daily heaped upon them by men immeasurably their inferiors as regards manhood and civilization, if they hesitate to vindicate their right to freedom of speech, or falter in their determination to drive back into the fens and marshes, where it properly belongs, the 'institution' which Washington, and Jefferson, and Madison, alike condemned, but of which Pierce, and Douglas, and the doughfaces of the North, acting under the lash of the Slave Power, have become the willing propagandists."

The General, speaking of the cowardly assault on Mr. Sumner, adds: "Upon receiving the blows, given in quick succession, and with great force, Mr. Sumner attempted to rise from his seat, to which he was in a measure pinioned, by his legs being under the desk — the legs of which, like all the desks of the Senate Chamber, have plates of iron fastened to them, and these plates are firmly secured to the floor. His first attempt to rise was a failure, and he fell back into his chair, and the blows of his assailant continued to fall mercilessly upon his uncovered head. His second attempt ripped up the iron fastenings of his desk, and he precipitated himself forward. He was prostrate on the floor, and covered with blood. The assault was justified and even applauded by Douglas, Toombs, and their fellow Senators, and by every Representative of the people, save two" (Humphrey Marshall, of Kentucky, and Henry W. Hoffman, of Maryland), "from the Slave States, and by every Representative of the people, North and South, who speaks the sentiments or sustains the measures of the Administration of the country."

That General Webb, Editor of *The New York Courier and Enquirer*, hitherto one of the bitterest enemies of the Anti-Slavery cause, and the instigator of the Pro-Slavery riots of 1835, should now be found battling, side by side, with the Abolitionists, is, to say the least of it, "the very biggest phenomenon of the Nineteenth Century." We hope the General won't backslide from the faith.

In October, 1835, the General, speaking of the friends of the oppressed, said: " These dangerous men" (that is, the Abolitionists, the true friends of the country) " must be met! They agitate a question that must not be tampered with! They are plotting the destruction of our Government, and they must not be allowed to screen themselves from the enormousness of their guilt, under canting pretences!" * * * * * * " And now, we ask the Citizens of the United States, if they are prepared to bring such a catastrophe upon the country, to gratify the *visionary projects of a band of canting fanatics?*" * * * * * * * * * " Are they willing, by giving countenance and currency to *such* a man as William Lloyd Garrison, to put in jeopardy the fair fabric of *our* liberty—the last and the only hope of Civil and Religious freedom on earth?"

The good book assures us that "the wise man's eyes are in his head." The General's eyesight was "considerably obscured"—in 1835.

As respects the great pioneer and leader of the Anti-Slavery cause, he has the consolation of reflecting, that when the falsehoods of the day are withered and rotten, he shall be respected and esteemed. And if the name of General James Watson Webb, and his co-workers, should descend to posterity, they will be known only as the recorded instruments of part of his persecutions, sufferings, and misfortunes.

The Governor of South Carolina, in his "Message," for the year 1854, said : " South Carolina must hereafter exist as a *military people*. The history of our country for the last ten years affords abundant proof that, as long as the Union endures, there is to be no peace for the Slaveholder. An eternal warfare against his *rights* and *property*, under the associated influence of the people and States of the North, has been solemnly and deliberately decreed. For this reason it is essential that the State should be prepared at any moment for every emergency."

South Carolina is rather a talkative little State. She has about 274,567 "genuine white inhabitants," and about 393,580 party-colored ones. But these "white inhabitants" make up for their paucity of numbers by an immensity of brag and bluster, which is truly terrible to listen to. See what South Carolina has done in a military way. In 1775, after the battle of Bunker Hill, Congress voted that each State should raise its contingent of Soldiers, for the common defence. *South Carolina asked that her soldiers might remain at home, in consequence of her "peculiar institutions." The request was granted, and her soldiers stayed at home.* Compare her revolutionary services with New England. In the nine years of the Revolution, South Carolina sent into the continental army 6,417 soldiers; Connecticut, 32,039. Yet Connecticut had not so large a population as South Carolina. At the same time, Massachusetts sent into the continental army 83,162 soldiers. The six Slave States sent only 59,336 soldiers to that war, while New England alone sent 119,305, besides Militia.

Nevertheless, the children of South Carolina are taught to despise such names as Bunker Hill, Lexington and Monmouth, when compared with Eutaw Springs, Cowpens and Fort Moultrie. The Northern child, when asked, "Who was the greatest man of America?" is apt to reply, "George Washington;" the Carolina child pertly answers, *John C. Calhoun!* The Southern child needs an honest "History of the United States of America."

The following Table shows the number of "Troops" and "Militia" furnished by the several States, for the support of the Revolutionary war, from 1775 to 1783, inclusive:—

NORTHERN STATES.	No. of Continental troops.	No. of Militia.	Total number of Troops.	Conjectural estimate of Militia.
New Hampshire	12,496	2,093	14,598	3,700
Massachusetts	67,937	15,155	83,092	9,500
Rhode Island	5,908	4,284	10,192	1,500
Connecticut	32,039	7,792	39,831	3,000
New York	17,781	3,312	21,093	8,750
Pennsylvania	25,608	7,357	32,965	2,000
New Jersey	10,727	6,055	16,782	2,500
Total	172,496	46,048	218,553	30,950
SOUTHERN STATES.				
Delaware	2,387	376	2,763	1,000
Maryland	13,912	5,464	19,376	4,000
Virginia	26,672	4,163	30,835	21,880
North Carolina	7,263	2,716	9,969	12,000
South Carolina	5,508		5,508	28,000
Georgia	2,679		2,679	9,930
Total	58,421	12,719	71,130	76,810

Yet, so great is the spirit of "brag" in that chivalrous State, that a Senator from South Carolina had the effrontery to attribute the independence of the country to the Slaveholders of that State. The records of the country disown the suggestion. The State of South Carolina itself, by authentic history, disowns it. We have "peculiar" and decisive testimony on this head, under date of March 29, 1779, from the Secret Journals of the Continental Congress: "The committee appointed to take into consideration the circumstances of the Southern States, and the ways and means for their safety and defence, report that the State of South Carolina (as represented by the delegates of the said State, and by Mr. Huger, who has come here at the request of the Governor of the said State, on purpose to explain the circumstances thereof), is unable to make any effectual efforts with Militia, *by reason of the great proportion of citizens necessary to remain at home, to prevent insurrection among the Slaves, and to prevent the desertion of them to the enemy.* That the state of the country, and the great number of these people among them, expose the inhabitants to great danger, from the endeavors of the enemy to excite them to revolt or desert." (*Life of Gen. Greene*, vol. i., p. 105.)

"There is not," said a Member of Congress from South Carolina, "a gentleman on the floor who is a stranger to the feeble situation of our State, when we entered into the war to oppose the British power. We were not only without money, without an army or Military stores, but were few in numbers, and likely to be entangled with our Slaves, in case the enemy invaded us." (*Annals of Congress*, 1789, 1791, vol. ii., p. 1474.)

Similar testimony to the weakness engendered by Slavery was borne by Mr. Madison, in debate in Congress: "Every addition Georgia and South Carolina receive to their number of Slaves, tends to weaken them and render them less capable of self-defence." (*Annals of Congress*, vol. i., p. 340.)

Dr. Ramsey (the Historian of South Carolina), a contemporary observer of the scenes which he describes, exposes this weakness: "The forces under the command of Gen. Provost marched through the richest settlements of the State, where are the fewest white inhabitants in proportion to the number of Slaves. The hapless *Slaves, allured with the hope of freedom, forsook their owners, and repaired in great numbers to the Royal Army.* They endeavor to recommend themselves to the British by discovering where their owners had concealed their property, and were assisting in carrying it off." (*History of South Carolina,* vol. i., p. 312.) The same candid historian, describing the invasion of the next year, says: "The Slaves a second time flocked to the British Army." (Vol. i., p. 336.)

At a still later period, Mr. Justice Johnson, of the Supreme Court of the United States, and a Citizen of South Carolina, in his elaborate life of General Greene, speaking of the Slaves, makes the same admission: "But the numbers dispersed through the Southern States was very great; so great as to render it impossible for the Citizens to muster free men enough to withstand the pressure of the British arms." (Vol. ii., p. 427.)

From the letters of Gen. Otho Holland Williams, of Maryland, one of the noblest men of the time, the intimate friend and right-hand man of Gen. Nathanael Greene, many passages could be quoted in proof of the abject state of South Carolina during the War of Independence. One or two will suffice. Gen. Williams, writing to his brother, in Maryland, after the capture of Charleston by Sir Henry Clinton, says:

"You may rely on it, my dear brother, that the enemy have had such footing and influence in this country, that their success in putting the inhabitants together by the ears has exceeded even their own expectations; *the distraction that prevails surpasses anything I ever before witnessed,* and equals any idea which your imagination can conceive of a desperate and inveterate civil war. There are a few virtuous and good men in this State and in Georgia, but a great majority of the people *is composed of the most infamous scoundrels that ever existed on earth.* The daily deliberate murders committed by pretended Whigs and reputed Tories (men who are actually neither one thing nor the other in principle), are too numerous and shocking to relate. The licentiousness of various classes and denominations of villains desolate this country, impoverish all who attempt to live by any other means, and destroy the strength and resources of the country, which ought to be collected and united against a common enemy."

Toward the close of the war, Gen. Williams thus writes to a brother Officer, Major Edwards, vindicating General Greene from the slanderous charges heaped upon him:

" The late revolution in South Carolina is owing not only to a change of circumstances, but to a change of men in the Government of that country. How daringly impudent is it for those who have been rescued from misery and dejection, to arraign the virtue that saved them. Gen. Greene exercised a superior judgment, changed the system of Military operations in that country, and used the only possible means of recovering it — and dare the ingrates now accuse him of any interested design, or any view of ambition, other than that which receives its highest gratification from the thanks and approbation of a '*free* people'? And do the devils dare to treat with neglect and contempt that little corps of gallant men who saved them from despair! There are sensible, amiable characters in Carolina, but I always feared the *majority were envious, jealous, malicious, designing, unprincipled people.* Come one, come all of you away and leave them! I am glad to hear the Northern troops are returning. Though I can not flatter myself with the pleasure of seeing them rewarded as they deserve, there will be something done for them; they will not starve on the same fields in which they have bled."

General Williams' original letters, from which these extracts have been made, are now in the possession of his grandson, residing in Baltimore.

But " never mind all *that*," South Carolina is growing martial —" a crisis is approaching," as witness the following paragraph from the " Message" of Governor Adams, delivered in the South Carolina Legislature, on the 27th day of November, 1855:

" The agitation in relation to Slavery continues to increase, and is rapidly tending to a bloody termination. Measures, which it was hoped by some, would give quiet to the country and dignity to its deliberations, have served but to redouble the efforts and augment the power of Abolition. Civil war is a direful calamity, but its scourges are to be endured in preference to degradation and ruin. The people of South Carolina are alive to the issue, *and are mindful of their obligations;* they are calm, because they *are prepared and self-reliant. They have not forgotten their history, and will not fail to vindicate its teachings.* The right to provide new guards for their future security, has been sealed by the blood of *their* ancestors, and it will never be surrendered."

The imperious spirit of South Carolina is not confined to that fussy little State. The whole row of cotton-growing States are agitating the re-opening of the African Slave-Trade, with all its horrors and its hideous enormities. The entire South is wild with excited clamor about its "rights," and about the wrongs which it claims to have suffered at the hands of the "infidel Abolitionists of the North." Pampered with official patronage, puffed up by political victories, the Slave Power defiantly shakes its fist in the Nation's face, crying, "More! more!"

Men of America! Shall Slavery rule the Nation? Or shall not the spirit of freedom be heard and felt in her Councils?

"ALL MEN ARE CREATED EQUAL: THEY ARE ENDOWED BY
THEIR CREATOR WITH CERTAIN INALIENABLE
RIGHTS; AMONG THESE ARE LIFE,
LIBERTY, AND THE PURSUIT
OF HAPPINESS."

APPENDIX A.

COLORPHOBIA IN THE "FREE STATES."

In Heaven, according to the theology of America, a " colored man" may sit down with the just made perfect, his sins washed white " in the blood of the Lamb:" but when he comes to a certain Baptist Church in Boston, Massachusetts, he can not own a pew. And there are few Churches where he can sit in a pew at all.

In the earlier years of the Anti-Slavery effort in Boston, before it became absolutely certain that the clergy were to be "out-and-out" opposers and not helpers of it, the prayers of the Churches, on Sundays, were hundreds of times requested, in the ordinary form, by Anti-Slavery men and women, in behalf of Slaves whose cases were then before the public, and hundreds of times refused. To ascertain whether any change had taken place between the years 1831 and 1851, an Anti-Slavery man made trial as follows. The Old South Church (Rev. Dr. Blagden's, equally with Park Street Church the head-quarters of Boston orthodoxy) had for many years maintained in its vestry a daily morning Prayer-meeting. Finding it customary to present requests, sometimes verbal and sometimes written, that particular bodies or individuals might be made the subjects of special prayer, one morning in May, 1851, while the Boston court-house was in chains, and the case of the kidnapped Sims yet unfinished, he handed in the following note:—

"The prayers of this congregation are requested in behalf of a brother who is now in imminent danger of being torn away from the religious privileges of Boston, and carried as a Slave to Georgia, where the laws forbid him to read the Bible; also, that God would be pleased to arouse the Churches of this city to a sense of the duty of *not* delivering again to his Master" (that is, Kidnapper) "the Servant" (that is, the Stolen man) "who has escaped from his Master" (that is, his Kidnapper) "unto them."

This note was presented during the singing of a hymn. The chairman (Rev. Dorus Clarke), having cast his eye over it, beckoned to Deacon Safford, who sat near him, and after he also had read the note, they held a brief whispered conference together. The purport of this could only be conjectured, but as the note was not read to the meeting, nor any allusion whatever made to it, it was manifest they had decided that the poor man who had fallen among thieves belonged to another parish; that they were neither his "keepers" nor his "neighbors," and that the interests of *their* Zion would prosper quite as well whether he were adjudged a Slave or a freeman.

In Boston, as in New York, the "colored" man is turned out of the Omnibus, out of the Burial-ground. There is a burial-ground in the neighborhood, and in the Deed that confers the land it is stipulated that no person with Negro blood in his or her veins can ever be buried there. Nowhere but in the jail and on the gallows has the black man equal rights with the white in American legislation.

A Congregational Church in New Haven, Connecticut, parcelled out in its Cemetery, a side lot for the burial of "Niggers." But it became necessary to enlarge the Cemetery and bury whites on the other side of the "Niggers," so that they now — "to the great mortification of the more respectable members of the Church" — occupy the centre. One "brother" proposed to erect a wall three feet in height, on both sides of the "Nigger ground." This was assented to, with a proviso that the wall be five instead of three feet. The pastor of the Church thought "a wall five feet in height altogether too·low," and proposed one of seven. The good man evidently thought there would be a practical difference between a wall of seven and one of five feet. A "Nigger"-soul might be capable, he thought, of jumping over a five-feet wall, but could be kept at bay by the height of a seven-barred gate; "*black* souls" being inferior to white ones in leaping according to the Pro-Slavery or "Lower Law" estimate.

Alexander Crummel, a colored young man of the city of New York, made application to become a candidate for "*holy* Orders.*"* He received from his Bishop the usual circular in such cases, in which he was encouraged to "belong to the General Theological Seminary," located at New York. In the Statutes of the Seminary it is expressly said, "Every person producing to the Faculty satisfactory evidence of his having been admitted a candidate for holy Orders," &c., "shall be received as a student of the Seminary." He was, however, referred to the Board of Trustees. A Committee was appointed to consider and report, consisting of Bishop Doane, Rev. Drs. Milnor, Taylor, and Smith, and Messrs. D. B. Ogden, Newton, and Johnson. The next day (June 26, 1839), Bishop Doane, on request, was excused from further service on this Committee, and Bishop Onderdonk, of Pennsylvania, appointed to fill the vacancy. This Committee reported, June 27th, that "having deliberately considered the said petition, they are of opinion that it ought not be granted," and they recommended a resolution accordingly, which, on motion of Rev. Dr. Hawks, was adopted. Mr. Huntington moved that the subject be referred to the Faculty, which was lost. Bishop Doane, June 28th, asked leave to state to the Board his reasons for dissent, with a view to the entering of the same on the minutes. Leave was not granted. During these proceedings Mr. Crummel was advised by the Bishop of New York to withdraw his petition, and was assured that "the Faculty were willing to impart to him *private* instruction."

In the minutes of the proceedings there was a careful avoidance of all allusion to the cause of excluding Mr. Crummel, leaving it to be inferred that it was for some cause besides his "color," which was not the fact. Mr. Crummel afterward became a member of the Theological department of Yale College, New Haven, Connecticut, but not being treated there as white students are, he was compelled to complete his education in Europe.

This unchristian prejudice has stood in the way of the emancipation of thousands of Slaves; and it will be at once perceived that, should the position of the "free colored people," be conspicuously reversed in the "*free* States," the effect upon the emancipation of the Slave would be very great. They, then, who, in the "*free* States," keep up this prejudice are no less Slaveholders than their "brethren" of the South.

The Rev. Henry Ward Beecher, in a letter to the New York *Independent*, of September 4, 1856, says:—

"The most miserable creatures that we know of are those who attempt to unite a love of *Slavery* and of *Liberty*. Like all hermaphrodites, they are merely monsters. Every day, we meet men who hate Abolitionists more than they love liberty. They turn away from every step toward Liberty with aversion. They are eager to believe falsehood against Anti-Slavery men. They are reluctant to believe the truth. When any event occurs tending to deepen the public feeling in favor of liberty and against Slavery, they refuse to aid in publishing it. They eye it askance, with sneering jealousy. But the moment that means and opportunity are afforded to discredit such movement, they become zealous and active. We have never seen this more illustrated than in the case of the Slave-woman Sarah, whose substantial emancipation took place in Plymouth Church not long ago." (See p. 133.) "As much as we knew of the vindictiveness of the '*we-dislike-Slavery-as-much-as-anybody*' men, we were surprised at their conduct in this matter. There could hardly be a case to appeal more irresistibly to the human soul. Indeed, there were present in Church, at the time, *many Southerners, and several Slaveholders. Not one of them was unmoved. They wept, and contributed liberally.* Sarah behaved herself with such modest and womanly propriety, her case was so affecting, the Slave of her own father, sold by him to go South, bought by a Slave-trader through sympathy, who offered to sell her to herself for a hundred dollars less than he paid for her, her little daughter of four years old, kept from her by her own white father, the spontaneous uprising of three thousand strangers, and their eager charity to put into her hands that golden key which should unlock the door of her prison — all these things constituted one of the strongest cases that could arise.

"What has been the result? All papers and persons who had hearts worthy of men rejoiced in the deed and spread it abroad. But others, what did they? Scarcely a day had passed before rumors were set in motion that it was all a deception. Pro-Slavery papers, in New York, Boston, Philadelphia, Cincinnati, and elsewhere, were shocked that such a violation of the Sabbath-day and of the sacredness of a Church should be tolerated! The poor woman's character was grossly assailed, and she was charged with voluntary immoralities. Fabulous incidents were paraded — such as, that a diamond cross had been put into the contribution by some fair child of wealth, whose sympathies had been deceived, and it was assumed that probably the cross was a gift of love, and squandered upon a lie; whereas, no cross of any kind was ever contributed, and nothing except money, with the exception of a small common breastpin, worth one dollar, given by a poor man who had nothing else to give. Sarah's story was pronounced a forgery, the whole thing was declared to be a speculation, and finally, *it was blazoned abroad that she was tired of liberty, and had of her own accord gone back to her master and to Slavery.* This last story roused up the Slave-trader who had bought her of her father, and he sent the following letter to the Editor of the *The New York Daily Times*, which duly appeared in that paper:—

"'RICHMOND, *Wednesday, August* 6, 1856.

"'DEAR SIR: I saw a correspondence in your paper, that the Slave-girl, Sarah, had returned to me, which is a base falsehood, which I wish to correct. I had nothing to do with her going to New York, nor her coming away from there. I purchased the girl through motives of sympathy, for $1,200, and agreed to emancipate her on the payment of $1,100, which amount has been paid to me, and I have executed to her her emancipation papers in the usual way. I have not seen her, or had any control over her for the last two months. I understand that she is living in Washington City with a widow lady. Yours, respectfully.

"'F. SCHEFFER.'

"But there is a Southern side of this story. This Mr. Scheffer, who in the whole transaction has labored with a humanity worthy of all praise, and who has proved himself a man of feeling in spite of his ignominious trade, this man *was subject to such animosity on account of his simple kindness, that he was in danger of being mobbed, and was obliged, for a time, to seclude himself.* What is the condition of a community when its *Slave-traders* are liable to popular violence for humanity to Slaves? This was in Richmond, Virginia. In a State whose wealth largely depends upon the Slaves, it is not deemed safe to allow Slave-brokers and Slave-traders to possess over-nice feelings about their cattle. When Sarah returned from New York to Washington, for the purpose of collecting the subscriptions which had been made toward her freedom, she found multitudes who refused to pay their subscriptions. Some because she had been among the Abolitionists, and many of the clerks in Government employ refused to keep their promises, because, if known, it would cost them their places. On this account, *it became necessary to use all that had been raised for the purchase of Sarah's child, and to raise a hundred dollars more for the completion of her own purchase-money, and the child is still in bondage.*

"In another age this story will figure in history. Such incidents as these are characteristic of the age and communities in which they happen. And men will recount this incident as an evidence of the utter corruption both of human feeling and of moral courage, wrought in a '*free* Nation' by that universal corruptor — Slavery. For though the Slaves live *only* in the South, *the spirit of Slavery pervades the Nation* — a contempt of man in his weakness, a contempt of liberty, except for the strong, and a hatred of everything that works for liberty. Slavery, like a dismal swamp, is *local*, but its miasma is National. It has poisoned the very Constitution, the laws, the customs, and the people themselves, of a Nation which boasts of nothing so much as its Love, its hereditary Love of Liberty for all! "HENRY WARD BEECHER."

A Presbyterian Church in Philadelphia advertised burial lots for sale, with the particular recommendation of them, that no colored persons or executed criminals were buried in the cemetery.

The New York *Evening Post*, of May 21, 1857, says:

"Robert Purvis, of Pennsylvania, the 'light-complexioned mulatto,' who spoke so eloquently at the recent Anti-Slavery Convention against the Dred Scott decision, has a special reason to feel aggrieved by oppressive legislation and prejudice against the colored race. It appears that Mr. Purvis, who enjoys the advantages of wealth and a foreign education, and who once received from James Forsyth, Secretary of State, a passport recognising his citizenship, is the largest school-tax payer but one in the county where he resides, and yet the law forbids his children from attending the very schools he does so much to support."

In March, 1855, Miss Isabella Newall, a teacher in one of the Public schools in Cincinnati, Ohio, "discovered" a "Nigger" in her school, and immediately applied to the Board of Education of the City, soliciting his dismission, not for improper conduct, nor on account of his inability or unwillingness to receive instruction, but because his skin was "darker than that of some of the other scholars." The matter was brought before the Board, and appears to have received considerable discussion in that body, but it was finally decided he "must take his walking papers." The vote stood fifteen to ten. Upon the announcement of the result, two of the Board resigned, both members from the District in which the contemptible Miss Isabella teaches. The young Miss is said to be the daughter of a most "venerable" Pro-Slavery saint, having an extensive business connection in Kentucky, which may account for her repugnance to "Niggers"—especially educated ones.

The Cincinnati Times, of March 9, 1855, gives the genealogy of this poor boy, which we copy—"for the benefit of mankind:"

"The great-grandfather was a full-blooded *white man*, and a Methodist clergyman in the State of Indiana, where he died. The father, David E. Graham, was a Baptist clergyman, in Athens County, Ohio, where he preached to several white congregations. The wife of Allen E. Graham was *half Indian* and *half white* blood, making the grand-parents on the mother's side—the grandfather, one eighth African and the rest white. The grandmother had no African blood at all in her veins, but had a small portion of Indian blood. The mother of the boy is about one-sixteenth African blood, and about the same amount of Indian blood, but is of fair complexion. The boy Graham has one *thirty-second* part of African blood in his veins, and about the same of Indian. *The boy has fair skin, a high Roman nose, and light straight hair, and has no African features about him.*"

The cutaneous democracy of Ohio vindicated itself in the State Senate by the exclusion of William H. Day, Editor of *The Cleveland Alienated American*, a colored man of the highest respectability, and graduate of Oberlin (Ohio) College.

The "*free* State" of Illinois (may God save our feet from

ever touching her soil), passed, on the 24th February, 1853, one of the most atrocious laws ever written in a Statute-book. It is not enough for the "Evangelical" Pro-Slavery Lawmakers of this State to insist that no Slave shall be freed — it will not suffice to re-fetter every colored or party-colored man, who, in horrible anguish, had snapt asunder his chains. No! the "*free* and enlightened Democrats of Illinois" must begin the work of manufacturing Slaves — at the North where people shout themselves hoarse for " liberty, equality, and fraternity !" And the cursed business commenced, too, in a State that ought to have been proud of its liberties, but will for ever after this be a by-word among the Nations. Legree, or Satan himself, would have shrunk back with affright from such an iniquity. To be a Slaveholder is one thing — but to sell at Auction free Men in a "*free* State," is a more stupendous wickedness.

This infamous law is called, " *An act to prevent the immigration of free Negroes into the State of Illinois.*"

To cap the climax, the " act" provides that, after paying to the prosecutor one half of the money accruing from the prosecution and sale of "*free* Negroes," the remainder shall be kept as a distinct and separate fund, " to be called 'The Charity Fund,' and said fund shall be used for the express purpose of relieving the poor"!!! This is intended as a religious consecration to devilism.

"RAN AWAY. — Committed to the County Jail of Alexander County, Illinois, on the 31st day of October, 1854, by L. L. Lightner, County Judge, a Negro boy *about* 30 years of age, weighs about 155 pounds, dark copper color; has a small scar over his right eye, two upper front teeth out, and several jaw teeth gone. Calls himself Samuel Sears. The owner is requested to come forward, prove *property,* pay charges, and take him away. "W. C. MASSEY, *Sheriff of Alexander Co.*

"THEBES, ILLINOIS, *October* 31, 1854."

Look at the style of this advertisement. How glibly a Sheriff of ."*free* Illinois" uses the Southern phraseology, as if all his life had been passed on a plantation in Mississippi, Louisiana, or Texas, and the crack of the "Nigger"-driver's whip familiar to his ears.

The Government has lately reiterated the petty and pitiful injustice and lawlessness of refusing Passports to "colored" native Americans — Rice's Minstrels — who intended to travel in Europe, that refusal being based on the ground, that, although "born free" in the States of New York and Pennsylvania, they are not citizens of the United States!

"DEPARTMENT OF STATE,
"WASHINGTON, *November* 4, 1856.

"*H. H. Rice, Esq., New York City*:—SIR: Your letters of the 29th ultimo and 3d instant, requesting passports for eleven colored persons, have been received, and I am directed by the Secretary of State" (William L. Marcy) "to inform you that the papers transmitted by you do not warrant the Department in complying with your request. A passport is a certificate that the person to whom it is granted is a citizen of the United States, and it can only be issued upon proof of this fact. In the papers which accompany your communication, there is not satisfactory evidence that the persons, for whom you request passports, are of this description. They are represented in your letters as 'colored,' and described in the affidavits as 'black,' from which statements it may be fairly inferred that they are Negroes. *If this is so, there can be no doubt that they are not citizens of the United States.* The question whether '*free* Negroes' are such citizens is not now presented for the first time, but has repeatedly arisen in the Administration of both the National and State Governments. In 1821, a controversy arose as to whether 'free persons of color' were citizens of the United States, within the intent and meaning of the acts of Congress regulating foreign and coasting trade, so as to be disqualified to command vessels; and Mr. Wirt, Attorney-General, decided that they were not; and, moreover, held that the words 'citizens of the United States' were used in the acts of Congress in the same sense as in the *Constitution.* This view is also fully sustained in a recent opinion of Mr. Cushing, the present Attorney-General.

"The judicial decisions of the country are to the same effect. In Kent's Commentaries, vol. ii., p. 277, it is stated that, in 1833, Chief-Justice Dagget, of Connecticut, held that '*free* blacks are not citizens within the meaning of the term as used in the Constitution of the United States ;' and the Supreme Court of Tennessee, in the case of the State against Claiborne, held the same doctrine. Such being the construction of the Constitution in regard to free persons of color, it is conceived that they can not be regarded, when beyond the jurisdiction of this Government, as entitled to the full rights of citizens; but the Secretary directs me to say, that though the Department could not certify that such persons are citizens of the United States, yet if satisfied of the truth of the facts, *it would give a certificate that they were born in the United States, and free;* and that the Government thereof would regard it to be its duty to protect them if wronged by a foreign Government, while within its jurisdiction for a legal and proper purpose.

"I am, Sir, respectfully, your obedient servant,

"J. A. THOMAS, *Assistant Secretary.*"

Supposing Christ was now on earth, as he was once, what course is it probable that he would pursue with regard to this unchristian prejudice of " color"? There was a class of men in those days as much despised by the Jews as the party-colored native Americans are by the " genuine white" portion of the population; and it was a complaint made of Christ that he was a " friend of publicans and sinners." And if Christ should enter, on some sabbath morning, into one of the " evangelical" Pro-Slavery Churches of the "*free* North," and see a " Nigger" sitting afar off by himself, would it not be just in his spirit to go there and sit with him, rather than to take the seats of his richer and more prosperous brother?

> " A poor wayfaring man of grief,
>   Hath often crossed me on my way,
> Who sued so humbly for relief,
>   That I could never answer nay.
> I had not power to ask his name,
> Whither he went, or whence he came;
> Yet there was something in his eye,
> Which won my love, I knew not why.
>
> " Once, when my scanty meal was spread,
>   He entered — not a word he spake —

Just perishing for want of bread,
  I gave him all; he blessed it, brake,
And ate, but gave me part again:
Mine was an angel's portion then,
For while I fed with eager haste,
The crust was manna to my taste.

"'T was night. The floods were out; it blew
  A winter hurricane aloof:
I heard his voice abroad, and flew
  To bid him welcome to my roof;
I warmed, I clothed, I cheered my guest,
I laid him on my couch to rest:
Then made the ground my bed, and seemed
In Eden's garden while I dreamed.

"I saw him bleeding in his chains,
  And tortured 'neath the driver's lash,
His sweat fell fast along the plains,
  Deep-dyed from many a fearful gash:
But I in bonds remembered him,
And strove to free each fettered limb,
As with my tears I washed his blood,
Me he baptized with mercy's flood.

"I saw him in the 'Nigger-pew,'
  His head hung low upon his breast,
His locks were wet with drops of dew,
  Gathered while he for entrance pressed
Within those aisles, whose courts are given
That Black and White may reach one Heaven;
And as I meekly sought his feet,
He smiled, and made a throne my seat.

"In prison, I saw him next condemned
  To meet a traitor's doom at morn;
The tide of lying tongues I stemmed,
  And honored him midst shame and scorn.
My friendship's utmost zeal to try,
He asked, if I for him would die;
The flesh was weak, my blood ran chill,
But the free spirit cried, 'I will.'

> " Then in a moment, to my view,
>   The stranger darted from disguise;
> The tokens in his hands I knew,
>   My Saviour stood before my eyes!
> He spoke, and my poor name he named —
> ' Of me thou hast not been ashamed;
> These deeds shall thy memorial be;
> Fear not, thou didst them unto me.' "
>
> MONTGOMERY AND DENISON.

There is power enough in true religion to melt down the most stubborn prejudices, to overthrow the highest walls of partition, to break the strongest caste, to improve and elevate the most degraded, to unite in fellowship the most hostile, and equalize and bless all its recipients. (See St. James ii. 2–9.)

APPENDIX B.

THE DOUGHFACE AND THE REV. JUDICIOUS TRIMMER, D. D.

I.—THE DOUGHFACE is a man facile and ductile in the hands of those who have him in possession, and who have an object to serve in moulding him.

John Randolph used, for the first time, the term "doughfaces." He applied it to Senators and Members of Congress from the "*free* States," and said: "We will drive you back! We will nail you to the counter, like base coin!" All Northerners were angry. John Randolph has kept his word. We are not aware that Mr. Randolph himself ever gave any explanation of the true orthography of the term which he employed, or of the precise sense in which he used it. Probably he was willing to allow it to be taken in all the senses suggested, according to the difference of humors and fancies; trusting, like a good rhetorician as he was, that each person would understand it in the sense that seemed to him most forcibly contemptuous. Backed up, however, by a quotation from Hosea, as explained by Matthew Henry's Commentary upon it, the spelling "doughface," and the idea of "dough-head," have pretty generally prevailed as the true orthography and real meaning of an epithet so essential at the present moment to the haters of oppression — to the true friends of the Slave.

The genuine doughface loves "our glorious Union." He venerates the American Eagle. If he has an enthusiasm, it is for the Star-Spangled Banner, and he says so on all occasions. He denies that there are any Legrees at the South; denies that Families are separated at Private sale, or at the Auction-block; denies that Bloodhounds are kept on the larger Plantations, to hunt up runaway "property;" denies that Women are flogged on their naked backs, or murdered in cold blood; denies that the Slave-breeding States sell tens of thousands of their "colored" Children every year; denies that young Women are picked out, like four-legged animals, and set apart as Breeders; denies that young Women are sold as Mistresses to any one who pays most; denies that fathers — often members of Churches — sell their own Children; denies that the Churches sanction Polygamy among their members, or are supported, in part, by the wages of Prostitution; denies that Education and the Bible are forbidden the Slaves and *free* people of color. He "would like to know how some people came to be so much wiser than our forefathers? Why didn't they abolish Slavery? Why didn't they mention Niggers in the Declaration of Independence, if they meant to include 'em?" He is confident that the Fugitive Slave bill, of 1850, and the Nebraska bill, of 1854, would have received their approval; in fact, he is inclined to think that the original drafts of them were made by Jay and Hamilton. "To be sure they emancipated their Niggers," but he doubts "whether they would have done it if they had foreseen the use some people would make of it. And if Washington did emancipate his Niggers, it was when he was on his death-bed, and, probably, after his mind began to wander."

The Doughface is "an American, in the true sense of the word." He is "not an Abolitionist, or a Disunionist, or an Amalgamationist, or anything of that sort—nothing but a *man ;*" that is all. He has been brought up to reverence the Union; he has no notion of dissolving it himself or having anybody else do it. He is also a great lover of "Law and Order." He considers Mob attacks on Kidnappers shameful outrages. He is not a Lawyer himself, but his "opinion is that such offences come under the head of high treason, in the first degree." He is confident he has seen a decision somewhere, to that effect, by Judges Taney and Kane. He is sure of one thing: That the entire safety of Society depends upon the maintenance of "law." The laws may be imperfect; they may seem wrong; but they must be supported. The only chance of getting better is to obey such as exist. He *is* an Abolitionist; *he* abhors Slavery. But with the Slave States none can legally interfere; the extension of the System can not be legally resisted; the Constitution guaranties the return of Fugitives. He is very sorry, but it can not be helped. He is particularly fond of quoting Daniel Webster's Speech against "South Carolina Secession" where it talks about "the broken fragments of a once glorious Union, dissevered, discordant, and drenched with fraternal blood," which he says, was "intended as a warning to posterity not to elect Anti-Nebraska members of Congress." He considers Slavery "a moral and political evil; and yet, what can be done to get rid of it, without some Greater evil happening?—that is the question." Again: "As to my own position and opinions on the Slavery question—all my friends" (he is a Commission Merchant in the lower section of New York city, and receives large consignments, of Cotton, Sugar, etc., from the South) "understand me very well, and know that I am opposed to it, root and branch, in All places, and under All circumstances." But he thinks that by weakening the South it gives the North greater commercial advantages and political preponderances. Nothing would give him greater pleasure than to help forward the Anti-Slavery cause, but really he has "*no time to attend to such matters. My Anti-Slavery friends must know, from seeing me so constantly pressed for time, in my Office, with my own business, that I can not do anything else.*" He has, nevertheless, written to his "particular" and "very respectable" friends, male and female, some rather strongly-worded letters, favoring the *Anti*-Slavery cause, but "would not, for the world," see lithograph copies of one or more of them in an Anti-Slavery book, as that would be certain to cause the transfer of his Southern clients into other hands.

The doughface admires the Southern character. He deplores the much misrepresented condition of the Slaves — "well fed and well clothed, and taken care of in their old age. What more do they want?" He is for ever talking about what he calls "the horrors of sectional strife," his great object being to "pour oil upon the troubled waters," to conciliate the conflicting interests of opposing localities and at all hazards to "Save the Union."* He did not justify the butchery of

* The history of Congressional proceedings for the last thirty years may be summed up in one sentence, namely, that the Slave Power legislators have demanded what legislation they wanted, with the threat that they would dissolve the Union if they did not get it; and that the legislators of the North have, with trembling hearts, granted all their demands, "to save the Union." The Lord have mercy on the poor souls who have not had the manliness to do what they knew to be their duty! Likewise on their constituents, who, for the sake of holding on to their Southern customers, have stuffed cotton in their ears, that they might not hear the cry of black brethren, praying for deliverance from worse than Algerine bondage!

Senator Sumner, of Massachusetts, by Brooks and Keitt, of South Carolina; but, then, if a man chooses to insult people, by telling the truth in plain language, as plain as that used in telling lies on the other side, he must make up his mind to take the consequences. In short, that though Brooks and Keitt were entirely wrong, still, they served Mr. Sumner exactly right.*

The doughface is a perfect enthusiast in his admiration of the Holy Bible, yet loves his own race better than any other, and has a peculiar horror of that kind of preaching which drives a man into the corner of his pew and makes him think the devil is after him.

II. THE REV. JUDICIOUS TRIMMER, D. D. — Dr. Trimmer began to study the "signs of the times." He became convinced that reformatory movements could not be "crushed out." He must look out for his interest, and like Uzzah who was a martyr to his extreme caution, he conceived it to be his mission to steady the ark. Radicalism he hated; but in order to head radicalism, he must turn moderate reformer. Abolitionists could not be held back from doing something, *unless it was by men who had some reputation as reformers*. By gaining such a reputation, Dr. Trimmer could be useful to himself in various ways. The conservatives would pay him for holding back the radicals, and the radicals would pay him for dragging along the heavy conservatives. He could get up a reputation as a reformer cheap. He could "pray for the enemies of our glorious Union," and that would catch the "moral-suasion Abolitionists." He could denounce "infidel reformers," and that would keep peace with the "conservative theologians." He could talk about Slavery as a "sin," but

---

* If the Union should happen to be saved, small thanks to Mr. Doughface and his time-serving friends and adherents.

denounce those who secluded themselves from the Churches which upheld the sin. After each Sermon or essay in favor of " gradual emancipation," he could assert his determination to live and die in his Church, whether it went for emancipation or not. Thus he would be able to get support and praise from both sides.

By preaching a little *Anti*-Slavery himself, he could keep itinerant brethren out of his pulpit. The Elders could say, " *our minister preaches on the subject, and we have no need of lecturers.*" He could thus hold the people under his hand, and could keep all things steady. He did not like Senator Sumner's speech, but thought Brooks had not done altogether right. He believed that Mrs. Stowe did injustice to the Slaveholder's character, but he thought her genius noble and fine. He did not vote for Fremont; he did not like the array of hostility to the South which the Republican party presented. He does not profess to know what is *politic*, or what is not; he seeks only to see the *truth*, and as he sees it to express it; and he thinks it would be just as well to let such simple persons as himself have a place in the world, to say their say, unharmed. He is *no* time-server; but he does not believe that all the truths of man's nature are violated by his friends at the South any more than by his friends at the North; neither is altogether right, or altogether wrong; still less that it is just for either side of the Republic to charge the other with crimes *never* committed. In this conviction he expects to live and die.

Dr. Trimmer pursued the same course in regard to " Christian union." He hated Sectarianism, he said, but he was equally afraid of come-out-ism. When a man came into the place to preach " Christian union," he proposed to exchange with his Baptist brother, and thus show how friendly they were, so as to " take the wind out of the sails of this *union* movement."

Mr. Judicious Trimmer, D. D., like the Editors of certain milk-and-water *Anti*-Slavery journals of New York, Boston, Philadelphia, Cincinnati, and other Cotton-ridden Cities, adopted this absorption system generally. That is, when any reform *began to grow popular*, he would engage in it just enough to keep "peace in the Church," and quiet the community, under the impression that the "minister" was a "reformer," and yet be careful not to render any real aid to radicalism. Words of reform were cheap. He could use them, too, with a "good conscience;" and as these reformatory words pleased the people, he became an adept in their use. At the same time, he kept at peace with his denomination. If any grew restless under the idea that the denomination was not advancing fast enough, Mr. Trimmer was just the man to be put forward to restore quiet. Was he not a *reformer?* and did he not remain in the Church? Did he not talk against Slavery and Sectarianism, and keep in the organization? Such a man must be right. Thus, you see, he formed a kind of breakwater on both sides, and catched any stray "donation" or "rise" in Salary which floated up from either side. He is "not a professed friend nor a professed enemy of Slavery"—he regards it as a "perplexing question"—and thinks it does not "professionally" belong to his calling, etc.

Mr. Trimmer went for "restricting and limiting evils"—but was not so fanatical as to think of abolishing them. Wherever there was a Church which was likely to lose some of their members by secession, he was just the man for that place. He could be *reformer* enough in words to keep the radicals quiet, and he never did any deed to disturb the others. On several occasions he attended "protracted meetings" with such Churches, and "healed all their breaches, by his judicious course." True, his meetings, with all his reform talk, left the Church dead on such subjects, practically; but Mr. Trimmer became all the more popular. *Some of the radicals complain-*

ed *of him as worse than a dozen opposers, for they said that his reputation as a reformer gave him double power to stab the cause.* Many young ministers took him as a "model." The seminaries taught his system of clerical tactics, under the head of "Pastoral theology," and the Rev. Solomon Straw-watcher, D. D., often referred young students to his success, as an illustration of the system. He won praise from all parties, and his wealth increased, thus showing how to obey that passage of Scripture which says, "Make unto yourselves friends of the mammon of unrighteousness."

The judicious trimmers know the infamous character of the "*heaven*-born institution." They know it is an "institution" opposed to God's law of love, and man's sense of right. They know it is a blight to every state which cherishes it, and a curse to the "free States." They know that it degrades labor; begets indolence, fosters violence, and drags down society to a permanent barbarism. They know that from the first it has been, and until it is destroyed it will be, a cause of dissension, and strife, and practical disunion, in the land. But they are time-servers, they have an eye to the golden calf. Therefore they cry to this hideous monster of perdition, "Be thou our God!" and bow to it, and worship it.

On the whole, the Doughface is the most contemptible specimen of humanity on earth.

The Slaveholders and their allies — the doughfaces — accuse the Abolitionists of having done the Anti-Slavery cause more injury than good; but this is denied; and no better reply to such nonsense can be given than that which we find in a letter of Wendell Philips, Esq., of Boston, Massachusetts, to a "friend" in England:

"My Dear Sir: Your letter needed no apology; it was a pleasure to receive it; such criticisms do us good, they show us how we strike strangers (distance of place performs the part of distance of time), and recall us to the duty of reconsidering our course, and the reasons on which it is based. It is not claiming much to ask that you will not suppose us so foolish as to wish the lives we give to a hard duty utterly thrown away, by a bad choice of means or misdirected effort. If we are in error, therefore, he does us a kindness who sets us right; and our gratitude should be in proportion to the worth of the cause such error harms — the value we set on ours, and our sincere conviction of the goodness of the means we use to forward it, we have shown by the lives we devote to them. Your letter objects to the language and temper in which the Anti-Slavery agitation is conducted, and the personal character it often assumes. You ask us to consider whether such a course is either justifiable or expedient; and I judge from a letter which enclosed yours, that you think our mistake in these respects, has injured the Anti-Slavery cause in the Slave States, and put back emancipation, especially in Virginia, Delaware, Kentucky, and Maryland.

"I will tell you my views on these points; though frequent experience leads me to doubt whether, except in rare cases, any but an American can fully understand our position. Napoleon, you know, always maintained that Wellington ought, according to all military rule, to have been beaten at Waterloo. The world, I believe, has never had the patience to listen to his explanation. The victory settled for us the military sufficiency of the means that gained it. Our case, allow me to say, is precisely similar. In 1830, the cause of the Slave was desperate enough. The reaction, after the intense political excitement of the Missouri question, was perfect; and the whole nation went to sleep. The pulpit was dumb, the press discreetly silent, and every politician avoided the fatal question with the instinct of self-preservation. Since then, the Anti-Slavery agitation, under Mr. Garrison, has achieved a wider and more immediate success than any similar cause ever gained in the world before. It has aroused the whole country, driven the South to that madness and those rash counsels, which, according to the Greek proverb, always precede destruction; swallowed up, like Aaron's rod, all the other political issues — Bank — Tariff — Internal Improvements, etc.; drew into the vortex of its own excitement all the great statesmen who had again and again pledged themselves never to touch the question, Webster, Benton, Clay, etc.; blotted out the lives of the two parties that have ruled us for half a century, and turned every man into Pro or Anti-slavery — unionist or disunionist — broken to pieces the two greatest sects, Presbyterian and Methodist, and is putting the rest on their good behavior; it has filled every pulpit, railroad car, lyceum, public hall, and private fireside, every arena, literary, religious or political, with discussion; witness (the last instance) Mr. Choate so desperate as to steal the occasion of a literary address for a caucus speech. In a word, it has taken up the Nation by the four corners, and shaken it out of all its old habits and trains of thought, turning it into an Anti-Slavery Debating Society; and all this, living in a country ruled by Public Opinion, and conscious that Truth is on our side, we do not despair of success. If God grant us as much during the next twenty years as we have had the past, our first of August will be near, if not over, unless some other and bloody Exodus is before us in the providence of God.

"I know you may say all this would have happened without Mr. Garrison and his friends. So, perhaps, the Reformation would have come some time or other, without Luther, and our Revolution without Washington or Adams. But he who maintained that either event would have taken place *as and when it did*, without these men, will recollect that the presumption is the other way, and that the burden of proof rests upon him. You may urge also, that the Anti-Slavery agitation would have succeeded better if differently conducted. But when the success has been so *unparalleled, the objector* must recollect that the burden of proof rests upon him, and that, until the contrary is shown, such unequalled success is conclusive evidence that the method of agitation was well devised. It may be very natural for parties whom Mr. Garrison has annihilated, and sects which he has broken to pieces, to find fault with him; *but it was hardly to be expected they should allege that the campaign in which they have been so signally defeated, by a miserable minority, was ill planned and worse executed.*

"What I wish you to observe is, that you are calling on the conqueror, in a case where accident could have no part, to prove his military capacity. He answers you, in Wren's epitaph, 'Circumspice!' Look around you. As you remark in your letter, all American discussions, political and religious, are carried on with such personality and frank and blunt censure as are distasteful to an Englishman. Granted. It ought then, to be no matter of surprise that the Anti-Slavery agitation shares in the national fault; nor should it be matter of special blame, that a man, in becoming an Abolitionist, did not cease to be an American in his habits and tastes. Indeed, we might claim that if there be *any* cause which could justify the most direct and harsh censure, and the utmost personality, it must be ours. Could we sit down together, and compare the Anti-Slavery with the religious and political press of the United States, I think that you would allow that its higher aims and purer principles have elevated and refined, as you think they should do, the tone of its discussions. Indeed, making fair allowance for difference of individual tastes, recollecting the priceless right we are battling for, and that our ranks are too poorly filled to refuse any man who offers his aid, I can say I have no fault to find with the language or temper of the Anti-Slavery press. To Alexander's criticism of their weapons, the Scythians made answer, 'If you knew how sweet freedom was, you would think it right to defend it even with axes.'

"Consider our position and recollect our object. Living in a land governed exclusively by Public Opinion — ruled by men not by laws — we are attempting to abolish a system of Slavery sanctioned by Public Opinion. To effect our object we must entirely change this Public Opinion. We are a minority; all the posts of influence are held against us, the pulpit, the press, the senate-house, and the market-place. Yet to succeed, we must reach every class in the community, the thoughtless and the thoughtful — the calm and the enterprising — the rude and the refined, the ignorant and the educated. In such circumstances, to expect every Abolition speaker to model himself on Dr. Channing is the greatest mistake. Dr. Channing spoke to the man of refinement and culture, with feelings sensitively alive to every consideration of duty and humanity. But with the exception of these, a few thousands at best, he was of no avail till lips more Saxon than his translated him for the benefit of the masses. The world has been criticising, for a century, the Methodist and the Moravian for their want of taste, and the rude familiarity with which they speak of things held sacred, and usually approached only with great decorum. But the Methodist and Moravian have touched more hearts than all the educated pulpits. The Quaker, while his words were half battles and stung like adders, made converts. He has become staid and decorous and ceased to grow. The fact is a new idea, the germ of Reform, is first a sentiment, then a thought — and afterward a principle. Hence almost all Reforms have originated among the masses and worked their way upward. I do not know that a single great Moral Reform has sprung from the schools; and when any Moral Reformer has appeared there, he has found himself speedily ejected and forced into the company of those who live in their sentiments, the mass of mankind. Their language is rough, blunt, and often coarse, as some over-fastidious ears count coarseness. Reformers are usually made of the same stuff, and share these faults. And one of a different stamp seeking to bridge over the space between him and his audience, borrows for the moment their vocabulary.

"You allude to the personality of our discussions. In a country like ours, governed, as I have reminded you already, entirely by Public Opinion, the opinions of those who either in the pulpit, at the head of the press, or in political station, represent and seek to mould the moral sentiment of the community, are practically *facts* of momentous import to all of us. Our immediate welfare and our future destiny are inevitably and deeply affected by them. *In such circumstances those persons have no right to complain if their opinions and actions are scanned and criticised with relentless scrutiny by parties so deeply concerned in them as we are. If they shrink from this responsibility they must quit the post which entails it.* The politician is our servant, whose acts it is our duty and right to criticise — the mistakes of the clergyman and the editor make our farms less valuable and our lives less secure — endanger free speech and jeopard the welfare of our children — they must expect to be vigilantly watched.

"If you object to our frequent judgment of *motives*, I need only remind you that such judgment is necessarily made upon a very close consideration of the thousand minute circumstances of a man's past history, present position, previous declarations, known associates, general character, &c., &c., *which none but those near at hand can properly estimate, so that we may be oftener right than your general knowledge of our country would lead you to think.* As to the expediency of openly stating that which is generally surmised, who can doubt that it is one powerful means of destroying the influence of the plausible arguments of designing men to point out to those they are likely to delude, the corrupt and interested motives by which they are led. It seems to me that nothing but very false charity would require that we should omit from our criticisms of

Webster the well-known fact, that he did not believe his own statements or rely on his own arguments, *and would never have used either but from calculations of political expediency and the hope of the Presidential chair.* Our cause must be very strong, indeed, when it can afford to forego, in its unequal battle with a Nation, so potent a means of opening men's eyes to the treachery of his conduct, and the fatal course on which he was leading the Nation. After all, *the masses judge of opinions more by the men who hold them than by the arguments on which they rest.* Our aim is to free the Slave, by changing the sentiment of this Nation. We must take human nature as we find it, and use all honest means to reach and mould the National heart.

"As for the here oft-answered objection about Delaware, Maryland, &c., it is one of the stale pretences of Pro-Slavery hypocrisy. Every candid man, of all parties, North and South, laughs at such statements. They served their purpose years ago, but have long since fallen into the kennel of exploded lies. Intelligent Southerners have again and again confessed that the agitation had weakened the whole system; Cassius M. Clay acknowledged it for Kentucky—Mr. Vaughan, his partner in the editorship of the Louisville Examiner, added his testimony for that and other States. If you wish more palpable evidence, take it in the clouded close of the life of John C. Calhoun, who sank to his grave, confessing that the days of Slavery were numbered, and throwing all the blame on the Anti-Slavery agitation. Indeed, if the Garrison movement, with the political efforts which have resulted from it, is putting back emancipation, how comes it that for twenty years the South has gone frantic with fear, and been calling on the North to quell it? threatening to dissolve the Union if it were not stopped, and rushing on the maddest course to regain the balance of power, which they felt was slipping from their hands. Do men usually exhibit such fear and hatred toward those who are confirming their power and adding value to their property? Have the manufacturers of your country offered a reward of £5,000 for the head of Sir Joseph Paxton? or did your landholders, during the late corn-law excitement, tar and feather the Dukes of Richmond and Buckingham? Judge the South by its *acts*, not its *pretences*—and you will easily learn by those alone the true effects of our agitation on Slavery even in the Slave States."

APPENDIX C.

THE DOMESTIC AND FOREIGN SLAVE-TRADE.

It has often been said that the Slave-Trade was still carried on from New York, Boston, Philadelphia, &c., but as the charge has been of a vague and general character, it attracted little attention. The world is, however, beginning to get light on the subject. There is now lying in Prison, in New York, a man (Captain James Smith) who has been tried, in the United States Circuit Court, before Judges Nelson and Betts, found guilty, and sentenced to two years' imprisonment, and to pay a fine of $1,000, for being engaged in the trade. The testimony in the case was ample, and although Smith protested against his condemnation, on the ground that he was a "foreigner," and not amenable to the laws of the United States, he did not deny the fact of his share in the business. He spoke of it to his friends, and related, with unconcealed exultation, the particulars of his wild and desperate career.

The Editor of *The New York Evangelist*, who had seen and talked with Smith in his prison, says that he told his story, not like a criminal making a confession, but rather with the freedom and pride of an old soldier relating his battles.

Nor did he intimate a wish that what he said should be kept private. Indeed, he had previously boasted to others his villanous deeds on the African coast. His disclosures, therefore, are public property. Some of these are curious. Whether he told the truth the world must judge. It is not very probable that a man would make up a story which implicated himself in a capital crime. Besides, his account is consistent with itself; it agrees perfectly with what was proven on the trial, and with the descriptions in Captain Canot's book. We believe, therefore, that Captain Smith let out the truth :—

"New York," said Captain Smith, "is the chief port in the world for the Slave-Trade." He repeated two or three times, "*It is the greatest place in the universe for it.* Neither in Cuba nor in the Brazils is it carried on so extensively. Ships that convey Slaves to the West Indies and South America are fitted out from New York. Now and then one sails from Boston and Philadelphia ; but New York is our headquarters. My vessel was the brig Julia Moulton. I got her in Boston, and brought her here, and sailed from this port direct for the coast of Africa." "But do you mean to say that this business is going on now?" "*Yes, all the while. Not so many vessels have been sent out this year — perhaps not over twenty-five. But last year there were thirty-five.*"

"Are there large shipping-houses engaged in it?" "Yes; I can go down to South street, and go into a number of houses that help to fit out ships for the business. I don't know how far they own the vessels, or receive the profits of the cargoes. But these houses know all about it. They know me. They see me sail out of port with a ship and come back a passenger. They sometimes ask me, 'Captain, where is your ship?'" (with a shrug). "They know what has become of her."*

---

* The profits accruing from a successful run to and from the West Coast of Africa are so great, that the captain generally hides all traces of his crime immediately after landing his cargo, by either setting on fire

"But how do you manage to get away without exciting suspicion?" "Why, you see, we keep close, and get everything aboard, and do not ask for our papers until we are just ready to sail. Then we go to the Custom-house, and take out papers for Rio Janeiro, St. Helena, the Cape de Verde islands, or any port we please — it don't matter where — and instantly clear." "But if you were seized at that moment, could the officers tell, by searching a ship, that she was a Slaver?" "Oh, yes, they couldn't help knowing. Besides, they must suspect something from seeing such an almighty crew. My little brig carried but 200 tons, and could be manned by four men. But I had fourteen before the mast. The moment of leaving port is the one of danger. But we don't lose time. A steamer is kept ready, and we get away immediately.* *Often two or three Slavers leave at once. We steam down the bay and*

or scuttling the vessel. In this way a steady market has been established for light swift-sailing schooners and brigs, which are built "for one voyage only."

* Formerly these vessels took out weapons to overawe the blacks as well as to fight off intruders; they also carried shackles enough to secure as many Slaves as they could carry. Now they depend upon their speed to elude cruisers, and instead of binding their human cargo, they simply carry a keg or two of sharp carpet-tacks; and, if the Slaves become restive, a handful or two of these sprinkled among them soon reduces them to submission. The Slaves being naked and closely packed, can not make any movement against their captors without being subjected to the most excruciating pain — every step which they take forcing the sharp points of the nails into their feet. They also stow the coppers away; and, if boarded by a cruiser before the Slaves are taken on board, the vessel presents the appearance of a legitimate trader. A few scattered bricks might perhaps be found, as well as a barrel of lime, on a close scrutiny; but the former may easily pass for ballast; and if anybody should be inquisitive enough to ask the use of the latter, why it would be the easiest matter in the world to convince him that it was required to purify the ship. Once on the Slave coast, however, and the Slaves on board, the bricks and mortar would serve just as well to fit up the coppers for cooking their food. Such are a few of the modern improvements.

18

over the bar, and then the ocean is before us, and we set our course for any quarter we please." " But when you reach the African coast, are you not in great danger from British Ships-of-War?" "Oh, no, we don't care a button for an English squadron. *We run up the American flag, and if they come aboard, all we have to do is to show our American papers, and they have no right to search us.*" "That may be very well when you are going in empty. But suppose you are coming out with a cargo of Slaves on board?" " Even then we can get along well enough, *if the Niggers will keep quiet. We put them all below deck, and nail down our hatches, and then present our papers. The officers have no right to go below. The only danger in this case is that they will stay on board too long, and the Niggers begin to get smothered and make a noise.*"

"How many Slaves could you carry on your vessel?" "We took on board 664. We might have stowed away 800. If she had been going to the Brazils, we should have taken that number. She would carry 750 with ease. The boys and women we kept on the upper deck. But all the strong men — those giant Africans that might make us trouble — we put below on the Slave deck." "Did you chain them or put on handcuffs?" "No, never; they would die. We let them move about." "Are you very severe with them?" "We have to be pretty strict at first — for a week or so — to make them feel that we are masters. Then we lighten up for the rest of the voyage." "How do you pack them at night?" "They lie down upon the deck, on their sides, body to body. There would not be room enough for all to lie on their backs." "Did many die on the passage?" "Yes. I lost a good many the last cruise — more than ever before. *Sometimes we find them dead when we go below in the morning.* Then we throw them overboard." "Are the profits of the trade large?" "Yes, sir, very large. My Brig cost $13,000 to fit her out completely. My last cargo to Cuba was worth $220,000."

"Did you ever get chased by the English ships?" "Yes; once a Man-of-War chased two of us. The mate betrayed me. I never liked the man. He was scared. He had no heart. You see, it takes a man of a particular constitution to engage in our business. When once at sea with a Slave cargo, we are in free bottoms. We belong to no country. We are under the protection of no law. We must defend ourselves. A man must have a great deal of nerve in such a situation when he is liable to be chased by ships-of-war, or perhaps, finds himself suddenly in the midst of a whole fleet. The Mate once served me a trick for which I should have been perfectly justified in shooting him dead. We were running in between the islands of Martinique and Dominique, when suddenly there shot out from behind the land an English steamer. The Mate thought it was a Ship-of-War, and so did I. He was frightened and instantly turned the vessel off her course. This was the very movement to bring down the enemy in chase. I saw the danger and flew to the helm, and put her back again, and we passed by in safety." "But are you not tired of this business?" "Why, I didn't want to go out the last voyage. I tried to get another Captain to take charge of my ship. I wanted to stay at home and get married.* But *good men* in our business are scarce. And I had to go."

A short time since, *The New York Daily Times* said, "The Slave-Trade is now actively carried on between New York and the coast of Africa. The conduct of the Federal officials on this subject is absolutely incredible. Vessels are fitted up almost every week, ostensibly for Cuban ports, or for legitimate trade on the coast of Africa, which almost any trader to that coast will not have a moment's hesitation in identifying as destined for the Slave-trade. Yet not one of them has the slightest difficulty in securing regular American papers.

* What a lovely husband the scoundrel would be! Who speaks first, young ladies?

"There are Merchants in our streets to-day who are making their tens and hundreds of thousands of dollars yearly by a traffic condemned alike by the laws and the public sentiment of the civilized world." Again: "There are hundreds of Merchants in New York, who are constantly and largely engaged in this traffic; who carry it on as their regular business— who grow rich by it, and live in splendid style, and claim and hold high rank in the rich circles of our metropolis by virtue of their wealth thus acquired. This fact is generally known, and not a week passes in which vessels are not cleared at the Custom-House, of whose destination and employment in the Slave-trade, the houses who ship crews for them, and even the Officials who prepare and sign their papers, are morally certain. New York and Baltimore are now, and have been for years, the great head-quarters of the African Slave-trade."

The Richmond (Va.) *Dispatch*, speaking of the African Slave-trade, says: "It is a notorious and undeniable fact, that the African Slave-trade always has been, is now" (Nov., 1856), "and in all probability always will be, carried on by Northern hands. The vessels engaged in the trade are built in and owned in New York and New England, and are manned mostly by New-Englanders."

The conscience of the Nation has been utterly debauched on the whole question of Slavery, and nothing short of a complete extermination of the "evangelical" Pro-Slavery Churches can work a cure of the wide-spread corruption. If emancipation is such an evil that Doctors of Divinity "can not pray for it," why should not the "evangelical" Merchants—members of those Churches—be allowed to import hundreds of thousands of Slaves every year, without forfeiting their standing either in the Churches or in Social life?

It is a common subterfuge of the Slaveholders and their allies, in order to shield themselves from the just condemnation of an indignant world, to claim that the transfer of the Africans from their native land to America has greatly *improved* their condition. As if the true method to civilize the ignorant and to enlighten the superstitious were to ravage their coasts — give their dwellings to the consuming fire — shoot down all who offer any resistance — seize and manacle such as can make no defence — drag them on board of Slave ships — pack them to suffocation in the holds of those "floating hells" — subject them to all the horrors of the middle passage — drive the survivors to unrequited toil under the lash, denying to them all the rights of our common humanity, forbidding them to learn to read the name of God, legally affirming them to be "goods and chattels, to all intents, purposes and constructions whatsoever," and trafficking in them as in cattle and swine! Why, then, prohibit the African Slave-trade, under such a penalty? Why not give unlimited encouragement to it? Why not let Christian philanthropy be as broad as the Atlantic, and Africa be depopulated afresh? What! put to death those benevolent men who kidnap benighted heathens for their good! What! brand those as pirates who forcibly remove the natives of Guinea· to the plantations of Carolina, seeing the result will be their temporal and everlasting welfare! Is not this the command of Christ — " Go ye into all Africa, and seize as many of its wretched inhabitants as ye can by fraud and violence, that they may be taken to Slaveholding America, where *my* Gospel is proclaimed!"

The Rev. Mr. Bushnell, an American Missionary on the Western Coast of Africa for thirteen years, in a letter to *The New York Evangelist*, in March, 1857, says:

"The Slave-trade is the great curse of Africa; it renders the wildest savages still more fierce and cruel, and baffles all attempts at civilization. Of course all other commerce is killed by this traffic. The country is rich in natural products and might furnish a large export. But all is kept down by this one trade. The moment a British squadron, hovering on the coast, puts the Slavers in fear and causes their trade to languish, other branches of industry revive. The chiefs, finding less demand for human flesh, bring down other commodities — ivory, palm oil, gold dust, dye woods, and ebony. Thus the instant the Slave-trade is checked, there springs up a legitimate commerce. But while that is in full blast, it kills everything else, for it is more exciting and more lucrative. The trade in Slaves is more profitable than trade in ivory, for it is easier to steal a child than kill an elephant.

"But the commercial loss is nothing to the moral desolation which it leaves behind it. The Slave-trade is the cause of almost all the wars between different tribes. It keeps them constantly fighting to procure fresh victims. It excites them to attack defenceless villages, and to seize men, women, and children. Thus it stimulates to burnings, to murder and to massacre. And it is shocking to think that it was 'Christian traders' who first taught the poor natives these arts of cruelty. And it is the cupidity of American traders which spurs on the natives to burning and butchery, and which brings upon this desolate coast all the woes of hell.

"A natural effect of such a trade in human flesh and blood is to produce a frightful disregard of human life. It has reduced the value of a man to the trifle that he will bring from the trader. Many a man has been bought for a keg of rum. Lately the price has risen, so that now an able-bodied man will fetch about $40, and a boy or girl half that sum.

"It is often said that these poor Africans do not suffer much, for that they are incapable of feeling. They are little above the beasts, and, like animals, all places are indifferent to them. On the contrary, they are a very sensitive race. Natives of that torrid clime, they are true children of the sun. Living in the open air, they drink in bright influences from sunshine and from sky. Their feelings are quick. They have a passionate love of music. The gondoliers of Venice, floating on their grand canal, are not more spontaneous and gushing in their melody than these Africans, floating on their inland waters. As the boat glides along the lagoons and rivers, the oarsmen keep time with a rising and falling strain. If any incident occurs in the sail they instantly improvise a rude poetry, and accompany it with a wild melody. Thus everywhere — in their boats or bamboo-huts, in every scene of gladness or of grief, at the wedding or the funeral — their hearts find vent in song.

"And do these simple children of nature feel nothing when torn from their homes and country? When I first landed on the coast, the Slave-trade was flourishing, and there were many factories near us. I often visited the barracoons, and such utter wo and despair I never saw on any human faces. Their lightness and gayety were all gone. Their songs were hushed, and they sat silent and gloomy. It was not a grief which burst forth in wild lament, nor a despair which nerved them to fierce resistance, but a wan and weary look, a despair which was speechless and hopeless, as of those doomed to die. There they sat upon the shore chained together, now turning a last fond look to the hills and palm groves in the distance, and now looking to the Slave-ship which began to show its dark hull on the horizon. Thus they watched and wept, their stifled sobs answering to the desolate moaning of the sea."

The Trade goes on briskly — the dealers separate husbands, wives, sons, and daughters; severing all the purest and holiest ties. Each year millions of dollars are invested in this infamous traffic, and thousands of its victims perish in the rice-swamps and sugar-field of the South; men whose purses are heavy with the gold gained as the price of blood by the sale of their Slaves, mingle in the highest social circles North and South, sit in Congress, or at the Communion Table, or stand in the Pulpit, in fellowship with the great majority of the Churches. The bloody Slave-whip is ever doing its cruel work, and the red-hot branding-iron hissing in the flesh of the wretched victims of cruelty, and sorrow and anguish unutterable dwell in the hearts of millions.

Such are some of the results of a long career of compromise with sin.

The Nation has sold itself to the Slave Power. That Power has hitherto had control of the Government, and is now to hold it until 1861. For the last twelve years, to go no further back, each successive Administration has performed some act of signal service to the Power which controls it.

Thus, from 1845 to 1849, Polk, Dallas & Co. were the political agents to do the business of the Slaveholder. They re-annexed Texas, made the Mexican war, and at great cost of money and men, plundered a sister Republic of an enormous tract of land, whence Slave States are one day to be made.

From 1849 to 1853, Taylor, Fillmore & Co. had the management of the political business. The senior partner in that firm, a man too honest to be in such a concern—for it was "a nomination not fit to be made" in more senses than one—soon died of "the Washington distemper," and the survivors managed as they saw fit. They had a whole Omnibus load of "Compromise Measures." The Fugitive Slave Bill was passed; Kidnapping became common; practical Atheism was proclaimed throughout the land as the first principle of Republican Government; the sentence, "No Higher Law," was added to the Litany of the Churches of Commerce, and the State Rights of the North were broken down by the Federal arm of Slavery.

From 1853 to 1857, Pierce, Cushing, Douglas, Brooks, & Co. had a general Power of Attorney to do all matters and things pertaining to the triumph of Slavery and the overthrow of Freedom; and most diligently did they do their work. This firm attended to the minute details of Slave-driving, and, while it encouraged Walker's fillibustering in Nicaragua, and Lecompte's bloody assizes in Kansas, it turned Dr. Jackson out of his postmastership at Cresson, Pennsylvania, because he helped to cure the wounds of Senator Sumner.

Now, from 1857 to 1861, if the firm does not break before, Buchanan, Breckinridge, & Co. are to carry on the same business at the old stand—sign of the Spread Eagle and thirteen Stripes.

APPENDIX D.

DOUGH-FACE RELIGION.

The American Tract Society.—The American Tract Society has, it seems, full liberty to rebuke "evangelical Christians:" 1. For sending children to dancing-school—but not for sending them to the Auction-block; 2. For reading novels—but not for preventing millions of colored men, women, and children from reading the Bible; 3. For covetousness—but not for compelling others to labor without wages; 4. For trading in intoxicating liquors—but not for trading in the bodies and souls of their fellow-men, or even of their "fellow-Christians;" 5. For attending horse-races—but not for driving men and women under the lash to the Cotton and Sugar fields; 6. For drinking wine—but not for robbing millions of men, women, and children of all Civil and Religious freedom; 7. For visiting the circus—but not for annihilating, by law, the Marriage relation.

Whenever the books of the Society allude to the existence of Slavery, it is as a system unknown to the people of the United States, but existing as a phenomenon in distant parts of the world. Hear them:—

"Suppose you were now in *Brazil*, and the owner of a large establishment to fit out Slave-traders with hand-cuffs for the coast of *Africa*, and could not change your business without considerable pecuniary sacrifice, would you make the sacrifice, or would you keep your fires and hammers going?" And again: "If a man only lives to make a descent on the peaceful abodes of Africa, and to tear away parents from their weeping children, and husbands from their wives and homes, where is the man that will deem this a moral business? Other men will prey upon unoffending Africa, and bear human sinews across the ocean to be sold. Have you a right to do it?"—(Tract No. 305.) Once more, speaking of the duty of rescuing the drunkard, it is asked: "What would you not do to pull a neighbor out of the water, or out of the fire, or to deliver him from *Algerine* captivity?"—(Tract No. 422.)

During the twenty-nine years of its existence, the American Tract Society has not published a line intended to touch the conscience of a Slaveholder. On the contrary, special care has been taken to expunge from its reprints of British, French, and German books every expression that could imply a censure on the stupendous National iniquity. This extreme sensitiveness is shown in the mutilation of a passage in its reprint of Mr. J. J. Gurney's "Essay on the Habitual Exercise of Love to God." On page 142 of the original edition, is the following passage:—

"If this love had always prevailed among professing Christians, where would have been the sword of the Crusader? Where the African Slave-trade? Where the odious system which permits to man a property in his fellow-man, and converts rational beings into marketable chattels?"

This was meat too strong for the digestion of the American Tract Society, and hence was carefully diluted, so that it might be swallowed without producing the slightest nausea. In the Society's edition, page 199, the passage stands thus:—

"If this love had always prevailed among professing Christians, where would have been the sword of the Crusader? Where the torture of the Inquisition? Where every system of oppression and wrong by which he who has the power revels in luxury and ease at the expense of his fellow-men?"

The Society, in its reprint of the well-known "Essays to do good," by the Rev. Dr. Cotton Mather, declares in the Preface:—"In this edition such portions of the original Essays are omitted, and such changes have been made in the phraseology, as might be expected after the lapse of more than a century since the work was written." The natural inference from this language is, that nothing had been omitted which could be of any interest to the reader of our time. Not so. In the original edition occurs this passage :—

"O that the souls of our Slaves were more regarded by us, and not using them as if they had no souls! That the poor Slaves which live with us may, by our means, be made the candidates of the heavenly life! that we might give a better demonstration that we despise not our souls, by doing what we can for the souls of our Slaves. How can we pretend to Christianity, when we do no more to Christianise our Slaves?"

But in the Society's edition (p. 44,) we read :—

"O that the souls of our Servants were more regarded by us! that we might give a better demonstration that we despise not our own souls, by doing what we can for the souls of our Servants. How can we pretend to Christianity, when we do no more to Christianise our Servants?"

Though "the Ethiopian cannot change his skin," yet *Slaves* have changed to *Servants* in somewhat "more than a century." This "might have been expected." Probably owing to the *bleaching process* going on in the South!

The Memoir of Mary Lundie Duncan, of Scotland, by her mother, first had a wide circulation abroad, then was published in full by Robert Carter and Brothers, New York, in various styles, and some as cheap as could be desired; but now it is published, in a mutilated form, by the American Tract Society. Both Mary Lundie Duncan and her mother hated Slavery, and loved freedom. Therefore the book would not be acceptable to the dear brethren who owned "niggers."

To send forth a book, with two or three short paragraphs on the subject of Slavery omitted, and call it "an abridgment of the original," is an insult to both author and reader.

The attempts of the "Managers" of the Society to defend themselves against these serious charges have been more numerous than successful. It was at first set up that the charge of mutilating the works republished by the Society was "unfounded," and that nothing of the sort—at least nothing of any consequence—had been done. But this position it was impossible to maintain against the array of facts brought to bear upon it. Obliged to admit the fact, the Managers of the Society—like their political sympathizers in Congress—have been obliged to fall back upon the "Constitutional" argument. Hear them :—

"Slavery may, for aught we know, be exactly what Wesley pronounced it, 'the sum of all villanies.' We must not be understood as denying *that*, or as committing ourselves to the doctrine that Slaveholding is an institution ordained by God, sanctioned by both the Old and the New Testaments, and every way compatible with Christian life and feeling. *Some* of us individually may lean to that view; but we must not be at all understood as committing or pledging ourselves, as a Committee, or the Society for which we act, to any such declaration of sentiment. On the other hand, *however great a sin and wickedness we might regard Slavery* to be, there is a *Constitutional* lion in the path. The very Charter under which we act forbids us to say a single word about it."

The friends of truth, however, longed for some more decided declaration on the subject than the milk-and-water apology of the Executive Committee. Their longings took the shape of emphatic demands for a Committee of Investigation, to examine and see whether the Executives were legally and constitutionally hindered from doing their duty and speaking the whole truth, or whether they were afraid to offend their masters, the Southern members of the Society.

On the 7th of May, 1856, the "leading Members" of the Society met at the Rev. Dr. Spring's church, New York, for the transaction of the " regular business," previous to meeting at the Tabernacle for the celebration of the Anniversary. Chief Justice Williams, of Connecticut, the President of the Society, occupied the chair. The attendance on the occasion was very large; all the available space, either for sitting or standing, both in the body of the Church and in the gallery, was occupied. Many "eminent Divines" from the Slave States were present. The meeting was opened with prayer by the Rev. Dr. Dewitt.

The REV. DR. KNOX, in behalf of the Executive Committee, of which he is a Member, then read a communication on the extremely happy condition of things in general. He assured his audience that "the Executive Committee of the American Tract Society had *no* secrets," and that "the funds gathered were *not* hoarded up or wasted." Also, that "he knew of *no* peculation." He admitted, however, that "some people" had assailed the Society, but "he knew of nothing that would blight or circumscribe the influence of an institution so purely *heavenly* in its character."

The Managers of the Society endeavored to push the regular business through and adjourn, so as to avoid the dust which these "insane sun-sweepers" would raise, should they proceed with their investigation enterprise. But the wires, though in the hands of experienced pullers, from some cause or other, would not pull right on this "interesting occasion." After a stormy time, Judge JESSUP succeeded in offering the following resolution:—

"*Resolved*, That a Special Committee of fifteen be appointed to inquire into and review the proceedings of the Executive Committee, and to Report to the next annual meeting, or at a Special meeting duly convened, to be called by said Committee at their discretion."

Dr. KNOX said that the Executives did not shrink from any investigation, and spoke of the pleasure it would give them to afford the investigators every facility in making searches.

After a time of unhallowed confusion, during which "Great is Diana of the Ephesians" was the prominent idea, the President "appeased the people," and, with violent voting, the Resolution was put and carried, and the Chair ordered to appoint a Committee of Investigation. The President then appointed a Committee of fifteen of his own friends, and added his congratulations to the Tract Society on their triumph over their Enemies. A prayer and benediction "closed the exercises" for the year 1856.

At the meeting of the Society on the 13th of May, 1857, the "Committee of Investigation" above referred to, submitted their Report, which patched up the difficulty with a "harmonious result," on this wise:—

"*Resolved*, That, in the judgment of your Committee, the political aspects of Slavery lie entirely without the proper sphere of this Society, and cannot be discussed in its publications; but that those moral duties which grow out of the existence of Slavery, as well as those moral evils and vices which it is known to promote, and which are condemned in Scripture, and so much deplored by evangelical Christians, undoubtedly do fall within the province of this Society, and can and ought to be discussed in a fraternal and Christian spirit.

"*Resolved*, That whatever considerations in the past may have seemed to recommend to the Publishing Committee the course pursued in its revision of certain works, yet, *in the future publication of Books and Tracts, no alteration or omission of the sentiments of any author should be made; but works not adapted to the design of the Society in their original form, or by a regular impartial abridgment, should be wholly omitted.*"

This only muddled the matter more and more. The men who used "great plainness of speech" went away from the Pro-Slavery concern, and took measures for the revival of another "American Tract Society," whose operations had been merged for some years in this one, and which should not be afraid to teach the truth concerning the "sum of all villanies."

THE AMERICAN BIBLE SOCIETY.—This Society dare not give a Bible to any one in the Slave States who has a drop of "colored" blood in his veins. They denounce—like their brothers of the Tract House—the "Bulls" of the Pope of Rome, and the laws of the papal countries which limit or prevent the circulation of the Protestant version of the Bible, while they are "dumb"—"as upright as a palm-tree, but speak not"—in regard to the laws of the Slaveholding States, which do the same thing in a hundred-fold worse form!

The Slave-power is felt, dreaded, and obeyed in the Pulpit, the Counting-house, the Office, the Workshop, the Political caucus, in the "Boards" of the benevolent and religious societies. Its pressure, like that of the atmosphere, is universal and unremitting, although habit may often render the people unconscious of its weight. For proof, see the "last Report" of the New York City Female Auxiliary Bible Society. This document, although containing not the most distant allusion to the American Moloch, was evidently written under fear of the demon. Speaking of the need of a wider diffusion of the Scriptures, the ladies assert, " of the 6,000,000 of families in the United States it is thought that one million is without the Bible." Do the ladies, in proof of the accuracy of their estimate, refer us to the millions of native-born "colored" Americans, who are by law prevented from reading the Bible? Ah, no! They dare not thus call attention to the abominations of Slavery; and, as if in terror at having excited a train of reflections which might possibly cause the Slaves to be remembered, they seek with trembling hand to direct the attention of the reader to a different class, for they add, in the same sentence, "*and of the millions of emigrants who land on our shores, nearly all are destitute of the sacred volume.*" Thus adroitly is the American reader's commiseration turned from the millions of his own countrymen, deprived by law of the means of reading the Bible, and excited for millions of foreigners, *who are at full liberty to read it if they please.*

The ladies ask, "What lever but the powerful Word can raise the prostrate masses of humanity?" The very question is virtually a declaration that the Bible is the only "lever" by which the "prostrate masses of humanity" can be raised. Now, what masses of humanity, let us ask these ladies, are more "prostrate" than the 4,500,000 of their own countrymen, deprived of marriage, robbed of every personal, domestic, and civil right, and sold in the Market, parents and children, like and with the beasts of the field? Yet, for these "prostrate masses," the ladies of the Bible Society bestow not one thought, utter not one word of sympathy, but they call the reader's attention to the "emigrants who land on our shores!" Could "Christian women" have manifested such heartlessness on such a subject, except through fear of the Demon?

A few weeks only before the ladies of the Bible Society assembled, a "sister," Mrs. Douglas, had been discharged from the gaol at Norfolk, Virginia, in which she had been for a month, in pursuance of a judicial sentence, for the "crime" of having taught a few children of "free" colored parents to read. Mrs. Douglas, speaking of the cruel treatment she received for teaching these poor children, all of them native-born Americans, says:—

"I used no books but the Bible, and those which illustrated it."

And what "greeting" did the ladies of the New York Auxiliary Bible Society send to their sister who had thus suffered for applying "*the only lever that can raise the prostrate masses of humanity*"? Greeting! why, the Demon forbid the Christians of the "free States" to notice the case.

The ladies of the New York Auxiliary Bible Society are "free" to eulogize the Parent Society, and this they do "in the *fear* of God." Hear them:—

"With a wide sweep, the American Bible Society passes over the *whole* field of benevolence, allying itself with all forms of *Christian* philanthrophy, and coöperating with all who 'look for the recompense of the reward.'"

If the effort to "raise the prostrate masses of humanity" in one-half of the States of the Union be indeed one form of "Christian philanthropy," it is to be regretted that the ladies did not point out the mode in which the Society had allied itself to *that* form.

THE AMERICAN SUNDAY-SCHOOL UNION.—This Association, when it once, by accident, happened to reprint an English Anti-Slavery tract, called "Jacob and his Sons; or, The Second Part of a Conversation between Mary and her Mother," which they had in their depôt for twenty years, it happened that a few copies of it were sent South, and it was discovered by a Slaveholder, in Georgia, capable of scenting danger afar off, that a certain passage in "Jacob and his Sons" was discourteous toward the "peculiar Institution." The whole South was instantly aroused. Newspaper editors and leading men, in Church and State, were vociferous in their denunciations of the Sunday-School Union, and demanded the instant suppression of the obnoxious book. A Vice-President of the Union, himself the owner of a large slave-plantation in South Carolina, pointed out the objectionable passage to the Committee of Publication, who, after an examination of the "odious sentences," acknowledged the impropriety of their maintaining a place in one of the books of the Union. The Committee then discovered that "Jacob and his Sons" had other *defects*, and obsequiously voted to have the book discontinued in the catalogue of the books of the American Sunday-School Union. And they printed a "Minute of the Committee," explanatory of their action, and caused it to be widely circulated in all the Slaveholding States, to propitiate their Masters. In the "Minute" it is said :—

"It" (Jacob and his Sons) "purports to be a description of the condition of Slaves, and though just and true when applied to some countries, was regarded as *neither just nor true when applied to ours;* this was the only exception taken to the passage, namely : that it was *not* true, in fact, if taken—as it naturally would be—to describe the condition of Slaves in the United States, and must, of course, make a *wrong* impression on the mind of the reader."

Such was the apology offered by the American Sunday-School Union to the traffickers in the bodies and souls of 4,500,000 of their fellow-men, all of them native-born Americans! The effect of this "Minute" was instantaneous. The Slaveholders were "appeased," and again took the Union into favor. The South Carolina Auxiliary Society lost no time in issuing a "Card," in which they said, "The Parent Society has given the most substantial evidence of its disposition to circulate and publish no work that is exceptionable in its character and spirit to the people of the Southern half of our glorious Republic."

The reader will doubtless have a curiosity to see the passage which was so seriously objected to. Here it is in full:—

"What is a Slave, mother?" asked Mary; "Is it a Servant?" "Yes," replied her mother, "Slaves are Servants, for they work for their Masters, and wait on them; but they are not hired Servants, but are bought and sold like beasts, and have nothing but what their Masters choose to give them. They are obliged to work very hard, and sometimes their Masters use them cruelly, beat them, and starve them, and kill them; for they have nobody to help them. Sometimes they are chained together and driven about like beasts." "Poor things!" said Mary; "but why do they not leave their Masters when they use them ill? The other day Margaret left you, mother, because she was tired of living here, though you never treated her unkindly; I wonder that the Slaves stay with their Masters, who are not kind to them." "They do not like to be Slaves," answered her Mother; "but they are not permitted to leave their Masters whenever they wish. Servants are paid for working for their Masters and Mistresses; and, if they do not like to stay, they may go and live somewhere else. But the poor, unhappy Slaves are obliged to stay with their Master as long as he chooses to keep them. And if the Master is tired of his Slaves, then he may sell them to another if he wishes."

"THIS IS A REBELLIOUS PEOPLE, LYING CHILDREN, CHILDREN THAT WILL NOT HEAR THE LAW OF THE LORD; WHICH SAY TO THE SEERS, SEE NOT, AND TO THE PROPHETS, PROPHESY NOT UNTO US RIGHT THINGS, SPEAK UNTO US SMOOTH THINGS, PROPHESY DECEITS."—Isa. xxx. 10.

Postscript, 1864.

AND now, in the eighteen hundred and sixty-fourth year of the Christ who came from heaven to die for the oppressed and the slave, and to redeem mankind with an universal redemption, into a common brotherhood of light and liberty, —the Slave power has done great things. Not contented with occupying its original bounds, it clamored for greater extension of territory. It shook its fist in the face of the nation, crying, "Give us all we ask for, or we will dissolve the Union!" It tried to get the nation into the same position that it got the negro into,—namely, trampled under foot. It howled about its wrongs, and clamored for its imaginary rights. Its wrongs were that it could not have its own way; its rights, to be soundly flogged into obedient submission to the law of the land, which for three-quarters of a century it had insulted and defied.

And so it rebelled. It waged war on the power which had nursed, and hugged, and protected it. It took the responsibility of trying to destroy the nation. The nation took the responsibility of defending itself, even at the risk of offending, and perchance destroying, its old pet and master.

And the black man "marches on!" No longer is his equality with his fairer-skinned brother only in the jail and upon the gallows. He is a soldier! The nation which for generations put its foot upon his neck and trampled him in the dust; which bound him with chains and scourged him with bloody thongs; which robbed him of his manhood, and pursued him with bloodhounds when, a fugitive, he tried to regain it; which set upon him fiends to whose savage nature the bloodhounds were angels of light;—that nation now comes to the poor, bleeding slave, and says, "We are in trouble. Come and fight our battles for us. Perhaps we will give you your liberty,—*perhap* not." At worst, your bondage will be no harder than it was before."

The contest rages! Not a family in the land but is mourning son, brother, father, or friends, sacrificed on the bloody altar of the Slave power. Streams of blood have flowed in defence of liberty. More will yet be shed! Thousands of millions of dollars have been spent in the bloody business. THOUSANDS of millions may yet be called for, and will freely come. Is it to stop? Is smiling peace to revisit this blood-stained land, and to crown it with prosperous happiness? Not till this matter is settled. The terrible work has gone too far to stop now. Slavery is not dead yet. It is pretending to be dead, only that it may be let alone and rise again to do mischief. It has had hard knocks, and is half dead. It would be madness not to kill the surviving half. We want peace, but not peace that will last only till our children shall grow up to partake of a legacy of blood and an inheritance of curses.

Slavery has throttled the Union! Let Slavery die! Slavery has made the Rebellion, and filled myriads of graves. Let it be put where it can never more rebel. Let it be placed beyond the power of ever filling another grave except its own!

Let Slavery Die!

PARTICULAR INDEX.

ABOLITIONISTS, to be lynched, 32.
    to be thrashed, 368.
Abraham's 318 armed "niggers," 55.
Accomplished "Lady's Maid" for sale, 126.
Adams, Rev. Nehemiah, D.D., 68, 212, 323.
Advance of Slavery, 89.
Aiken, William, his "property," 262.
Amalgamation, 251.
America not "civilized," 220.
American Bible Society, 422.
American Sunday-School Union, 425.
American Tract Society, 417.
Arrest of Free-men, 296.
Assassination, 231.
Astonishing ingratitude of Slaves, 277.
"Auburn-haired" runaway, 317.
Auction sales of slaves, 143, 186.
BARBARIANS, 243.
Barnes, Rev. Albert, 9, 117.
Baptist Association, Charleston, 81.
Beaten to death, 191.
"Beautiful nigger," 281.
Beecher, Rev. H. W., 97, 133, 384.
Bible, only for white people, 255.
Bigamy compulsory, 83.
Black lambs, 258.
Blacksmiths, coopers, and carpenters at auction, 180.
Black soldiers, 12.
Bleaching black people, 252, 280, 296, 300.
Bloodhounds, 293, 311, 320, 326, 339, 343, 349.
Blood-stained cow-hide, 297.
Bloodthirsty Christianity, 72.
Booksellers banished from Mobile, 249.
Border ruffians, 360.
Border-ruffian laws, 362.
Boy, ten years old, hung, 227.
Bottomless pit, 86.
Brady, schoolmaster, lynched, 166, 242.
Branded forehead, 342.
Brantley, Rev. W. T., 85.

Brownlow, "Parson," 330.
Brooks, "Bully," 367.
Buchanan, J., 91, 109, 241.
Buford's men—Kansas, 359.
Bull, John, D.D., not "nervous," 76.
Burning alive, 216.
Burns, Anthony, excommunicated, 298.
Bushnell's letter on Slave-Trade, 413.
Byberry kidnapping case, 286.
"CALL" for a "runaway preacher," 346.
Capheart, the torturer, 193, 220.
"Capital must own labor," 33.
Captain James Smith, slave-trader, 407.
Carnal weapons, 369.
Carpenter for sale, 27.
Carpet Tacks, to keep the "cursed sons of Ham" quiet, 409.
Character of society South, 186.
Cheating a "nigger," 147.
Cheever, Rev. G. B., D.D., 91, 96, 101, 270, 312, 350.
Chicago Fugitive Case, 322.
Children "in lots to suit purchasers," 121.
Children killed by their mother, 309.
Chopped to bits and burned, 199.
Christiana Fugitive Case, 283.
Christian thrown into a slave-pen, 80.
Church property in slaves, 79.
Cincinnati Platform, 112.
Clay, Cassius M., 240.
Cleveland lecture committee, 71.
Coffle-gang, 159.
Cold-blooded selfishness, 219.
Compromise, 128.
    Missouri, 132.
Corporation fines on free negroes, 296.
Correction, deserved or not, 253.
Cowhiding on the Sabbath, 211.
Crispus Attucks, 13.
Crummel, Alexander, 383.
Cuba, 103, 353.
Cursed be Canaan! 60.
Cushing, Caleb, his letter, 95.

429

INDEX.

Dahomey, King of, 114.
Dancing, a sin, 261.
"Dead nigger" sold, 177.
Death to Abolitionists, 27, 360.
Decrepit niggers, $15 and $30, 150.
Degradation of female slaves, 149.
Delaware, Ohio, Fugitive Case, 307.
Democratic Postmaster Circular, 39.
Dickey, Rev. J. H., 164.
Dickinson, Warren, Hill & Co., 156.
Dissolution of the Union threatened, 108.
Dog testimony, 225.
Domestic and foreign slave-trade, 407.
Double game of Franklin Pierce, 356.
Dough-face, 393.
Dough-face religion, 417.
Douglas, Mrs., put in jail, 255.
Downs, S. W., outrageous proposition, 43.
Editorial prospects, 243.
Empty negro stomachs, 190, 213.
Evangelical kidnappers, 69.
Exaggeration, not at all, 144.
Excommunication of Anthony Burns for running away, 298.
Faulkner, C. J., speech, 37.
Fears of slave-insurrections, 299.
Field parturition, 227.
Fillmore, Millard, 94, 241.
Five "niggers" = three freemen, 22.
"Foreign heathen," 269, 275.
Foreign slave-trade, 407.
Four hundred stripes on the back, 198.
Free negroes, 53, 244.
Freeman, Bishop, on "the sun behind a cloud," 255.
Fremont, J. C., candidate, 107.
"Fried Dog," 218.
Frozen to death, 189.
Fugitive funeral, 304.
Fugitives in Canada, 294.
Fugitive Slave Law, 68, 91, 128.
Furman, Rev. Dr., his estate, 82.
Garrison, William Lloyd, 374.
Gentlemen, work marked out for, 368.
Germans enslaved, 207, 347.
Getting rid of the minister, 33.
Giddings, Hon. J. R., 126, 131, 136.
Girl sold "for want of use," 127.
Government promises violated, 10.
"Grand nigger hunt," 290.

Graniteville ignorance, 26.
"Gratifying condition" of slave-market, 176.
Ham and his family, 60.
Hand-saw flogging, 217.
"Handsome piece of furniture," 153.
Hard masters, 200.
Harrisburg kidnapping case, 287.
Haxall & Brother, Richmond, Va., 192.
Henry, Patrick, 92.
Herbert kills his "German nigger," 207.
Hill's auction-rooms, 142.
Hopkins, Bishop, his book, 65.
House of Bishops, 259.
How, Rev. S. B.; funny exposition of tenth commandment, 75.
Human flesh at auction, 125, 130.
Humbugging poor "niggers," 253.
Hypocrisy, 60, 119, 253, 270.
Ignorance a political necessity, 233, 235.
Illinois, negro laws of, 389.
Imprisonment of black sailors, 16.
"Incendiary" literature burnt, 249.
"Infidel love of freedom," 299.
"Infidels," 267.
Ingraham, E. D., 283.
Irenæus Prime, 332.
Isabella the Spaniard, 353.
Jackson, Andrew, on negro soldiers, 17.
Jefferson's prediction, 19.
"infidelity," 72, 123.
opinion of slavery, 265.
Jeremiah the prophet, 101, 120, 366.
Joe Shicaway's "warm jacket," 192.
"Jobbing" negroes out, 79.
Johnson and wife, escaped, 281.
Journal of Commerce apologizes for Brooks and Keitt, 370.
Judicious Trimmer, Rev., D.D., 397.
Junkin, Rev. George, D.D., 70.
Kansas affairs, 358–366.
Kerr, Rev. Leander; ruffian speech, 75.
Kidnappers, 286, 311.
King of Dahomey, 114.
Knowledge is gunpowder, 234.
Lame negro runaway, 330.
Latter-Day Saints, 112.
Laws of Ohio trampled on, 309.
Lecompton, 365.

INDEX.

Lord, Reverend Nathan, D.D., LL.D., 59.
MADISON, James, 92.
Marks of the lash, 194.
Marriage denied to slaves, 57, 195.
Marrying "by the blanket," 215.
Marshall, Hon. Thomas, on slavery, 51.
Maryland slave markets, 124.
McDowell, J., speech, 87.
Meade, Bishop, on "servants," 252.
Men and women reared for market, 156.
Merciful safety-valve, 48.
Methodist missionary work, 246.
Minister *ducked* in Kentucky, 316.
Mobile book-burning, 249.
Morrill, Senator, speech, 10.
Mormons, 111.
Moses a radical Abolitionist, 67.
"Mules, hogs, and niggers," 180.
Munificent bequests, 190.
Murder of "Caroline," 198.
   of a slave mother, 222.
Muscogee Herald, sick, 31.
Mutilation and murder, 219.
NAKEDNESS and hunger, 190, 212, 221.
Negro burial in Boston and New Haven, 382.
Negroes must be contented, 254.
Negro habitations, 213.
Negro religion, 233.
Negro slavery not Bible slavery, 56, 74.
Negro soldiers' bones, 14.
Nelson, Rev. C. K., 78, 257.
New England rum, 178.
New Orleans morals, 230.
New York slave-trade, 408–411.
Nicaragua "mission," 115.
"Nigger Dave;" his execution, 216.
"Nigger in the river!" 336.
Northern submission, 372.
Not allowed to "mind the baby," 223.
OBSERVING the Sabbath, 221.
Officious Missourians, 328.
One hundred lashes, 218.
Onesimus, 65.
Ostend Correspondence, 354.
PADDLING a "nigger," 191.
Park Street Church, Boston, 381.
Passports not granted to free negroes, 390.

Pastor wanted, 76.
Patterson, his fingers and teeth, 308.
Paulding, Hon. J. K. 159.
Penalty for teaching negroes, 246.
Phillips, Wendell, letter, 400.
Pickens, his speech, 34.
Pierce, Franklin, 91, 208, 241, 297, 353.
Pinckney, Charles, testimony, 15.
Plumer, Rev. W. S., D.D., 72.
Plymouth Church, 133.
Polk, Right Reverend Leonidas, 56, 277.
   his crop of black babes, 258.
Pontius Pilate, 103.
Poor white folks, 239.
Possum-fat for "black lambs," 258.
Predestinated piracy, 60.
Prejudice and persecution, 9.
Presbyterian Synod of Kentucky, 54, 58, 163, 204.
Pro-slavery piety, 66.
Publicans and sinners, 267.
Pullam's blood, 317.
"Putrid carcass," 264.
QUAKERS, 160.
Qualifications of slaveholding legislator, 21.
Queer-colored "niggers," 55.
RANDOLPH, John, 103, 200.
Raced to death, 189.
Railroad "niggers," 209.
Reverend cowhider, 210.
Religious liberty (so called), 333.
Returning from church, 210.
Revolutionary soldier thrashed to death, 229.
Richmond Examiner, 104, 369.
Richmond "nigger" auctions, 140.
"Right of property," 350.
Right Reverend slave-breeders, 259.
Rights in jail and on the gallows, 10, 382.
Robbing a minister, 302.
Runaway "niggers," 277, 295, 297.
SABBATH slave-hunt, 301.
"Sale of land and other property," 149.
Sale of "niggers" at St. Louis Hotel, New Orleans, 182.
Sarah, in Mr. Beecher's church, 133.
"Save the Union," 63, 261.
Scarred bodies, 145.

432 INDEX.

"Scribes and Pharisees," 122.
Seminole outrages, 341.
Setting a "nigger" on fire, 204.
Shadrach, keeping an eating-house, 346.
Shannon, Governor, big supper, 208.
Sheriff's sale of men, women, and children, 176.
"Show your teeth," 144, 153.
Sims Fugitive Case, 381.
Slave auctions, none in Palestine, 74.
  after church, Lexington, 167.
Slaveholder "sold" by a runaway, 314.
Slave meetings, 234.
Slave mother hung, 179.
Slave revenge, 222.
Slave suicide, 162, 188, 343.
Slave-trade, domestic and foreign, 407.
Slave trafficking churches, 84.
Slavery better than liberty, 28.
  pushing Freedom towards Canada, 89.
  the basis of Democracy, 31.
Sleeping "accommodations" for the children of Ham, 216.
Smylie, Rev. J., defends ignorance, 77.
Soul bondage, 233.
Soulé, Pierre, 355–358.
South Carolina, action of Synod, 263.
  brag and bluster, 378.
  don't like missionaries, 246.
  ignorance, 24, 245.
  military disposition, 375.
  representation, 22.
  slave insurrection in, 314.
  weakness in the Revolution, 377.
"South-side" sophistry, 323.
Southern customers, 63, 108.
Southern disgust for "free society," 29.
"Southern Presbyterian" logic, 245.
Spurious Christianity, 270.
Stole the money, 238.
Stop thief! 59.
"Stow-aways," 282.
Stray "darkies" in Illinois, 329.
Strickland & Co's. book-shop, 248.
Stringfellow, Rev. Thornton, D.D., 73.

Stroud, Judge, 287.
Stuart, Rev. Moses, D.D., 65.
Stubborn runaway, 337.
Subterranean den, 316.
Sumner, Charles, 97, 157, 367.
Sunday-School Convention, 237.
Swindling the poor Indian, 341.
Sylvia in Canada, 325.
Sympathy for Mrs. Douglas, not much, 256.
TAMPERING with the mails, 235, 241.
Taney, Roger, 20.
Texas, annexation, 104.
The "*mild*" sort of slavery, 191.
Theological Seminary "niggers," 264.
Throat-cutting, 221.
Too white for a "nigger," 327.
Trimmer, Rev. Judicious, D.D., 397.
Tyranny and torture, 188, 291, 297.
UNBORN slave infants, valued at $150,000, 341.
Underground railroad, 282, 290, 307, 320.
United States officers, 286.
VENGEANCE on a poor "nigger," 206.
Violence and theft, 350.
Virginia now past help from guano, 45.
Virginia, originally fertile, 49.
  dilapidated military system, 300.
  "leprosy," 44.
  slave population, 154.
Virginius and his daughter, 279.
WASHINGTON an abolitionist, 106.
Washington's nephew, 12.
Webb, James Watson, 371.
Whipped to death, 204, 219.
White boy turned out of school for being a "nigger," 388.
"White niggers" advertised and sold, 42, 150.
White runaways, 327, 332, 335, 348.
White slave children, 280.
White trash, 25.
Wilkesbarre Fugitive Case, 284.
Winthrop, Hon. R. C., 16.
Wise, Henry A., "stump-tailed steer," 52.
Wives and slaves equal, 66, 226.
Women "thrown upon the market," 186.
Worked out in six years, 211, 227.

www.ingramcontent.com/pod-product-compliance
Lightning Source LLC
Chambersburg PA
CBHW022146300426
44115CB00006B/363